Globalization, Urban Form and Governance

Globalization, Urban Form and Governance

Fourth International Conference
ALFA-IBIS Preceedings

Edited by M. Carmona , J. Rosemann and M. Schoonraad

DUP Science -. 2001

Technical Support

Publicatieburo Bouwkunde. TU Delft

Editing and Layout

Roxane Crestian
Diego Sepulveda

English Revision

Marinda Schooraad

Published and distributed by:
DUP Science

DUP Science *is an imprint of:*
Delft University Press
P.O. Box 98
2600 MG Delft
The Netherlands
Telephone: +31 15 278 5121
Telefax: +31 15 278 1661
E-mail: DUP@library.tudelft.nl

ISBN 90-407-2273-0

Keywords: Globalization, Urban Form, Governance, Urban-Regional Sustainability, ITC

Printed in The Netherlands

Contents

Part IV
New Research

Introduction

Marisa Carmona and Marinda Schoonraad

Since the Nineties cities have increasingly been steered by the pace and scope of the processes related to the intensification of international trade and capital, the ICT revolution, the growing power of transnational companies and the political and economic conditions aimed at attracting Foreign Direct Investments. Over the past ten years the process of globalisation has been associated with the changing role of cities in national development strategies. National boundaries have rapidly been loosing their importance as trade barriers and cities have become more autonomous economic entities opening up their production, commercial and financial services to international competition. Politically, culturally and economically, nations and regions are forming new alliances and closing ranks and new forms of competition and co-operation are developing. Governments and International Agencies have argued that globalisation would enhance the trading opportunities of the less developed regions in a world-wide market and would promote their internal modernisation by transferring advanced management and technology from global firms. Structural adjustments, agglomeration economy and infrastructure modernisation appear simultaneously as requirements and as outcomes of the new age of globalisation.

Our IBIS network regards globalisation as an important component of current urban thinking, yet sees the city not as a purely macroeconomic imperative but as a social process of building and negotiating, in which different actors state their interests, propose solutions and generate decisions. The research atelier IBIS believes in a historic and holistic approach to understanding the city and recognises the diversity of urban realities within and between developed and developing countries.

Initially we intended to study the impact of globalisation on cities within the Latin American and European contexts according to the framework of the European Union-ALFA program, but later we included South Africa and Singapore. These two cases, although not fully representative of the African and Asian regions, are sufficiently important by themselves to aid in the analysis and comparison, in relative terms, of the opportunities and problems of cities with different levels of economic and social development. Thus IBIS research has posed the question of city transformation in a wider perspective of situations with regards to demographic and social features, level of urbanisation, historical and cultural developments and particularly opportunities and constraints to address globalisation.

Currently the number of network members has increased to 18 researchers, under the thematic framework of "Globalisation, Urban Form and Governance" and there is the prospect of adding 8 more researchers after this conference. This will result in 23 cities being included in the investigation.

This publication is the result of the fifth international conference of IBIS network which took place in October 2001 in which 22 papers where submitted for discussion and evaluation. Some important changes have been introduced to many of the papers presented to the Conference and finally an editing procedure has tried to organise the papers within a three-theme structure. A fourth part has been added with the new proposals presented to the research network.

The three constituent themes correspond to the three parts of this book:

- The first part on Globalisation is be concerned with the economic, technological and cultural impact of globalisation and structural adjustments on space, on the urban systems and relationships between cities and on the opportunities and limitations offered by internal structures for fostering economic growth and social development.
- The second part on Urban Form is be concerned with current policies and programs for sustainable urban development, infrastructure delivery and urban strategies. It necessarily focuses the issue of urban form and environmental planning.
- The third part on Urban Governance is concern with the effect of structural adjustment and the theory and practice of market, political and community enablement.
- Finally we have added a fourth part containing the new approved proposals in this research network.

With respect to the first Chapter on Globalisation, an important contribution to the Conference was the three keynotes lectures which where given by Saskia Sassen, Ricardo Toledo Silva and Sueli Schiffer. Since the papers of Toledo and Schiffer are included in this book, we will to comment largely on the keynote address of Sassen, which is a relevant issue in IBIS research.

Sassen presentation was entitled ‘Between Topographic Representation and Spatialized Power Projects’. She argues that examining a city or a metropolitan region in terms of its built topography is perhaps, increasingly inadequate in a global digital era. On the one hand, topography does not engage with what is currently the dominant discourses on globalisation and digitalisation, discourses 'which evict place and materiality and hence what we might call the topographic moment'. Yet she argues that the digital and the global are deeply imbedded with the material and the local in the case of a global city. Topographic representations of such a city fail to capture the fact that components of a city's topography may be spatialisations of global power projects and/or may be located on global circuits, thereby destabilising the meaning of the local or the sited, and hence the topographic representation of such city. Sassen explains use of the term topography in this case refers to its literal meaning. She distinguishes between the topographic representation of key aspects of the city and an interpretation of these same aspects in terms of spatialised economic, political, cultural dynamics. She states that this is an analytical exploration into the issue that attempts to do a re-reading of the city through representation of its relationship to topography. The focus is on the spatialisation of power projects arising from globalisation and digitalisation. This bring a particular perspective to the discussion on urban topography and spatialisation since both are associated with dispersal and increased locational options for firms, markets and households with resources/power. She argues that topographic representations fail to capture the fact that cities continue to be key sites for the spatialisation of power projects even in a global digital era. Topographic representations also does not allow one to capture the fact that cities are key sites for the spatialising of a different type of power project, perhaps better thought of as contestatory. Here her argument is that global cities allow the emergence of new types of political movements arising out of conditions of often acute disadvantage. A topographic representation of poor areas of a city would simple capture the physical conditions of disadvantage: the poor housing, the bad transport infrastructure, and the decaying schools.

Spatialized Power Projects. Sassen argues that cities have long been key sites for the spatialisation of power projects whether political, religious or economic. "We can find this spatialisation of cities in the structures and infrastructures for control and management functions of past colonial empires and of current global firms and markets; it can also be seen in the segregation of population groups that can consequently be more easily produced as either cheap labour or surplus people; in the choice of particular built forms used for representing economic power, such as the preference for the "Greek temple' to house stock markets; in what we refer today as high-income residential and commercial gentrification to accommodate the expanding elite professional classes, with the inevitable displacement of lower income households and firms; it can be seen in the large-scale destruction of natural environments to implant particular forms of urbanisation marked by sprawl rather than density and linked to specific real estate development interests, such as the uncontrolled strip-development and suburbanization to be seen in the Los Angeles region". The dominant interpretation propose that digitalisation entails an absolute disembedding from the material world and that place no longer matters. Sassen argues that many suggest that the type of place represented by major cities may have became obsolete from the perspective of the economy, particularly for the leading industries as these have the best access to, and are the most advanced users of, telematics. Sassen has always criticised the simple representation of the global information economy as place-less, where there is no longer a spatialisation of current type of power. This argument has been convincingly developed in The Global City (new fully updated edition Princeton, NJ 2001). Sassen's particular reading of digitalisation and globalisation seeks to detect the implications of the digital and non-digital domains and thereby to insert the city in mapping of the digital, both actual and rhetorical-mapping from which the city is easily excluded. It is a reading that seeks and localises in concrete built environments. The risk in this type of effort, as recognised by Sassen, lies in generalising, using metaphors and figurative language - in brief, to hover above it all. The importance is how to reintroduce place in economic analysis and how to construct a new narrative about economic globalisation, one which includes rather than expels spatial, economic and cultural elements that are part of the global economy as it is constituted in cities.

This paper of Sassen forms an important backdrop to the papers presented in the different sections of this publication.

Part I refers to the impact of globalisation processes in cities through four papers.

Ricardo Toledo Silva points out some methodological problems on dealing with urban physical analysis related to poorly documented realities, like in Latin America, where solutions are motivated by assumptions or misguided references to research in Europe and America. From that statement, he attempts to clarify what are the limits between urban research and design practice, and from that point, which research methodologies could be developed to improve urban planning and research.

Sueli Ramos Schiffer refers to the discussion on the new trends of economic and urban development in the largest Latin American cities, in terms of demographic stabilisation, the irreversible decline in manufacturing jobs and the relative share of this stabilisation in the total national value-added production. This discussion leads to the need to promote appropriate public policies and urban plans addressing the inevitable fate of these cities becoming predominantly tertiary by the urgent renewal of obsolete areas, largely dependent on a comprehensive and integrated macro-plan for the city – clearly aside from the political will.

Paul Drewe points out in his paper that there is no direct link between ICT and spatial structure. As the spatial impacts of these new technologies are still uncertain, design-oriented research has a place to demonstrate and to visualise the possible futures that could be. In that sense, he introduces the "design studio" as a team which joints both fields in order to integrate land use planning and urban technology networks in particular transport and ICT.

Mario Lungo discusses the changes in traditional patterns of socio-spatial segregation in Latin American cities due to the effects of the globalisation process. On one hand, he emphasises the explosion of the gated-communities as a homogenising trend in cities, in spite of historical and structural differences in cities. On the other hand, the validity of the relation between socio-spatial segregation and urban land regulatory framework is analysed through the case of the San Salvador Metropolitan Area, looking for future research themes in this line.

Roberto Rocco intends to investigate the conditions and processes occurring in two distinct economic regions (Sao Paulo Metropolitan Area and the Randstad in the Netherlands) in the reshaping of urban structure, and the assessment of how local forces might be contributing to these changes. In this vein, he points out that the definition of an identity for both agglomerations as recognisable units for attracting FDI constitutes a target in itself and permeates the whole research project towards the understanding and establishment of new boundaries for the analysis of metropolis.

In Part II, 6 papers refer to the issue of sustainability of urban development.

Silvia de Schiller analyses the relation between urban tissue and environmental quality to demonstrate the environmental impact of building form, firstly at the urban scale by quantifying the heat island and secondly at the urban design scale by analysing the local microclimate. The paper shows the results of measurements during different seasons in the Buenos Aires Metropolitan Area compared to a small city in Patagonia, Argentina, in order to demonstrate that the transformation of urban tissue affects the quality of urban space and sustainability of urban form due to the regional climatic variations as well as the social, economic and political forces of globalisation.

Stephen Read writes about the relation between urban centrality and public space referring to urban space as a mechanism when considering the city as a functional object. In this sense, he points out that this relation ends in multiple overlapping processes and that the respective scales are co-ordinated within public space by the fact that they are grounded in material flows in a real urban spatial connective context. The case of the Pijp neighbourhood in Amsterdam shows how the structure may order the details of urban circumstance and the patterns of social interface in the city, differentiating volume and scale of movement and activity resulting in the recognition of urban centrality and periphery.

Alvaro Arrese presents a piece of work about the restructuring of central areas considering as case study the main urban project for the waterfront in Buenos Aires framed by the globalisation process, the "Puerto Madero" project. The new methodological discussions in urban planning are related to the possibility of breaking down the barriers between the research project and the urban project itself through the application of new design concepts in order to preserve social life and environment while enhance urban quality.

Diego Sepulveda This paper is part of a wider study that analyses the role of public space in restructuring Latin American cities. The concept of urban morphological zones to identify structure of and projects in public space is used. The research deals with two cities: Santiago in Chile and Cordoba in Argentina. The morphological zones are identified in terms of the spatial transformation process that has taken place in the city over the past century. These zones constitute the analytic unit used to analyse the potential of the public square. In order to simplify the research, five processes have been selected which correspond to morphological zones: Renewal, Consolidation, Gentrification, Development and Re-functioning.

Americo Villegas Ormachea presents a study on the urban tradition of the Inca culture in the Peruvian Andes, stating that there are social and cultural continuities as a result of the relations between the traditional or historical urban structures and present development, which corresponds with the magnitude and importance of the physical frame. The main question is what kind of relations existed between urban form and society in the Inca period and the colonial society and what are the present consequences of this relation.

Cecilia Marengo refers to the process of urban expansion in Cordoba City, an intermediate city in Argentine. The city growth is enhanced by private and public investment, by the decentralisation of activities and the suburbanisation strategies of private entrepreneurs. She questions the consequences of urban expansion in terms of the effectiveness of public policies to reduce internal imbalances in the urban system and in the kind of relationship between expansion and urban fragmentation.

The Part III contains 8 papers dealing with globalisation and governance.

Diego Carrión points out that the lack of a collective city project has provoked spatial disintegration and deterioration of the urban image in the metropolitan area of Quito. This resulted from the fact that urban agents have been operating without any policy guidelines and/or controls. This has contributed to the deterioration of natural areas, scattered housing developments, and has impacted on the location of commerce, services and industry. He introduces the General Spatial Development Plan of Quito based on the premises of productivity, environmental sustainability, improvement of the quality of life and levels of governance.

Maria J. Bazan Lopes presents the analysis of urban planning in cities of the South Cone in Latin America during the XX century influenced by restructuring processes. She analysis both national and local contexts including the planning objectives of the plans. The paper refers to the evolution of ideas, discourses and practice taking into consideration three cases: one primary city (Santiago de Chile) and two secondary cities (La Plata and Rosario, Argentina), from the "city beautiful" to the "strategic approach".

Beatriz Cuenya writes about the "Retiro Project" in the centre of Buenos Aires, which constitutes the most important transportation node of the country, the extension of the administrative area, a middle-high cost residential area, public parks and the most emblematic precarious settlement. She points out the main facts and factors, which have affected the decision-making of the project in order to create a competitive centrality by stitching fragments of the old city to create a second-generation metropolis.

Ana Falu presents a preliminary hypothesis on research into strategic planning to restructure cities in order to create centralities in intermediate cities in Latin America, considering as city case Cordoba, Argentina. The institutional power has shifted from the central entities to local governments, with regards to foreign direct investments, privatisation of assets, concessions and deregulation of infrastructure and urban utilities, land uses and strategic urban projects. In this context, the traditional aspiration of restructuring the city through development of centralities seems to be hindered by market opportunities enhancing the concentration of real estate in particular locations.

Raul di Lullo and Ana Kantarovsky relate the case of San Miguel de Tucuman, Argentina, to the hypothesis that selective private investments establish conditions that have been influenced by trends for the development of public space in the inner centre of the city. They point out that the decisions taken in the private realm, in the absence of clear policies and effective enforcement capacities, impacts on the public domain with regards to their achievements and failures without the possibility of mediation regarding collective interests. Its roots can be found in the persistent governance crisis and in the lack of a proactive mindset prevalent in the state institutions.

Hao Hu and Jurgen Rosemann introduce the case of the housing system in China, which has been a major component in the economic reform since 1979. They state that the huge housing needs, low affordability and oversupply of high-end commodity housing is experienced The paper focuses on the analysis of the evolution of the housing market and develops some recommendations concerning the improvement of housing policies with regard to the economic globalisation, by including the private sector under market conditions as the key variable determining the post-reform urban development in China.

Jose F. Chanez describe the environmental, social and economical conditions of urban centres in Latin America related to water management problems and makes general suggestions for further analysis. The main questions posed are: Is it possible to apply the principles of the Dublin Declaration to Latin America? What managerial arrangements are necessary for its practical solution? Do poverty and social deterioration complicate its application? How does the informal sector interfere in water management? What managerial arrangements are necessary in order to apply these principles to Latin America urban centres?

In Part IV, we present four new research projects in the framework of the Alfa-IBIS Network.

Alejandro Suarez Payeron introduces the case of the Metropolitan District of Mexico, through a historical study about the restructuring of the central area since the city of Tenochtitlan of Aztec times to the present. He explores the future development and expectations of the old central area under the impact of globalisation.

Ana Sugranyes focuses on the housing policy of Chile over the last 20 years, specifically related to the low cost sector and the changes introduced by a "residential mobility program" designed in 1996 with the purpose of developing value for low-cost dwellings in the real estate market and to limit the building of cheap and low-standard housing units.

Ernesto Philibert-Petit will work on a project about sustainable design for regions and cities in Latin America with interdisciplinary virtual teams working and researching simultaneously. This project will develop a virtual vehicle linked to the existing infrastructure of the Virtual University of the ITESM (Technological Institute of Monterrey).

Jorge Ozorno starts a project that comprises a comparative analysis of different cities that generate a framework to propose a conceptual approach to a theory of architecture for Latin America given that globalisation has accelerated the process of colonisation and has impeded a local form of "urbitecture".

Two other research projects were presented, the one on the redesign of waterfront in Valparaiso, by Eliana Muga and the redesign of waterfront in Antofagasta by Glenda Kapstein. Both proposals will be presented in the next book (number 6) of this series.

Finally **Marisa Carmona**, co-ordinator of the IBIS network, makes a short evaluation of the first common research: Strategic Planning and Urban Projects, Responses to Globalisation from 15 Cities (DUP-Science 2001) and presents a second theme for a forthcoming collective project: Globalisation and Changes in Urban Morphology. The paper starts with a discussion on how globalisation has affected developing societies. Growing financial opportunities have not meant any improvement in the distribution of wealth, nor have improved urban governance and public participation. In this context the analysis of the restructuring urban morphology is presented in relation to the technological, the demographic, infrastructure and institutional changes of agglomeration economies.

Part I

Globalization

1

City Renewal under Globalization

Urban Process in the Periphery of Capitalism. Methodological Challenges in Evaluating a Poorly Documented Reality.

Ricardo Toledo Silva[1]

Urban and regional systems provide prominent support for social and economic life, and nobody ignores the shape and the main features of his or her surrounding environment. Most people have a feeling of how urban matters should be conducted, and this feeling is the main motivation for political choice at local level. The proposition of politically feasible alternatives in urban management is strongly dependent on the ability of politicians and policy makers to capture the prevailing movements of this social will.

Urban planners, architects and other professionals dealing with physical propositions have widely accepted this immediate interpretation of the social will as the main information input for design alternatives. Good practices in urban planning and design have been associated with the quality of this overall interpretation of the urban and social processes, in many cases considered as part of the design process itself. Many of the notorious interventions of modernism on city planning and design were underpinned by information organised in this way, tributary to the individual skill of the designer to capture his or her reality, as opposed to a systematic treatment of urban data.

In contexts where urban information is poor, this approach has been the only possible response of rational planning practice to a predominantly spontaneous and informal process of city growth. Urban planning and design in Latin America have generally matched this archetype, whereas a chronic lack of conveniently aggregated information reinforced a professional attitude of modernist/reformist planners and architects skilled more for an expeditious glimpse at the scene and immediate formulation of physical propositions than for the systematic analysis of the context over which they should act. One of the most radical and controversial examples of this practice in Latin America was the case of Brasília, the capital city of Brazil, whose plan and design incorporated the ideal of a new and more fair society, later proven to be more of a political wish than of a true tendency in Brazilian social development. This does not reduce the intrinsic qualities of Brasília as a revolutionary experiment of urban design and architecture, and the legitimacy of that exercise at that time. Likewise, many other modernist inspired initiatives of urban planning and design also have their intrinsic value and legitimacy.

---

1 *Faculdade de Arquitetura e Urbanismo* at the University of São Paulo, Brazil.

Contemporary urban planning and management, however, cannot predominantly rely on particular skills to interpret social and political will anymore. On the one hand, urban systems have gained more complexity, larger scale, and are the object of a myriad of conflicting interests that imply growing risks of misinterpretation. On the other hand, urban information systems have new prospects of benefiting from the fast evolution of information technology in general, even if most of this new potential may not be ready for immediate use. One of the main points of this article is that we cannot ignore the existence of this new potential in urban information no matter how difficult it is to deal with.

Apart from its incorporation in urban planning and design practices, the evolution of information technology determined important changes in urban and regional research methodology. The traditional border between research on urbanisation and on urbanism[2] tends to diminish, since the new information tools give an unprecedented visibility to the links that articulate different scales and sectors of the regional and urban processes. Similarly the separation between research carried out under the aegis of urban sociology, using predominantly a substance language, and of urban geography, identified with a space time language, also tend to decrease. But this does not render the conceptual framework of urban research easier or trivial. On the contrary, the basic conceptual difficulties of working at the interface between substance and space-time languages, earlier raised by Harvey (1973), have grown with the sophistication of analytical tools. More than ever urban and regional research risks the confusion of causes and consequences, hypotheses and assumptions, conclusions and proposals.

If in professional design practice the formulation of propositions based on a number of unproved hypotheses is still an acceptable approach, given the relatively recent influence of modernism (and of so called post-modernism as well), in urban research it is completely unacceptable. This raises the question that has never been totally solved by most schools of architecture, urbanism and urban planning: what are the particular foci and acceptable methods of research in architecture and urbanism that distinguish research itself – in the sense of proven innovation – from creative professional practice in these fields?

The attempt to establish clearer limits between urban research and design practice guided many academic works in urbanism, especially during the sixties and seventies, to embrace either the schools of urban sociology and their evolving branches and variants, or spatial modelling methods based on land markets and transport flows, developed by urban geographers and transport engineers. For an general but well founded view of urban sociology and its evolution to the contemporary sociospatial approach, see Gottdiener (1994, chapters 6 and 7). Those theoretical schools developed after Henri Lefèvre, that considered real estate to form a particular circuit of capital within the overall capitalist process of accumulation (inclusive Castells 1975 and Harvey 1973, 1978) were particularly welcomed by researchers dealing with the built environment, since they opened theoretical clues for hypotheses specifically referred to the urban process

2 One of the best definitions distinguishing urbanisation from urbanism has been given by Gottdiener (1994). For him urbanisation "... refers to the city formation or building process (...) and tries to understand the rise and fall of great cities" (op. cit. p.103). Urbanism, on the other hand, "... takes the city formation process as given and seeks to understand the ways of life that transpire within this container" (idem).

Without entering into further detail of each theoretical school, there are two basic problems that are recurrent in the relationship between urban theory, research methodology and the concrete urban systems under analysis/intervention by planning and design professionals. The first, which seems to be common to researchers from both advanced and emerging countries, is the entanglement of architects and planners in a sociological perspective when attempting to explain the urban structure, in such a way that the return to a spatial framework over which eventual conclusions should be drawn and physical solutions proposed, is jeopardised. This first problem may lead to two particular manifestations in the final documentation of academic research (thesis, report):

- the work as a whole assumes the shape of a thesis on sociology or urban geography (depending on the specific hypotheses and theoretical choice underpinning the analytical framework) and its quality will depend on the skill of the author to internalise the concepts and the particular logic of a language that is frequently strange to his/her original formation;
- when faced with the unsolvable conflict between the analytical work developed in sociological language and the hypotheses in spatial language, the researcher forces connections that lead to conclusions for a spatial response that in fact are not logically tied to the analysis.

In this second variant the quality of the final work is always poor, regardless the internal coherence of each part. Such a disconnection between socio-economic analysis and technical propositions is very common not only in academic work but also in many urban and sectoral plans produced by specialised planning offices.

The second main problem associated with the relationship between urban theory, research methodology and the concrete object of analysis – an existing city or region – is the mismatch between the conditions under which a given theoretical approach has originally evolved and its empirical support, and those under which the system considered for analysis actually develop. Whenever the empirical support of the original theory is sufficiently clear and analogous data can be retrieved in the context to be researched, it is possible to retrace the methodological path proposed and to effectively test the hypotheses taken in the new context. Since these two conditions are fulfilled, there would be no problem, in principle, for testing theoretical hypotheses originated in advanced capitalist countries with empirical evidence relevant to emerging countries. It would be roughly the same as reworking theoretical pieces supported by empirical evidence of one advanced country for the context of another advanced country. This has been quite common between American and French scholars dealing with social research in both countries, as in the case of the prolific exchange among those working on the theories of regulation during the 70's and 80's (see Boyer 1990).

However in trying to transfer theory and research procedures between countries whose urban information bases are deeply unequal, researchers have frequently generated imperfect analogies with quite questionable results, both theoretically and empirically. The first condition for theoretical transfer, that is clarity on the methodological procedure to produce empirical evidence, is not always fulfilled in the specialised literature on urban research. When this happens, the testing of hypotheses in another context different from the original is jeopardised even if both keep a reasonable balance in terms of availability of information. The second condition for transfer, that is the use of relevant local information to retrace the original methodological path, is more frequently unfulfilled when the transfer takes place between fully developed and emerging contexts.

A recurrent problem that is a corollary of the information imbalance is the replication of theoretical hypotheses whose empirical support was unclear even in the original construction. This is likely to happen much more amid scholars working in poorly informed contexts than with those working in well informed societies. Put in another way, the researcher working in a poorly informed context is more vulnerable to accept a biased theory as its basis than the one working with full availability of information. Since the former has always dealt with dramatic limitations in information, it is very difficult for him / her to device where exactly is the problem of the transfer, whether it is in the unclear empirical support of the original work or in the poorly informed receiving context. For the researcher experienced to deal with abundant information in daily research practice, it is much easier to question the empirical consistency of the original theory. This is why we have argued that this second problem of matching urban theory, methodology and research is more frequent in cases of theoretical applications that originate in advanced countries and attempt to explain urban processes in emerging countries.

Whenever sufficient information is produced and dealt with in the receiving context, this second problem tends to be offset. An example is the case of housing schemes in São Paulo, in the seventies, whose users' satisfaction was systematically surveyed by the São Paulo State Institute of Technological Research (Motta 1975). At that time there was a generalised feeling that official housing schemes, built and designed according to a strict and non creative mass housing orthodoxy, would perform very poorly in terms of users' satisfaction. The original hypotheses of that research presupposed severe functional and constructive inadequacy, leading to recurrent problems of vandalism, rejection, etc.

Even if those hypotheses were not openly associated with the contemporaneous European literature about rejection of mass housing, the researchers themselves, all young sociologists, architects and geographers in the early 70's, were deeply motivated by those critical positions, truly expecting a generalised rejection of the existing housing schemes to be revealed by the research. But the results of the survey, applied on a statistically representative population of the official housing schemes then existing in São Paulo, did by no means show a systematic rejection. The rigor of the methodology, based on a framework of human needs and performance indicators developed by Blachère (1965) at the *Centre Scientifique et Technique du Bâtiment* (France), by clearly contradicting the initial hypotheses, permitted a serious review of the research assumptions and deeply influenced the following works of that research group.

This particular feature of sociological and of urban research, that is the direct involvement of the observer with the research object and a strong theoretical presumption of results, is not always understood by those dealing with other fields of scientific and technological research. While for many branches of research the object may be completely detached from the observer and faithfully reproduced elsewhere (e.g. a given chemical or biological substance) the social systems in general and the urban and regional systems in particular have unique attributes – including the particular geographic location – that render them non replicable as such, and inexorably attached to the observer himself. This is why urban research is so complex and so much in need of adequate skills in combining qualitative and quantitative research methods. It is also why urban policy has so frequently been subject to pseudo scientific formulations, based on unproven hypotheses, unrelated to a systematic appraisal of the local context.

Today, with the emergence of market based policies as one of the main components of the globalisation of the economy, the attempts to apply oversimplified models for analysing urban systems have blossomed everywhere. These models are not present as such in any original work of urban research literature. Rather, they have been widely found in dissemination literature associated with sectoral policy and financing, such as examples of planning and management tendencies matching the new movements in privatisation and re-regulation of urban services, real estate businesses, and other fields of economic activity linked to urban management. Once again, the conflict between urban policy practice and research emerges. For the professional activity of urban planning and design it is often impossible to escape the adoption of oversimplified schemes of management imposed by financing agencies. But in the domain of research, even when carried out by the same professional compelled to accept oversimplification in his/her daily activity, this is not acceptable.

In contrast to the preceding modernist rationale of an expeditious glimpse underpinning reformist propositions, and from the mathematical modelling techniques that characterised transport and communications planning, the oversimplified approaches to urban management deviate from archetypes based on particular cases combined with de-contextualised segments of notorious research works. Some of the most recurrent examples of these contemporary archetypes in urban management are:

1. the formation of new centres inside predominantly monocentric urban complexes,
2. the inexorability of de-industrialisation and the emergence of modern services in main 'global' cities,
3. the 'end of territory' due to the generalisation of virtual flows and nodes,
4. the formation of urban enclaves, etc.

None of these ideas is true or false by itself, but the recurrent combination of them to explain very different urban processes gives rise to a very uncomfortable feeling of escapism from deeper analysis.

It would be deeply unfair to attribute this combination of contemporary platitudes to this or that author particularly. Most of the concepts above have been the object of consistent research involving theoretical hypotheses sustained by robust empirical evidence developed for the original contexts – spatially and timely – under investigation. This is the case of the seminal work of Sassen (1991) about global cities, that showed a qualitative change in the relationship between financial centres worldwide, based on evidence systematically analysed for the cases of New York, London and Tokyo. However the direct – and partial – transfer of her theoretical framework to particular cities of emerging countries with insufficient regard for the methodological revaluation and retracing of empirical evidence, will certainly lead to quite questionable results. The same is likely to happen in relation to conceptual categories of social exclusion and urban segregation based on studies carried out by Marcuse (1997) originally focussed on the U.S., should no critical retracing of the theoretical and empirical links that originated those categories take place in the context to be tested. In brief, oversimplified approaches are bad not because of the quality of the original concepts that may have inspired them, but because they do not capture the underlying dialogue between theory and practice that forged that particular concept in the original work.

Analogously to the already described mismatch between sociological analysis and spatial structure in several urban research experiences of the late 60's and 70's, oversimplified approaches using mixed pre-digested theoretical concepts also do not succeed in associating the analysis of a particular context with the contents of spatial/physical propositions related to this same context. But differently from the first case, in which the quality of each part could be recognised as internally valuable academic exercises despite the incoherent structure of the whole work, the direct transfer of pre-digested archetypes would hardly have any value as a research practice.

Back to our initial considerations of the new prospects of urban information and its inescapable inclusion in urban research regardless of the particular theoretical school involved, it is important to highlight the role of information itself as a tool for social change.

The production, control and treatment of robust urban information is one of the basic preconditions for democracy in urban management. If on the one hand the modernist reformism of the 60's and 70's has been shown to be inapplicable in these days of stringent fiscal discipline, on the other hand the progress and generalisation of information technology and the formal commitments of the managerial state regulation systems to social control and accountability[3] open a new front of social commitment to urban planners, designers and managers. More than in the ready reformist proposition, this commitment is based on the building up of complete and generalised urban information systems that effectively enable vulnerable groups to fight for their rights.

Information today is not a mere input in the formulation of consistent technical proposals in the planning process, rather it is the means through which social groups exercise their will in the political arena. Traditional planning has been somehow replaced by market driven management practices[4] whose main legitimating feature, from a social standpoint, would be accountability and social control. Should these dimensions be not explored by means of an effective democratisation of information, the system will be fully appropriated by a commercial logic, regardless of the political party in charge of local or regional government at that time. The right of voice and vote conceded to vulnerable group representatives in local or sectoral boards will be ineffective should no clear information be available about the policies and projects involved.

In a previous article (Silva 2000) we have shown that, in the field of public networked services, traditional indicators of coverage do not represent an acceptable proxy to universal access anymore. Apart from being connected to a network, effective access to public networked services depends on the localised capacities of production and distribution, as well as on the specific provisions for universal access provided by the regulatory framework. Assessing these capacities and connecting the technical data involved with regulatory provisions require sophisticated information organisation, treatment and interpretation. Should these capabilities not develop and be effectively transferred to users, social participation and public accountability would be impaired.

Therefore the production and management of sound information systems, alongside urban research, is more than a requirement for the sake of academic precision. It is the spine of the new prospects of democratic control over management. In the work of building up this new relationship between urban research and management practice,

3 The understanding of present regulatory reform held in most countries, apart from the main economic and institutional aspects discussed in the literature – e.g. Majone, ed. 1988 – requires also some acquaintance with the foundations of the managerial reform of the state. The prospects and basic limitations of social control and public accountability in the context of the managerial reform of the state can be seen, among others in Kettl (2000). The basic idea is that despite its market driven character, the managerial reform process opens new spaces for democratic control that have not been properly used so far.

4 The twilight of planning as a tool of urban policy and its replacement by a market based concept of management has been assessed by Barnekov (1989), in light of the neo-conservative reform of the 80's in Britain and in the US.

design professionals – perhaps a whole generation of them – will be bound to keep aside, temporarily, their usual tools of analysis and proposition.

More than a design study, a research project within to the context of emerging cities and urban agglomerations must address a sensible response to the construction of a democratic urban management process, since this construction is a precondition for the development of new design approaches that, analogously to past modernist reformism, embody a truly social engagement. This implies an receptive attitude to explore multiple hypotheses originating in different theoretical contexts, to be tested upon a growing information structure whose adequacy – of the information structure itself – would be simultaneously tested.

The importance of such a receptive attitude towards research, and the difficulties involved in this, justifies in our view the emphasis on methodological discussion within Alfa Ibis research network, regardless the matching of each individual project to usual forms of academic production in architecture and urbanism. The research experience carried out under this framework has assumed the dual responsibility of producing consistent projects individually and to overcome meaningful methodological problems in urban research collectively. The basic studies that formed the origin of the Alfa Ibis research program (see Carmona, Burgess and Kolstee 1997) departed from the recognition that well accepted but unproven concepts associated with economic adjustment – e.g. urban productivity and city-wide urban management – were sufficient to explain the complexity of urban process in emerging countries. Thus an innovative attitude towards research methodology is intrinsic to the central objectives of Alfa-Ibis, implying a permanent revision of ongoing doctoral projects. In this last general conference held in Delft in October 2001 this attitude has been reaffirmed, being the rigor of methodological criticism, more than academic purism, and a constructive position in favour of a common objective in promoting, from the standpoint of urban research, new tools for the democratisation of urban planning and management practices.

References

Barnekov, T. (1989) – *Privatism and urban policy in Britain and the United States.* The Oxford University Press. Oxford.

Boyer, R. (1990) – *A teoria da regulação. Uma análise crítica.* Nobel. São Paulo.

Castells, M. (1975) – *La question urbaine.* Maspero. Paris.

Burgess, R.; Carmona M., Kolstee, T. (1997) – Contemporary macrocconomic strategies and urban policies in developing countries: a critical review. In *The Challenge of Sustainable Cities.* Ed by R.Burgess, M..Carmona and T.Kolstee. Zed Books. London & New Jersey. pp 19-21.

Gottdiener, M. (1994) – *The new urban sociology.* McGraw-Hill. New York.

Graham, S.(2000) – Constructing premium network spaces. *International Journal of Urban and Regional Research.* Vol. 24/1. Pp. 183-200. Blackwell Publishers. Oxford.

Harvey, D. (1973) – *Social Justice and the City.* Edward Arnold. London

Harvey, D. (1978) – The urban process under capitalism: a framework for analysis. *Urban Regional Research.* vol. 2: 1. Edward Arnold, London.

Kettl, D.F. (2000) – *The Global Public Management Revolution: A Report on the Transformation of Governance.* Brookings Institute. Washington D.C.

Motta, C.F.A., coord. (1975) – *Nível de satisfação em conjuntos habitacionais da Grande São Paulo.* IPT – Instituto de Pesquisas tecnológicas do Estado de São Paulo. Publicação nº 1061 (2 vol.). São Paulo.

Majone, G., ed. (1988) – *Deregulation or re-regulation? Regulatory reform in Europe and the United States.* Pinter Publishers. London.

Marcuse, P. (1997) – The ghetto of exclusion and the fortified enclave. New patterns in the United States. *American Behavioral Scientist.* Vol. 41 / 3. SAGE Periodicals Press. Pp. 311-328.

Sassen, S. (1991) – *The Global City. New York, London, Tokio.* Princeton University Press. Princeton, NJ.

Silva, R.T. (2000) – The Connectivity of the Infrastructure Networks and the Urban Space of São Paulo in the 90s. *International Journal of Urban and Regional Research.* Vol. 24/1. Pp. 139-164. Blackwell Publishers. Oxford.

2

ICT and Urban Design

Paul Drewe

Outline

Dealing with ICT, a design studio has been created, dedicated to the "Network City". There is no direct link between ICT and spatial structure. And the spatial impacts of the new technology still involve high levels of uncertainty. That is where design comes in as it can demonstrate and visualise **what could be**. The future urban agglomeration is one of the test-beds. The approach is one of design-oriented research aiming at **possible futures**. This approach might be referred to as "research by design", but certainly also involves "design by research". It is, not unlike many aspects of ICT, not a simple matter of either/or.

I. ICT and Urban Design, a Paradigm Challenge

"Why have cities not, long since, been identified, understood and treated as problems of organised complexity? If the people concerned with the life sciences were able to identify their problems of organised complexity, why have people professionally concerned with cities not identified the kind of problems they had?"(Jacobs, 1961: 434). Almost 40 years later the question is even more challenging and urgent: because of ICT.

Box 1

bookstores → bitstores
stacks (in libraries) → servers
galleries → virtual museums
theatres → entertainment infrastructure
schoolhouses → virtual campuses
hospitals → telemedicine
prisons → electronic supervision
banking chambers → ATMs (automated teller machines)
trading floors (stock exchange) → electronic trading systems
department stores → electronic shopping malls
work (in offices) → telwork
at home → @ home

According to Mitchell (1995), a citizen has a choice between actual physical buildings and the corresponding virtual ones. The recombinant architecture implies mutations of traditional buildings (shown in box 1) The latter, to some extent, continue to exist, offering alternatives to virtual "buildings".

Seen as a transport technology, ICT, generally speaking, introduces **choice** for households and business firms. Not unlike the rail, road and air network (in especial the road network when it comes to urban form) it increases the action space, that is the reach of jobs and facilities accessible to users (Dijst, 1995). Accessibility by road also has been a key factor in the evolution of multinodal urban structures: from interaction between two urban systems, exchange of persons, goods and information, via interference (a partial change in the functional structure), to the development of a new joint urban system leading to the creation of new functions (Jacobs, 2000). A shift from automobile travel to electronic communication is a shift to a higher speed. And a higher speed, in turn, means a higher reach.

What are the implications of applying this kind of reasoning to spatial concepts?

From the Dutch history of spatial concepts, for example, two main themes can be distilled: concentration **or** deconcentration (dispersal), multifunctionality (mixed land use) **or** monofunctionality.

The compact city, the dominant concept in recent years, is an example of concentration combined with monofunctionality.

With ICT, however, the either/or thinking of the past is better replaced by multiple-option thinking. At least, that is part of the paradigm challenge.

Only multiple-option thinking - say, concentrating **and** deconcentrating, multi-functionality **and** monofunctionality - can cope with the challenge of organising complexity.

A spatial concept reflects a planning actor's view of a desirable spatial structure (and the interventions necessary to implement it). In the Netherlands there are national, regional and local planning actors who act increasingly with private partners. And there are households and companies with their own view of what is spatially desirable. Yet planning actors and decision-makers on the national level try to impose top down uniform blueprints of spatial structure such as the compact city. This is hardly a good practice of organised complexity. A new approach, embracing the principle of subsidiarity, could stimulate multi-option thinking bottom up; also taking the form of online planning.

II. Networks as Central Concept

Dupuy (1991) distinguishes three, interacting levels of network operators that (re)organise urban space as shown in Figure 1.

Level one involves the suppliers of technical networks. They are specialised and organised in sectors.

On **level two** we find functional networks of common-interest users centring on consumption, production, distribution and personal contacts. To each of these networks specific location factors apply.

It is at **level three** that the operators of functional networks make actual, selective use of technical networks for their special purposes. The resulting networks represent virtual cities. Virtual means being functionally but not formally of its kind. These virtual cities tend to clash with how planning actors usually view a desirable spatial structure.

Figure 1

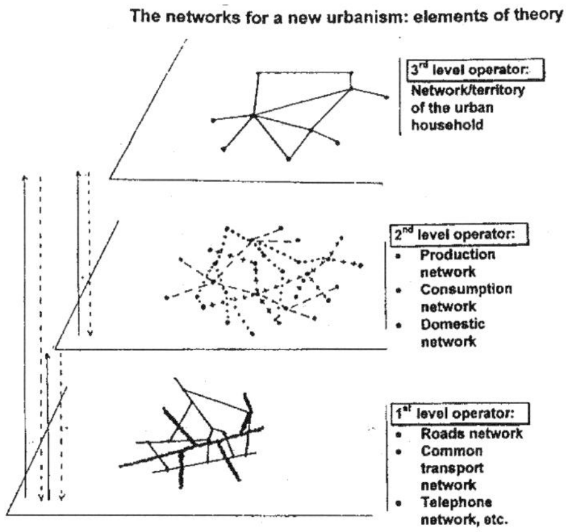

The three-layered has been successfully applied to the Internet three times on the European and national levels (Drewe 1999 a, b; 2000 a).

In each case, **level one** corresponds to the Internet infrastructure. The ISP transit backbone has been chosen, as it is closest to the users. On **level two**, the "Internet industry" is analysed, that is the commercial domain as it leads over other domains. And, finally, **level three** refers to actual traffic on or performance of the Internet.

With suppliers of technical networks at level one, networks are urban-technology based. All kind of technical networks are involved: water, sewer, energy, transport, conventional telecommunication and ICT. The behaviour of the different operators is in itself an important research topic what with the policies of privatisation and liberalisation and the issue of social exclusion or universal service.

In order to illustrate how important urban technology is for urbanism or spatial planning, let us single out the road network and the private car (because it has never been property conceptualised spatially). Mainstream urbanism has rather been dominated by zonal thinkers like Le Corbusier as opposed to network thinkers such as Cerda, Wright or Rouge (Dupuy, 1991). Creating monofunctional zones for dwellings, work and facilities (recreation) naturally induces traffic between those zones. The rise of the automobile and the accompanying expansion of the road network have produced a "mobility problem" that is still unsolved today.

More generally speaking, the Athens Charter of 1933 that served as a blueprint for post-war urbanism is based on two false premises:

"(a) It is desirable to concentrate functions into giant packages; (b) The geometry within each package is homogeneous. Nevertheless, a city contains so many complex human functions that it is impossible to isolate them, let alone concentrate them, so that imposing a simplistic geometry on urban form inhibits the human activities that generate living cities" (Salingaros, 2000: 15).

III. The 'Network City', a Design Studio

The Network City design studio is another example of the search for new concepts. It is a co-operation between the Ministry of VROM and the Faculty of Architecture at Delft University of Technology (http://www.networkcity.nl). The studio involves staff members, PhD students, students in their final year and representatives of VROM's central directorate.

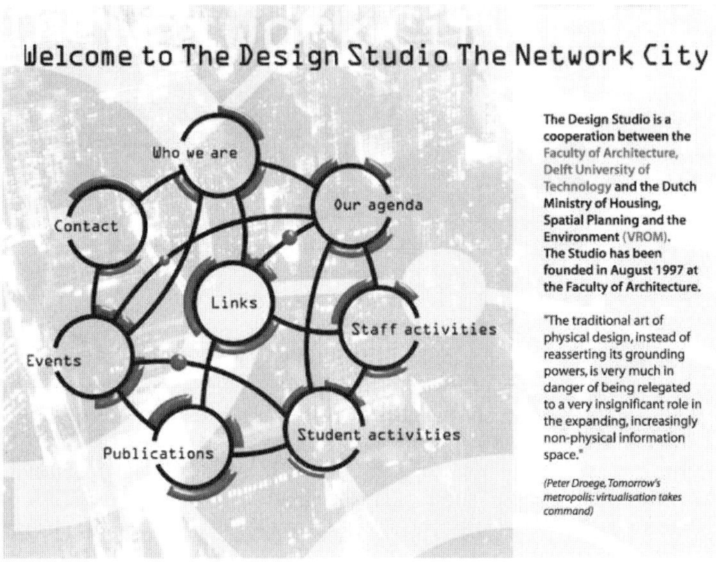

The studio approach is one of design-oriented research aiming at possible futures – as design can demonstrate or visualise what could be. Possible futures relate to the long term. In order to bridge the gap between a distant future and today's practice, a number of location specific test-beds has been chosen: among them "the future urban agglomeration".

Conventionally, urban agglomerations (in the Netherlands) are approached as a hierarchy of areas, looking from the inside out:

- the (historic) city centre (as the "pedestrian city"),
- pre-war inner-city neighbourhoods,
- post-war residential suburbs (or housing estates),
- recent expansion areas (including the VINEX locations),
- the outer periphery (villages and the nearly countryside).

As a contrast, it is possible to design the future agglomeration also from the outside looking in. Each type of area must be able to function according to its own potential, integrating (mixing) different functions as much as possible. The future urban agglomeration can be conceived of as a network of complementary, synergetic locations, a network that is not hierarchically ordered. Complementarity constitutes a certain coherence which makes that the whole is more than the sum of its parts. But coherence or cohesion also requires both old and new means of communication: private cars, however, reducing, automobile dependence; (individual) collective transport; seamless multimodal mobility; and, of course ICT connectivity. This is indeed a challenging design task; how to organise complexity. Post-modern architects, considering urbanism as " a bastion to the denial of reality" will disagree with this approach to urban agglomerations. They find concepts such as identity, complementarity or coherence suspect as the entire notion of urbanism:

"Urbanism or the building of settlements has not only become impossible, but no longer needed or, even worse, undesirable, complicating things. Urbanism ceases to exist" (Koolhaas, 1998).

An illustrative example of a networked city is the concept of an "integrated metropolis" developed by Roberts et al (1999).

According to Roberts et al the shape of cities is moving towards a polycentric or multi-centred form which functions as a whole. Attention is focused on transport interchange (nodal connections between the networks), the high street and the sub-centre.

Urban designers, traditionally, have focused on the square and on site-based problems. The integrated metropolis offers the opportunity of extending the traditional concept of the public realm. It is rather turning into a place of connections between modes of transport, between public and private. Rather than replacing the physical by the virtual or digital, the extended concept of public realm comprises both traditional physical interactions (exchanges of goods, face-to-face social interactions) and virtual interactions (the exchange of information) (MacCormac, 1996).

In designing the integrated metropolis, one does not have to start from scratch, however. There are quite a few "classics" that offer sources of inspiration (Drewe 2000b).

What needs to be done is to develop rules or codes for electronic or digital connectivity: "In order to define a coherent, working urban fabric, the pattern language of electronic connection (which is only now being developed) must tie in seamlessly to the language for physical connections. Already some authors misleadingly declare that the city is made redundant by electronic connectivity. Such opinions ignore new observed patterns which correlate electronic nodes to physical nodes in the pedestrian urban fabric" (Salingaros, 2000, 8).

To illustrate what the network at the "Network City" design studio is about, here are some topics that relate to the future urban agglomeration, that is the relation between ICT and urban form:

- how to design a new residential area, talking into account ICT and hence in contrast to a VINEX location
- can the New Urbanism approach from the United States inspire the design of a new residential area in the Netherlands, including a code for ICT; once again, in contrast with a VINEX location
- and, vice versa, can the Dutch approach to urbanism make a contribution to planning a location in the United States including ICT and elements of new urbanism
- how to plan emergent Edge Cities in the Netherlands, compared to the US experience and what role can the urbanist play in this
- how can the national planning concept of "network cities" be applied to a corridor of two cities outside the Randstad and what would the planning and decision-making process be like

- how to plan and design "the future urban agglomeration" in the periphery of the Netherlands as ICT-based network urban nodes
- how can the urbanism of networks be changed into sustainable network urbanism: in designing interfaces between ecological and urban infrastructures
- how to design a mixed residential-work environment interfacing with new wet grassland, using "light urbanism" and ICT
- how to combine ICT (a neighbourhood telecenter) with sustainable construction to revitalise a waterfront area
- design aspects of ICT applications in an existing neighbourhood: catering to the needs of the elderly (Caso, 1999)
- can ICT be used to help with the revitalisation of a deprived neighbourhood in a Dutch city empowering its residents
- the same question only this time applied to cities in Latin America
- design of personal travel services as part of a larger project on sustainable multimodal mobility including, among others, a design theory for intermodal transfer points in multimodal passenger transport networks.

IV. Where do we go from here?

The work carried out so far in the design studio as well as a number of emergent (mainly Anglo-Saxon) concepts lead to the same conclusion: the need of an integrated planning of land use and urban technology networks, in particular transport and ICT. Siembab (1999) – for example – pleads for "a bricks and bits strategy for livable communities" including land use, transportation and ICT. He illustrates this idea with a demonstration project in **Los Angeles** ("Blue Line Tele Village"). Graham and Marvin (1998) list three areas in which urban ICT initiatives are already occurring:

- integrated transport and IT strategies (urban and regional teleworking initiatives, new communication corridors, road information informatics),
- city-level new media and IT strategies,
- information districts and urban televillages,

There is a wide range of possibilities as, for example, demonstrated by the Global Bangemann Challenge with more than 600 submissions covering 11 themes and 18 winners (Drewe 2000b)

Of course, there is still a lot of work ahead. An integrated planning of land use and urban technology networks (including ICT) needs to be developed. And urban ICT initiatives are to be stimulated. In particular those that tackle the "digital divide" in cities (Drewe, 2000b).

If ICT is not taken seriously and dealt with in a professional manner, Kolhaas after all may be proven right in calling urbanism "a bastion to the denial of reality". Or is Dorothy Parker right when she wrote way back "you can't teach an old dogma new tricks".

References

Caso, O.: The city, the elderly and telematics, PhD. Thesis, Faculty of Architecture, Delft University of Technology; Delft University Press, Delft, 1999.

Dijst, M.: Het elliptisch leven, actieruimte als integrale maat voor bereik en mobiliteit, PhD. thesis, Faculty of Architecture, Delft University of Technology, Nederlandse Geografische Studies, Utrecht, 1995.

Drewe, P.: The Internet- beyond the "hype", how to position the Randstad Holland, Design Studio "The Network City", Faculty of Architecture, Delft University of Technology, 1999a.

Drewe, P.: The Internet- The Randstad and the 'rest' of the Netherlands, Design Studio "The Network City", Faculty of Architecture, Delft University of Technology, 1999b.

Drewe, P.: The Internet – how to position capital cities on the European net, release 1.1, Design Studio "The Network City", Faculty of Architecture, Delft University of Technology, 2000a.

Dupuy, G.: L'urbanisme des réseaux, théories et méthodes, Armand Colin, Paris, 1991.

Graham, S. and Marvin, S.: The richness of cities, urban policy in a new landscape, Working Paper 3, Centre for Urban Technology, University of Newcastle, 1998.

Jacobs, J.: The life and death of great American cities, Vintage Books, New York, 1961.

Jacobs, M.: Multinodal urban structures, a comparative analysis and strategies for design, PhD thesis, Faculty of Architecture, Delft University of Technology, 2000.

Koolhaas, R.: Amnestie voor de hedendaagse stad, in W.J. Beek et al (eds), De onvermijdelijke culturele revolutie, SMO, Den Haag, 1998.

Maccormac, R.: An anatomy of London, Built Environment, 22, nr. 4, 306-311, 1996.

Mitchell, W.J.: The city of bits-space, time and the infobahn, MIT Press, Cambridge, Mass. and London, 1995.

Roberts, M., Lloyd-Jones, T., Erickson, B. and Nice, S.: Place and space in the networked city: conceptualizing the integrated metropolis, Journal of Urban Design, 4, no. 1, 51-66, 1999.

Salingaros, N.A.: The structure of pattern languages, Division of Mathematics, University of Texas at San Antonio, 2000.

Siembab, W.: Integrating telecommunications into metropolitan policy and planning: a bricks and bits strategy for livable communities. Paper presented at 'Cities in the Global Information Society: An International Perspective', University of Newcastle, November 22-24, 1999.

3

Rethinking Urban Form and Development in Latin America

Sueli Ramos Schiffer[5]

Introduction

The new trends of economic and urban development of the largest Latin America cities are discussed, focusing on the need to promote appropriate public policies and urban plans, and addressing the inevitable fate of these agglomerations to become predominantly tertiary.

The 21st century is subjecting Latin America public management and urban policies to a new reality, characterised by a strong decline in the population growth rate. This recent trend of very little population increase is something new to planners and public management alike, and something that must be addressed. The immediate outcome of possible demographic stabilisation (*Table 1*), together with the irreversible decline in manufacturing jobs, and the relative share of this stabilisation in the total national value-added (*Table 2*), is a new prospect for city planning in Latin America. This is because the historical paradigm of the public sector to provide infrastructure for city expansion has changed. Peripheral city areas, in particular, were densely occupied, and became consolidated with no infrastructure and with environmental deterioration, long before any possible improvement could be implemented by the public sector.

On one hand, urban plans should aim at preserving the history not only of possibly degraded city centres, but also of the early manufacturing areas that are now obsolete. On the other hand, they should give support to the effort of improving housing conditions, especially for the low-income population. This population is marginalised as a result of the on-going globalisation of the world economy, and its social inclusion is more than ever dependent on how well national and local public policies can steer the right course.

Public policies are urgently needed to renovate parts of the city that, despite their visual unattractiveness due to deterioration or abandonment, are nonetheless representative of past historical periods, so that future generations may live alongside their historical roots. At the same time, the evidence from recent research[6], which indicates that there is a correlation between violence and deteriorated neighbourhoods or urban areas with a critical lack of adequate social and basic infrastructure, requires

5 Full Professor of the University of Sao Paulo School of Architecture and Urban Planning, Brazil.

6 See: Cardia & Schiffer (2000) and WHO Project on Urbanization, Youth and Risk Factors for Substance Abuse, Geneva: WHO (2000); and Lehrer (2000).

stronger action from urban management in order to promote acceptable urban environments.

The effectiveness of these policies will be largely dependent –clearly besides political will– on a comprehensive and integrated macro-plan involving the entire urban or metropolitan area and focussing on renovating specific urban areas[7]. Such urban renewal should be contemplated as a strategic investment needed to address the Latin American short-term prospect of lower economic and population growth.

Demographic Trends and Urban Form

The urban pattern that developed after the period of early industrialisation in the late 1800s, in most Latin America cities, preserved the radial form that expanded out from the colonial nucleus, according to a trend whereby lower income groups settled in the outskirts. The traditional downtown centre witnessed on-going degradation after the mid-20th century, when new centres emerged to house the advanced tertiary activities. This superseding process is still ongoing – any newly created centre depreciates the previous one. It is governed by market rules and lacks governmental control over the preservation of the city's memory.

Owing to the recent trends of manufacturing globalisation with intense modernisation, following the introduction of electronics and robotics on assembly lines, a number of old manufacturing areas were abandoned in the main industrial centres of Latin America as from the early 1980s. All these historical spaces dating from the 19th century risk being strongly degraded or replaced by modern buildings, leaving behind no memory of that period save pictures and stories. Meanwhile, peripheral areas expanded mainly to accommodate lower income housing, which cropped up with no planning or infrastructure.

The 1980s also evidenced the final stages of the urbanisation process in most of Latin America (*Table 1*), partially responsible for the intense population growth rate, especially from 1950 to 1980. Nonetheless, what is remarkable is that even despite the lower population growth rates of today, in comparison with previous decades, the urban population in the Latin American and Caribbean region rose by 147.2 million in absolute numbers from 1980 to 1999 [8]. In 1999, 75% of the total population of this region was urban, in contrast with 65% in 1980 *(Table 1)*.

This population growth places heavy demands on housing, jobs and public services, especially considering that the geographical distribution of these basic needs within major cities has followed a very irregular pattern. In nearly all Latin American countries, there has been a relative higher population growth in the lower income groups without any essential change in the income distribution indicator (*Table 2*) and a significant growth in the unemployment rate[9]. These factors are aggravating the already serious deficiencies in the social and urban infrastructure in the outskirts, where the lower-income population lives, particularly regarding housing, transport and telecommunications.

What is also constant in Latin America is the extreme concentration of the urban population in a few oversized agglomerations. Considering Latin American and

---

7 See Zancheti (1999) for an approach integrating historical heritage and urban planning.

8 Data from the World Bank: 2001 World Development Indicators (Table 3.10).

9Table 2.4, taken from "The World Bank: 2001 World Development Indicators," indicates that the unemployment rate is expressively higher for the labor force with a lower educational level.

Caribbean countries, the average share of urban population living in agglomerations with more than 1 million inhabitants rose to 32% in 2000 (*Table 1*). The percentage of total urban population living in the largest cities of the Latin American countries presented in Table 1 is also impressive. Over one third of Argentina's whole population lived in Buenos Aires in 2000; Mexico City is responsible for 25% of the national urban population, representing roughly 24 million persons in 2000, whereas Sao Paulo City housed about 12 million inhabitants in the same period (*Table 1*).

Most of the major cities in Latin America now face an absurd reality. On one hand, there are particular districts with fair infrastructure and reasonable accessibility, and with a great number of empty old buildings. On the other hand, there are peripheral and/or downtown districts with scarce basic infrastructure, and with a growing number of squatter settlements and slums. Urban planners and urban management have to face this reality, and to put in place urban renewal projects for obsolete or degraded areas in prospective plans for urban and regional development.

Another important fact that must be addressed in prospective urban studies and plans is the projected annual population growth rate by age blanket for Latin American countries (*Table 1*). Basically, in all the countries listed in *Table 1* as well as all of Latin America and the Caribbean, a negative growth rate is expected for the population age 0 to 14, contrasting with high annual growth rates for the population over 65, in the next decades. The social and physical infrastructure needs of the population in the urban areas must be determined and realigned in line with this ageing population growth trend.

In recent years, the World Bank Group[10] has sought to develop a loan program strategy to promote historical heritage conservation in developing countries to reduce poverty[11]. Their report "Poverty Trends and Voices of the Poor" (January 2001), quantified for 1987, 1990, 1998, and projecting scenarios for 2015, by world regions, point to a growing population living with less than 1 or 2 dollars a day. In the Latin American and Caribbean region, the number of people living on less than US$2 a day has been 159.0 million since 1998, with a prospect to rise to 161.6 million in 2015, under a low case growth scenario.

It is clearly implicit from recent World Bank Group documents [12] that investing in cultural and historical sites is an alternative for unemployment and for waning job offers in the manufacturing sector. The proposal studied today and signalling the growing relevance of international loans and grants to conserve historical assets [13] are mostly directed at developing countries where poverty is swelling rapidly and the prospects for effective economic development are extremely unfavourable in the current context of economic globalisation.

---

10 The World Bank Group consists of five institutions: IBRD – The International Bank for Reconstruction and Development; IDA – The International Development Association; IFC – The International Finance Corporation; MIGA – The Multilateral Investment Guarantee Agency; and ICSID – The International Centre for Settlement of Investment Disputes.

11 For detailed information see The World Bank: "Partners in Transforming Development: New Approaches to Developing Country-Owned Reduction Strategies" (March 2000), and "Poverty Reduction Strategy Papers; Internal Guidance Note" (January 2000) (http://www.worldbank.org).

12 The main documents from The World Bank Group web site under the topics: 'Poverty Net', 'Culture' and 'Cultural Heritage' are listed in the *references* of this paper.

13 The relevance of this issue can be assessed in the announcement by the Bank's President James Wolfensohn concerning the text of the '*World Development Report 2002/2003*', entitled "Sustainable Development with a Dynamic Economy: Growth, Poverty, Social Cohesion, and the Environment" (http://worldbank.org/wdr/2002/index.htm).

However, political will and financial credit may be not enough to guarantee the success of urban renewal projects, which are required if 'success' is to be measured in terms of quality of preservation and renovation of an urban area. Also needed are the commitment by newcomer residents and the instilling of a sense of citizenship in the entire population.

The complexity of the research, action and management required for integrated urban planning for urban renewal and development is undeniable, especially when more than one municipality is involved. The methodological approach suggested below, for the development of integrated urban planning parameters for historical, technological, legal/institutional and financing issues is, in fact, new to most Latin American countries, if we consider modern cities.

Some successful experiences have been made in different places in Latin America, mainly UNESCO world heritage cities, such as Olinda, Sao Luiz and Salvador in Brazil, Coro and la Vela in Venezuela, Trinidad in Cuba, and Mexico City, among others[14]. The developed countries have innumerable examples of renewal projects for inner cities, such as South Bronx [15] in New York (late 1970s). Re-development projects have also been implemented, especially aiming at revitalising old seaports such as the Docklands in London and the Old Port of Rotterdam, or waterfront areas such as Battery Park in New York, Faneuil Hall in Boston and Nyhavn Canal in Copenhagen [16]. Puerto Madero in Buenos Aires is one of the few examples of the successful revitalisation of a waterfront area in Latin America[17].

Certainly the most comprehensive and largest project of urban and regional industrial renewal was developed in the Emscher region within the Ruhr District in Germany. Under the auspices of the Internationale Bau Austellung – IBA, a regional association of 17 municipalities comprising a total land area of 802 km^2, over 100 different projects have been carried out since 1989. The area that previously housed the main German coal, steel and related industries, experienced a great decline in economic production[18], with the obsolescence of the manufacturers, out-migration of the qualified labour force and population, and contaminated soil as a side effect of these industries (Latz & Partner, 1996).

The project was designed to safeguard the history of the area by preserving the existing vegetation and renovating some industrial buildings for new use. At the same time, seven development areas were set aside within the region, involving housing, offices, shopping, and leisure activities for the neighbourhood areas (Walker, 1997), in addition to the creation of the Emscher's Park according to ecological principles.

Nevertheless, few studies have been carried out in developing countries focusing on deteriorated manufacturing areas and the possibility of undertaking urban renewal projects for historical areas of low-income housing land use.

The recent Brazilian redevelopment project which aimed at revitalising an old manufacturing area, organised by the Santo André Municipality (within the metropolitan area of São Paulo) with the co-operation of internationally renowned planners –named

---

14 For further information on and evaluation of the main projects implemented in Latin American world heritage cities, see Milet & Pontual (1999), and Zancheti (1995; 1998).

15 See: Shnidman (1999).

16 See: Halpern (1995) for an evaluation of American case studies, and Roca Cladera (1995) for detailed European examples.

17 The renewal project of Puerto Madero was carried out under the management of the Corporación Puerto Madero, as described by Bertolini (2001).

18 See Maggi (2000) for further assessment of the IBA project.

'Projeto Urbanístico Eixo Tamanduatheí'[19] – is a relevant example of the complexity of the institutional framework and of the lack of adequate supra-municipality tools needed to undertake redevelopment and renewal projects[20] within an urban agglomeration boundary.

A Methodological Approach to Prospective Urban Plans

The planning of any public policy intent on preserving the historical development of major cities in Latin American countries should begin by reviewing the city's economic development and any consequential spatial changes. This is needed to determine how the historical periods of the built-up environment should be divided and what assets must be preserved in each period. Usually the older parts of these cities are marked by diverse and pronounced contrasts in urban occupation, characterised by the conservation of few important old buildings and a very unattractive landscape. In spite of this physical handicap, some old sites have impressive assets, rich in achievements that are part of their national histories.

The development of parameters aiming at conservation and urban renewal of the historical centres and obsolete manufacturing areas of Latin America's most important major cities should pursue a multidisciplinary methodology. Focusing on the development and the land use of the entire urban agglomeration, the selection of sites to be renewed should bear in mind social, economic, political and cultural aspects of the built-up environment, rather than focus on isolated historical monuments.

In this sense, research developed with an eye to building according to public policy parameters, in such a way as to preserve the historical course of a city through urban renewal and redevelopment, must include a diversified set of approaches, such as:

- *Institutional* - establishment of an appropriate regulatory and programmatic framework to allow project implementation within a regional scale;

- *Historical development* – assessment of the development of particular urban sites and their specific role within the urban structure, aiming at determining the boundaries of the area to be renewed and the relevant buildings to be restored, as well as preserving the historical identity of the area for visitors and local inhabitants;

- *Socio-economic* – proposals for new land use priorities must take into account the needs of the population previously living in the area and the socio-economic relevant land use demands for the whole urban agglomeration;

- *Financing* – forms of economic partnerships between the public and private sectors: from the planning to the implementation stages; legal structure and criteria to finance the acquisition and/or renting of the housing/buildings in the renewed area;

19 See: Prefeitura Municipal de Santo André (2000).

20 According to Burns (1963:14), "*redevelopment* is taken to mean the process which involves clearance of property and the building of new structures according to a definite preconceived plan with a layout different from that of the area before redevelopment was undertaken," whereas "*urban renewal* is taken to mean the process by which a large area of a town –say the whole town center– slowly renews itself and thereby gradually changes its character to fit in with the needs of contemporary society."

- *Legal planning and control tools* – establishment of general norms and possible restrictions for urban renewal projects; development of the institutional framework required for management and social control of the urban renewal process;

- *Community participation* - Several different social and economic agents, whether public, private or non-governmental groups, trade unions, and the local and urban population must be encouraged to commit themselves and must have a pre-established role set forth in the public policy;

- *Economic* - assure the promotion of social and cultural initiatives, especially to promote employment and re-qualification of the local labour force;

- *Information system* – creation of relevant indicators that will allow urban management and the community to have long-term control over the implementation and preservation of the renewal project, and enable any future changes to be made smoothly.

Research and projects aiming at urban development with the renewal of specific areas should also be based on the following premises:

1. The understanding that the adequate preservation of the historical development of a city is crucial to foster the population's sense of citizenship and to gain its commitment to the quality of both urban life and the surrounding environment;

2. The renewal project for a particular area must enable the population to identify a particular built-up environment as the outcome of a social-economic process that has partially shaped the city's history and its present urban form;

3. The renewal projects should have the foremost goal of addressing the most evident local social problems, which, in the case of Latin America, would be the extreme lack of social housing.

In summary, the proposal of parameters for urban development should be based on architectural, technological, cultural, economic and social factors aiming at revitalising select areas and at proposing new land uses, according to an integrated macro-urban plan, but without neglecting the role of some specific sites in the past history of the area.

Conclusions

Similar to what occurred in most major cities of developing countries before the 1990s, most of Latin America's largest cities are becoming a tertiary-oriented region. In terms of land use, on-going manufacturing deconcentration and modernisation processes have strongly and chiefly impacted the old manufacturing districts. In these zones, today, large areas are occupied by degraded or abandoned manufacturing plants, in which neither private capital nor public management has invested.

Proposals by urban planners today should focus on designing parameters for urban conservation and redevelopment, in order to urge public management to earmark subsidies and create public policies tailored to revert the frequent, deleterious intervention in old neighbourhoods that often robs the zones of their historical local characteristics. At the same time, the urban plans must focus on creating alternatives for employment, social housing and construction of adequate neighbourhoods, in a regional context of lower rates of population growth and economic development.

In this sense, urban researchers and policymakers must urge that interdisciplinary studies be taken up, essentially rethinking the urban development trend, in which urban renewal must be part of integrated macro-urban plans designed to take into account the entire urban agglomeration. They must also advocate the participation of multiple agents, both private and public, to design urban policies successfully and enforce their suitable implementation, in order that historical areas may be preserved and that assistance to the lower income local population may be assured.

The most problematic issue that the major Latin American cities will have to deal with in this new century is the drawing up of poverty relief policies. The quality of life of a neighbourhood, measured by urban and infrastructure indicators, such as social, leisure, health, and educational equipment factors, among others, is closely connected to the level of violence and to the population's sense of citizenship, and cannot be neglected by the local and regional management if any improvement in social inequalities is to be achieved.

References

Bertolini, M. (2001). "La costanera del Sur. *Revista TGM (34)*. P. 20-25.

Cardia, N. & Schiffer, S. (2000). São Paulo Secondary Data Analysis. In: WHO Project in Urbanization, Youth and Risk Factors for Substance Abuses. Geneva: WHO.

Halpern, Robert (1995). *Rebuilding the Inner City*. New York: Columbia University Press.

Latz & Partner (1996). "Duisburg Nord Lanscape Park, Emscher, Germany. Landscape planning and regeneration". *ELASA UN Paper 1996*. (http://www.stu-uni-hannover.de/~voell/elasa/archive/UN96).

Lehrer, E. (2000) Crime-fighting and urban renewal. *Public Interest* (141), pp. 91-103.

Maggi, C. (2000). *INEF Report. Key factors of structural changes in North Rhine-Westphalia.* Duisburg: Gerhard-Mercator-Universität. (Heft 45/2000).

Milet, V. & Pontual, V. (1999) *Evaluacion de la Gestion y de las necesidades de capacitacion técnica en las ciudades del patrimonio mundial de América Latina.* Canada: Organization of the World Heritage Cities / ICCROM / CECI.

Prefeitura Municipal de Santo André (2000). *Cidade Futuro: Projeto Urbanístico Eixo Tamanduatheí.* Santo André: PMSA.

Roca Cladera, Juana (1995). *Rehabilitación urbana. Análisis comparado de algunos países de la Unión Europea.* Madrid: Ministerio de Obras Públicas, Transportes y Medio Ambiente. Dirección General para la Vivienda, el Urbanismo y la Arquitectura.

Shnidman, E.S. (1999). Charlotte St. in the South Bronx – Urban Renewal that Worked. *Realty Times*, April 21, 1999.

The Nordic World Heritage Office (1999). *Sustainable Tourism and Cultural Heritage. A Review of Development Assistance and Its Potential to Promote Sustainability.* The World Bank: Washington.

The World Bank (1998). *Culture and Sustainable Development: A Framework for Action.* The World Bank: Washington.

The World Bank / UNESCO - United Nations Educational, Scientific, and Cultural Organization (1999). *Proceedings of the Seminar Culture Counts. Financing, Resources, and the Economics of Culture in Sustainable Development.* The World Bank / UNESCO: Florence, October 4-7.

The World Bank / UNESCO - United Nations Educational, Scientific, and Cultural Organization (1999). *Culture Counts. Towards New Strategies for Culture in Sustainable Development.* The World Bank / UNESCO: Florence, October 4-7.

The World Bank / UNESCO - United Nations Educational, Scientific, and Cultural Organization (1998). Conference *Understanding Culture in Sustainable Development: Investing in Cultural and Natural Endowments.* The World Bank / UNESCO: Washington, September 28-29. (http://wbln0018.worldbank.org)

The World Bank. Poverty Reduction and Economic Management (2001). *Poverty Trends and Voices of the Poor. Fourth edition.* The World Bank: Washington.

Walker, R. (1997). "Germany Greens its 'Brownfields,' offering a post-industrial model." *The Christian Science Monitor* (Dec.3, 1997)
. http://www.csmonitor.com/durable/1997/12/03/intl).

Zancheti, S.M (org.) (1999) *Conservation and Urban Sustainable Development.* Recife: CECI/UFPE.

Zancheti, S.M. et al. (orgs.) (1995). *Estratégias de intervenção em centros históricos.* Recife: MDU/UFPE.

Zancheti, S.M. et al. (orgs.) (1998). *Revitalização do Bairro do Recife: plano, regulação e avaliação.* Recife: CECI/UFPE.

Table 1. Latin American selected countries. Population data.

Countries / Region	Total population (in millions)	Urban population (% of total population)		Population in urban agglomerations of more than one million (% of total population)		Population in largest city (% of total population)		Average annual population growth rate (1999-2015) (Ages)		
	1999	1970	1999	1980	2000	1980	2000	Total	0-14 (%)	65+ (%)
Argentina	36.6	78	89	42	41	43	38	1.0	-0.1	1.6
Brazil	168.0	56	81	32	34	16	13	1.1	0.0	2.9
Chile	15.0	75	84	33	36	41	43	1.0	-0.5	3.1
Ecuador	12.4	40	62	23	32	29	29	1.5	-0.3	3.0
Mexico	96.6	59	74	28	28	31	25	1.3	-0.2	3.2
Uruguay	3.3	82	91	42	37	49	41	0.6	-0.2	0.7
Venezuela	23.7	72	87	28	29	21	15	1.5	-0.2	3.9
Latin America & Caribbean	508.2	57	75	29	32	27	25	1.3	-0.1	2.8

Source: The World Bank: World Development Indicators 2001 (Tables 1.5; 2.1; 3.10).

Table 2. Latin American selected countries. Social-economic data.

Countries/Region	Gross Domestic Product (US$ millions)		Manufacturing value-added (% of GDP)		Services value-added (% of GDP)		Total Unemployment (% of total labor force)		Distribution of income (percentage share of income) *		Gross National Income per capita (US$)
	1990	1999	1990	1999	1990	1999	1980-82	1996-98	40% -	10% +	1999
Argentina	141,352	283,166	27	18	56	67	2.3	16.3	..	..	7,550
Brazil	464,989	751,505	25	23	53	61	2.8	7.8	(4) 5.7	46.7	4,350
Chile	30,323	67,469	20	16	50	57	10.4	7.2	(3) 6.3	46.9	4,630
Ecuador	10,686	18,991	19	21	49	50	..	11.5	(2) 9.4	33.8	1,360
Mexico	262,710	483,737	21	21	64	67	..	2.3	(3) 7.6	41.1	4,440
Uruguay	9,287	20,805	28	17	56	67	..	10.1	(1) 10.0	32.7	6,220
Venezuela	48,593	102,222	20	14	44	59	5.9	11.4	(4) 8.3	37.6	3,680
Latin America & Caribbean	1,136,103	2,052,720	24	21	55	62	..	..	..	..	3,800

Source: The World Bank: World Development Indicators 2001 (Tables 1.1; 2.4; 2.8; 4.2).

.. no data / * survey years: (1) 1989; (2) 1995; (3) 1996; (4) 1997

4

Globalisation, Socio-Spatial Segregation and Urban Land Regulation: What are the Links?[21]

Mario Lungo [22]

I - Introduction

In addition to its historical character, socio-spatial segregation is a social process with a spatial dimension. For this reason the research question is intrinsic to its complex development and forms, especially in urban areas (Marcuse, 2001). Socio-spatial segregation also has to be taken into account in analysis and formulation of policies to address its negative consequences. Each social group and society have their own perception on the consequences of segregation. Unfortunately, in most instances this question is omitted from the analysis and policies.

Socio-spatial segregation is a clear example of an issue whose features and determining factors differs historically among distinct countries. In some of them, mainly developed countries, the predominant questions are linked to ethnical and racial relationships; in others, most of developing countries, social and economical differences are the basis of socio-spatial segregation.

However, the differences between developed and developing countries do not imply that in the cities of the developed world manifestations of socio-spatial segregation linked with social distinction (Bordieu, 1979), social distance (Chamboderon and Lemaire, 1970), and with different income levels of the inhabitants, do not exist. Neither does this mean that cities in developing countries are exempt of socio-spatial segregation manifestations that are based on ethnical and racial questions. It is clear from the literature that these differences are the source of a particular focus between academic research and policy design to address this problem in distinct countries. In the developing countries ecological explanations of socio-spatial segregation predominate as well as the development of quantitative indices (Brun and Rhein, 1994). In developing countries, however, research on socio-spatial segregation is limited, and attempts to quantify segregation is in its infancy and face statistical limitations (Schteingart, 1997).

In Latin America, the analysis of socio-spatial segregation in the 60´s and 70´s was influenced by Marxist theory, but this approach lost influence at the beginning of the

---

21 This document written for the October 2001 ALFA-IBIS Conference, is broadly based on the ongoing research for the TUDelft. A preliminary version, with the collaboration of Sonia Baires, was presented at the Lincoln Institute of Land Policy seminar "Segregation in the City", Cambridge, Massachusetts, July 2001

22Executive Director of the San Salvador Metropolitan Area Planning Office (OPAMSS) and Professor of the Organization of Space Department, Universidad Centroamericana "José Simeón Cañas".

80's. More recently, the interest in this theme has been linked to the analysis of the effects of the globalisation process. Several of these analyses focus attention on the question of liberalisation of the land market (Sabatini, 1997; Jaramillo 1997); whilst others focus on the new forms of socio-spatial segregation (Arizaga, 2000; Caldeira, 2000; Robert, 1998; Torres, 1998; Portes et al, 1997).

But the differences in socio-spatial segregation between distinct countries have been diminishing over the last years. Globalisation, in our opinion, is a process that tends to homogenise socio-spatial segregation manifestations in many of the countries. The massive flows of capital, goods and people have introduced social and cultural transformations in all countries that are changing the social geography and landscapes of cities and metropoles.

In the cities of developed countries, intense international migration flows are modifying the traditional localisation of racial and ethnical communities, resulting in melting processes sometimes conflictive sometimes integrative. In several cities of developing countries, the increase of the immigrant population of neighbouring countries, is generating pockets of socio-spatial segregation never seen before, like in the case of San José in Costa Rica, that accommodate a high percentage of immigrants coming from Nicaragua.

The increasing limitation of available urban land, the growing urban population, the environmental restrictions (as in the case of Bogota's Sabana), the new logic and forms of commercial and service centre localities and the construction of new road infrastructure networks, are among the factors, transforming socio-spatial segregation patterns in the large Latin American cities.

In these cities there is another phenomenon, which is strongly linked to the issue of socio-spatial segregation: the large and growing area that most researchers call the "informal city", especially illegal neighbourhoods and slums.

The combinations of all these factors produce multiple segregating dynamics. Among its current manifestations we find a type of elite suburbanization, that is located outside the cities and break with the traditional central grid (i.e. Buenos Aires and Santiago de Chile). The spatial pattern consists of residential projects for high-income groups within low and medium income residential zones (i.e. San José and San Salvador). As part of this dynamic "gated communities" emerge, a residential form preferred by the richest people.

These transformations occur in the midst of an intense state modernisation process that is promoting the liberalisation and privatisation of urban management. In this current context, the traditional methods of urban land regulation are clearly obsolete, in the light of increasing urbanisation in general terms and socio-spatial segregation problems in particular.

Based in the previous statements, the following double and preliminary hypothesis can be developed:

Firstly, as the globalisation process advance, new forms of socio-spatial segregation tend to be increasingly similar in the Latin American cities, in spite of historical and structural differences;

Obviously there is not a direct causality between globalisation and socio-spatial segregation, and the fact that globalisation is the cause of growing inequalities in world development, does not imply more socio-spatial segregation. We need to identify the linkages that exist between these two processes. One of the most important linkages is the functioning of the land market; in this regard we must understand the important role of urban land regulation.

In addition, the question of territorial scales must also be considered to analyse the issue of socio-spatial segregation. It explains the fact that in several Latin American cities, this phenomenon is diminishing at urban macro level but at the same time, increasing at urban micro level. Globalisation, as is postulated by many researchers, is not a new process and, its consequences and effects are deeply conditioned by the history and the geography (Harvey, 2000).

Secondly, as more transformations of socio-spatial segregation occur, the urban land regulatory framework becomes more obsolete and it doesn't contribute to the reduction of socio-spatial segregation.

If it is true that the functioning of land markets play an important role in the linkages between globalisation and socio-spatial segregation, the critical analysis of urban land regulatory frameworks and their instruments, emerge as a priority research and policy-making theme.

The analysis of the links between globalisation and the new forms of socio-spatial segregation through the functioning of urban land markets require the analysis of current urban land regulatory frameworks, especially for cities that have a weak urban planning tradition and a short urban tradition, like San Salvador. In general terms, this kind of research can contribute to research on the sustainability of current Latin American urban development. There have been limited studies in Latin America on this issue despite the fact that it has great importance for the formulation of policies on urban social sustainable development (Polese and Stren, 2000).

The following section discusses the changes in the traditional patterns of socio-spatial segregation in Latin American cities, emphasising the explosion of the gated communities as one of the most common new forms of socio-spatial segregation. The following section analyses the relation between socio-spatial segregation and urban land regulation, using the case of the San Salvador Metropolitan Area. In the last section we pose some preliminary conclusions looking at future research themes on this issue.

II - Changes of Socio-Spatial Segregation Forms in Latin American Cities and their Relation with Globalisation Processes

The more visible manifestation of socio-spatial segregation in Latin American cities, especially during the accelerated expansion of the last half of the XX century, was the dramatic spatial separation between the residential areas of the highest income groups and the residential areas of the poor people, a scheme that reveals other differences such as ethnical and racial ones. This pattern of residential occupation of urban land was in line with urban planning approaches based on the spatial separation of activities through zoning.

Current globalisation processes are contributing to substantially modify the grid prevailing in the last decades of the XX Century and the dominant approach of urban planning. This will change not only the new forms of territorial activities, services and housing locality, but it will also make way for a new approach to city development theory, where strategic planning and large urban projects will play an essential role.

These changes are visible since the early 80´s and today they are a common trend which has to be managed in the majority of the great Latin American cities. In this context, socio-spatial segregation assumes new forms that tend to be alike in most of these cities.

We can identify three types of urban interventions that have strong consequences for the emergence of socio-spatial segregation forms:

- Large urban projects, including the large historical centre revitalisation projects. Some of these projects imply a gentrification process that move the poorer inhabitants from this old zone (like a kind of involuntary eviction), and the occupation by new high income people.
- Building of a new urban network and big shopping centres. These projects are generally linked with the relocating of productive activities and services (free zones, harbour reactivation, financial zones, etc.), and with interregional and international trade increased by the globalisation process.
- Construction of gated communities in areas of high and medium-high income. These residential units assume distinct forms depending on each city, ranging from luxury apartment buildings in the central zones to complexes of individual houses, with large green and play spaces and surrounding protection walls. In many cases these projects are territorially linked with a new road infrastructure network.

It is obvious that large urban projects do not inevitably produce socio-spatial segregation processes, neither do historical centre revitalisation projects, but we can observe examples of gentrification in some of them. Here again, it is necessary to analyse this phenomenon taking in consideration the issue of territorial scales (Sabatini, 2001).

A good example of the first urban intervention type and its role in the accentuation of socio-segregation is a large urban renewal program in the downtown of old Santo Domingo, in Dominican Republic, promoted by the Balaguer government in the late 80's (Lozano, 1997). The inhabitants of these neighbourhoods had been largely evicted to the city's periphery and the few residents that remained in this zone suffered from a total habitat fragmentation since several streets dissecting the traditional neighbourhoods. On these new streets, buildings dedicated to trade and services were constructed replacing the former houses.

This urban renewal project was closely linked with an economic strategy that sought the reactivation and redeployment of activities in the context of the structural adjustment and the opening of the Dominican economy to the outside world. In addition, the Balaguer regime aimed to obtain political legitimacy and gain the support of the urban middle classes that would benefit from the drastic process of urban renewal.

Spatially this program provoked the creation and increase of popular neighbourhoods on the periphery of Santo Domingo. The population evicted from the old central areas added to migrant populations, coming from rural areas and settled in the periphery since the 60's and 70's.

As said before, a particular manifestation of the urban renewal projects constituting the revitalisation programs of historical centres have been a strong force in the urban politics in Latin America during the last decade of the XX Century (Rojas, 1999). Effectively, even if it wasn't an objective, in many cases the historical centre interventions brought a widespread modification in the resident population. This process of gentrification is transforming the landscape in the historical central areas of San Juan, in Puerto Rico; Cartagena, in Colombia; and other cities on the continent.

This phenomenon is also visible in many cities of developed countries and is related to what we could call "globalisation of urban lifestyle" in some urban social sectors. It deals with, in most cases, people with medium or high incomes that seek the status that characterise the residential complexes build in those zones.

Old industrial zones, harbour and rail infrastructure renewal processes that attract new inhabitants are also prevalent. One outstanding example is the renovation of the Buenos Aires sector known as Puerto Madero, that transformed an abandoned zone into a celebrated project where one of the essential actions is the recuperation of public space. This is one of the most important postulates of contemporary urban planning and one of the priority actions to execute in order to promote urban social integration.

Another successful example is the city of Barcelona, where urban planners have opted to prioritise the development of multiple public space projects (Ajuntament de Barcelona, 1992). In Latin America we could find similar efforts such as the public space recovery made possible by the construction of a subway in Medellín (Metro Medellín, 1998), or in large projects like el Eixo Tamanduatehy, in Santo André, Sao Paulo, that suggest, the mixing of social classes through the creation of spaces and public activities, and the requalification, and construction of housing for medium and low income people.

There are others projects of urban renovation with the specific goal to ameliorate living conditions in slums without causing the eviction of the inhabitants. Much of these zones are located near valuable central areas. Amongst these types of projects, an outstanding example is the program of the Rio do Janeiro Municipality nominated Favela Bairro (Prefecture of the city of Rio do Janeiro, 1999; Duarte et al, 1996). It has been taken as example for the Inter American Development Bank and the World Bank to promote projects of urban upgrading with an integrated approach in Latin American cities. Moreover, linked to the discussion on the results in terms of upgrading living conditions for the beneficiary population, the role of those projects in the changes in the traditional grids of socio-spatial segregation is an interesting research theme to explore in the future.

III - Socio-spatial segregation patterns and the expansion of gated communities

An earlier research project indicate, with sufficient clarity, the dominant trend of the reduction of "spatial polarisation" (understood as physical distance) in some principal Latin American cities (Portes, 1989; Portes et al, 1997). In the frame of the economical crisis caused by external debt and the beginning of structural adjustment programs, factors such as the impoverishment of middle class sectors and the expansion of informal settlements (slums and illegal neighbourhoods), are causing important transformations in the historical patterns of spatial and social class segregation. Among the most important changes were the establishment of an impoverished middle class in poor working neighbourhoods or in peripheral zones where the urban land costs are lower (Bogotá, Kingston and Santo Domingo), and the expansion of precarious housing into zones of high income sectors or to vacant zones (Bogotá, Montevideo, Port au Prince, Guatemala, San Salvador).

This dominant tendency differs depending of each country and showed some exceptions. One noticeable exception is the case of Santiago, where the urban services resettlement, the creation of more municipalities as part of the decentralisation process and the eviction of 30,000 families to the city's peripheral zones, generated residential pockets for high income people, further deepening the spatial polarisation, and socio-spatial segregation. Sabatini (1997) analyses in detail these distinct dimensions of socio-spatial segregation in Santiago. Other exceptions are several Central America cities, where the coercive politics of the state have impeded the invasion of public and private urban land (Guatemala and San Salvador), or the public policies are trying to respond to the housing demand of low-income people (San José de Costa Rica).

Two elements are remarkable here: firstly, on the basis of different residential resettlements we encounter labour market transformations, characterised by flexibility in terms of working contracts with consequences for unemployment and informality, similar to the result of the previous tendency, the strong process of middle class impoverishment and the enlargement of the social exclusion. Secondly, the role of public policies, even in obscure forms, which can encourage the modification or reduction in segregating trends.

Since the 80's but especially in the 90's, new socio-spatial segregation forms that tend to complicate and limit the possibilities of social integration have appeared in many Latin American cities. Among these we find gated communities. There are several design differences and origins between distinct cities: buildings or luxury apartments (Sao Paulo), individual houses condominiums (Santiago and San Salvador), chacras and country clubs (Buenos Aires). These types of residential complexes tend to spread over Latin America, as an ideal model of housing for middle and high-income people.

Like much of other Latin American cities, San Salvador experienced a clear separation between residential areas of social distinct sectors since the end of the XIX Century. Following a similar urban pattern, the socio-economic elite migrated progressively from the central zones where they would be found at the beginning of XX Century to the city's north-western zone in the 30's, and consolidated their presence in certain neighbourhoods between the 50's and 70's. The middle class also moved into the same direction.

Meanwhile the low-income sectors settled in the northern and eastern zones. With the industrial development during the 70's and the creation of an important manufacturing belt, a large number of workers tend to reside in municipalities located to the north-east of the San Salvador Metropolitan Area. Many of those municipalities experienced the highest population growth rate in the Metropolitan Area (i.e. Soyapango and Apopa had average annual growth rates of 12.6% and 14.7% between 1971 and 1992 respectively).

However, the spatial separation has never been completely clear cut. In San Salvador, the public land occupation between the 50's and 70's, on the borders of the rivers and creeks that cross the city from north to south, resulted in large numbers of people living in slums located in the interstices of high and middle income residential areas, population that provided a wide range of services in those areas. At the end of the 70's we find, a spatial separation pattern less stark than at the beginning of the Century.

Here it is important to say outright, that the existence of different social communities in the same urban zone does not mean they are integrated. The issues of social inclusion or exclusion are conditioned by territorial features but they are not explained only by them. Limited physical separation between residential neighbourhoods of poor and rich people does not mean inevitable social integration, and the existence of poor neighbourhoods near rich ones is related to the characteristics of the poor people's houses and their locality within the urban frame.

A recent survey on urban poverty led by The World Bank in the San Salvador Metropolitan Area shows some interesting preliminary outcomes. 82% of the households interviewed reported household formation in this urban agglomeration, in terms of change of neighbourhood only 6.9% indicated that they the intention to move to a different neighbourhood in the coming year.

This situation is explained by at least three factors:

- firstly, job location (high percentages of the poor people work in their own houses or in the nearby rich neighbourhoods);
- secondly, house tenure characteristics (almost half of the interviewed reported to be owners and to have their houses fully paid);
- thirdly, most of the houses belonging to the poor people are well constructed even the though some do not have vehicular access.

The functioning of the urban land market, specially the informal one, emerge here as an important linkage between residential location and socio-spatial segregation.

IV - Linkages between Socio-Spatial Segregation and Urban Land Regulation

It is widely known that a major weaknesses in urban land use regulation is the level of abstraction and generalisation of norms that are applied over very different, complex and dynamic urban realities. This situation explains the inadequacy and obsolescence of most of the current urbanisation norms and their inability, in many cases, to accomplishing their role as guiding instruments for urban development. For the same reason, these norms do not only not contribute to the reduction socio-spatial segregation but actually stimulate it and, obviously, are inadequate in the face of new forms of this phenomenon.

This section aims to analyse the relationship between socio-spatial segregation and urban land regulations. The first problem is how to operationalise the concept of urban land regulation; the second refers to the development of indicators in order to measure it. In Latin America, there are several interesting efforts concerning these problems. A study conducted in 220 municipalities in Sao Paulo (Rolnik, 2000), developed an indicator of territorial exclusion based on the conditions of housing and their urban insertion, with the idea of relating them with the concept of social exclusion.

To develop this indicator, the study constructed a matrix with four types of information: housing occupation conditions, urban locality, infrastructure available and number of rooms, that can be transformed into dichotic variables (adequate or not). In order to contextualize the data, the results were cross-tabulated with other variables corresponding to the city level: rate of population growth, aggregate income per capita, municipal income per capita and percentage of household heads earning less than two minimum wages.

The results of this study showed a total lack of correlation between urban regulation and territorial exclusion, revealing that land use regulations have a limited influence on control of socio-spatial segregation, and that this regulation function as a fundamental instrument for delimitating land market segments.

In San Salvador increasing urbanisation since the 50's and the industrialisation of the economy have accelerated rural migration to the main city creating a true Metropolitan Area. More recently this tendency has been accompanied by an important international migratory flux due to the armed conflict during the 80's. This has not only lead to increasing monetary income for the country but also promotes important social and cultural transformations. More than 20% of Salvador's population can be found outside the country, and a clear example of its economic implication is shown in the land market and housing modifications in all cities and small villages inside the country.

In October 1986 the earthquake in San Salvador deepened the deterioration of the historical centre increasing the resettlement of banks and other financial offices from the centre to the city's north-eastern sector, near the exclusive residential zones. At the same time, the economic elite started a new spatial displacement, this time into the south-western sector, building gated private condominiums.

With the boom experienced by the construction sector after the 1992 Peace Agreements, this concept of private residential complexes extended not only to the elite but also to sectors of the middle class, as a response to increasing post-war criminality and violence. The gated communities of El Salvador take many forms, underlining the following:

- individual residential units, sometimes a condominium, located in the southern suburbs, on the road to the pacific coast;
- luxury flat towers in traditional zones of high income sectors.

In contrast to Buenos Aires, where gated communities seem to expand further from the Metropolitan Region limits; in San Salvador, the increasing limitation of available urban land and environmental restrictions, and the high risk of building in vulnerable zones, have given rise to a model of gated communities that are more urban than suburban. The buildings and much of the medium residential complexes that have been built during the last 10 years are found in the central city of the Metropolitan Area, producing densification of it or in the vacant land in peripheral municipalities. This type of densification with measures that deepen the social separation through physical barriers like walls and security doors, do not have a positive impact on socio-spatial segregation.

This function clearly appears when observing the housing density map defined by the urban regulation in the case of San Salvador Metropolitan Area. Only in three of the fourteen municipalities composing the Metropolitan Area have densities been limited to between 50 and 200 inhabitants per hectare; in the rest the densities allowed are more than 400 inhabitants per hectare (predominantly the zones have densities between 800 and 1000 inhabitants per hectare). The first three are located precisely where the housing for the high-income sectors is. The others municipalities are where middle and low-income populations live.

We, as in most of the others Latin American cities, are faced with a very common type of socio-spatial segregation legalisation. In addition to the effect of these densification norms on the price of urban land (that can reach proportions of 1 to 30 between the more densely populated zones and the less dense zones in the Metropolitan Area), urban regulation also tend to create strong differences in infrastructure, public facilities and urban services.

In order to undertake a more specific analysis, we chose two housing projects to compare the effect of the existing norms related to the following items:

- minimum area lot;
- housing density per hectare;
- maximum percentage coverage of lot area;
- area of green recreation, ecological protection and social facilities (the last destined to build schools, health units and market buildings etc.).

The chosen projects are "Palmira", located in the Municipality of Nueva San Salvador, in the south-eastern zone of the Metropolitan Area, classified as low density because of the restriction of one house per lot, and "Cumbres de San Bartolo", located in the Municipality of Tonacatepeque, in the north-eastern zone of the Metropolitan Area.

The size of the first urbanised area is 369,443.20 m², consisting of a total amount of 144 lots. The size of the second area is 337,685.51 m², consisting of 2,500 lots. The two projects are constant changing and still in the process of construction. The plan for "Palmira" only contains individual lots and one house per family. The other one is planned for attached housing.

The project "Palmira" is located in a zone where many similar projects exist, the average size lot is 3,000m², and in a Municipality where low densities prevail and the densification of previously existing projects is forbidden. The project "Cumbres de San Bartolo" is located in a zone of high density close to other similar projects and the minimum lot size is 50m².

Table 1 shows the observed difference between the green and recreation area per capita due to the application of current urban norms. For the project "Palmira" there is 13.8m² per inhabitant; for "Cumbres de San Bartolo" there is only 1.36m². If we add to the common area the vacant space left in each individual lots (since only 17% coverage of the 3,000m² lot is permitted "Palmira" whilst in "Cumbres de San Bartolo" 90% coverage of the 55m² is allowed), the spatial differences between the two projects are more pronounced. It is evident that urban regulation norms underline the inequalities in land use and encourage socio-spatial segregation.

Table 1. Evaluated projects: comparative norms analysis

PROJECT / IND ICATOR	**San Bartolo**	Norm Applied	**Palmira**	Norm Applied
Total land area	337,685.51m²		369,443.20m²	
Number of lots	2,500		144	
Inhabitants	12,500		720	
Net density (inh/hectare)	835	800	26	50
Average lot area	55m²	50m²	3,000m2	from 1,000 to 5,000m²
Allowed coverage	90%	90%	between 25% and 10%	between 25 and 10 %
Green and recreation area	17,030.05m²	5%	9,930.00m²	4%
Green ecological area	27,807.85m²	5%	24,447.90m²	6%
Social facility area	27,204.23m²	6.4% of total area	1,182.00m²	8.00 m² x lot

Source: OPAMSS´ Archive

The compared projects are typical of their respective zones. It is clear that socio-spatial segregation at macro-territorial level is increasing based on current urbanisation norms, particularly those regarding allowed densities, from where the majority of the other norms are derived.

As a researcher has pointed out, the price of urban land, and the affordability costs of it are both cause and consequence of socio-spatial segregation (Ward, 2001). The role of the function of urban land markets on this issue is easily visible.

V - Conclusion

The brief analysis made of the new socio-spatial segregation forms emerging in Latin American cities during the last years allow us to visualise the importance of developing the hypothesis over their similarities. Here we find an important future urban research stream. These studies must follow a historical approach, take in consideration the different territorial scales and the particular perceptions of social groups on this issue.

Concerning the second hypothesis, the relationship between socio-spatial segregation and urban land regulation, is a changing and indissoluble link, as is shown with the example of the San Salvador Metropolitan Area and the research outcomes of the cities of Greater Sao Paulo cited before. We also think that it is another important research theme to explore.

In addition to this question it is necessary to incorporate the economic dimension of socio-spatial segregation: externalities, costs, impact on urban efficiency and productivity in general, and urban land prices and affordability costs in particular.

In order to create of a set of new urban land regulation instruments to reduce the negative impacts of the socio-spatial segregation, it is necessary to accomplish two requirements:

- firstly, to abolish the general and abstract character that prevail in most Latin American urban development regulatory frameworks; and
- secondly, to incorporate the new socio-spatial segregation dynamic described above.

New urban land regulation instruments are politically necessary to fight against this phenomenon and promote a more democratic and sustainable urban development. This is a very important question for urban policy makers, urban managers and all citizens.

Moreover, beyond the changes in the relation between urban land regulation and the reduction of old and new forms of socio-spatial segregation, we believe that as a key question to build socially sustainable cities, it is necessary revive an integrating urban component par excellence: the public space. Around it a complex debate is developing among urban planners, urban policy-makers and urban social organisations, especially since new forms of urban public spaces are emerging that are changing our conception about them. A good example is the use of shopping centres as recreational places in many Latin American cities that have created some serious doubts.

To do more comprehensive studies, more integral research on the issue of socio-spatial segregation and new and qualitative and quantitative measurements of this phenomenon is needed. To construct specific data about it is another challenge for the future.

Finally, in general terms it is clear that new forces, the globalisation process amongst others, are restructuring the spatial form and the urban society of Latin American cities, particularly since the second half of the XX Century, and socio-spatial segregation is being transformed by this.

References

Ajuntament de Barcelona (1992): *Barcelona. Public Space*, Barcelona.

Arizaga, María Cecilia (2000): "Murallas y barrios cerrados. La morfología espacial del ajuste en Buenos Aires" in Nueva Sociedad No. 166, Caracas.

Bourdieu, Pierre (1979): *La distinction*, Editions de Minuit, Paris.

Brun, Jacques y Catherine Rhein (1994): *La ségrégation dans la ville. Concepts et mesures*, Jacques Brun et Cathrine Rhein (eds.), Éditions L'Harmattan, Paris.

Caldeira, Teresa P.R. (2000): *City of Walls. Crime, Segregation and Citizenship in São Paulo*, University of California Press, Berkeley-Los Angeles-London.

Chamboredon, Jean-Claude y Madelaine Lemaire (1970): "Proximité spatiale et distance sociale. Les grandes ensembles et leur peuplement", Revue Française de Sociologie, Vol. XI, pp. 3-33, Paris.

Duarte, Cristiane; Silvia, Osvaldo; e Brasileiro, Alice (1996): *Favela, um Bairro*, UFRJ, Rio de Janeiro.

Harvey, David (2000): *Spaces of Hope*, California Unversity Press, Berkeley-Los Angeles.

Jaramillo, Samuel (1997): "El papel del mercado del suelo en la configuración física de las ciudades latinoamericanas", draft, Urban Land Markets in Latin America Project, Lincoln Institute of Land Policy, Cambridge.

Lozano, Wilfredo (1997): *La urbanización de la pobreza*, FLACSO, Santo Domingo.

Metro Medellín (1998): *El espacio adecuado*, Medellín.

Marcuse, Peter (2001): *Enclaves Yes, Ghettoes No: Segregatin and the State*, paper presented to Lincoln Institute of Land Policy Seminar "Segregation in City", Cambridge.

Peña, Rosa Amalia (2000): *Normas y regulaciones urbanísticas. Su papel en la segregación socio-espacial en el Area Metropolitana de San Salvador*, master degree thesis in social sciences, FLACSO, San José.

Poduje, Iván (2000): "Formas y externalidades de la expansión metropolitana en Santiago de Chile 1990-2000", Paper to Seminar "Expansión y densificación de las ciudades latinoamericanas", organized by LILP and OPAMSS, October 2000, San Salvador.

Portes, A., Carlos Dore-Cabral y Patricia Landolt (1997): *The Urban Caribbean. Transition to the New Global Economy*, The Johns Hopkins University Press, Baltimore and London.

Portes, Alejandro (1989): "Latin American Urbanization in the Years of the Crisis", Latin American Research Review, Vol. XXIV, No.2, Alburquerque.

Robert, Federico G. (1998): "La gran muralla: aproximación al tema de los barrios cerrados en la región metropolitana de Buenos Aires". Paper to Seminar "El Nuevo Milenio y lo Urbano" organized by the Instituto de Investigaciones Gino Germani, November 1998, Buenos Aires.

Rojas, Eduardo (1999): *Old Cities, New Assets*, IDB, Washington.

Rolnik, Raquel, (2000): "Impacto da Aplicacao de Novos Instrumentos Urbanísticos em Cidades do Estado de Sao Paulo", Revista Brasileira de Estudos Urbanos e Regionais 2, ANPUR, Recife.

Sabatini, Francisco (1997): "Liberalización de los mercados de suelo y segregación social en las ciudades latinoamericanas: el caso de Santiago", draft, Urban Land Markets in Latin America Project, Lincoln Institute of Land Policy, Cambridge.

Sabatini, Francisco (2001): *Residential Segregation Patterns Changes in Main Chilean Cities: Scale Shifts and Increasing Malignancy*, paper presented to Lincoln Institute of Land Policy Seminar "Segregation in City", Cambridge.

Schteingart, Martha (1997): "La geografía social de la división urbana. El caso de Mexico", draft, México.

Torres, Horacio (1998): "Procesos recientes de fragmentación socio-espacial en Buenos Aires: la suburbanización de las élites". Paper to Seminar "El Nuevo Milenio y lo Urbano" organized by the Instituto de Investigaciones Gino Germani, November 1998, Buenos Aires.

Ward, Peter (2001): *Squaring the Circle: Whither or Wither Segregation Cities*, paper presented to Lincoln Institute of Land Policy Seminar "Segregation in Cities", Cambridge.

5

FDI and World Cities: Establishing Parameters for Comparison

Further Discussion on Methodology for the Comparison of the Randstad and São Paulo Metropolitan Area

Roberto Rocco

Introduction

Within the framework defined for the Alfa-Ibis Network - Globalisation, Urban Form and Governance - the aim of this research to be conducted within TU Delft PhD program is to assess and map how foreign direct investment (FDI) is operating in São Paulo Metropolitan Area, Brazil, and the Randstad, The Netherlands. The conditions and processes occurring in the two case studies will be investigated in order to understand the way in which global capital is operating within distinct economic arenas (Latin America and Western Europe) in reshaping urban structure and to assess how local forces might be contributing to these changes.

In this text, the objectives of the research will be clarified and refined and the objects of study outlined: the agglomerations of the Randstad and São Paulo Metropolitan Area (MASP). Finding an identity for both agglomerations as recognisable units for the study of FDI constitutes a target in itself, and it permeates the whole research project. In fact, we believe that the profound changes that cities have undergone in the last few decades demand a new approach to the understanding and establishment of new boundaries for the metropolis as a study unit. However, here some exploratory hypotheses will be advanced and possible tools for the complexity of the task of comparing two 'world cities' will be investigated.

New Economy, New Boundaries

Transformations in the urban structure of cities during the 90's have been largely described as related to national development strategies and to the process of 'structural adjustment' linked to the Globalisation agenda. Starting from the mid 70's to the early 80's, governments in most developed countries shifted towards a neo-liberal programme, generally prescribed by international organisations like the IMF and the World Bank, which, at least in the case of Latin American developing countries, followed the so-called Washington Consensus agenda[23]. Changes in foreign trade, financial flows and

---

23 The 'Washington Consensus' is a term coined by John Williamson (Williamson, 1990, ch.2). Williamson argued that there was a set of policy reforms which most of official Washington thought would be good for Latin American countries. This set of policy reforms could be summarized in ten propositions:

foreign direct investment began accelerating, parallel to a huge improvement in digital communications and data processing technologies. Cities, being the *locus* of such rapid transformations, have experienced a process of flexibilisation, deregulation of land use policies and various strategies for increased competitiveness, thus becoming more autonomous towards the processes operating in worldwide markets. Governments and international organisations supported the shift towards the urban bias and an unprecedented rapid process of change in regional and urban structure started to manifest itself in most developed and developing countries, especially those in the middle income range.

Simultaneous processes of decentralisation of production and concentration of capital, goods and services at regional level followed the worldwide changes of production and managerial processes and the re-organisation of economic activities at global level- mainly at the financial level. The Randstad in the Netherlands and São Paulo in Brazil are two significant examples to which Foreign Direct Investment has been relocated and important changes in the behaviour of real estate capital has taken place in order to adjust the metropoles to new infra-structural requirements.

Both cases, the Randstad and São Paulo, present us with peculiarities that impose new approaches to the delimitation of the case study. The Randstad is a dense, yet polycentric and discontinuous agglomeration whose boundaries are not legally defined. Can it be understood in terms of a single metropolitan body? São Paulo Metropolitan Area, on the other hand, has a legal administrative status, but how much of the extremely extended urbanised area is actually connected to the dynamic processes related to globalisation occurring in some parts of its metropolitan body?

In fact, the specialised producer services offered by both agglomerations, which might characterise them as 'world cities', are concentrated in very particular areas of both agglomerations. However, they have ramifications, through the chain of contracting and subcontracting, use and demand, scattered administration and governance, which stretch throughout the agglomerations and reach far beyond the territory of the metropoles themselves, pervading the respective national territories where each agglomeration is located, and have international impact. Still, there is a lack of knowledge in determining recognisable entities where FDI operates. As a hypothesis, we believe that the impacts of the changes brought by FDI in real estate, land price, infrastructure and urban facilities are far less concentrated and have impacts upon the ensemble of the two metropoles as a whole.

---

1. Fiscal discipline. 2. A redirection of public expenditure priorities toward fields offering both high economic returns and the potential to improve income distribution, such as primary health care, primary education, and infrastructure. 3. Tax reform (to lower marginal rates and broaden the tax base). 4. Interest rate liberalisation. 5. A competitive exchange rate. 6. Trade liberalisation. 7. Liberalisation of FDI inflows. 8. Privatisation. 9. Deregulation (in the sense of abolishing barriers to entry and exit). 10. Secure property rights.

Williamson later said: "*Ten years ago I invented the term "Washington Consensus". While it is jolly to become famous by inventing a term that reverberates around the world, I have long been doubtful as to whether the phrase that I coined served to advance the cause of rational economic policymaking. My initial source of concern was that the phrase invited the interpretation that the liberalizing economic reforms of the past two decades were imposed by Washington-based institutions like the World Bank, rather than having resulted from the process of intellectual convergence that I believe underlies them. (...) However, I have gradually developed a second and more significant concern. I have realised that the term is often being used in a sense significantly different to that which I had intended, as a synonym for what is often called "neoliberalism" in Latin America, or what George Soros (1998) has called 'market fundamentalism'*" (Williamson, 1999).

Therefore, by assessing how FDI operates in the two case studies and alters the urban and regional configuration, it is possible that new boundaries emerge, challenging the prevalent definition of their official or assumed boundaries.

Beaverstock, Smith and Taylor (1999) identify two "basic approaches" to the question of the nature of cities in the world economy today: the 'demographic' approach and the 'functional' approach. The first is based on a tradition that is largely concerned with the size of cities, and can be represented by the 'megacity project', which "is exploring the human and ecological implications of contemporary and future huge population concentrations" (Beaverstock, Smith and Taylor, 1999).

But how big must a city be in order to be considered a megacity? There seems to be no theoretical basis from which to assert that a city with 5, 8 or 10 million inhabitants is qualitatively different from one with fewer inhabitants (Gilbert, 1996). *"Perhaps for this reason different authorities use widely differing definitions of a megacity. Although Richardson (1993) and UNDIESA and UNU (1991) use the eight million benchmark, UNCHS (1987:29), Ward (1990, xvii), and the World Bank (1991:16) use ten million, while Dogan and Kasarda (1988: 18), implicitly use four million."* (Gilbert, 1996). One of main difficulties, advances Gilbert (quoting Richardson, 1973), would be to separate the effects of size from those of other variables. "Certainly, attempts to examine the relationship between size and the benefits and pathologies of urban growth have produced very little in the way of reliable results. There is seldom a clear relationship between size and any single variable of welfare or illfare", says Gilbert.

On the other hand, according to Beaverstock, "the functional tradition is to be found [today] in studies of world and global cities which are interpreted as integral to contemporary globalisation processes". (Beaverstock et al., 1999). This research tends toward the latter tradition, but it is necessary to clarify the concepts in this specific case.

São Paulo can be characterised as both a third-world megacity AND a world city, but that is certainly not the case for the Randstad, which, among other things, is not an officially constituted political entity.

Therefore, it seems imperative to characterise the two objects of this study as two comparable entities. The notion of 'world city' was chosen for this. Under such characterisation apparently dissimilar agglomerations can become comparable, as they are inserted in the same framework of analysis and a common economic background (globalisation), where they can be contrasted and "evaluated" with reputable parameters, which are discussed further.

Therefore, the exploratory assumption here is that it is possible to characterise the Randstad as a 'world city', therefore comparable with another 'world city', São Paulo (whose characterisation, seems somewhat easier and already achieved by many authors[24]), due, among other factors, to its conurbated physical characteristic.

The concept of 'world city' might vary and the inclusion of a given city in this category is disputable and may vary from author to author according to the adopted methodology. However, there seems to be a general consensus about which are the leading world cities in a globalised world -New York, London and Tokyo- each corresponding to a certain global arena: North America, Western Europe and Eastern Asia, respectively. However, since Friedman's inaugural hypothesis (Friedman, 1986)[25]

24 GaWC elaborated a table with 15 sources where 79 cities are cited. São Paulo is cited by 10 sources, the same number as Amsterdam. Rotterdam is cited 3 times and The Hague once. Utrecht, the other of the four large cities that constitute the Randstad is not cited. The Randstad, as indicated before, does not appear as such. See Table 1, Appendix. (Idem)

25 Peter Hall (Hall, 1997) claims that Patrick Geddes already recognised world cities and defined them, as

and Sassen's seminal work (Sassen, 1991) the inventory of 'world cities' below the highest level seems yet unclear and their role in attracting, co-ordinating and materialising direct foreign investment is yet to be better understood. This has a direct connection with the parameters established in order to 'rank' world cities or to determine the degree of their participation in cross-border networks.

The Randstad and São Paulo are agglomerations that have undergone different historical processes of urban and social structuring and currently are going through an accelerated process of capital concentration: rapid development of telecommunication and digital technologies; decentralisation of production processes and acceleration of financial inflows and Foreign Direct Investment (FDI) (Castells 1992, 1995; Sassen, 1991, 1994, 1998, 1998 (a); Santos 1990, 1993(a), 1993(b) UNCTAD, 2000). The nature and speed of this process have created new forms of organisation of capital and labour in urban space, and produced transformations in the conditions for social reproduction as compared with the previous welfare period. It has also induced the creation of new institutional and legal tools for the transformation of urban space.

As Sassen (1994) indicates, the specific field of urbanism requires the understanding of how this "new global economy" structures itself in urban space through specific projects and actions in digital and basic infra-structure, new building program requirements and the articulation of intra-urban spaces.

Following Sassen's line of argument, the dispersion of economic activity has accompanied the appearance of new forms of spatial centralisation. They are related to high-level managing and operation control. National and global markets, as well as globally integrated operations require 'central' spaces where the outcome of globalisation takes place (Sassen, 1994, p.14). The digital industry and the necessary network of services that allow a city to become 'global', also need a large physical infrastructure that contains strategic nodes with hyper concentration of certain processes, activities and material infrastructure. According to Sassen, Harvey and Santos, among others, these are essential for the implementation of globalisation.

---

long ago as 1915, in a book called: Cities in Evolution (Geddes, 1915). Hall also published an early book called "The World Cities" (Hall, 1966), where he defines world cities in terms of multiple roles:
1.Centres of political power, both national and international, and of the organisations related to government; 2.Centres of national and international trade, acting as entrepôts for their countries and sometimes for neighbouring countries; 3.Centres of banking, insurance and related financial services; 4.Centres of advanced professional activity of all kind, in medicine, in law, in higher learning, and the application of scientific knowledge to technology; 5.Centres of information gathering and diffusion, through publishing and the mass media; 6.Centres of conspicuous consumption, both of luxury goods for the minority and mass-produced goods for the multitude; 7.Centres of arts, culture and entertainment, and of the ancillary activities.
Therefore, it may be argued that, just like Globalisation, world cities are far older than we usually assume when trying to characterise the new developments of capitalist economy since the mid 70's. However, we follow GaWC suggestion and take Friedman and Sassen as the inaugurators of the world city study agenda. We do this with due recognition of the theories that assert that Globalisation is not really a new phenomenon, but an acceleration of various phenomena related to production, communication, transportation, etc, resulting in an intensification of some phenomena related to Capitalism (Santos, 1993). This acceleration has incisively changed urban form and function in what we call world cities, however it has evidently taken shape after mid 70's. Hall implicitly recognises this as he asserts: "This definition, I would argue, still applies thirty years later. But it does need amplification and modification, because of the phenomenon of globalisation and its impact on the urban system, coupled with what can be called the informationalisation of the economy, the progressive shift of advanced economies from goods production to information handling (...)" (Hall, 1997).

In order to build a framework though which both agglomerations may be compared, and as a first approach to the research object, the work that has been conducted within the frame of GaWC (Globalisation and World Cites Study Group and Network) by the aforementioned Beaverstock, Smith and Taylor (1999)[26] was chosen. This is based on the level of **advanced services** offered by cities around the world. This choice is based on the consistent methodology of this study, which will be used in this research when searching for evidence of FDI investment and its impacts on the built environment of both agglomerations. It also enables the examination of the boundaries of the research objects, whose idiosyncrasies and particularities are to be discussed further in the doctorate research and might constitute one of the first attempts to develop a consistent comparison of the two world-cities.

The Randstad as a World-City

Source: Expedic/ MapPoint Tech., Microsoft 2001

Map 1. The Randstad Region in the West of the Netherlands.

Why question the status of the Randstad as a world city? Actually, it is more a matter of terminology and delimitation of boundaries, than an actual questioning of the Randstad as a centre for decision-making, specialised producer services and concentration of intellectual, technological and communication resources, which among other factors characterise a world city. The term 'Randstad' does not appear as such in most published papers outside the Netherlands, nor does it in GaWC's inventory.

---

26 Beaverstock, J.V. et al. (1999), "A Roster of World Cities" in Cities, 16 (6), 445-458.

According to M. Paul de Jong[27], the name 'Randstad' was first used in the 50's by the then President of KLM Dutch Airlines, to define the urban area that his company served from the newly inaugurated Airport of Schiphol. The use of the term then spread. It was incorporated in the common Dutch vocabulary and today roughly designates the urban agglomeration situated in the west of the Netherlands, adjacent to the North Sea, which includes the major Dutch urban agglomerations. The word appears in the reputable Dutch dictionary *Verklarend Woordenboek der Nederlandse taal*[28], that put forward the following definition: "*het stedengebied van Holland (de provincies Noord-Holland en Zuid-Holland) en Utrecht, gezien als één grote stad langs Nederlands westrand*" ("The urbanised part of Holland (the provinces of North Holland and South Holland) and Utrecht, which are seen as one large city along the Dutch west coast").

Therefore, although it is a recognised term, the so-called 'Randstad' urban agglomeration does not enjoy legal status, which would provide it with clear boundaries and easy compilation and assessing of data. The Central Bureau of Statistics of the Netherlands, for instance, does not publish any specific information on the 'Randstad Region'. "For us it is not an official segmentation", says Mrs. M. Kern, employee of the CBS Infoservice. The CBS only gathers and provides information at the level of Provinces, EGG-Regions and COROP-Regions, and of course, at the municipality level.

There are a number of authors who deal with the Randstad as a whole[29]. Recently, task groups such as the 'Regio Randstad' and the 'Delta Metropool' have undertaken the task to give substance to the Randstad.

The 'Regio Randstad' is a shared task group of the Dutch provinces of North Holland, South Holland, Utrecht and Flevoland. Its head office is located in the city of Utrecht and it has a representative office to the European Union in Brussels.

The 'Delta Metropool' is an alliance of city councils, other public authorities and private institutions in the urbanised 'delta' located in the midwestern region of the Netherlands, which "have joined forces to develop a 'metropolis'"(Delta Metropool, 1999, p.4). Delta Metropool is therefore an initiative of the four main municipalities in the region (Amsterdam, Rotterdam, The Hague and Utrecht) which have signed a joint declaration in 1998.

As for the Regio Randstad, the 'Randstad' region comprises the totality of four provinces: North and South Holland, Utrecht and Flevoland. This would include a population of approximately 7,3 million inhabitants, or 46,2% of the total population of the Netherlands, in a surface area of 8.313 km^2.

27Ministerie van Landbouw, Natuurbeheer en Visserij.

28 Koenen, M. J. en Endepols, J., Verklarend handwoordenboek der Nederlandse taal. Groningen: Wolters-Noordhoff N.V., 1969 (1897).

29 See specific bibliographic section below.

Map 2. The 4 Provinces that constitute the Randstad, according to Regio Randstad.

Delta Metropool is of course concentrated on the municipal level, but the exact boundaries of the Randstad does not feature as an issue in the published material we have had access to.

The methodology used to define the boundaries of the Randstad in the first instance has to be clarified, but at first glance it seems a political choice, which is of course supported by the geographic situation and complementary economic role the cities and provinces involved play in the ensemble, as well as the advancing conurbation of some areas, with a large movement of people, vehicles, merchandise, etc. We can perhaps identify both organisations with different political agendas: The Delta Metropool is an initiative of the four powerful municipalities that lead the region whereas the Regio Randstad is related to the provincial and national agenda.

Geographer André Mulder points out that the limited size of the Dutch territory and its historic development has contributed to the creation of institutional planning and control at a national level. Paradoxically, also due to particular historical developments, Dutch cities (municipalities) have conserved many of their prerogatives in the control of the area within their jurisdiction. This is particularly true for the most important municipalities that form the Randstad: Amsterdam, Rotterdam, The Hague and Utrecht, which compose the Randstad. By being able to attract much of the investment and the generation of employment in the post war period, these cities managed to remain relatively independent in certain instances of decision-making. They have sometimes challenged the more centralised planning of the national ministries and have many times 'de facto' disregarded provincial power. In a certain way, they were able to determine the direction of their own development, but also indirectly influenced the development and planning of the neighbouring municipalities - smaller neighbouring cities and 'dorpen' (little villages).

Since the post war period, the Dutch central government has attempted to finance the costs of infrastructure and dwelling production for future generations, in the framework of the Welfare State, through a system of taxation and shadow pricing. This, despite of the relative independence of the municipalities, has allowed general conditions that are **homogeneous** throughout the national territory in general, and in the Randstad in particular.

It is clear, however, that, in many ways, Amsterdam enjoys a certain dominance in the Randstad and the Netherlands as a whole in the provision of sophisticated producer services. In fact, in GaWC's classification (see complete table elaborated by GaWC at appendix- table 1), Amsterdam is the only Dutch city to be included in the rank of 'world city'. The inventory was constructed based on the level of advanced producer services offered, following Sassen (1991) and Castells (1995) propositions for the identification of a world city network. Cities are ranked Alpha, Beta and Gamma, according to the level of certain advanced producer services offered. "Global service centres are identified and graded for accountancy, advertising, banking/finance and law." (Beaverstock et al., 1999)[30]. The cities were divided in Prime, Major and Minor centres based on the offering of these services.

Amsterdam appears as a Gamma World City. The other Randstad cities to appear in the GaWC inventory are Rotterdam, The Hague and Utrecht, but they appear only as minor centres for accountancy services. The following table compares the main cities of the Randstad with São Paulo, according to the GaWC listing.

Table 1. A Roster of World Cities (by presence of selected specialised producer services)

Service/ City and ranking at 'world cityness' according to GaWC	Accountancy	Advertising	Banking	Legal
Amsterdam (GAMMA World City)	Major	Major	Minor	Minor
Rotterdam (Some evidence)	Major	DNA	DNA	DNA
The Hague (Some evidence)	Minor	DNA	DNA	DNA
Utrecht (Minimal Evidence)	Minor	DNA	DNA	DNA
São Paulo (BETA World City)	Minor	Major	Major	Major

DNA: Does Not Appear
Source: Beaverstock, J.V., et al (1999).

Therefore, according to the GaWC, Rotterdam and The Hague present only 'some evidence' of 'world city-ness' (in a score of 1 to 12), and Utrecht presents only 'minimal evidence'. Clearly, the types of specialised services taken into account favours Amsterdam in the methodology employed. This dominance may be masked by some methodological questions that would have to be clarified by further research. Transportation and communication services, as well as institutional operations, if taken into account, would certainly put Rotterdam and The Hague as relatively important world cities. The international airport of Schiphol also plays an important role in the structuring of the region.

Hall (1997) identifies a tendency on the part of business to migrate from traditional centres to suburban locations close to airports – "a trend long observed in the United States, but now becoming evident in Europe also, in developments around London Heathrow, Paris Charles de Gaulle, Amsterdam Schiphol or Stockholm Arlanda". This provides a basis to include the international airport of Schiphol as an important structuring element in the Randstad into the research agenda. Hall also underlines the

30 A full list of international companies used for the assessment is presented in the appendix.

importance on the train transportation system in the structuring of many urban networks and regions. This puts Utrecht, as the operating centre for railway transportation in the Netherlands, in a distinctive position. The importance of train transportation is of special interest, since the proposed rapid train transportation system might change the balance between the cities in the Randstad. As London, Paris and Amsterdam form what the EC's Europe 2000+ report calls the "National Capitals Region", the impact of the rapid train system connecting London, Paris, Brussels, Rotterdam and Amsterdam (but not the Hague and Utrecht) might have decisive implications for the structure of the Randstad, either accentuating the dominance of Amsterdam or, to the contrary, strengthening the metropolitan characteristics of the region as a whole. For Hall (1997), "(...) it seems certain that they [London, Paris and Amsterdam] will constitute an effective central core of the European urban system."

GaWC's inventory is only one of the possible ways of evaluating 'world city-ness', as it takes into account, roughly speaking, the location of firms and/or the number of their employees[31]. In the case of the Randstad, the services discussed (accountancy, advertising, banking/finance and law) may be offered and employed in a wide area, as there is evidence that the whole region works as an extended metropolitan area.

In fact, many authors support the idea of a polycentric urban region with metropolitan characteristics. Kloosterman and Lambregts (2001), for instance, identify the Randstad with this model, which they define as:

- (...) A number of historically distinct cities that are located in more or less close proximity (roughly within current commuting distances).
- They lack a clear leading city, which dominates in political, economic, cultural and other aspects and instead, tend to consist of a small number of larger cities, that do not differ that much in terms of size or overall economic importance, and a greater number of smaller cities.
- The member cities are not only spatially distinct, but also constitute independent political entities." (Kloosterman & Lambregts, 2001).

The authors list as examples of polycentric urban regions the Kansai-area (Japan), the Rhine-Ruhr region (Germany), the Po Valley (Northern Italy) and the Dutch Randstad. Quoting Hohenberg and Lees (1985, p.242), they affirm that the Randstad "goes beyond the rather thin definition and is a prime example of a network system in a relatively pure form". They also stress the fact that "recently, research into polycentric urban regions has moved up higher on the agenda, now transportation and telecommunication technologies increasingly enable polycentric urban regions to achieve agglomeration economies of comparable magnitude as large monocentric cities." (Kloosterman & Lambregts, 2001).

31 A complete account of the methodology is to be found in Bearverstock et al., 1999.

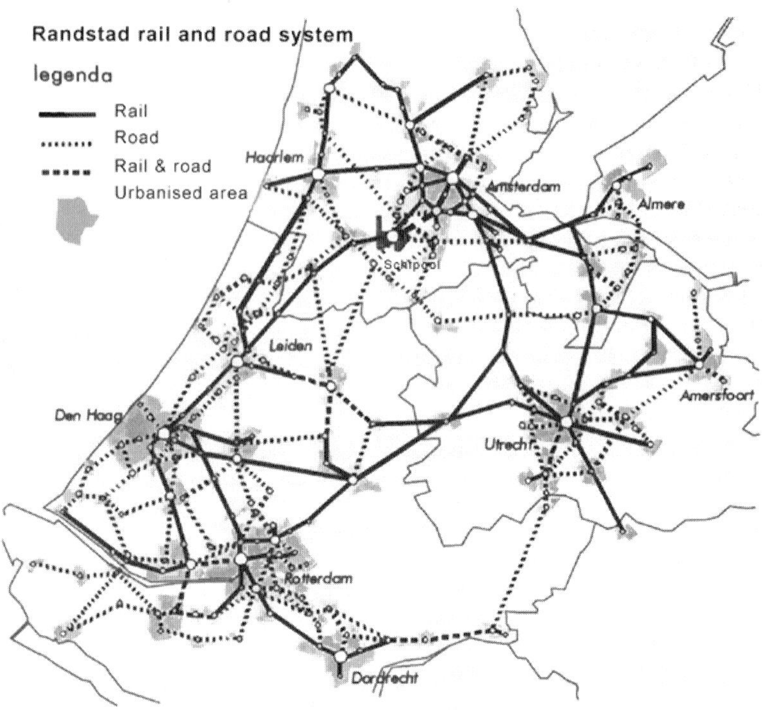

Source: Deltametropool

Map 3.Randstad Network of Transportation.

They provide the theoretical basis to study the Randstad as a metropolitan body, which could be summarised in their description of the clustering of activities occurring in that region, which they assess through the study of start-up business in 13 selected cities in the Randstad region in 4 selected years out of a ten-year time period.

For Kloosterman and Lambregts, "These linkages between the constituent parts of the polycentric urban regions are crucial in helping to create agglomeration economies for all parts concerned on a higher level than the individual parts (cf. Batten et al., 1995)". The authors identify the formation of urban networks "in the sense that they constitute a contiguous travel-to-work area", thus furnishing us with an important element for the understanding and comparison of the two agglomerations.

Localisation economies are mostly found where a high supply of highly specialised labour is available. The concentration of resources and investment that enables a city to become a recognisable area for FDI operation are within the boundary created by the travelling and commuting times of workers and consumers (see Map 3), since, according to Kloosterman and Lambregts (quoting Scott, 1998, p.92), "the daily journey to work represents a particularly expensive kind of transaction per unit of distance". Apart from a small number of high-ranking functionaries who might travel large distances in order to carry on the administration of larger (national or international) networks of producer services, the majority of workers and consumers must be within this boundary, which is notably elastic and may vary according to the efficiency and reliability of the means of transportation available. Therefore, research has indicated that daily movement of workers and consumers are of utmost importance in defining these boundaries, since there seems to be a recognisable limit for competitive clustering of activities.

As indicated by the authors, such clustering of activities (which might determine the shaping of a polycentric agglomeration with metropolitan characteristics) can only be verified empirically, as the formation of localisation economies depends upon a series of ever changing factors related to an economy that is increasingly mobile, scattered and detached from old determining factors of localisation. However, the concentration of infrastructure, resources and a highly skilled labour force has a tendency for concentration that has been the subject of many studies, engaging research in a new agenda for the study of polycentric agglomerations and economies of localisation.

Using empirical evidence based on start-up businesses, rather than concentrating on "linkages in terms of commuting patterns and of (potential) functional relationships between the individual components", they conclude that the Randstad is "becoming more of a uniform milieu rooted in the same kind of localisation economies and social networks that are instrumental in creating a highly specialised inter-urban economy" (Kloosterman and Lambregts, 2001). As mentioned before, they used data collected in 13 different municipalities, which they identify as the largest historical urban centres of the Randstad[32], therefore dispensing with what they call the 'new cities', such as Almere, Zoetermeer or Hoofddorp.

According to Kloosterman and Lambregts, "judged by the trends in business formation, the polycentric urban region Randstad seems to be on the way to become more of an economic region that hinges on the same strategic sources of competitive advantage, namely highly skilled labour".

Furthermore, they also identify an interesting feature: the Randstad is structuring itself in two "wings". The northern wing clearly headed by Amsterdam and Utrecht and the southern wing by Rotterdam and The Hague.

---

32 The cities used in Kloosterman's and Lambregt's study are: Amsterdam, Rotterdam, The Hague, Utrecht, Zaanstad, Amersfoort, Dordrecht, Leiden, Delft, Alkmaar, Haarlem, Hilversum and Schiedam.

São Paulo (MASP) as a World-City

Source: Expedic/ MapPoint Tech., Microsoft 2001

Map 4.The Metropolitan Area of São Paulo (MASP) and the Surrounding Region.

Is it possible to use approximately the same methodology in order to evaluate economic cluster formation in the São Paulo Metropolitan Area (MASP)? In the case of MASP, we are dealing with an ensemble of 39 municipalities that cover almost exactly the same area as the Randstad (according to the methodology used by Regio Randstad), with a population more than double that of the Randstad and with a continuous urban occupation.The Metropolitan area of São Paulo (MASP) covers an area of 8.051 km^2, with 39 municipalities and 137 districts. It houses a population of approximately 17.5 million inhabitants (approximately 10% of the total Brazilian population), with a GNP of US$147.1 billion in 1997 and a per capita income of approximately US$8.758/year (1997[33]). (see Map 5)

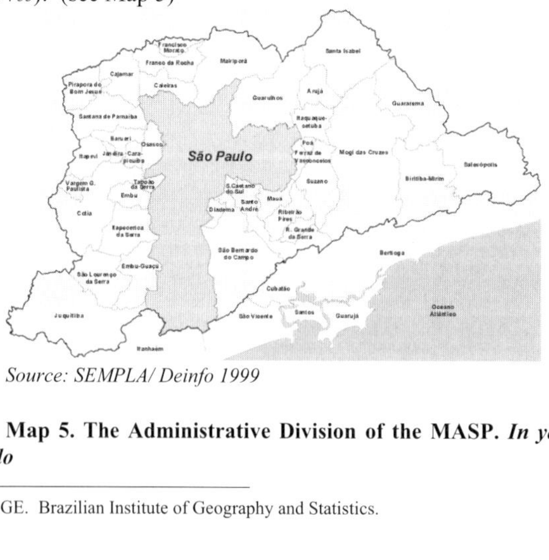

Source: SEMPLA/ Deinfo 1999

Map 5. The Administrative Division of the MASP. ***In yellow, the municipality of São Paulo***

33 IBGE. Brazilian Institute of Geography and Statistics.

The region appears to be the 'organising' centre for the whole Brazilian economy, which produced a GNP of US$730.4 billion in 1999 - compared, for example, with US$397.4 billion in the Netherlands[34]. The total amount of FDI in the country for the year 1999 was approximately US$33 billion (US$34.2 billion for the Netherlands in the same period[35]). São Paulo is therefore certainly a mega-city, but not, as it may appear at first sight, a primate city. Brazil lacks a primate city, for although there is a great concentration of people and production in the MASP, there are other big metropolitan areas distributed in the Brazilian territory. (See comparative data on primacy of four selected Latin-American countries in appendix).

We should try to describe some features in order to understand some of the traits of São Paulo. Although it is structured in a radial-concentric pattern, it doesn't have a typical Central Business District (CBD) as can be found in most American and Latin American cities. Instead, there are 9 distinct dynamic areas for commercial real estate development, which can be grouped in 4 main business districts regions (See Map 6). They roughly correspond to various "waves" of real estate development, following periods of national economic growth. They are: 1.Centre (Sé), 2.Avenida Paulista, 3.Avenida Faria Lima/Vila Olímpia and 4.Avenida Berrini/Marginal Pinheiros. They developed more or less parallel to each other, in a westerly direction. Investment in real estate is concentrated in the Southwest sector of the metropolis. There are other less important centres in the surrounding municipalities of Santo André, São Bernardo e São Caetano (South-East of the MASP), as well as in the edge-cities of AlphaVille and Tamboré (North-West of the MASP).

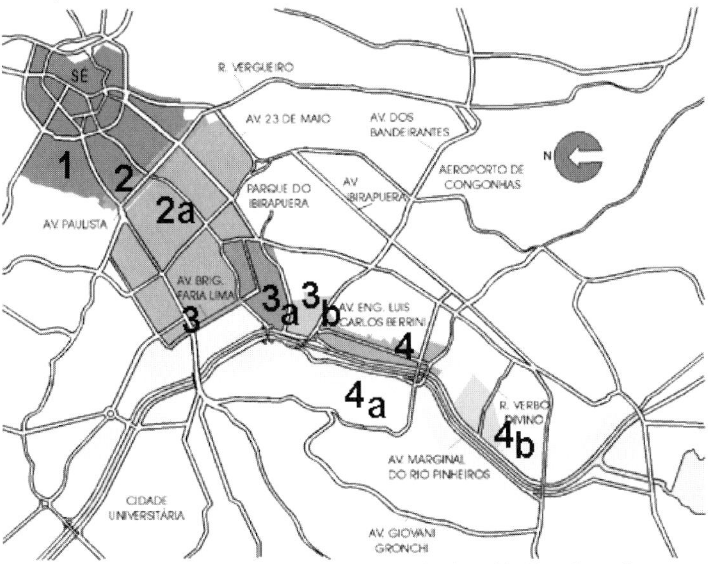

Source: Bolsa de Imóveis de São Paulo, 2001. Map developed by Sírio Cançado.

Map 6. The Main Areas for Commercial Real Estate Development in the MASP. : 1. Sé (Centre), 2. Avenida Paulista, 2.a. Jardins, 3. Avenida Faria Lima, 3.a. Itaim, 3.b. Vila Olímpia, 4. Avenida Berrini, 4.a. Marginal Pinheiros, 4.b. Rua Verbo Divino.

34 World Bank, World Development Indicator database, April 2001.
35 Idem.

Therefore, the land price system and investment isn't as clear as in other agglomerations where they usually decline with distance from the CBD. Like in other urban areas with large suburban commercial development, land prices are positively correlated with accessibility, but in a very complex way where both producers and consumers make trade-offs between the price of land and its characteristics in terms of location, accessibility, quality, and other attributes. The outcome of numerous locational decisions by businesses, households and government produces a complex urban mosaic of business districts, shopping centres, government centres and residential neighbourhoods characterised by four dominant business centres, where the ancient core of the city is not necessarily the most dynamic area for real estate investment, despite its good accessibility.

However, it is inconceivable to analyse this specific area as detached from the broader ensemble, as the whole region functions more or less organically, despite public transportation deficiencies. Much of the public investment has been devoted to give São Paulo a modern and comprehensive road system, privileging private cars (See Maps 7 and 8).

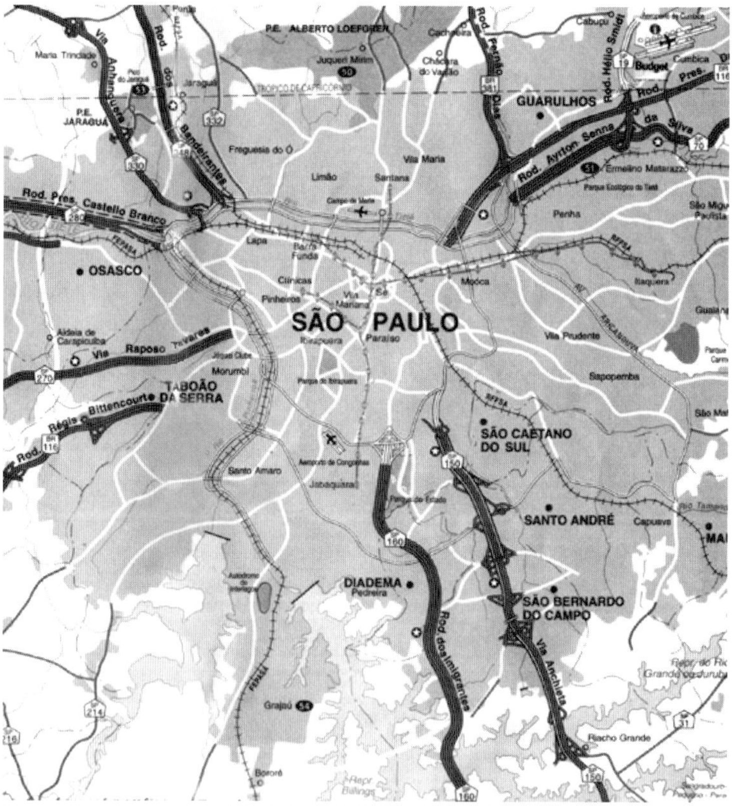

Source: Secretaria Municipal de Turismo de São Paulo. Ap. 1997.

Map 7. Main Road System of the MASP into the City of São Paulo.

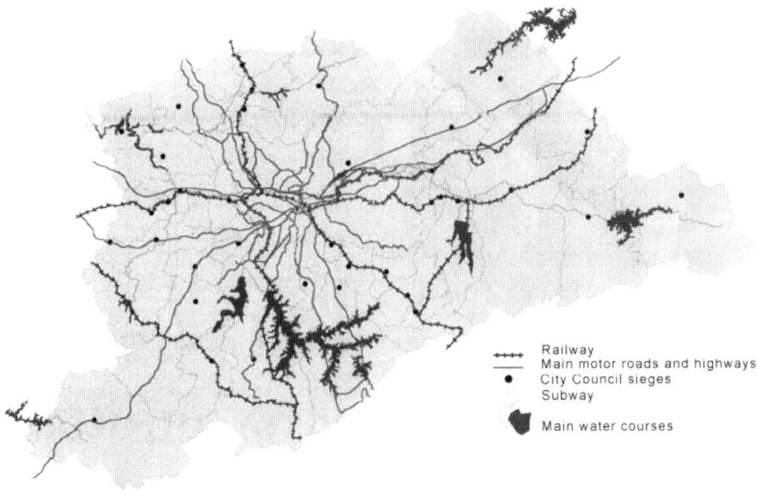

Source: CESAD-FAUUSP/ Map elaborated by INFURB_FAUUSP, 1998

Map 8: Main Road and Railway Network of the MASP.

According to Santos (1996), urban expansion in São Paulo has followed a radial model since the introduction of motorcars early in the XX century. The radius of the built-up area did not exceed one kilometre until 1870. In the beginning of the XXI century however continuous urban development spreads 80 kilometres from east to west and 40 kilometres from north to south. (See Maps 5 and 7).

For Santos, the city's land-use pattern has been strongly influenced by land speculation, which since the end of the last century, has ensured that the built-up area has expanded, leaving large areas of undeveloped space. This process has increased the price of serviced land and has helped accentuate social segregation.

São Paulo generally corresponds to the "Multiple-Nuclei Model" proposed by urban geographers C.D. Harris and E.L. Ullman (1945). Harris and Ullman were confronted with the problems of the mature American industrial city. In this model, there is an explicit recognition of the importance of the automobile and the tremendous impact that major arterial highways and expressways have on the structure of the city. The transportation improvements resulted in the development of many different employment centres within the city resulting in decentralisation out of the CBD. This model did not dispute the basic understanding of the previous models, but it did account for the rapidly expanding complexity of residential areas within larger cities of the mid-20th century, where individual employment centres were capable of generating their own patterns of residential structure at a more local level, resulting in a much more complicated pattern of overlapping residential zones. Although originally intended to explain the developed industrial city of the XX century, this model roughly fits the description of São Paulo in the second half of the last century. The main differential feature of São Paulo is that public investment in roads and freeways, largely based on the model adopted by Robert Moses in New York (CARO, 1975), has been indisputably concentrated in the Southwest sector of the city. Also, different from its counterparts in the industrial developed world, São Paulo has experienced an uncontrolled and unparalleled growth in the second half of the XX century. (Table 2)

Table 2. São Paulo Metropolitan Area Population Growth 1950-2000

Year	1950	1960	1970	1980	1990	2000
Population	2,333,346	4,005,631	7,866,659	12,183,634	15,183,612	17, 500,000 (aprox.)

Source: IBGE

A large part of the metropolis does not comply with official development control regulations (Grostein, 1987). This represents a major difficulty to the research. However, although FDI generally operates in areas that are well served by infrastructure and regulated by urban regulations, whose adequacy may certainly be disputable, this lies outside our field of study.

However, the MASP also fits the definition of "urban basin", given by French geographer Bernard Kaiser (1963). For Kaiser, an urban basin is an urban-regional complex that has a highly dynamic metropolis as its political and administrative core, which controls one or more smaller city networks. In a general manner, these urban systems and networks are the heritage of earlier economic cycles. Because of capital accumulation during these cycles, they have entered progressive activities, then structured urban-industrial processes and attracted large masses of workers from impoverished areas. São Paulo is an example of such a model.

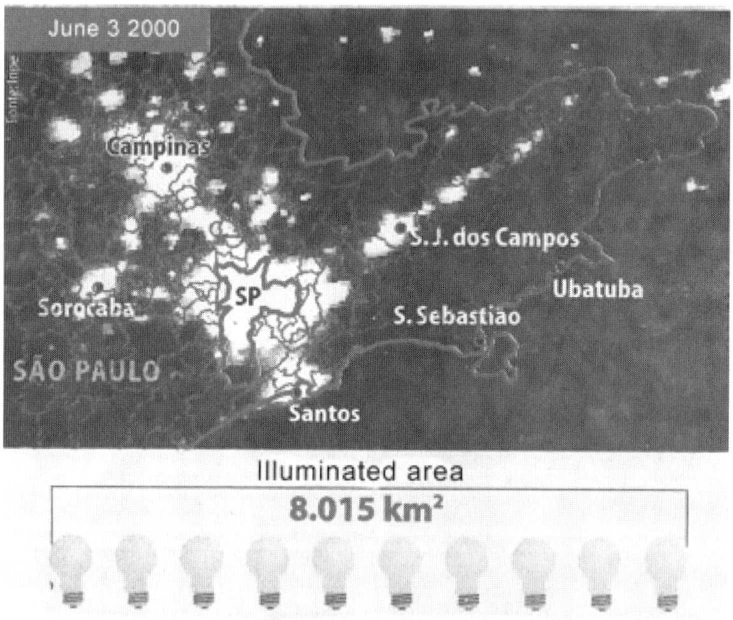

Source: INPE/ Pub. FSP: August 5, 2001

Map 9. The 'Urban Basin' of São Paulo Illuminated By Night. It includes important cities such as Campinas, São José do Campos, Santos and Sorocaba, which lie outside the MASP. The total illuminated area depicted in this map was estimated in 8.015 km2 in June 2001.

"São Paulo began to grow rapidly during the last quarter of the nineteenth century on the basis of coffee production. Modernisation transformed the productive structure, the transport and communications systems, and the consumption structure of the region, changes reflected in the city's built environment. However, until the 1960s, Brazil lacked adequate modern transportation and there was no national market. São Paulo supplied the south and southeast, the only region of the country with a well-developed system of ports, railways, and roads. When the construction of Brasilia, and the opening of new roads into Amazonia finally unified the country, São Paulo region benefited enormously. It became the undisputed economic centre of Brazil. Not only did its manufacturing and commercial activities thrive but it also developed into the country's main financial centre. Until 1960, finance had been mainly controlled from Rio de Janeiro, the headquarters of major public financial institutions such as the Central Bank and the National Bank for Economic Development. The transfer of these functions to Brasilia and the integration of Brazil into a single market gave São Paulo the opportunity it needed to take over." (Santos, 1996)

According to Cordeiro (1988: 158), between 1968 and 1984, São Paulo banks increased their share of the country's total bank deposits from 26 per cent to 42 per cent. By 1985, 33 per cent of Brazilian banks had their headquarters in the city. Many important banks moved their main offices from Rio de Janeiro to São Paulo; by 1989, 18 of the 23 foreign banks operating in Brazil had their principal Brazilian offices in the city, only five in Rio de Janeiro (Cordeiro, 1990). The growing financial clout of the city attracted other economic activities. São Paulo increasingly controls the country's advertising business. In the early 1980s, its advertising billings were already higher than those of Rio, and by 1985 São Paulo companies controlled two-thirds of the billings. Today, São Paulo contains 60 per cent of the major agencies and nine of the eleven agencies with more than 250 employees. It is also now the country's major intellectual centre, with the largest university and research complex in Brazil and with a substantial proportion of the major scientific publishers.

According to Santos (1996), "São Paulo is not only Brazil's dominant economic centre but has established itself as a major world city. In the process, it has begun to change its form. Without losing its industrial importance, it has become a centre of services and the indisputable hub of commercial decision-making. As industrial employment has begun to move out to nearby cities, São Paulo has been transforming itself into an informational complex. This is reflected in the growth of technical, scientific, and artistic employment in the city. From 205,000 workers in 1971, the total rose to 460,000 in 1981 and 760,000 in 1990 (National Household Survey, 1971, 1981, and 1990). Whereas the city's total workforce increased by 119 per cent between 1971 and 1990, the labour force in informational activities increased by 271 per cent; this sector's share of total employment expanded from 6.3 per cent to 10.4 per cent during the same period. In the process São Paulo's share of Brazil's gross national product has declined from 25 per cent in 1970 to 20 per cent in 1987. This decline, is the result of its loss of manufacturing activity, which fell from 44 per cent in 1970 to 31 per cent in 1987." (Santos, 1996)

As a result, former industrial districts of the MASP are giving way to new residential, commercial or recreation areas. According to the international consulting company CB Richard Ellis, 19,1% of former industrial area in the MASP is today occupied by services and other non-industrial related activities. The MASP has 25 million m^2 of built industrial real estate, a large percentage of which currently may be in process of transformation. Bamberg Real Estate Co., a Brazilian real estate company, estimated that 300 to 400 thousand m^2 of built industrial real estate is sold each year for non-industrial activities.

Studies conducted by the "Bolsa de Imóveis de São Paulo" (São Paulo Real Estate Stock Exchange, a private company) indicate that different industrial regions of the agglomeration have different tendencies of occupation. Therefore, large former industrial sheds in the eastern sector of the city have a tendency to become high-rise residential areas, whereas former industrial areas in the Southern sector give way to high technology office towers or shopping centres (Folha de SPaulo: July 29, 2001, Imóveis, p.2).

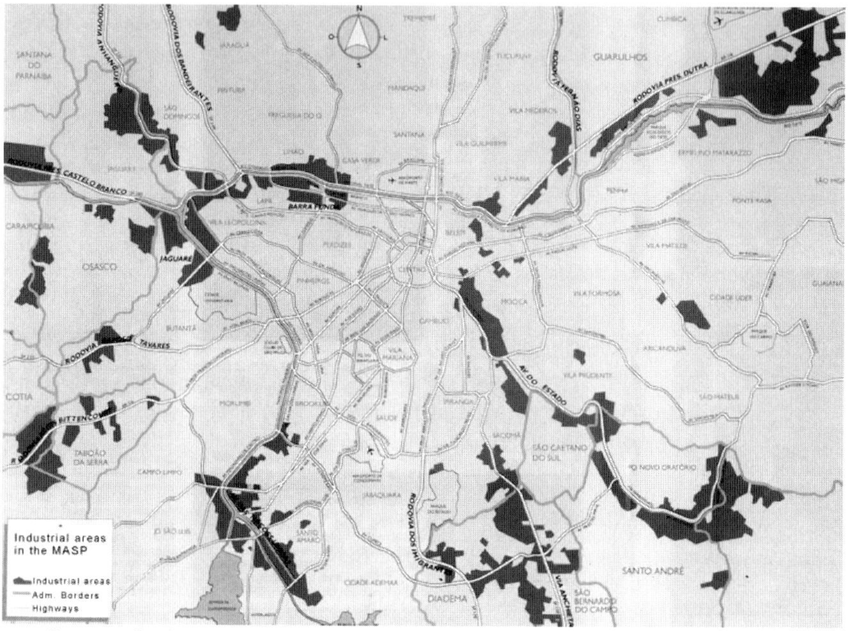

Source: Bolsa de Imóveis de São Paulo, 2001. Map elaborated by Sirio Cançado.]

Map 10. Industrial Regions in the MASP.

How much of this movement is triggered by FDI should be evaluated, but the presence of some of the main real estate companies of the world in São Paulo[36] is a sign that it should have a great influence on the city's real estate market.

36 Such as CB Richard Ellis, Jones Lang Lasalle, Cushman & Wakefield Semco, etc.

Conclusion

Therefore, the task to evaluate how FDI is operating in both agglomerations has to be carried away taking into consideration each agglomeration's features and economic framework. However, we can identify some tools in order to start addressing the problem.

The dynamic areas for FDI in both agglomerations might be identified by using the measurement of start-up businesses proposed by Kloosterman and Lambregts, complemented by the localisation of a significant set of offices for specialised services in the territory, as proposed by GaWC: accountancy, advertising, banking/finance and law firms. (See complete list of firms proposed by GaWC in appendix). However, we could try to enrich this list by aggregating some highly dynamic sectors of activity, which operate transnationally, such as real estate and building companies, assurance companies, telecommunications, and hotel/convention centre chains. The names and numbers of firms would have to be established following a similar methodology as that used by GaWC, which is based on the assessment of global competence of service firms in terms of the geography of their presence in cities. GaWC deals with 'significant presence' only, which means assessing data collected firm by firm and establishing a threshold of presence in a number of cities in order to define the global capacity of firms (Beaverstock et al., 1999).

GaWC supports this method by asserting that "setting up an office to provide advanced producer services is a very expensive undertaking for a firm since it is the nature of service provision that it takes times to build up clientele. Furthermore, operating in this many cities [15], inevitably means working in different legal frameworks and cultural settings. In short, to have 15 or more offices shows a firm to be committed to developing a significant cross-city provision for their particular producer service." (Taylor & Walker, 2001)

But, different from GaWC, we would then proceed to the identification of the exact location of offices in both agglomerations. This would give us a rough idea of areas where globalisation is 'taking shape', so to speak, and provide us with a first clue in order to identify:

- New real estate development that might be the direct result of these firms' operations in the Randstad and MASP.
- New real estate developments that might follow FDI logics in choosing specific areas in the city.
- Public investment or partnerships in order to provide these areas with the necessary infrastructure.
- Real Estate price development in such areas in contrast with the rest of the agglomerations.

(This complements methodology previously submitted to Alfa-Ibis Network and TU Delft.)

Appendix:

Table 3.Cities in World Research

City/Source	FI	F2	PK	DK	SS	FG	No	RP	HY	CO	TH	KA	LP	RE	SK	Sum
Amsterdam	No	***Yes***	***Yes***	***Yes***	***Yes***	***Yes***	***Yes***	***Yes***	No	No	No	No	***Yes***	***Yes***	***Yes***	**10**
Rotterdam	***Yes***	No	No	No	No	No	No	***Yes***	No	No	No	***Yes***	No	No	No	**3**
The Hague	No	No	No	No	No	No	No	No	No	No	No	No	No	No	***Yes***	**1**
São Paulo	***Yes***	***Yes***	No	***Yes***	***Yes***	***Yes***	***Yes***	***Yes***	No	No	No	***Yes***	No	***Yes***	***Yes***	**10**

Source: Beaverstock, J.V. et al., "A roster of world cities", Cities, 16 (6), (1999), 445-458.

Sources:

F1: Friedmann (1986, Table 1)
F2: Friedmann (1995, Table 2.1)
PK: Knox (1995, Figure 1.1)
DK: Keeling (1995, Table 7.1)
SS: Sassen (1994a, from chapters 1 and 2)
FG: Finnie (1998) adapted in Graham (1999, Figure 1)
NO: Nomura (in Rimmer, 1991, Figure 4.1)
RP: Petrella (1995, p. 21)
HY: Hymer (1972, p. 50)
CO: Cohen (1981, p. 308)
TH: Thrift (1989, p. 70)
KA: Knox and Agnew (1989, Figure 2.18)
LP: The London Planning Advisory Council (1991, p. Figure 1.2)
RE: Reed (1981, p. 59-60)
SK: Short and Kim (1999, Table 3.10)

Table 4. The GaWC Inventory of World Cities

- Elaborated by Beaverstock, J.V. et al., "A Roster of World Cities", *Cities*,16 (6), (1999), 445-458.
- Cities are ordered in terms of world city-ness with values ranging from 1- 12

A. Alpha World Cities
12: London, Paris, New York, Tokyo
10: Chicago, Frankfurt, Hong Kong, Los Angeles, Milan, Singapore

B. Beta World Cities
9: San Francisco, Sydney, Toronto, Zurich
8: Brussels, Madrid, Mexico City, Sao Paulo
7: Moscow, Seoul

C. Gamma World Cities
6: Amsterdam, Boston, Caracas, Dallas, Dusseldorf, Geneva, Houston, Jakarta, Johannesburg, Melbourne, Osaka, Prague, Santiago, Taipei, Washington
5: Bangkok, Beijing, Montreal, Rome, Stockholm, Warsaw
4: Atlanta, Barcelona, Berlin, Buenos Aires, Budapest, Copenhagen, Hamburg, Istanbul, Kuala Lumpur, Manila, Miami, Minneapolis, Munich, Shanghai

D. Evidence Of World City Formation

Di Relatively strong evidence
3: Athens, Auckland, Dublin, Helsinki, Luxembourg, Lyon, Mumbai, New Delhi, Philadelphia, Rio de Janeiro, Tel Aviv, Vienna

Dii Some evidence
2: Abu Dhabi, Almaty, Birmingham, Bogota, Bratislava, Brisbane, Bucharest, Cairo, Cleveland, Cologne, Detroit, Dubai, Ho Chi Minh City, Kiev, Lima, Lisbon, Manchester, Montevideo, Oslo, Rotterdam, Riyadh, Seattle, Stuttgart, The Hague, Vancouver

Diii Minimal evidence
1: Adelaide, Antwerp, Arhus, Baltimore, Bangalore, Bologna, Brazilia, Calgary, Cape Town, Colombo, Columbus, Dresden, Edinburgh, Genoa, Glasgow, Gothenburg, Guangzhou, Hanoi, Kansas City, Leeds, Lille, Marseille, Richmond, St Petersburg, Tashkent, Tehran, Tijuana, Turin, Utrecht, Wellington Definitions

World city-ness values produced by scoring 3 for prime centre status, 2 for major centre status, and 1 for minor centre status.

Table 5. Major Latin American Cities: Population Relative to the National Total, 1950-1990

City	Percentage (c. 1950)	Percentage (c. 1960)	Percentage (c. 1970)	Percentage (c. 1980)	Percentage (c. 1990)
Buenos Aires	29.1	33.7	35.6	34.8	33.4
Mexico City	12.2	14.8	18.5	20.7	18.5
Rio de Janeiro	5.6	6.2	7.2	7.2	6.6a
Santiago	25.4	28.9	32.3	34.8	35.0[a]
São Paulo	4.5	5.7	8.4	10.2	10.4[a]

Source: Villa & Rodríguez (1996), based on national census figures.
a. Preliminary figures.

Table 6. Indices of Urban Primacy, 1950-1990 in 4 selected Latin-American Countries

	Index of primacy and populations				
Countries and cities	(c. 1950)	(c. 1960)	(c. 1970)	(c. 1980)	(c. 1990)
Argentina (Bs. As.)	4.0	4.0	4.0	3.8	3.5
Buenos Aires	4,622,959	6,739,045	8,314,341	9,723,966	10,886,163
Brazil (Rio and São Paulo)[a]	0.8	0.7	0.8	0.9	0.9
Rio de Janeiro	2,885,165	4,392,067	6,685,703	8,619,559	9,600,528
São Paulo	2,333,346	4,005,631	7,866,659	12,183,535	15,183,612
Chile (Santiago)	2.4	2.6	2.8	2.9	2.9
Santiago	1,509,169	2,133,252	2,871,060	3,937,277	4,676,174
Mexico(Mexico City)	3.0	2.8	2.7	2.8	2.0
Mexico City	3,145,351	5,173,549	8,900,513	13,811,946	15,047,685

Source: Villa & Rodríguez (1996) based on National population censuses and DEPUALC project.

Accountancy

Arthur Anderson
Coopers & Lybrand
KPMG
Ernst & Young International
Price Waterhouse

Advertising

Abbott Mead Vickers
Dentsu
DMB&B (Magnus Group)*
Grey Worldwide*
JWT (Thompson)*
Lowe Howard-Spink*
Ogilvy & Matter Direct Worldwide *
Publicis
Saatchi & Saatchi*
TMP
Young & Rubicon

Banking and Finance

- ABN-AMRO*
- Barclays
- BBV Group
- Banker's Trust
- Citibank*
- Compagnie Financière de Paribas SA
- Crédit Suisse
- Creditanstalt-Bankverein
- Dresdner Bank Group
- J.P.Morgan
- HSBC
- NatWest Group
- Standard Chartered Group
- UBS

Law

- Allen & Overy*
- Baker & McKenzie
- Bryan Cave
- Clifford Chance*
- Coudert Brothers
- Dorsey & Whitney
- Freshfields *
- Graham & James
- Hogan & Hartson
- Jones, Day, Reavis & Pogue
- Leboeuf, Lam, Greene & MacRae
- Miller, Canfield, Paddock & Stone
- Skadden Arps
- Squire, Sanders & Dempsey
- White & Case
- Wilson, Elser, Moskowitz, Edelman & Dicker

References

Ab'Sáber, Aziz, (1997), "Metropolização e Globalização: Desafios e Reposição Conceitual", in Globalização, Metropolização e Políticas Neo-Liberais. São Paulo: EDUC.

Batten, D.F. Casti, J. & Thord, R, (1995), Networks in Action, Berlin, Heildelberg: Springer Verlag.

Beaverstock, J.V., Smith, R.G. & Taylor, P.J., (1999),"A Roster of World Cities", in Cities, 16 (6).

Caro, Robert A. (1975), *The Power Broker: Robert Moses and the Fall of New York*, New York: Vintage Books.

Castells, M. (1995); The Informational City, Oxford: Blackwell.

Castells, M., Mollenkopf, J. (ed.) (1992), H. Dual City: restructuring New York. New York: Russell Sage Foundation.

Cordeiro, H.K. (1988) "Os principais pontos de controle da economia transnacional no espaço brasileiro." Boletim de Geografia Teorética 16-17: 153-96.

Cordeiro, H.K. and D.A. Bovo (1 990) "A modernidade do espaço brasileiro através da rede nacional do telex." Revista Brasileira de Geografia 52: 107-55.

Cordeiro, H.K. (1993), "A 'cidade mundial' de São Paulo e o complexo corporativo do seu centro metropolitano", in Fim de Século e Globalização (org. Milton Santos), São Paulo: Hucitec-Anpur, pp.318-331.

Delta Metropool (org.), (1999) Planning Metropolis: Urban Growth and Social Patterns, Delft: Deltametropool.

Friedmann J (1986) 'The world city hypothesis' Development and Change, 17, 69-83

Friedmann, J & Wolff, G (1982) 'World city formation: an agenda for research and action' International Journal of Urban and Regional Research, 3, 309-344

Gilbert, Alan (ed.) (1996); The Mega-city in Latin America, Tokyo, New York, Paris: United Nations University Press.

Grostein, M.D., (1987), *A Cidade Clandestina: Os ritos e os mitos. O papel da 'irregularidade' na estruturação do espaço urbano no município de São Paulo. 1900-1987.* São Paulo: FAUUSP.

Hall, Peter (1966) The World Cities (Heinemann, London)

Hall, Peter (1997), "Mega-cities, World-cities and Global-cities", Mega-cities lectures series, Megacities Foundation Rotterdam (February 1997, Rolzaal, The Hague).

Harris, C. & Ullman, E.L. (1945), "The Nature of Cities", in Building the Future City, Annals of the American Academy of Political and Social Science, 242 (1 Nov, 1945): 7-17.

Hohenberg Paul M & Lees, L.H. (1985), The making of Urban Europe, 1000-1950. Cambridge, Massachusetts and London: Harvard University Press.

Kaiser, Bernard (1963), Types des espaces des pays sous-dévéloppés, Paris: Centre de Documentation Universitaire.

Kloosterman, R.C., LAMBREGTS, B.; (2001) "Clustering of Economic Activities in Polycentric Urban Regions: the case of the Randstad", in Urban Studies, 38 (4), 717-732.

Santos, M.; Souza, M.A.; Scarlato, F.C. e Arroyo, M. (orgs.) (1993); Fim de século e Globalização. São Paulo: HUCITEC/ANPUR.

Santos, Milton (1990); Metrópole corporativa fragmentada: o caso de São Paulo; São Paulo: Secretaria de Estado da Cultura : Nobel.

Santos, Milton (1996) " São Paulo: A growth process full of contradictions", in *The Mega-city in Latin America*, (ed. Alan Gilbert); Tokyo, New York, Paris: United Nations University Press.

Santos, Milton, (1993) (a); "A aceleração contemporânea: tempo mundo e espaço mundo", in SANTOS, Milton et al. (org.); Fim de Século e Globalização, São Paulo: Hucitec/ ANPUR, pp.15-22.

Santos, Milton. (org.), (1993) (b); Novo mapa do mundo: fim de século e globalização; São Paulo: Hucitec, 1993. 341 p. Série 'Geografia : Teoria e Realidade'.

Sassen, Saskia (1991) The Global City (Princeton University Press, Princeton)

Sassen, Saskia (1994) Cities in a World Economy (Pine Forge Press, London)

Sassen, Saskia (1994a) 'The urban complex in a world economy' International Social Science Journal 139 43-62

Sassen, Saskia (1999) 'Global financial centres' Foreign Affairs 78(1), 75-87 Short, J R, and Kim, Y-H (1999) Globalization and the City. Harlow: Longman

Scott, A.J. (1998); Regions and the World Economy, The Coming Shape of Global Production, Competition and Political Order. Oxford: Oxford University Press.

Taylor, P.J. & Walker, D.R.F (2001).; "World Cities: A First Multivariate Analysis of their service Complexes", in Urban Studies, vol. 38, no.1, 23-47.

UNCTAD (2000), World Investment Report. Geneva: UNCTAD.

Villa, M. & Rodríguez, Jorge; "Demographic Trends in Latin America's Metropolises, 1950-1990" in GILBERT, Alan (ed.) (1996); *The Mega-city in Latin America*, Tokyo, New York, Paris: United Nations University Press.

Williamson, J. (1999), "What should the Bank think about the Washington Consensus? ", Paper prepared as a background to the World Bank's World Development Report 2000, Washington: World Bank, July 1999.

Quoted by Gilbert (1996)

Dogan, M., and J.D. Kasarda (eds.) (1988) *The metropolis era.* Vol. 1: *A world of giant cities.* Vol. 2: *Mega-cities.* Sage.

Richardson, H.W. (1973) *The economics of urban size.* Saxon House.

UNCHS [United Nations Centre for Human Settlements (HABITAT)] (1987) *Global report on human settlements 1986.* Oxford University Press.

UNDIESA [United Nations Department of International Economic and Social Affairs] (1986) *Population growth and policies in mega-cities: Seoul.* Population Policy Paper no. 4. New York: United Nations.

UNDIESA and UNU [United Nations University] (1991) *Summary report and recommendations of the symposium on the mega-city and the future: Population growth and policy responses*, 22-25 October 1990, Tokyo.

Ward, P.M. (1990) *Mexico* City. Belhaven.

World Bank (1991) *Urban policy and economic development: An agenda for the 1990s.* Washington DC.

Part II

Sustainable Urban Development

6

The Impact of Building Form on Urban Transformation in the Framework of Sustainability

Silvia de Schiller

Abstract

The relation between urban tissue and environmental quality is presented in order to demonstrate the environmental impact of building form. The results are used to detect the relative importance of design decisions. Two scales of impact are considered; at the urban scale the heat island is quantified, using mobile temperature recording, while at the urban design scale local microclimate is simulated and measured. The urban heat island was measured in the denser areas of Buenos Aires, as well as a smaller city in the colder region of Patagonia. At the urban design scale, the key variables considered are direct solar impact and shade, wind protection and acceleration, and energy demand for heating, cooling and lighting. These variables are analysed during different seasons of the year. The impacts considered affect the building form under study, the neighbouring buildings and the adjacent outdoor spaces. The analysis is applied to a series of alternative building forms in a typical block found in the traditional orthogonal grid of Buenos Aires to show how the transformation of urban tissue as a result of global trends affects the quality of urban space and the sustainability of built form.

Introduction

It is argued that global trends in urban design, related to the changing urban morphology, produce significant environmental impacts that influence urban sustainability. These impacts depend on the specific climatic conditions as well as the historic trends of urban development and present day tendencies. The studies presented in this paper use the city of Buenos Aires as an example of urban transformation developed within the regular orthogonal street pattern, typical of the Spanish Latin American cities.

The development of this grid, based on the original layout of the city according to the requirements established in the colonial era, presented in previous papers (de Schiller, 2000, de Schiller, 2001), has been preserved over time despite the significant changes of the building form. In recent decades, these changes have accelerated, giving rise to environmental impacts that are explored and analysed in a series of studies, including those presented in this paper.

The methodology combines measurements in urban spaces, observation of the use of urban space and simulations of sun and wind in different urban conformations to analyse the influence of building form on environmental impacts at the building and urban scale. This frame of reference is used to detect the relative importance of design decisions. The sustainability of the built environment depends not only on the control of energy use and physical resources, but also on the quality achieved, including the thermal comfort of outdoor spaces for urban living. Attractive and comfortable spaces will encourage users, affect perceptions and thus contribute to sustainability in the long term.

The paper also presents the techniques and concepts for analysing the influence of building form on environmental impacts at the building and urban scale.

At the urban design scale, the key environmental variables considered are direct solar impact and shade, wind protection and acceleration, summer breeze, cooling by night radiation and energy demand for heating, cooling and lighting. These variables are analysed during different seasons of the year. The impacts considered affect the building form under study, the neighbouring buildings and the adjacent outdoor spaces. The analysis is applied to a series of alternative building forms in a typical block found in the traditional orthogonal grid of Buenos Aires. A real case, the 164m high 'Le Parc Tower' built within one urban block, was taken as a base for the analysis with alternative designs of equivalent volumes with different heights and identical floor area.

In order to evaluate environmental conditions in alternative urban tissues, laboratory studies were undertaken with models in the CIHE multiple sun heliodon and low speed wind tunnel. Comparative studies of interface between building form and urban space analyse the effect of configuration of public and private open areas as well as the influence on car dependence, pedestrian access, street vitality and capacity to perform urban functions and facilitate variety of uses.

The urban spaces were also analysed, using local measurements of temperature, humidity, radiation and wind speed to detect local variations in microclimate. Observations of users reactions, especially comparative pedestrian flows in streets with different conditions and spatial configurations were also made, as reported in previous papers (de Schiller, 2000).

Thermal responses to the environment are shaped by the environmental conditions in which man evolved (Baker, 2000). Indoor comfort is also affected by the outdoor conditions which are experienced every day on the way to and from the office, school and shopping. This paper therefore attempts to balance indoor comfort and energy demand for conditioning indoor spaces with the environmental conditions in outdoor spaces.

Urban Heat Island

One of the most noticeable environmental impacts of urban development is the heat island phenomenon, resulting in increased temperatures related to density. Studies of the Buenos Aires heat island show differences of 3° within the city boundaries, centred on the areas with high population and building density. Further differences are expected between the City of Buenos Aires, with a population of over 3 million, and the outer edges of the Buenos Aires Metropolitan Area, with a total population of about 12 million inhabitants.

Additional studies (de Schiller et al, 2001) show that this phenomenon is not restricted to the large metropolitan areas but is also found in smaller settlements with lower densities and less favourable conditions for the formation of the heat island. For example, the City of Rio Gallegos also has an urban heat island of 3°C, despite the open urban tissue, the smaller population and high average wind speeds.

Surveys of the heat island intensity show considerable differences according to climatic conditions and time of day, so the measurements, though variable, are clear indicators of impact. The urban heat island is largely a result of energy use in the built environment, though energy use in the transport sector and heat storage in building materials and paved surfaces also contribute to the total impact. The urban heat island is therefore a consequence of inefficient use of energy resources. On the other hand, it also has an impact on energy use, reducing demand in winter but increasing demand for cooling in summer, as well as affecting comfort conditions in outdoor spaces.

Significant variations in environmental conditions can also be detected at the micro-urban scale, which are considered in later sections of the paper, following a review of recent trends in urban development.

Recent Trends in Urban Development

A series of major stages in the transformation of urban form are considered, through the analysis of tissue configurations within the typical Latin American grid. Five steps in this sequence are analysed, from the introduction of a single high rise building in a city block among the compactness of low rise high density perimeter blocks to the open model with free-standing high rise towers.

A critical factor is the tendency to favour high-rise development in the new urban legislation under revision in Buenos Aires, as this building form has a strong influence on energy demand and environmental quality. This paper provides a framework for the evaluation of sustainability, with instruments to detect, qualify and quantify design decisions and planning strategies.

Building control and urban zoning regulations have been introduced in order to assure minimum conditions of natural light, natural ventilation and access to sunlight within buildings and the urban tissue. The free-standing tower was allowed and promoted as a way to achieve higher urban densities, without compromising environmental quality. Zoning regulations in New York, Boston, London and other metropolitan centres permitted higher buildings and denser development for buildings with set-backs from the street boundary that allowed views of the sky from the sides of the towers, rather than over the roofs as was provided in the more conventional development along continuous street frontages.

Planning and building codes have promoted different forms at different periods. The tower on the podium improves daylight to adjacent plots, while allowing larger floor areas on the valuable lower floors. The free-standing tower increases the unbuilt area of the plot, to provide more 'urban space', vegetation potential and natural drainage. The classic form of the New York skyscraper with the tapering upper floors also responds to lines of access to light required in the building codes. The Kavanagh building in Buenos Aires (Figure 1) adopted this form although the requirements of the building code at the time were very different, an early example of the influence of globalisation.

Sun in Urban Space

Sun is regarded as a benefit in the northern latitudes of Europe and the American continent, and legislation promotes access to direct sunlight. For many years, housing standards have required exposure to a certain minimum period of sunlight in the main rooms of the dwelling at a given season of the year. For example, the standards for the United Kingdom require 1 hour of sun in the principle rooms of each dwelling during the winter solstice (MoHLG, 1965). However, the evaluation of solar access is rather more complex in warmer tropical and sub-tropical climates where summer shade is also desirable and direct sun can cause severe overheating.

Regulations for sunlight in the colder climates of northern Europe concentrate on solar access in the principal indoor areas of the dwelling as the occupants use them more than the outdoor spaces in winter. However, in warmer climates, sunlight and shade in external areas is a factor that influences the habitability and use of outdoor space.

Therefore, different and specific requirements for solar access and shade can be identified when analysing alternative urban tissues, considering seasonal adaptation in response to climate.

For the cool season, access to direct sunlight is required for certain minimum periods in the principal rooms of the dwelling. Access to direct sunlight is also needed in a proportion of the public pedestrian circulation. The requirement here is not a period of time but a proportion of the total surface and a reasonable distribution during hours when the sun's elevation is over a certain angular limit. Access to direct sun is also desirable in part of the private outdoor space, especially areas designed for children's play, clothes drying, passive recreation, etc. Here, the hours of use may be more critical, as the solar access to neighbouring buildings and spaces must also be assured to achieve social and environmental equity, while ensuring solar access to the building under analysis.

Figure 1

A new building typology, the Kavanagh Building, completed in 1936, forms a landmark in Buenos Aires with a characteristic tapering profile.

When inaugurated, this building was the highest reinforced concrete building in the world. It clearly shows the global influences of urban images that originate in North America influenced by the building codes of New York.

Old and new buildings within the conventional grid.

New architectural development within the existing urban tissue maintaining the street profile of Santa Fe Avenue.

For the warm season, exposure to summer sun is critical. Therefore, it is essential that building forms are designed to avoid large sunlit surfaces of the eastern and western facades. Buildings should also provide partial shade in the areas of pedestrian circulation, as well as spaces for tree planting to provide **sun protection** at midday when the sun is close to the zenith. Trees and vegetation are important elements to provide partial shade, as larger public and private open spaces may receive little shade from buildings at midday in summer.

In part, these criteria respond to traditional concepts of **solar access**, while others contemplate the requirement for options and choice, expressed in the definition of the ideal urban climate (Katzschner, 2000): "provision of spaces with comfortable micro-climate within reduced walking distances'.

Surveys and Tests of Solar Access and Shade in Urban Space

Using these criteria, heliodon studies were made to evaluate solar access and shade in the different dense urban tissues within the traditional urban block found in the centre of Buenos Aires of about 100m x 100m with a street width of 17m. All alternatives have the same built volume in order to compare the resulting environmental quality as shown in figures 2a - 2e. Five different forms were selected to characterise different models that are representative of urban development trends at different periods. Given the tradition of individual development within plots with limited frontage, rather than the comprehensive development of a whole city block, most of the models are symmetrical.

This allows equal development opportunities in terms of square meters, but does not necessarily achieve equal environmental quality.

- With the traditional form, called the ***'gruyere',*** the patios perforate the low continuous built form. Originally of even height with central open space, the plot coverage is very high in central areas where 8-10 storey buildings are inserted.

- Though the **perimeter block** was a theoretical objective of Buenos Aires planning codes in the past, it was seldom achieved in practice due to the fragmentation of land ownership and the succession of individual developments. It is rather more typical of Central Europe and hence the alternative denomination of the 'Berlin Block'. It is also difficult to control unauthorised development of the inner patio, which is hidden from the public streets surrounding the block.

The environmental conditions in areas of vehicular circulation have not been considered here, though shade and avoidance of uncomfortable reflections are desirable and partial sunlight is also favourable in winter, when low angle sun is excluded.

In some cases there are variations with the spacing and orientation of the buildings within the blocks, while others are symmetrical. Street and block orientation can also be varied.

In addition to the performance of the typical blocks, the environmental impact of one block was studied in relation to the surrounding blocks. In the first case, the effect of one block was considered with blocks of a similar type surrounding it, while in the second, the effect of inserting one type in a development of a second type was evaluated. For example, an isolated tower inserted in the traditional urban tissue will have a different effect from that of a tower surrounded by other towers.

BUILDING FORM AND THE EVOLUTION OF URBAN DEVELOPMENT

Different stages of urban development in Buenos Aires are characterised by five alternative building morphologies with the same volume.

The photos show tests carried out with models in the solar simulator.

Building forms

Figure 2. Existing tissue
Figure 3. Single free-standing tower
Figure 4. Four free-standing towers
Figure 5. Perimeter block, Berlin type
Figure 6. Parallel row buildings

Figure 2

Conventional tissue, typical of Buenos Aires urban development, with compact older low-rise buildings with limited patios, mixed with higher buildings permitted under former codes and zoning regulations. This example shows the first stages of density and height increase within the conventional plot subdivision .

Access to sun and daylight within buildings is limited, but the street environment has certain favourable aspects and low building height allows some top lighting and natural ventilation.

Figure 3

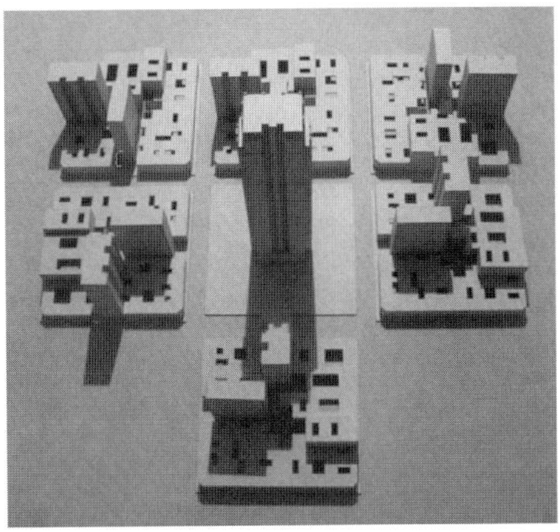

The ***single free-standing tower,*** placed in the centre of a typical urban block, is based on the actual case of the Le Parc Tower. This is the ideal and extreme case, with the provision of green space within the dense and compact urban tissue. This intervention interrupts the continuity of the street profile and reduces contributions to urbanity:

In contrast to the ideal model proposed by Le Corbusier, the green space is private with a clear barrier segregating the development from the public sphere, and excluding urban activities.

Figure 4

Four towers within the block, with a lower building height are also found in Buenos Aires, with variations in form and placement on the site. This alternative was called the **'upside-down table'**.

Figure 5

The ideal ***perimeter block***, the Berlin type, with a large central patio and continuous regular development along the street frontage. This form is rarely found in Buenos Aires due to the fragmentation of land ownership, though past zoning regulations have attempted unsuccessfully to achieve this.

In contrast with the Buenos Aires situation, the core of the Berlin model allows semi-private activities in a protected environment. .

Figure 6

Two or three ***parallel rows*** of buildings: this alternative is rarely found in central areas, but the parallel block was used frequently in social housing schemes outside the central area in the 50's and 60's.

The prototype is related to the forms studied by Walter Gropius in the Bauhaus during the pre-war period.

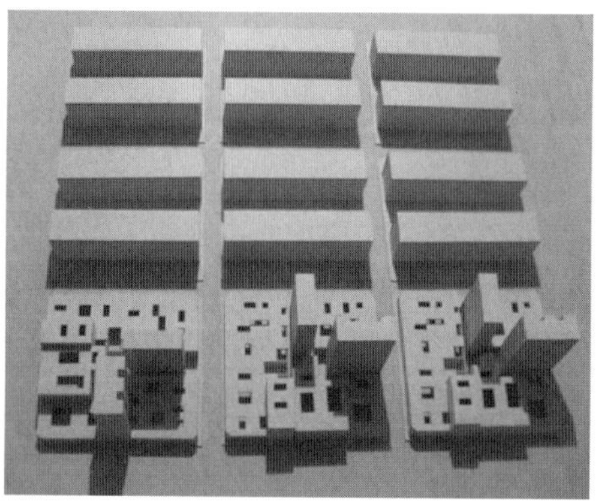

Figure 7

The paradigm of the model for the free-standing tower: Le Parc Tower, on the left, surrounded by other free-standing tower buildings.

Despite the high population density the streets have little urban activity.

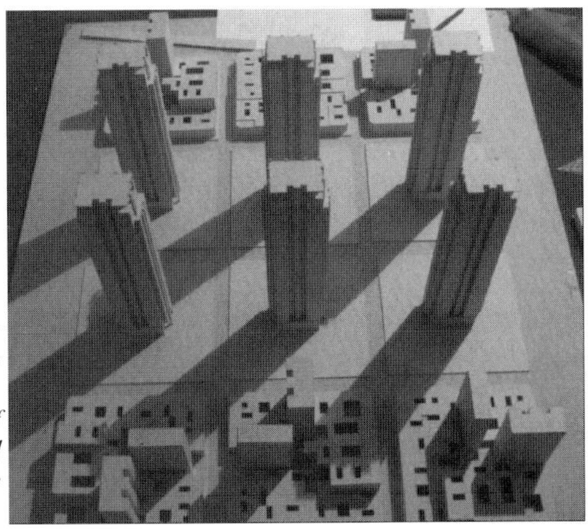

Figure 8.

A series of towers, with shadows corresponding to 10:00 during the equinox.

This example of multiplication of the tower typology can be compared with the single tower inserted in the conventional tissue shown in Figure 3.

Figure 9

North Diagonal Avenue in the centre of Buenos Aires.
The regular level of the cornice was established when this avenue was cut through the existing urban tissue, and is one of the few streets where this has been maintained over time.

Wind and Ventilation in Urban Space

The impact of wind in urban areas, as with solar access, affects various aspects of urban and building performance, such as heat losses of buildings and comfort in public and private outdoor spaces. Although, unlike sun and shade, **wind is invisible and unpredictable,** laboratory tests and site measurements were carried out to determine the influence of this environmental variable in the quality of outdoor urban space.

The wind speed measurements were made in two stages: firstly around high buildings that interrupt the existing urban tissue (de Schiller, 2000) and secondly in a series of traverses across a sector of the central area. In both cases the increase of wind speed at pedestrian level depended on the height and form of the surrounding buildings, with a very clear tendency to significant increases close to high towers. CFD simulations and measurements in urban spaces in the centre of Buenos Aires supplemented studies in the low speed wind tunnel, carried out in earlier research.

According to the characteristics of the wind pattern, three areas were identified:

- Around high buildings where wind speeds increased significantly above the urban average. During the traverse measurements velocities of 2 - 5m/s were measured.
- Traditional compact urban tissue had low wind speeds, from 0,3 to 1m/s.
- In areas of transition between the edge of the central area and the open port area, wide avenues, etc had intermediate velocities.

Table 1 shows the general results of the laboratory tests and site measurements, classified in ranges of wind velocity in the public pedestrian circulation areas.

Table 1. Classification of Wind Speeds

Type of block	Wind speed at pedestrian level
Existing tissue	Low
Isolated tower block	Very high
4 tower blocks	High
Perimeter block with patio	Low
Parallel blocks (Bauhaus)	Low – Medium

Although pedestrians are unable to plan their route across urban spaces to avoid wind, a study of pedestrian flows in sectors of Buenos Aires was carried out in order to detect a tendency in the behaviour and positive use of outdoor urban spaces. The survey not only showed that pedestrian flow are lower in windy areas than in potentially sheltered areas, even on calm days, but also that pedestrians try to avoid potentially windy urban spaces altogether.

Energy Demand and Urban Form

To obtain an initial idea of the potential variations in energy demand that result from altering the built form, different thermal and energy indices were compared:

Form factor: this is the simplest indicator which demonstrates the relation between the external surface area and the built volume, assuming an average thermal conductivity over the whole external envelope. This is expressed as metres^{-1} (m^2/m^3).

Weighted form factor: as the proportion of the total envelope consisting of better-insulated roof surface can vary from 4 to 50%, this factor gives a better indication of the relative heat losses of different forms. The weighted form factor indicates larger losses for high towers compared with lower developments with larger roof surfaces.

Energy Evaluator: a spread sheet was used considering heating requirements according to building form, window size, thermal qualities of the construction, exposure to wind and sun, geographical location, internal design temperature, heating plant type and efficiency, etc (Evans, 2001). This approach takes into account that a significant proportion of housing still does not use air conditioning, and therefore the energy demand for cooling in summer is negligible.

LT method: this method includes heating, cooling, ventilation and lighting demand. This method takes into account the form, orientation and distance from the facade (Baker and Steemers, 2000). The other variables considered are building type, window size as a proportion of facade area and the internal gains. The most important concept of the LT method is the distinction between passive and active zones: passive zones at distances of up to 6 meters from the facade can have natural lighting and ventilation, while spaces further from the facade need artificial conditioning.

Energy-10: based on an annual hour by hour simulation of building performance, this method (Balcomb, 1999; Evans and Torres, 1999) generated similar values to the LT Method, though using climatic data for Buenos Aires, rather than the more generic data used for the LT Method.

There are a number of alternative evaluation criteria, including heat loss related to building form (form factor), heat loss according to the variation in external surface and thermal insulation (weighted form factor), percentage of passive floor area, proportion of wall surface area exposed to winter sun, proportion of wall surface exposed to summer sun from the west, etc. **When evaluating the energy demand of different forms, comparative values are required rather than precise absolute values.**

Table 2 shows the results of the evaluation for form factor and passive zones, while Table 3 shows the potential and actual exposure to winter sun. It should be noted that the symmetrical forms have similar exposure to winter sun from the north and summer sun from the west. The dense traditional urban tissue has the highest losses due to partial shading on patios, followed by the perimeter block.

Table 2. Form Factor and % Passive Zones

Type of block	Form factor FF	Weighted FF	Passive %
Existing	0.16-0.19	0.15-0.18	0.35-0.45
1 Free-standing tower	0.14	0.15	0.64
4 Free-standing towers	0.18	0.19	0.72
Perimeter block with central patio	0.15-0.19	0.16-0.20	0.68-0.95
Parallel blocks	0.14-0.17	0.15-0.19	0.50-0.75

Table 3. Solar Access in Winter compared with North Facing Walls

Type of block	% Walls facing north	% Wall with winter sun
Existing	25 %	15 %
1 Free-standing tower	25 %	25 %
4 Free-standing towers	25 %	25 %
Perimeter block with central patio	25 %	20 %
Parallel blocks	40 %	35 %
Existing	10 %	8 %

Table 4. Roof Area as a Proportion of Total Envelope and Total Floor Area

Type of block	Roof area / envelope area	Roof area / floor area
Existing	50 - 67 %	20 - 33 %
1 Free-standing tower	4 %	2 %
4 Free-standing towers	9 %	5.5 %
Perimeter block with central patio	16 - 29 %	7 - 17%
Parallel blocks	13 - 33 %	10 - 15 %

The results show that the variation of the form factor for different alternatives of the same building type was greater than the variation for averages of different types.

The low traditional urban tissue has a low percentage of passive zones, but if the 'active' internal zones of the top floor obtain lighting and ventilation through the roof then the percentage rises to over 70%, comparable with other building forms (Table 4).

Temperature Variation in Urban Space

The variations in urban temperature were studied at two scales: the urban heat island at the city scale and local variations at the micro-urban scale.

At the city scale, the temperature increase that forms the Buenos Aires urban heat island is strongly related to building density. Temperatures were measured using miniature data loggers on the outside of vehicles making urban circuits. The measurements do not show a direct relation with building types (de Schiller, 2000).

The heat island varies with time and climatic conditions, with a tendency to increase in the evening when the measurements were taken. Within the Capital district with a population of 3 million out of the 12 million in the whole of the metropolitan area, temperature differences of 3°C were measured, centred on the dense urban areas of the centre, Belgrano and Palermo.

At the local scale, similar differences were measured over much smaller distance around buildings and in different points across the street canyon. Once again, considerable differences and variations were observed with a tendency to increase around tall buildings and wide and deep street canyons.

Radiation

The dimensions of the street canyon also affect urban cooling at night, according to the exposure to the sky on clear nights. This is beneficial in summer to promote cooling of air in urban spaces and the users within these spaces.

On the other hand, enclosed spaces such as patios and narrow streets retain heat in winter and improve thermal comfort, though they may suffer from poor access to winter sun.

The angular view of the sky allows the sky factor to be measured to assess this variable. It is closely related to the geometry that provides wind protection.

Mapping Thermal Comfort

Humidity, temperature, radiation and wind speed can be combined in a single thermal index to predict thermal comfort. Although the PMV index (ISO 7730, 1994) was not developed for application in urban spaces, it was found to give meaningful results when evaluating the impact of urban microclimate in pedestrian areas.

During the traverse survey mentioned earlier wind speed, temperature, relative humidity and radiation were measured. The general climatic conditions at the time were a light wind, cool temperatures and little radiation around sunset. Using these measurements, the PMV was determined assuming warm outdoor clothing and metabolic rates corresponding to walking, A range of Predicted Mean Votes PMV from 0,2 to 1,0 was measured, indicating a variation from comfortable to cool, at the same time and within a radius of 700 metres.

This is a significant difference that can be perceived by pedestrians as they walk through the city. A significant part of the difference is caused by variations in wind speeds, though radiation and temperature differences also contributed to the result.

Graphical Evaluation of Results

The multiplicity of variables, spatial, environmental, seasonal, etc., makes the evaluation of alternatives very difficult. The following graphical method has been used to explore the comparative advantages of different urban forms. In this example, the relative importance of seasonal variations is analysed.

Firstly a rank order is made for the different variables for each alternative urban tissue, numbered from best (1) to worst (5) for winter and summer conditions.

Table 5. Evaluation of Sun and Shade using Rank Order for different Spaces in different Seasons

Alternative tissue	Facades		Sidewalks		Gardens	
	S	W	S	W	S	W
Existing	4	5	2	4	1	5
1 Free-standing tower	5	1	5	1	5	1
4 Free-standing towers	5	2	4	2	4	2
Perimeter block with central patio	3	4	1	5	2	4
Parallel blocks	1	1	3	3	3	3

The ranking for the three spaces is combined to have one ranking for summer and winter. A weighting system can be used, for example if it is considered that sun on facades is more important than sun in gardens or on sidewalks. However, in many cases, the weighting system does not affect the rank order, so arithmetic averages can be used directly.

Figure 10 shows that single isolated towers provide best solar access in winter for all three criteria, but it is also the worst in summer, with least shade. On the other hand, perimeter blocks are most favourable in summer, though less advantageous in winter. The existing urban tissue is slightly worse in both summer and winter. The parallel blocks have a good performance in both seasons. If winter is considered to be the critical season then the left hand scale can be used to rank the alternatives while the right hand scale indicates the priorities for summer. In the case of Buenos Aires where there is a balance between summer and winter, the centre of the graph shows the most favourable solutions; parallel blocks in this case.

Figure 10

Evaluation of sun and shade in summer (S) and winter (W).

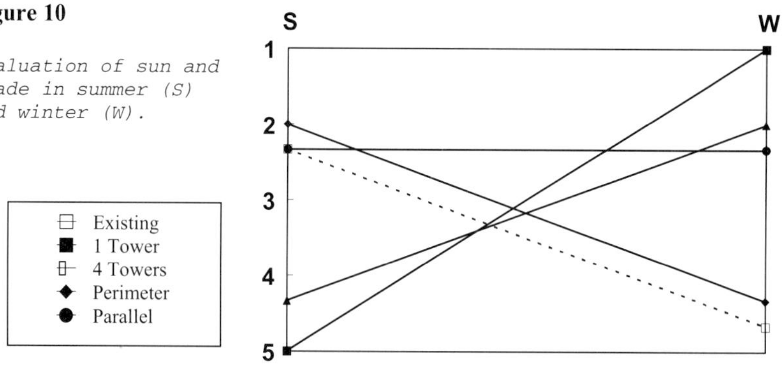

In the case of wind, a similar procedure is adopted. Three aspects of wind impact are considered: on facades for heat loss effects, in public pedestrian spaces and in the gardens or private open spaces within the plot. Air movement is favourable in summer for thermal comfort, but excessive winds are undesirable. In winter, wind protection is required.

Table 6. Evaluation and Ranking of Wind and Air Movement on Facades, and in Public and Private Outdoor Spaces.

Alternative tissue	Facades		Sidewalks		Gardens	
	S	W	S	W	S	W
Existing	5	1	3	1	3	1
1 Free-standing tower	1	5	4	4	5	5
4 Free-standing towers	2	4	5	5	4	4
Perimeter block with central patio	4	2	2	2	2	1
Parallel blocks	3	3	1	3	1	3

Figure 11

Evaluation of combined wind effects in summer (S) and winter (W).

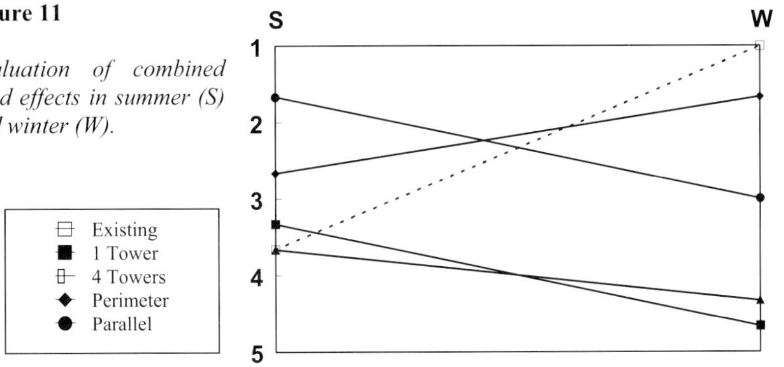

Different criteria for evaluating energy demand related energy can be considered in the same way to obtain a composite ranking of alternatives.

Energy requirements for heating are related to the weighted form factor, energy for lighting ventilation and eventually air conditioning will increase as the percentage of the passive zone decreases, energy for air conditioning in summer depends in grand part on the exposure to western sun, etc. The results of the ranking for these factors are shown in Table 7

Table 7. Evaluation of Energy Demand for Heating, Lighting and Cooling

Alternative tissue	Heating/ cooling		Lighting/Ventilation		Solar gains	
	S	W	S	W	S	W
Existing	2	1	5	5	2	5
1 Free-standing tower	1	2	3	3	5	2
4 Free-standing towers	5	4	2	2	4	3
Perimeter block with central patio	4	5	1	1	3	4
Parallel blocks	2	3	4	4	1	1

Figure 12

Mean ranking of alternatives with respect to energy in summer and winter.

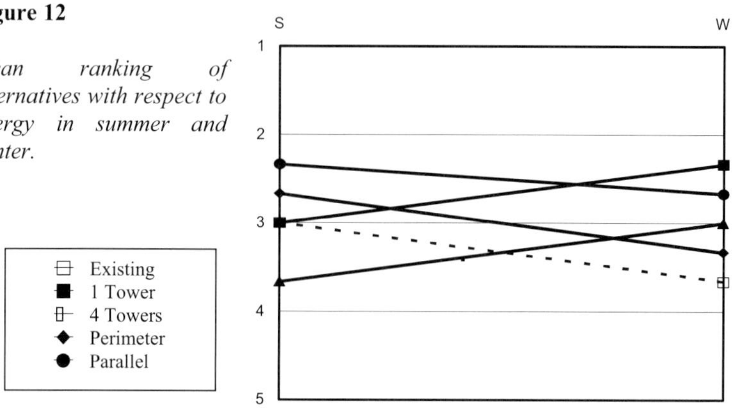

In this case, the parallel blocks perform well in summer and winter, though the single tower has certain advantages in winter. The most unfavourable are the 4 towers and the existing tissue, the former in summer and the later in winter.

The combination of different variables for different seasons will be affected by factors such as:

- Building types: buildings with high energy demand, such as offices will have a rank order that differs from low energy demand buildings of the residential sector.
- Regional climate: the balance between the importance of summer and winter changes in different climatic zones.
- Local microclimate: windy areas close to the coast and on exposed slopes will have different requirements from protected urban centres.
- Planned activities: spaces for passive outdoor recreation will have more demanding requirements than pedestrian circulation.
- Subjective values: as comfort is a subjective sensation, methods are required that allow alternative value criteria.

Figure 13

The towers of Catalinas Norte seen from the Buenos Aires waterfront with the Nature Reserve in the foreground.

This area of the centre has been transformed in the last thirty years as a result of the introduction of new building typologies, the paradigm of the model.

Figure 14

The same urban development seen from within the city forming an apparently continuous front along Alem Avenue, although the free-standing towers produce an open tissue.

Conclusions

The study of the relation between built form, urban tissue and microclimatic conditions, presented in this paper, provides evidence of environmental impacts that affect sustainability as a result of the transformation process. The measurements made show that there are significant variations in urban microclimate that are produced by different conformations of urban tissue. The different urban tissues related to architectural form are representative of evolving theories of urban development in Buenos Aires in the framework of the Latin American orthogonal grid.

Two alternative and complementary lines of study carried out to evaluate the impacts of building modification, reflect different ways in which new urban and architectural forms are inserted in the existing city grid. In the first set of examples, different building types of identical volumes were inserted in one block surrounded by existing tissue, and in the second set the complete tissue is transformed with the repetitive insertion of the same building form to create new paradigms. The five different volumetric typologies selected represent evolving concepts and application of built form as well as a sequential process of urban transformation.

The methodology developed for the evaluation of these alternatives integrates complementary measurements of environmental variables at the city and micro-urban scale with different building and urban forms. These are tested with laboratory simulations, which allow a comprehensive understanding of the phenomenon.

The impact of various environmental factors can be combined in indices such as Predicted Mean Vote, PMV (ISO, 1994), which provide a useful method to integrate variables. The results of the application of the PMV index, originally developed for indoor environments, show that it also provides valuable conclusions for outdoor conditions, although the values obtained are less precise.

A graphic evaluation method, based on a qualitative ranking system, allows a comparison of results in winter and summer, allowing a visualisation of the balance between different and often-conflicting environmental requirements.

The result of this analysis, rather than identifying a preferred or ideal urban tissue, provides a way to understand the consequences and impacts of different planning requirements and the quality of the resulting urban character.

However, it is clear that the most recent building typologies introduced in Buenos Aires do not provide the best balance of environmental conditions in the spaces surrounding them.

Three factors have been identified that contribute to the deterioration of environmental conditions in urban spaces:

- The introduction of design features and building technologies that improve the indoor conditions in buildings often have an unfavourable impact on the quality of the outdoor spaces.
- The same building form has a different performance and provides different quality of adjacent outdoor paces depending on the local climatic conditions. Therefore local environmental requirements and specific design strategies should be identified in order to select appropriate building forms.
- The tendency to design individual and free-standing buildings on their own plot in the existing urban grid reduces the possibility of a coherent design for the outdoor spaces to produce favourable micro-climatic conditions.

In all three cases, there is a common factor that depends on the regional climatic variations as well as the social, economic and political forces of globalisation, that characterise the North-South divide. In warmer climates, the outdoor space has a far greater potential for active and prolonged use than similar spaces in colder climates, altering the balance between indoor and outdoor space use and conception.

Finally, it is argued that the sustainability of urban spaces will depend in part on the environmental quality of the outdoor morphological configuration. The surveys of pedestrian behaviour (de Schiller, 2000) support this hypothesis, showing that improved environmental quality attracts users of the urban space. The promotion of urban activity through control or improvement of environmental conditions will therefore contribute to the sustainability of urban development.

Acknowledgements

The research presented was carried out as part of the project 'Sustainable urban form: environment and climate responsive design', within the EU ALFA-IBIS Program 'Globalisation, Urban Form and Governance', co-ordinated by TU Delft, under the supervision of Profs. Ian Bentley, Georgia Butina Watson and Elizabeth Wilson, of the Joint Centre for Urban Design, Oxford Brookes University.

Some studies and laboratory tests were undertaken with support from the University of Buenos Aires in the framework of the UBACyT Project A-022 'Sustainable Architecture: evaluation of the impact of design decisions', with the assistance of Prof. John Martin Evans for the instrumentation of microclimate measurements and application of graphic evaluation methods.

The students Markus Vogl, from the University of Munich, and Paul Feldkamp, from the Technical University of Delft, prepared the models and assisted with the laboratory studies of solar impact in the heliodon as part of their academic activities carried out during their training at the Research Center Habitat and Energy from May to September, 2001, under the direction of the author.

References

Baker, N & Steemers, K. (1998), *The LT Method 2.0*, Cambridge Architectural Research, Cambridge.

Baker, N. (2000), *We are all outdoor animals*, in Koen Steemers and S. Yannas, Architecture City Environment, Proceedings of PLEA 2000, James and James, London.

de Schiller, S. (2000), *Sustainable cities: contribution of urban morphology*, in Koen Steemers and S. Yannas, Architecture City Environment, Proceedings of PLEA 2000, James and James, London.

de Schiller, S., Bentley, I, Butina Watson, G. (2000), *Sustainable Urban From, Environment & climate responsive design*, in Sustainable Cities: Sustainable Development, Proceedings of the 17th Interschools Conference, Oxford Brookes, Oxford.

de Schiller, S. (2001) *Sustentabilidad y transformación del tejido urbano en la cuadricula Latinoamericana*,

Katzschner, L. (2000), *Urban climate maps – a tool for calculations of thermal conditions in outdoor spaces*, in Koen Steemers and S. Yannas, Architecture City Environment, Proceedings of PLEA 2000, James and James, London.

ISO EN 7730: 1994 (1994), *Moderate thermal environments, Determination of PMV and PPD indices and specifications of the conditions for thermal comfort*, International Standards Organisation, Geneva.

Leveratto, M. J., de Schiller, S., Evans, J. M. (2000), *Buenos Aires heat island, intensity and environmental impact*, in Koen Steemers and S. Yannas, Architecture City Environment, Proceedings of PLEA 2000, James and James, London.

7

Neighbourhood Spatial Process: Notes on Public Space, 'Thick' Space, Scale and Centrality

Stephen Read

1. Urban Centrality

To talk of urban centrality and public space may sound a little old fashioned, the subject of wishful thinking or misty-eyed nostalgia. The city is of course changing - seemingly torn apart by the exploding scales and speeds of the processes playing themselves out there, and we sometimes think of the dynamism of these spatial processes as being foreign to the city as it once was, and often still is in its historical cores - as if the new 'space of flows' is conceptually incompatible with a fundamentally static 'space of places' (Castells, 1996). But the richness of these traditional 'places' is just as much a product of life patterns in motion as is the fragmentation of the experiential and social fabric of the city on it's periphery. The city and change are no strangers to each other and cities have burst beyond the constraints of their edges before. The space of the city has always existed in a tension between inside and outside, between the local and larger scales, and between inhabitant and the traveller, trader or stranger. It is possible to overstate present-day change and to imagine that all that we know about cities from their histories is becoming irrelevant - and also to lose sight of the importance of centrality and a rich diversity of scales in *any* story about the city. Those who claim the city is becoming uniformly generic without centrality and peripherality, and without public space, haven't been shopping in my neighbourhood. Of course there is a new city emerging and of course it is recasting the question about the nature of the city - but it is forcing us to reappraise our concepts of what *both* the old city of centres and peripheries *and* our new dispersed 'generic' city are. The two continue to coexist alongside one another - as indeed they did before the terms generic or edge city were ever coined. And the reappraisal can do as much to help us to understand what the nature of centrality is as it can help us to understand what the diffusing and invading generic city is.

I'm going to approach the problem of public space in a way that may sound strange at first - by talking about urban space as a mechanism. I will try to avoid some of the more difficult issues of meaning by considering the city as a functional thing - as something that *works* at a simple level of everyday activity and experience. The city is of course complex but one of the remarkable things about it is that although it seems to be such a difficult thing to describe and analyse in any way which explains its workings, we seem to *use* it very easily indeed. Perhaps there is something about the way we deal with the city at a very everyday, very intuitive level which may be a key to its understanding.

Of course meaning comes back into this as well. A lot of questions about the city and our relation to it - and our relation to neighbours and strangers within more or less public space - are about the way the city acts at the same time as a physical environment and as a model in everyday life of less tangible things like society, community, and so on. It is more than a metaphor, it is a demonstration in the real world of the workings of social and cultural systems. And the important thing is that it happens right there before our eyes - in our sensible experiential world - and it happens in such a way that we are immersed in it. So it is at the same time the real thing and a representation of itself which we latch onto and use as a model or metaphor for understanding the workings of things like society and community. So the city is at one and the same time both a material environment (made up of both people and things) that we engage in a very direct way - and a material grounding for a mental construct supporting all sorts of ideas that we take for granted as constituting our lives, often without crediting the city for doing any of these things. It's like language in a way, an only half-seen background to our everyday lives which nonetheless supports constructs of everyday meaning and knowledge.

But if the city is a machine, what sort of machine is it? What is clear is that it is not the sort of machine that has a very clear programmatic aim, or necessarily any built in programmatic aim at all. Nor is it a machine for supporting something like community or neighbourhood or economy or anything like that, though it may eventually do all these things as a lucky consequence of what it was doing in the first place. I suggest that the city is, or rather has been in its best moments, a machine for supporting intelligibility and for supporting interface - interface between people, and particularly interface between people operating and doing things at different scales. We are talking here about networks of course and about the ways networks at different scales overlap each other and then interface in the urban field. I believe that we can talk here about both virtual networks and those networks of social and economic contact and interaction built into the spatial infrastructures of streets squares and public and private transport networks, but here I will be considering these effects as they play out within and affect the quality of public space.

But the city, because it is not programmatically specific, is also a machine for change. The city, as a field or background for human activity, will absorb the dominant activities of the time - form 'permanences' (Harvey, 1996) or encrustations of relatively ephemeral programmatic and institutional stuff around the urban spatial network structure, which can change as the city changes from for example an industrial base to a services base to an entertainment and tourist base. The city organises and structures human activity, but it does this according to a principle of scale not a principle of programme, and different scales are held in relation to each other in a way which supports intelligibility and coherence.

2. Space, Public Space, and Relations between Local and Higher Scales

If what I have just said is true, urban space is not just the simple physical stuff, or the void between the physical stuff, that we draw on maps. Urban space is at the same time both physical and mental. Lefebvre has taught us that if we want to understand anything about urban space we have to look at both these aspects together and never reduce the urban to simply the physical or simply the mental (Lefebvre, 1991). Space, or rather ideas about space, are also ways that we understand and construct our world.

Recently there has been a lot of talk about space as flux. This is a space with multiple overlapping dynamics, one which emphasises multivalent connection. It is about extension continuity and unity, about a field whose centralities and voids are defined by and emergent out of the dynamics that play out within the field.

There is another kind of space with which many of us (especially designers) are even more familiar, which involves codes for the production of our physical environment, some of which are so familiar they have become almost invisible. This space is much more closely tied to issues of territory and bounding. It is about the parts which make up wholes, about areas which are assumed to have a certain autonomy and about the relations between them. Many of our familiar ideas about neighbourhood, about urban functional zones and so on are based in a basic framework of bounded areas and the relations between them.

This conception of space leads to a fundamentally different view of neighbourhood - or more generally 'the local' - and its relations with the rest of the city than does that of the idea of different scales of network interfacing each other in a structured manner. On the one hand we have a patchwork of local zones with relations between themselves, and on the other we have relations between local networks and higher scales - these higher scales acting as network systems in their own right and mediating relations between local zones.

In fact if we look at neighbourhoods in a lot of more traditional cities it is clear that neighbourhood is not this clearly bounded phenomenon. Neighbourhood seems difficult to delimit spatially and seems to be something which *emerges out of* urban processes, rather than being the result of bounding intended to *control* urban processes. The second spatial framework mentioned above has been used for the more planned production of urban space but the first (that of flux) has always produced urban space, especially where the more conscious and deliberate process of the second has not dominated. Today, the first spatial process is again becoming more insistent and taking over from the second as the flows in our urban landscape speed up and escape the control of the spatial techniques and practices of planning and design. The space of flux has always produced urban space in more organic settlements, where preconceived ideas of neighbourhood or of urban programme do not form a prestructuring framework. Rather the prestructuring framework in organic settlements is more directly influenced by everyday life processes and their patterns, especially those related to mobility.

The notion of a *public* space is one of those seemingly self-evident ideas which benefits from a more rigorous inspection. We tend to define public space in opposition to the notion of private - rendering it crudely homogeneous and failing to account for its complexity and unevenness as a field for social activity and meaning. In fact public space has always been highly uneven in the way it supports urban activity and urban society and in its accessibility and meaning, and it is not at all clear within the public-private polarity what the exact dimensions of public space are as they affect issues of social power and empowerment. The concepts public and private are not absolute, they acquire meaning in context and in relation to one another. Public and private serve to organise contrasts within different paradigms while across paradigm boundaries meanings can differ profoundly - the public of the *public sector* is something different to that of the *public realm* and is different again to that of the *public interest*. Clearly then, the public-private polarity presents epistemiological and terminological problems, and is less straight-forward than it is sometimes taken to be. In relation to the public of social groupings in a larger society, what in fact seems to happen is that segments of society pursue their own limited interests in opposition, or at least in differentiation, to a wider public - clearly segmenting the amorphous idea of *the public* or *the public realm* by scale (Borret, 2001). This scale segmentation can be taken further and related not just to more formal social organisational structures, but also to multiple, more mobile, less clearly articulated, but nonetheless real issues of everyday identification in urban space. The public may then be defined not in opposition to the private but rather in terms of the relations between multiple publics.

3. Urban Fabrics and their Typologies

To talk about produced social environments as typologies or shapes of layout is ineffective without talking at the same time about typologies or shapes of use. And as soon as one starts talking about use, we can no longer talk about that layout without considering the way that everyday patterns of use and activity weave an area into the surrounding fabric and beyond. In a sense the interwoven patterns of peoples everyday activities *becomes* the fabric of the city of our social and cultural experience. The expanding everyday processes of the new city and new patterns of use are producing new environments on the periphery. But they are also often emphasising the dynamic, connective, integrative aspect of use and space in centres and giving rise to programmatically different ways of using the city in the centre that nonetheless (in many or most cases) do not fall outside of the capacities of central urban space for programmatic adaptation and change.

The city sometimes looks to be unravelling - processes of mobility and habitation are disengaging from each other as the city expands beyond the centre. The historical centre is characterised by proximity and contiguity - mobility connects all places with all other places within a context of high densities of people and things. Local and larger scales confront one another and contiguous flows of people, goods, money and information energise and enrich each other. On the periphery with mobility patterns historically directed towards the centre, mobility tends to concentrate in engineered infrastructures and to disengage from the functionally and experientially diluted fabric through which it is woven. The dense, integrated experience of the city is lost as habitation is consigned to capsular interstices between high speed arteries where the direct friction between local and larger scales is evaded. Relationships of scales and patterns of activity in the periphery become very different to those in the inner cities. The question is; how is the environment on the periphery we are sketching out here public, and how does its public-ness relate to that of our traditional city centre model?

The public space that one enters as one steps out one's front door in a neighbourhood like that of the Pijp in Amsterdam (see Figure 7b) is not an empty neutral form. The local intrinsic qualities - what is immediate and seen - mask another space whose qualities are extrinsic and which comprises a pattern of known and understood relations, relations with friends, neighbours, work, shops, facilities, meeting points, entertainment. There is no doubt that many of these relations are undergoing transformation but many remain grounded in the public space of neighbourhoods such as this. What I would like to do is examine how these relations are grounded in old and new types of neighbourhoods, and what the consequences might be for public space.

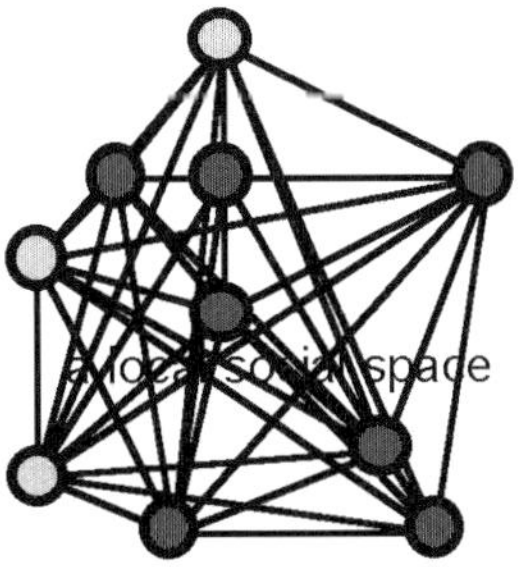

3.1 A Neighbourhood within the Inner City

Figure 1. A Local Relational Space.

Social spaces are constructed in use, and the ways experience and identity are grounded in urban space are multiple and highly specific. Meaning is constructed in the way places are inhabited and experienced in relation to each other, and then insofar as these spatial relations and meanings are shared, they become one of the ways that social groups define and identify themselves. A local social space therefore may consist of the shared experience and the shared significance of locations and relations within a field of connective possibilities, and crude representations of the set of relations can be constructed using node and edge diagrams. Local spaces may, in a mixed neighbourhood, consist of the dwelling places of the members of an ethnic group along with the places - shops and cultural facilities - they use and with which they identify. It may also simply be the locations of the houses of a group of friends along with the cafe they frequent and the supermarket where they bump into each other.

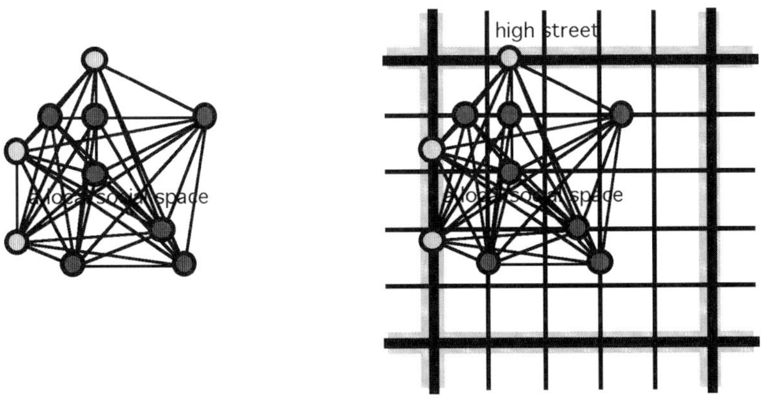

Figure 2. An Inner-City Neighbourhood. Local relational space superimposed over the physical layout. Mapping trajectories through the physical layout generates the social space.

The diagram is of course a gross simplification, and represents relations between nodes as abstracted topological connections. But consider how these connections are going to be translated into movement through the actual geometry of the layout, and one gets a sense of the way that members of the same group could meet on the street in the course of their everyday activities. Mapping trajectories through the physical layout therefore generates the social space one finds on the street.

Figure 3. Overlapping Local Relational Spaces Superimposed Over The Physical Layout.

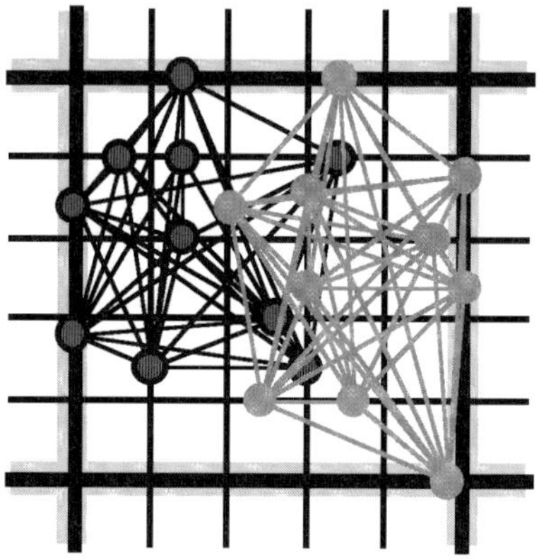

Many of these local social spaces will of course coexist and overlap in the same urban area. Superimposing just two of them already begins to give a sense of the huge density of connections and relations that are starting to be generated. What is also interesting is the way, if you map trajectories of people through the streets of the layout you can show how people using different local social spaces will come into daily contact with each other - building a dense web of social interface and co-presence - a *thick* urban social space.

The local social space in a traditional urban neighbourhood is also subject to certain characteristic urban scale differentiations and hierarchies, as in the difference between streets which are quiet and residential and those where shopping and facilities concentrate - typically on the high-street, where local people *and* those from outside the neighbourhood are co-present. Within the normal compass therefore of a person's daily neighbourhood activities and within the local walkable neighbourhood, there are not one but two scales of urban activity. Contact and co-presence is made on a daily basis not only with immediate neighbours but also with people from outside the neighbourhood who use the shops and other facilities on the high streets. Although the high streets serve as traffic arteries they are in no way specialised as such. I will illustrate this further in my discussion of the example.

It is interesting to note that the neighbourhood 'territory' is not simplistically bounded, but is defined in a relational way and that it is this that allows and supports the social and cultural overlap and diversity that we find in traditional urban space.

3.2 A Neighbourhood on the Periphery

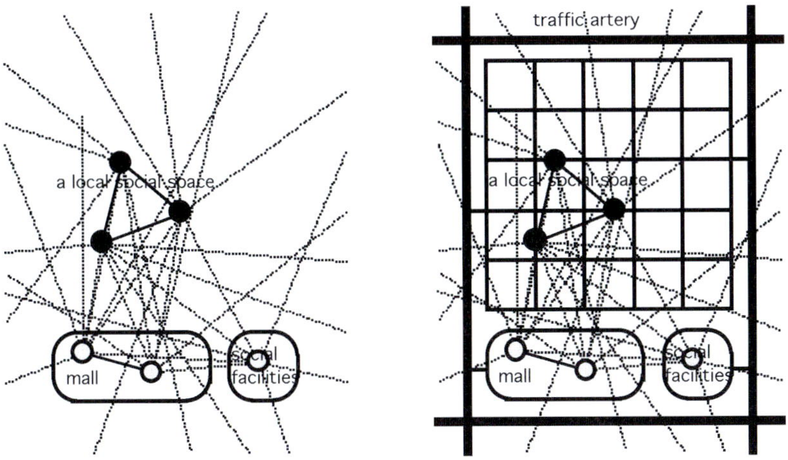

Figure 4. A Neighbourhood on the Periphery. Local relational space superimposed over the physical layout.

In contrast, neighbourhood and community on the periphery is in general founded on territory that is about the bounding or encapsulation of land - generally in the interstices between specialised movement routes. These neighbourhoods tend also to be more socially and culturally homogeneous while social and commercial facilities tend to become segregated from the housing and concentrated in more 'generic' capsules of malls and 'centres' of various types, accessed through the specialised mobility network. Relations which may have been local in the centre, embedded in the neighbourhood and in the local social space, have become distantiated and accessible only through the specialised mobility network.

3.3 The Territorial Gradient; capturing the Spatial/Social Typology

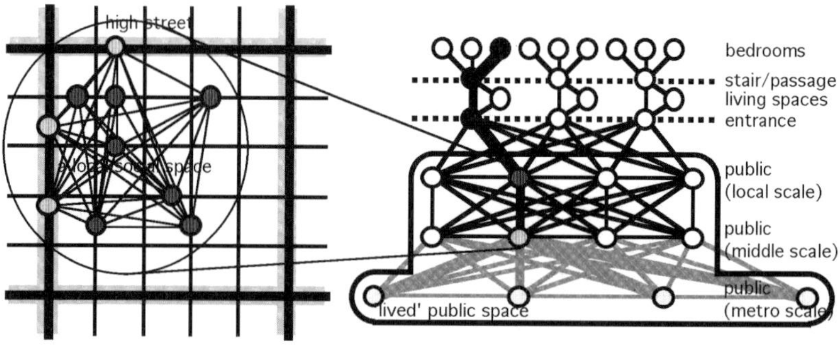

Figure 5. An inner-city neighbourhood. Territorial gradient.

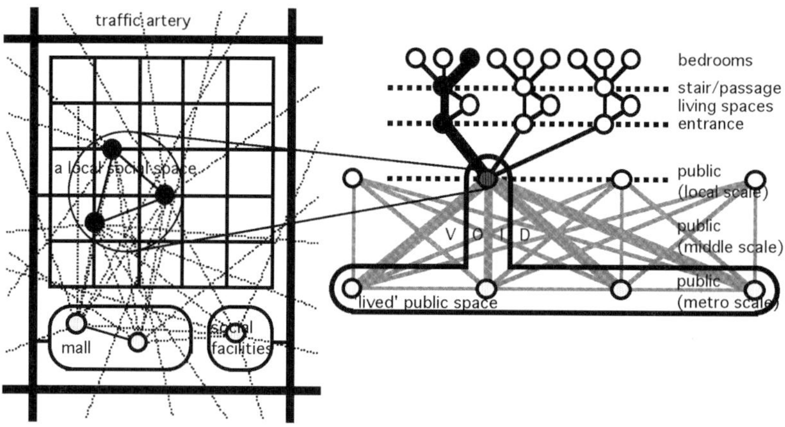

Figure 6. A Neighbourhood on the Periphery. Territorial Gradient.

Julia Robinson has coined the term *territorial gradient* for these diagrams (Robinson, 2001). They represent a schematic section through the gradient of privacy that a person experiences in his or her everyday life - from the largest public scale to the most intimate and private - marked off in steps from bottom to top. There is a sequence from the very private, the bedroom, through gradations of involvement with others within the dwelling, then through local social space - through different scales of public space - and eventually to those 'generic' public spaces, the 'centres', malls and other facilities attached to no particular public. Historically, when the city encompassed the daily lives of almost all people, this largest scale was associated with the public centre of the city. As the lives of people escape the bounds of the old city of course the new accessibility and *centrality* (at this regional scale) of the periphery siphons many of the facilities associated with this scale off into the periphery.

The local social space in the area on the periphery is much reduced compared with that in the urban centre. This is not to suggest that no distantiated relationships exist in social patterns in the inner city, simply that in the process represented by the change from urban life to suburban, relations which were local have tended to become distantiated. The relative social homogeneity of new residential areas and the use of private transport in local areas means that relations between different local social spaces are effectively eliminated. These factors have a serious consequence for the 'shape' of public space as it is defined by these relations. Consider the outline I have traced around the public space that is effectively experienced by the people whose territorial gradients are drawn here. The *thick* shape of the public space for the inner-city neighbourhood is a consequence of the richness of connection between local relational and social spaces. The thinness of the experience of public space in the neighbourhood on the periphery is a direct consequence of the lack of this richness of connectedness and co-presence.

Another serious transformation in the 'shape' of this set of relations is the loss of the scale represented in the centre by the high street. The simple pattern of mobility network and attached 'capsules' means that the largest generic and the smallest local scales predominate and the middle scales of direct connection to adjacent areas is lost, along with the economic and cultural advantages this kind of connection can be seen to generate in inner city areas like the Pijp in Amsterdam.

Central public space is much richer in relationships, as local social spaces come in contact with each other, and in the relationship of the local with a 'middle' scale in the high street. This illustrates further how peripheral spatial layouts suffer a loss in the experience of 'the public'. If the meaning and quality of public space are dependent on this spatial connective richness and breadth, the territorial gradient demonstrates how 'public space' in the periphery, even that in well-designed 'new urbanist' neighbourhoods with all the obvious *intrinsic* qualities designed in - the house styles, the street furniture, even the 'corner shop' - may be experienced quite differently. It is the *extrinsic* qualities of space - demonstrated by the territorial gradient - that make the difference, and here it is difficult to find common ground between the 'space of many publics' of the traditional centre and this 'space of a rather depleted public', no matter how visually attractive, on the periphery.

4. The Spatial Mechanics of the Local and Middle Scales

I have done a lot of work establishing that there is a two part hierarchy - corresponding to the high-street, residential street distinction - in normal central urban space which has a fundamentally spatial basis. I have argued that the distribution of activities is not simply based in an historical narrative of decisions and events but rather that it is fundamentally based in a spatial patterning which influences the ways people move. Flows of people through the traditional urban spatial grid tend to concentrate in a higher level network called the *supergrid*, and I have argued elsewhere that this two part hierarchy of supergrid and less-used, usually residential, streets is fundamental to our everyday experience of the historical city. I have argued further that it underpins the mechanisms of interface and intelligibility that I am talking about here (Read, forthcoming 2002).

We can understand from our experience of traditional urban space the characteristic distinction in any local area between relatively busy streets and relatively much quieter ones. I am arguing that this is a principle feature of the spatial mechanism - one that designers often understand intuitively. When we look at plans of cities we can usually pick out with some degree of accuracy which are going to be the busy streets just by their geometrical attributes. My work with spatial models has established this systematically and I have been using these models to investigate the relationship between the high-street and the area around it. In particular how the relationship between high-street and area radically influences the character of both high street and the lesser-used streets comprising the area (Read, 2001).

It is in fact this interaction between the high-street and the area - between therefore the scale of the local neighbourhood and the urban scales just above that of the neighbourhood - which seems to determine a lot of the character and commercial and social functioning of urban spaces.

4.1 The Pijp Neighbourhood in Amsterdam

I will use the example of the Pijp neighbourhood in Amsterdam in order to discuss the spatial/social mechanics of the local and middle scales.

Figure 7a. Ferdinand Bolstraat, the Pijp

Figure 7b. Jacob van Campenstraat, the Pijp

Figure 7a shows a high-street space in the Pijp and Figure 7b a quiet residential street. What is significant is the way the readability of the urban environment - its knowability and usability therefore - are connected to the simple code that is reflected by this bipartite ordering. The city at the level of its particulars is manifestly rich and complex, but the complexity of the detail with which we are confronted in our daily interaction with the city is referenced to this intuitively known and understood spatial order, rendering complexity knowable and the well-functioning urban context *thick* with meaning and information. Multiple particulars relating to street-scene and the life-patterns of people become meaningful and intelligible with respect to each other through their relation to this order. Particular locations become related to the wider city while they at the same time maintain their local particularity and distinctiveness.

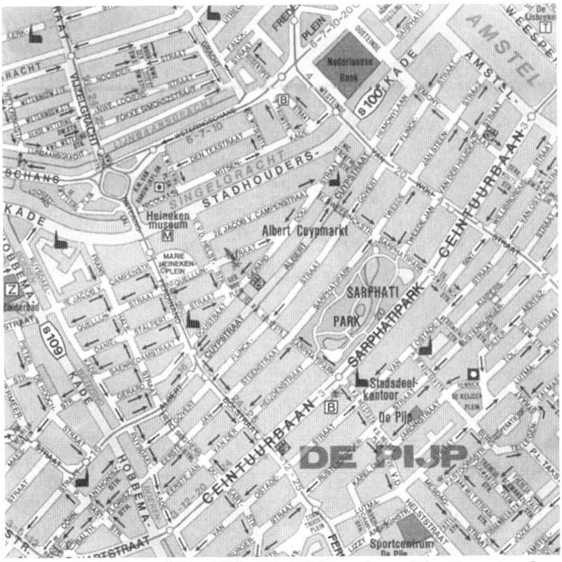

Figure 8. Map of the Pijp Neighbourhood in Amsterdam.

The Pijp is crossed by four strong high-street axes, two running roughly north-south, two running east-west, making it an area which is powerfully connected to the rest of the city. The radial north-south axes are the Ferdinand Bolstraat and the van Woustraat, and the circumferential east-west axes are the Stadhouderskade and the Centuurbaan. I will concentrate on these streets and the area around them.

I want to first look at how the interface between the scales of the area and the supergrid is constructed in the patterning of streets. There is nothing spatially forced or complicated about the spatial layout, minor streets simply meet supergrid streets at right angles, more often than not crossing them so that a four-way crossing is established. If we look at the way these spaces are used, the first thing that can be said is that the characters and the types of function supported on the circumferential, east-west supergrid streets are different to those supported on the radial supergrid streets.

Figure 9a. The Stadhouderskade - running east-west. Figure 9b. The Centuurbaan - running east-west.

The extremely good accessibility from the rest of the city of this circumferential axis, the Stadhouderskade and the Ceintuurbaan, is reflected functionally in the concentration of computer, carpet, curtain, furniture and household goods stores which clearly serve a much wider area than just the local neighbourhood.

Figure 10a. The Ferdinand Bolstraat - running north-south. Figure 10b. The van Woustraat - running north-south.

The characters of the Ferdinand Bolstraat and the van Woustraat, the north-south axis, are very noticeably different. Although they both also carry high volumes of motor traffic, the volume of pedestrian movement on these two routes is very much higher and the types of shops supported here reflect a much closer link with the immediate neighbourhood. Many smaller stores are supplemented by the high-street clothing, electrical goods and general household goods chains.

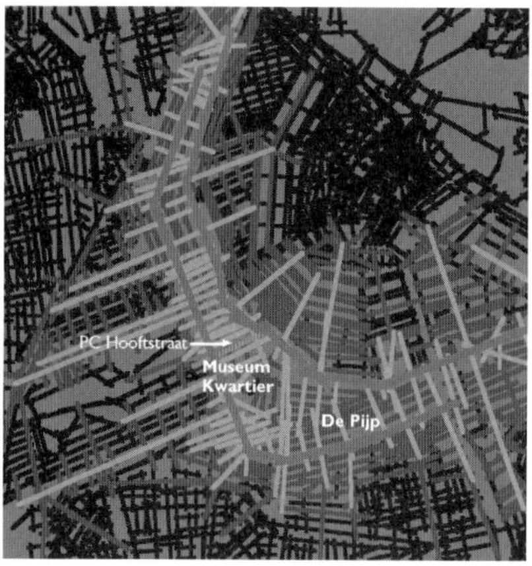

Figure 11a. The Pijp: point depth diagram showing direct links from the Stadhouderskade and Centuurbaan with the interior of the area (in green).

Figure 11b. The Pijp: point depth diagram showing direct links from the Ferdinand Bolstraat and van Woustraat with the interior of the area (in green).

It is clear if we look at these diagrams that the openness of the area grid and the transparency of the area from the north-south axes is quite significantly higher than it is from the the east-west axes. The block geometries are such that there are more than twice the density of inner-area streets that connect with the Ferdinand Bolstraat and the van Woustraat as connect with the Ceintuurbaan and the Stadhouderskade. The visual link down these inner-area streets is strong and direct - the green spikes represent direct sightlines and permeabilities from within the area. The area therefore has a strong east-west bias, orientating itself on the Ferdinand Bolstraat and the van Woustraat and making them the dominant local-area shopping streets.

From within the area the Ferdinand Bolstraat and van Woustraat are felt as a constant presence. Much of this is related to the awareness of movement and to the awareness of a higher intensity of activity along these routes. This movement and higher activity are picked up visually, and serve to orientate and to signal the spatial structure, which they do without ever becoming intrusive.

But while it is clear that the Ferdinand Bolstraat and the van Woustraat relate strongly to the local area, the link with the wider city is also strong, and the people on these streets and the clientele in the shops are by no means restricted to people from the local neighbourhood. Rather this is also a popular medium-priced shopping area for people from other parts of Amsterdam and even for visitors from out of town.

While spatial hierarchies are reflected functionally through a concentration of shopping and activity in the circuit defined by the crossing of the high-street axes, this is by no means the end of the story. The openness of the area engendered by the simple open grid ensures that though the functional hierarchies are clear they are by no means rigid. Shopping penetrates the interior of the area, where rentals are cheaper and where non-prime positions are taken by second-hand shops, bicycle and other repair shops, specialist food shops, restaurants, cafes etc.

Figure 12a. Gerald Douplein

Figure 12b. Albert Cuyp Market

The interior of the area seems to serve to some extent as overflow space to the major supergrid spaces. It is apparent that the openness of the grid serves to soften and blur the structure, and that the blurring that this openness engenders allows a freer use of space both for movement, and commercially - where shops which serve the local area and which cannot afford the high-street rentals find places which are still exposed, though at a lower intensity, within these blurred movement patterns. The whole 'interior' of the Pijp between these four major supergrid streets therefore has its activity levels raised. The most remarkable example of this slippage of commercial functions into the interior of the area is the Albert Cuyp Market, the largest daily street market in Amsterdam, which occupies a whole inner-area street strung between the Ferdinand Bolstraat and the van Woustraat - in a sense becoming an extension of the shopping frontage of these shopping streets.

Figure 13a. Frans Halsstraat.

A contrary effect to this infusion of movement and activity into the interior of the large 'block' bounded by the major high-street spaces, can be observed on the other sides of the Ferdinand Bolstraat and the van Woustraat. Here the grids are also extremely open but the effects of the pull of strong high-street spaces does not work *across* the area itself, given that the spaces on the other sides of these areas exert a much weaker attraction than do the four streets already mentioned.

These areas then, while being highly open and transparent, as well as highly intelligible and strongly located because of their visual openness - are by-passed by the major movement patterns. Here high clarity and intelligibility combines with a quiet ambience, the whole adding up to a quality in the total environment whose parameters are rather difficult at first sight to pin down. These areas are popular with young professionals and other urbanites in spite of their high densities and very small houses.

5. Summing Up: *Places* of Flows

Multiple overlapping processes and their respective scales are coordinated within public space by the fact that they are grounded in material flows within a real urban spatial connective context. The grounding of these processes draws the spatial factor into the equation with its specific configurations of spatial connection, permeability and resistance. The Pijp shows how the structure produced within this spatial context may order the details of urban circumstance as well as patterns of social interface in the surface of the city, differentiating volumes and scales of movement and activity, and formally articulating the city as a intelligible field for everyday use.

What I can begin to propose, is that certain spatial layouts, characterised by openness and transparency at the local scale, combined with strong connection to their surroundings at the scale immediately above the local, offer the necessary spatial-structural qualities to support the sort of structured diversity, overlap and busy-ness characteristic of well-functioning central urban locations. They enable a multiplicity of use which is at the same time spatially and functionally articulated and intelligible. These environments absorb and sustain a life of the city, structured around but not determined by the scales of the local and the wider city. The particular social and cultural vitality of these environments is underpinned by a rich overlap of social and cultural meanings constructed within relational spaces - where individual and group territories are specific and clear without being exclusive, and relations between the local and the middle urban scales is strong and direct.

These environments also underpin a potential for change. It is the strength of places like the Pijp that they are capable of changing in tune with changing times - in fact it is often on the streets of places like this that we first notice that social or cultural change is taking place. Here periodic decline has always been followed by new awakenings, with new street cultures and economies growing up to replace older ones as wider social and economic orders are transformed. The 'permanences' - comprising particular material encrustations of function and culture - break down as social and economic conditions change, but the underlying structure, founded in space and in mobility remains, around which new encrustations, emerging from new social and economic conditions, may form.

Urban centrality is constructed on movement flows and activity patterns within the urban spatial matrix. It is constructed on a dynamic and is itself dynamic. A conception of urban centrality and place founded in these ideas may offer a framework both for investigating the shifting fortunes of urban centres and locations as they respond to shifts in the scales and circuits of these flows in the city the region and beyond, and for designing vital urban places capable of supporting a rich mix of urban life and culture.

References

Borret, K. 2001. 'On Domains: the Public, The Private and the Collective', OASE 54, Winter 2001, 50-61.

Castells, M. 1996, *The Rise of the Network Society*, Blackwell, Oxford.

Harvey, D. 1996, *Justice, Nature and the Geography of Difference*, Blackwell, Oxford.

Lefebvre, H. 1991, *The Production of Space*, Blackwell, Oxford.

Read, S. 2001, ''Thick' Urban Space: Shape, Scale and the Articulation of 'the Urban' in an Inner-city Neighbourhood of Amsterdam.' As yet unpublished paper presented at the Third International Symposium on Space Syntax, Georgia Institute of Technology, Atlanta.

Read, S. forthcoming in *Space Syntax I*, 2002, 'The Patchwork Landscape and the 'Engendineered' Web; Space and Scale in the Dutch City', Available as working paper.

Robinson, JW. 2001, 'Institutional Space, Domestic Space and Power: Revisiting Territoriality with Space Syntax.' As yet unpublished paper presented at the Third International Symposium on Space Syntax, Georgia Institute of Technology, Atlanta.

8

Research and Project Buenos Aires and De La Plata Riverfront

Design Concepts for Restructuring Central Areas

Alvaro Daniel Arrese

1. Introduction

In the face of the rapid change that cities are experiencing, the role of architects and town planners is to analyse which conditions and in which manner practice can influence the urban transformation process towards reconstructing urbanity and defining new spaces for the development for social life. This general objective, which constitutes an influential venture of present architecture and urbanism, is intimately related to the ethical commitment of these disciplines, which were born "to contribute to the general well-being". As Alain Touraine rightly pointed out "our experience is fragmented and the institutional role was substituted by important financial organization strategies, techniques and measures..."1. The new economic order generates growing social exclusion, threatening life and urban spaces, contributing to violence and insecurity.

With the aim of achieving security, closed and "walled suburbs" are growing on the urban fringes, while older residential areas start to decay and deteriorate, and the city ceases to be a homogeneous and open space. There are urgent and interrelated tasks to rebuild the cities, and simultaneously, the conditions of urbanity. These tasks seek to simultaneously find new concepts, tools and the necessary theoretical support to resolve new problems, as traditional urban planning instruments have shown their incapacity to respond to this new situation. In the new setting, the public and private sectors play new roles in which the responsibilities of authorities increase. They must determine policies and plans to frame private actions with the aim of achieving general well being.

In this perception, the roles of analysis and of the urban project must be radically re-evaluated if we want to meet the challenge of our times. This research attempts to contribute to the task of breaking down the barriers separating both worlds. These differences refer to old methodological discussions on the relation between the general project sciences and the project design itself. Science refers to universal regularities and design to specific situations to be solved, since each city constitutes a special case with its own landscape, its own history and its own problems. These can be studied with the typical rigor of scientific analysis, but their singularity can only be solved by the synthesis of design decisions.

Urban planning has adapted objective and scientific methodologies in order to reach certain results in a rigorous manner. In contrast, the direction of the project is sometimes unclear and unpredictable and those involved never know for certain what the outcomes will be. Once reached, however, the results become clear, are easily verifiable and can immediately be carried out. Inversely, we could say that planning becomes tedious and clinical in the short term, as its results only become obvious over much longer periods. In the short term they seem abstract, inflexible and theoretical, contrary to the realisation, apparent reality and immediacy of the project results.

Despite the differences mentioned, sometimes the results of the methods used in the scientific approach are as concealed and unpredictable as the ones from the project approach. In fact numerous discoveries in the history of science were made when casual experimenters obtained different results from those they were expecting to find. However, while both science and projects use very different thought processes, languages and methodologies, the results can be evaluated with balanced objectivity. As a result, instead of talking about the unbridgeable differences between planning and project, it would be better to think in terms of "how and when" they complement each other.

As we know it is impossible to plan without a project, or to sketch huge projects without the general guidelines that only plans can provide. For these reasons, this study uses the project to verify concepts and also as the subject of investigation, referring not only to the spatial order from determined needs, but also to the internal handling of the project tools and procedures, that simultaneously builds and embodies theory. One of the main objectives is to build a theoretic model from the project development and research into its tools, procedures and results.

The research includes the scientific analysis of the specific case and its context. A validating design strategy verifies the formulated concepts in projects that serve as conclusions to the scientific analysis. This was done without evaluating whether the results contradict old cultural habits or concepts and images accepted as unchanged. However, there are ethical reasons that led me to the responsible acceptance of reality in all its complexity, with both advantages and inconveniences. There is a contradiction in this: working within reality but ignoring past solutions. The knot of the problem should be untied and solved, but results from this operation should challenge old and established beliefs. In this case, keeping them will only hide them under the consoling veil of past convictions.

2. The Buenos Aires Riverfront Case

The River Plate constitutes the most valuable environmental, landscape and productive resource of the city of Buenos Aires. Its position facing the city, guarding the access to the River Plate's basin and the entry door to the heart of South America have played a dominant role in its four-century destiny. This site, open to the interior as well as to the rest of the world, located between a fresh water sea and an ocean of grass, had also provided important support for its legend and urban imaginary. The city has throughout its history shown a consistent ability to achieve a reasonable balance between its riverside recreation, circulation and port uses. This intention couldn't always be carried out successfully because of the accumulation of physical and cultural complexities. To turn around the assigned spatial limitations to the role of the city constituted a two century long battle. The transformation into a port city by converting the natural moorings on an alluvial river into reasonably practical port infrastructure took a similar period of time. Not an easy task, as stated by the different port layout proposals, the unscketched developments and the ones finally built, from the vessels of the Riachuelo to Puerto Nuevo. It also required the improvement of river and land access from different points, through the use of towrope tugs, channel construction with permanent dredging of supply routes, etc.

From the XIX century, the riverfront was changed for each technological port change or improvement in maritime and land accessibility, as landfill was used as an exclusive resource to solve new functional demands. The port and its supply system inserted progressive barriers between the city inhabitants and the riverside coast, every time increasing the distance. To consolidate the successive riverfronts as public spaces in the shape of promenades, parks, yacht piers or swimming facilities demanded similar efforts, as those required for the port. The city, meanwhile, had sprawled outwards, embracing the surrounding towns in a continuous urban agglomeration. Today, in spite of all the effort, the city has lost its two fundamental horizons, the green from the "pampas" and brown from the river, with the riverfront again under pressure.

The Central Area has been revitalised, because the global economy requires infrastructure that creates a new centrality. Large areas, that previously housed transport infrastructure, pose new opportunities for strategic development linked to central areas. An urban corridor is inserted between the city core and the coastal landscape, and in the future, apart from a complementary highway, various complex developments, which were formulated in an ad hoc manner, outside any planning process, will result in contradictory and opposing development. These projects cover an approximate surface of 1.023ha and stretch over 8km of the north-south corridor. The corridor is a key element in connecting parts of the of the Buenos Aires area and constitutes the eastern limit of the central area. Thus the relation between the original city core and the riverside landscape, which was originally one of its borders, is affected by a variety of different projects today:

- *Puerto Madero (140ha)*:
  In the beginning of the 90's, the effective land recovery of the area was initiated as a limited expansion of the Central Area for administration and residential use.
- *The Riverside Highway (25ha)*:
  Projected as a movement corridor to complement the saturated coastal corridor at regional level, this highway will connect the south and north of the metropolitan area with Puerto Nuevo. As a result of the development of Puerto Madero, its construction was interrupted, leaving a final decision on different alternatives and possible layout pending.
- *New Port Enlargement Project (270ha)*:
  This project would improve the river port access, docking, loading and storage capacity and will incorporate a new land-fill area on the northern limit of the Central Area, as a result of the dredging and deepening of its access channel.
- *Retiro Project (75ha)*:
  Currently still being investigated, this project would provide for residential and green areas in a part of the railway shunting yard, simultaneously solving the problems with transport transfers which occur here.
- *Tandanor (9ha):*
  This section was abandoned as shipyards and later privatised, with a suspiciously 'permissive' regulation for its future development.
- *Santa María del Plata (71ha)*:
  The landfill was carried out in the sixties to house Boca Juniors Athletic Club Sport City. today there is some conflict and uncertainty over its future development.

- *The North Preliminary Port (35ha) and the Southern Dike (48ha)*:
  The Urban and Environmental Plan, currently to be approved, extends the future development areas into these directions
- *The Ecological Reserve (350ha):*
  Twenty years after the landfill which created it, it's still not effectively incorporated into the stock of green spaces in the city, as current public use is restricted by accessibility issues.

Until now, these projects have been developed with a total lack of co-ordination between them, as if they were autonomous and self-sufficient fragments in the general framework. If the development takes place, some areas will compete fiercely to accommodate new central area uses, while others will strengthen uses incompatible with the existing ones. Also, it is necessary to evaluate the impact of all the projects on ground level movement, which is presently insufficient and difficult to enlarge.

As the final resolution of this confusion, on which the future relation between the city and its coastal landscape depends, as well as the future quality of urban life, I have proposed an integral evaluation of all of these operations and the establishment of parameters which allow the selection of some and the rejection of others. Further projects are used to verify the results of analysis and evaluation as final proof. The conversion of the area under study may then provide an opportunity to adapt Buenos Aires to new demands, to provide in its needs and recover the coastal landscape. The case imposes a definition with respect to the relationships to be established between city and nature, the appropriation of the recovered areas and the historical "calling" of the city. It also brings its own accents to the relationships between project and urban planning, infrastructure and urban space, leisure and public space.

3. Project and Urban Planning

The effectiveness of regional and urban plans is clear by now, as well as the need to frame them within general strategic guidelines at both scales. However, the different roles that the project can play in this respect are not clearly defined. With the exception of diagnosis, no step of planning can ignore the project. In the same way the urban project cannot ignore planning. The best urban experiences of the last few years, however, are the result of a successful combination of plans and projects. In these stages, as we know today, the project is not an unchanging element: it needs different approaches and actions to aid its formulation, while it constitutes an analysis tool and allows the selection between many alternative solutions to a defined problem.

The project constitutes, therefore, a tool for the development and spatial documentation of plans, allowing for the pursued objectives and operations on a scale at which the impact can be considered. In this step, it performs the same role as the model in the human sciences: a scale simulation practice, which allows the validation of certain hypotheses, inscribed in a defined framework showing the spatial results of one proposal.

The model of human sciences has two basic components: a fixed and unchangeable nucleus, supported by theory, and a flexible periphery, which allows different adaptations. The nucleus of the urban project would be defined by the theoretical premises, the general objectives and directions of plans and the urban structure in which the problem to be solved is inserted. The periphery "much more variable" refers to the contingent, the resolution of the different fragments and their links with the structure, etc.

Also, the synthesis and determination of the project elements has the clear value of materialising the future for ordinary people, showing that the prospect of a better future is possible in a circumscribed operation. Its implementation shall induce transformations in the neighbouring area that must be taken into account within the provisions of the plan. This is the reason why an urban project can change into a strategic project. In other words, an engine of the transformation developed by responsible planning, which shall lead to future actions to achieve the stated aim. Its realisation will clarify the general outlines of the plan, too abstract for ordinary citizens. A good project must "materialise" in a precise manner such expectations, rising from the plan as a flower.

The project also becomes an analysis tool for future decisions with regards to the development of an action. Naturally, this could be studied from the starting point of considerations tied to the stated fixed urban problem (structure, fragment infill, uses, etc.) with independent considerations regarding its development. When a project is developed, from its analysis new elements will flow to determine its shape. The project shows the real dimension determined by the problem, and allows a comparison of this reality with the theoretical considerations foreseen until then. Questions arise from the scientific analysis of an urban problem, while certainties arise from the project analysis destined to solve them, supplied by the precision of elements which constitute the project.

Once an action is defined, the comparison of the different project alternatives allows the refinement of the decision making process. In the light of comparative analysis, the final alternative is selected or else all of them are ruled out, and a new one is outlined. The precision of tools and documents of the project allows an objective comparison of costs, urban behaviour and foreseeable future scenarios resulting from the materialisation of each alternative, etc. The comparison of alternatives is a useful tool at the time of finding solutions to very specific problems, i.e. potential tracing of a highway or subway, opting between different densities and form configurations of an area, etc.

For these reasons, the investigation makes use of the project, performing different roles and objectives, in different stages of its development. Some projects are used to determine the appropriateness of some intervention, or to choose the most convincing option between many alternatives. Also, one of the main objectives of this work is to propose in which condition and shape the coastal corridor of Buenos Aires and the transformation of its surrounding area will take place, and which conditions and shape will dictate the re-establishment of the coastal landscape. Current developments should incorporate these ideas. Because in the development of public spaces and its infrastructure, "how" becomes inseparable from "what", as design constitutes a substantial part of them. The project, used in this case as a verification tool, will allow the verification of the validity of the approach and the chosen premises.

Infrastructure as Elements of Urban Design

Similar to a century ago, the general movement and accessibility of each of the areas constitute important conditions for the existence of urban activity. There is neither general mobility nor accessibility, without the infrastructure canalisation of the growing circulation flows. This defines physical appearances that cannot be ignored. The relationship between circulation infrastructure and urban design in the nineties changed to reaffirm that presence. The new Barcelona roundabouts and the OMA development for Lille (1994) 16 are good examples of this in their different ways. In both cases the circulation grids and the commodity characterise service areas in relation to the whole development. The circulation commodities and the service dependencies established themselves as structural components and as major determinants of urban form. To ignore the present role of urban mobility, or to attempt to camouflage its components with the aim of preserving historic urban values, challenges the survival of the city. It can also have consequences similar to those in the brand new De Resident (Rob Krier) 17 residential development, in the centre of The Hague. As costly and severe, as the ones suffered with the irresponsible intrusion of overpasses into the heart of the cities in the fifties and sixties.

In view of this erratic and confusing process, it needs to be remembered that the terrain, which is now known as the "Natural Park", is a result of man's deliberate action, undertaken with specific objectives and not a work of nature. The same wild appearance is also a result of men's actions or lack of actions with regard to the changes in its final use, as is the abandonment and inaccessibility that it suffered in its first years of existence. Once the landfill had been developed, the barrier of Madero Port prohibited access to the area. The new terrain was located on the other side of a zone inaccessible to the public and for common mortals it didn't exist because they couldn't see it.

As result of this quiet abandonment, wild native species of the Paraná and Plata riverbanks settled in the area. The same species are found in the prolific Paraná Delta, located to the north of this terrain, only 60 km away. The extension of this delta exceeds the area of the metropolitan district of the city and today constitutes its most important natural reserve *(Gobierno de la Ciudad de Buenos Aires, 1998).* The political decision to convert the landfill into a Natural Park and Ecological Reserve safeguarded the fate of this public space threatened by the failure of the central area expansion and the incipient process of privatisation.

However, in practice it poses a conflict of interests between the inhabitants and natural species, as the conservation of the latter does not allow the use of the area with the characteristic intensity of a public park. Access is restricted, limited to specially prepared educational visits. Meanwhile recurring "unintentional" fires has destroyed the natural resources to be preserved. With the start of the effective urban rehabilitation of the Madero Port Area and the dismantling of this barrier, the terrain of the Reserve became closer to the city and today this empty site has become unacceptable in the heart of the Central Area.

Leisure and Public Space in a Democratic City

With the increased overcrowding of the big metropolis, nature has disappeared from the domestic scenery of many people, becoming more abstract and degraded. Therefore, leisure time becomes one of the few opportunities to encounter organic life. Public space can correct part of this insufficiency. An authentic democratic city must provide leisure spaces to allow its inhabitants to fulfil their lives. By reusing old port areas, cities could have privileged public meeting spaces, rediscovering its original landscape for the leisure of its inhabitants. Today, in contrast to the 19th century, this opportunity can't be only contemplative, as our cultural habits have intensified the need for a direct physical contact, widespread and active, between men and nature. The current trends in global society have produced results opposed to this spirit, with an unequal access and segmentation of public space. These facts penalise the more defenceless sectors of society with greater inequality. To understand the quantitative importance of the Reserve with regards to the supply of green spaces in the city of Buenos Aires, the following comparative analysis is of value:

The total supply of green spaces within the city limits of Buenos Aires is 863ha and together with the landfill of 350ha form 40% of the total green spaces. The total area of the public parks system would reach 584ha if the use of the landfill were included. This would correspond to 59% of this area. The landfill would constitute the largest park in the city, four times larger than the Palermo Woods (Parque Tres de Febrero) which is the second largest in size at 90ha. To maintain its use as a public space with restricted access, the indices would improve from a purely statistical point of view, without a direct effect on the quality of life of the inhabitants.

As a conclusion to this comparative evaluation, the relevance of the area and the requirements of the city indicate the need to incorporate it effectively as part of the stock of public parks with free entry for all. It needs to be remembered as stated before that the reserve is a man-made creation and not a creation of nature. It is of indisputable value to assign the landfill to use as a public park of the River Plate coast. This will fulfil the aim of improving the quality of urban life and respond to the role that the coast has played throughout the life of Buenos Aires.

4. The Analysis Conclusions as Project Starting Points

Determination of Guidelines at Regional, Metropolitan and Urban Levels

Aside from the proposal to extend the port, choosing the route and alternatives for the Coastal Motorway, analysing the proposals for the area and their compatibility and establishing the use of a public park for the area of the Ecological Reserve, it only remains to measure how these decisions contribute to the improvement of the relation between the city and its landscape. The Project plays an important role in this verification, moving through the existing tensions in the contemporaneous worlds of nature, economy and culture, expressed in the current transformations in the central area of the city, in urban road infrastructure, urban infill and in the actual roles of a metropolitan central park. In the case of the motorway, the vision of the project and the quantitative evaluation of its relative advantages will have to overcome the cultural prejudice that has opposed the implementation of an alternative for the Coastal Highway. When the public park in the Ecological Reserve is considered, the vision of the development should keep in mind: that the landfill was a planned decision, destined to house a public park and demonstrate the fact that a landfill doesn't necessarily mean separating the city from the river.

The principal guidelines adopted for developing the project are provided by conclusions extracted from different topics of the current research and by personal convictions, established after years of professional practice, research and teaching.

General Guidelines with regards to Urban Mobility

- To guarantee the current general mobility demands of major urban transformations, as the spatial model based on a strict relation between architecture and circulation, which guided it throughout more than a century, has now lost validity.
- The reformulation of that model should convert the present day components of urban movement, such as overpasses and motorways, into structural models of the urban composition, where its scale and urban imprint makes it impossible to attempt to disguise it within the public urban space.

General Guidelines with regards to the Relationship between City and Landscape

- Centres can rediscover their landscape, because of the current world trend of extensive port transformation. In this process, it becomes a democratic imperative to prioritise the development of public space on available land at the waterfront. In this way, the lifestyle of all the inhabitants will be improved and the central area revitalised.

General Guidelines with regards to Regional and Metropolitan Levels

- The Metropolitan Area of Buenos Aires (AMBA), similar to its counterpart Sao Paolo, with it's population, economic and cultural activities is one of the most important centres of South America. Its Central Area contains the country's most important administration, financial and cultural services, and the second most important in South America.
- The AMBA is connected with the country's most important production centres and with the Mercosur, through the La Plata-Santa Fé coastal corridor and the Buenos Aires-Sao Paolo and Buenos Aires-Valparaiso supranational corridors. The coastal north-south corridor forms a metropolitan segment of those corridors and a key piece of the urban structure of the Metropolitan Area of Buenos Aires.
- The half radius-concentric structure of Buenos Aires was developed over four centuries and both general characteristics and principal components should be preserved. The coastal corridor, within it, defines its diameter. As a result, it channels the north-south circulation at an urban and regional level, it controls the eastern development and guarantees the city-landscape relation. To solve its congested metropolitan and regional circulation will guarantee its force as a basic structural component at those levels.
- As part of the green space provided within the metropolitan area, the public park of the Reserve will fulfil a notable role for its extension, exceptional riverside location and guaranteed accessibility, directly linked with the corridor. At a regional scale its characteristics are only comparable with the area of the Pereyra Park and the Palermo Woods, Ezeiza and Northern Riverfront with respect to its easy accessibility. Due to its exceptional location on the riverfront, it is unique among similar facilities.

General Guidelines with regards to an Urban Level

- The relationship between Buenos Aires Central Area and the landscape of the River Plate should be re-established, avoiding interference with the coastal corridor road infrastructure. The Public Park of the Reserve is established as a key feature in this reconstruction, guaranteeing the public riverside use while developing the provision of public urban spaces.
- At an urban level, the coastal corridor will also channel the north-south circulation, allowing vehicular accessibility to the Central Area and Port. In this last case, it should be stated that the vehicular accessibility is dominant, given the insufficient railway capacity linking the Port of Buenos Aires. To solve the actual circulation capacity of the urban corridor, therefore, will guarantee its force as a basic structural component at this level.
- The regional and urban circulation of the corridor will be differentiated, assigning different roles to the elements, which constitute them. The ground level avenues will exclusively channel the urban traffic and the Riverside Motorway, as it was stated, the one accommodating passing regional traffic and the other supplying the port. From these assigned roles, new junctions or ramps would not be developed within the stretch in question.

Particular Guidelines with regards to the Central Area

- To link the new areas from the east of the corridor in functional, visual and symbolic terms, the dominant structural patterns from the Central Area should be extended.
- The different historical layers of the Riverside of Buenos Aires should be related in a continuous manner, linking the river landscape to the centre of the city again.
- Taking into account the saturation of the urban corridor, new residential or administration developments to the east should be avoided.
- The Central Park will improve the residential conditions of the southern and northern central sectors, considering at this level its contribution to the green space supply for daily use.
- The existing interstitial spaces between built developments should be secured for effective uses and converted into urban spaces.
- The railway track, which runs in front of Puerto Madero, constitutes essential infrastructure to supply the port and should be preserved until another option is developed.

Particular Guidelines with regards to the Motorway Development

- Functional

- It should allow for the integration of the new urban areas with the central core, without interrupting the city-shore relation.
- Its layout should be as close to Madero-Huergo Avenue as possible to separate them from the dwellings and offices of Puerto Madero.
- To determine the number of lanes, the traffic studies stated in this research will be considered.

- Morphological

- It should merge together with the surrounding valuable built environment, blending the regional, urban and architectural scales.
- Its profile should take advantage of the difference of level of the slopes of the former riverbank to reduce its impact and resolve the pedestrian connection between the historic centre and the new areas.
- The longitudinal sector, freed from the road layout, will become a green zone, over sixty meters wide in its narrowest stretch, to reduce the impact of the overpass on the buildings of Puerto Madero.
- New horizontal barriers, such as exit and entry ramps, will be avoided in the city–coast relation.

Particular Guidelines with regards to the Park

- Functional

- The park should respond to the massive demand of users, which corresponds with a central metropolitan park. To answer the same demands means to contemplate its general accessibility, as well as the required provision of vehicle and pedestrian circulation infrastructure
- The supporting infrastructure ought to relate to the recreational and cultural uses, which characterise a contemporaneous active park, to the benefit of a direct physical relationship between man and nature.
- To provide extensive access and to equip the park conveniently will unavoidably modify the actual "wild state" of the area. The park will fulfil simultaneously recreational, pedagogic and scientific objectives, as they are compatible.

- On behalf of the preservation of the zoological species settled there, a sector could adopt the characteristics of a protected natural park with restricted access, without affecting the public use of the rest of the property
  - Morphological
- Its terrain will be integrated with the basic urban layout through the extension of the dominant structural patterns in the Central Area, embodying the potential of the site, determined by its shape, construction process, levels, etc.
- The Park needs a design to build its artificial landscape. The vernacular plant species, which today inhabit it, could be used for the park landscape design, providing its special character. This presence should be handled without the need to falsely hide its planned character and the degree of abstraction that characterises every human product.

Personal Convictions

The idea of availability and indetermination is not incompatible with the actual concept of beauty. In the field of design, this concept is currently associated, not only to the utilitarian idea of satisfaction of a need, but also to the essential truth of its mental and material construction. It has the strength and to the potential capacity to arouse in its use and contemplation the poet within every human being. When these objectives are achieved, everything that results purely from decoration and accessory is not needed, resulting in useless added "beauty".

The park landscape, from this point of view, should clearly show its artificiality, as a terrain needed and constructed and to find its beauty therein: In its production as well as in its dimension, in the river alluvial processes and the landfill, in the water displaced by the land and the man-made geometry taming the natural world. Also in the confrontation of these products with the river, a true natural monument which borders its shores. Within this framework of vision, in the invitation for the use of its docks, in the material of its water course, in its enormous sky and the clarity of its perfect horizon.

An actual concept of the beauty of truth is complex and not mere reductionism, and embraces the mental production, the production material and the delight of its processes. As in public spaces the shape constitutes an object that is inseparable from its use, its design isn't dictated only by the program. If we want active and plural users, its shape should suggest a certain facility to house these needs, and in this manner to complement them. Its design should reaffirm the program of requirements, suggesting a particular tension between use and shape, determination and availability.

5. The Project

5.1 Riverside Motorway

Between all distinct alternatives up to date, the project adopts the historic layout from the beginning of the 80's, taking into account the corrections developed by the 1999 program, Buenos Aires and the River. This layout is the one that best complements the on-grade urban corridor, as it accompanies it, side by side. It also takes advantage of the land reserves conveniently provided for this use, which is currently vacant and segregates the city with its gigantic empty site. By locating the motorway project on the eastern border, and by adopting a straight layout to soften the urban impact, the demolition of three buildings is required. The demolition is justified by the future function and by the fact that they have no significant inherent value. In the same way, the project meets the provisions adopted in the 70's to formulate the initial project, considering the highway as an infrastructure for regional traffic crossing in the north-south direction, which should also give access to the port and not interfere with the urban circulation distribution. This is the reason why additional motorway exit ramps were not foreseen in the stretch under consideration. According to the present-day provisions and the contemplated sections for the future in the Illia and Buenos Aires Motorways, which join the planned section, the width of the motorway was planned with eight lanes (thirty meters wide). This allows the incorporation of ample landscaped zones between the overpass and Puerto Madero, 60 meters wide in the central section, which will reduce its impact. In this zone the railway which currently crosses the area can circulate without changes, as this infrastructure is essential until the railway ring to connect the different lines is completed. Its retention has been a project premise.

Implementation Method

Over and above the abstract considerations with respect to the convenience of burying or elevating the viaduct, neither the variable topography of the "barranca"(plateau border) which characterises the surrounding environment, nor the clear level differences between them such as in front the Government House, has been considered. The project takes advantage of the change of levels in the city to accommodate the overpass, locating it to coincide with the highest ground level of the urban core. In the northern and southern stretches, the overpass maintains the levels adopted for the central stretch, which facilitates its connection with the foreseen Buenos Aires–La Plata Motorway and the President Arturo Illia Motorway junction. In these extreme sections the road will play an important role in establishing order and conveying specific urban values, related to the enhancement of urban mobility.

Northern Stretch

It extends between New Port and Retiro station on the one side and the Presidente Perón Avenue crossing on the other. In this stretch, in which the connection with the port is made, the highway will be elevated as in all the alternatives known until now. To determine the definitive outline in this stretch the consideration contained in the "Buenos Aires and the River Program" (1999) were adopted. This controversial stretch initially threatened the existence of slums located here for many years. The considerations proposed the simplification of the outlines in front of Retiro Station, allowing the permanent settlement of the current inhabitants. With respect to the Northern Dike (Dársena Norte) stretch, the highway is retained as an elevated overpass. In so doing, the project avoids entry ramps to the tunnels of the following stretch that could generate new segregation elements affecting the relation city-shore. Some sectors of this stretch house shops and parking places under the motorway route, while others will remain as free spaces, as gigantic urban loggias, which are framed in the vision of new developments and the riverfront landscape. Bars and restaurants will be distributed in its shade.

Central Stretch

In this stretch, which extends from the Presidente Perón and Belgrano Avenue crossing, the route meets with the highest level of the urban corridor. Both will course parallel at the same level without generating new visual or physical obstructions. This layout uses the ground level cut materialised by thick masonry to connect the historic city with the new eastern developments and the riverside landscape. Crossing under the level urban corridor, the historical axial pedestrian circulation can be extended to the Puerto Madero and Southern Riverfront Avenue direction without vehicular interference. The manifestation of this crossing point at the major historic, representative and symbolic site of the city, will join the most valuable archaeological foundations with the pedestrian public space. In spite of having the most valuable heritage, it has not yet been recognised as being of value as real estate. In this way the remains of the fort, successive coastal defences and Taylor Customhouse will definitely be revalued, opened to view and within reach of the porteños. The project uses the Colon´s monument as a meeting point of a trident pedestrian promenade, opened to the east and developed in the vast space of the square. The inclusion of heritage in this descending promenade makes the place richer and defines different sequences (remaining places, viewing points, etc). With this operation the city centre will simultaneously gain a closer and more direct relation with the shore landscape. It is necessary to connect this crossing point with Calatrava's proposed bridge for Dike Three, and this with the new bridge of the project over Cohipo's Lagoon. In this way, a variable and rich axial promenade will reach the Río de la Plata in different sequences, relating the successive fronts of the city shore. In this stretch, parking areas and shops will be located under the highway, defining a new profile on Madero Avenue.

Southern Stretch

The elevated viaduct allows the connection of the 25 de Mayo with the Buenos Aires-La Plata Motorway, to be constructed in this sector without inconvenience. The project will avoid the introduction of conflicting elements, such as entry ramps to the tunnels, sloping sections, etc., which characterise the other solutions and will result in a greater impact of the motorway as a segregation element affecting the urban areas to the east of its route. As in the Northern stretch, some sectors of this stretch will house shops and parking places under the motorway, while others will remain as free spaces.

5.2 Reserve Park

Site Definition

To fill the entire Reserve land surface for its use as a public park within a reasonable time limit will produce numerous material difficulties. As a matter of fact, these levels could not be achieved over the last twenty years. To maintain the current level of the Reserve will delay its use as a park into the distant future. Today, traffic areas can only use the top of the protective embankments, while the rest are ponds and marshland of doubtful interest to the human species. To follow the traces of these trails to see the river horizon entails a 45 minutes monotonous walk, without major visual attractions, only relieved by the singing of a benteveo bird. A direct relation between the aquatic and the terrestrial was established, returning the greater part of the floodarea to the river and retaining the rest of the land for more effective human use. To achieve these goals, the existing controversial embankment that coincide with the urban axis was broken, allowing the incorporation of land for public recreation and bringing together the new riverbank and the South Costanera historic centre. This decision provided a huge aquatic heart and two terrestrial areas. The opening was carefully evaluated from a structural point of view, keeping a percentage of the primitive structural landfill and the transversal embankment in its entirety.

Accessibility and Vehicular Layout

A primary vehicular circuit for these areas was developed, which establishes a maximum pedestrian range of two hundred meters (two blocks). A landscaped promenade, which includes a maximised coastal development in front of the internal and external waterfront of the project, was created. The circuit, which is accessed from the northern and southern ends, is formed by wide boulevards, served by landscaped buildings for parking. We can differentiate three varied basic components:

1. The extension of Brazil Avenue within the property, which becomes the southern park access. This route ends in a cul-de-sac and a lookout pier, which extends towards the river.

2. A new coastal avenue, to be developed on the structural embankment, defines the northeastern front in a rectilinear manner. The avenue terminates in a cul-de-sac in front of the yacht harbour.

3. A circular shaped connection links these two diagonals with different coastal situations (surrounding the pond, opposite Costanera Sur, crossing both amphitheatre extremes, in front of the port piers). Its design recovers two latent site circles: the bulrush lagoon and the northern border, where a chinampas labyrinth is created.

Pedestrian Accessibility

Three important pedestrian access routes were established, two of them coincide with the previously mentioned northern and southern vehicular access, and a third with the urban axis, crossing Costanera Sur with a bridge. On this axis, which passes under the motorway and crosses dike 3 over Calatrava´s Bridge, the different historic sites of the urban riverside are shown in a continuous promenade. Triangular pedestrian squares were arranged to coincide with the northern and southern access, as complements of the central axis suitable for gathering, contemplation and resting.

Zoning

The superposition of the decisions taken in points I, II and III define seven basic areas, using these layouts as limits of five different areas: Northern Trapezoid, River Amphitheatre, Yacht Harbour, Southern Triangle, Sport Area, Natural Species Protection Area and Western Front of the Costanera Sur.

1. Northern Trapezoid: The northern trapezoid consists of the vehicular and pedestrian access to the park from the north, a pedestrian access square, the Chinampas circular labyrinth as one of the edges of the circle, a yacht harbour support area, northeastern coastal riverfront and free relaxation areas. The chinampas labyrinth symbolises the pre-Columbian-American way of creating new land on water, which reached its peak in Tenochtitlán and Xochimilco. Landscaped buildings are proposed on the southern avenue, which links the piers, to complement the services of the yacht port.

2. River Amphitheatre: The river amphitheatre is a vast space destined to house a variety of mass gatherings, such as large musical events, light and sound shows in the river front, etc. It is formed by two huge embankments facing each other, which descend to the water, a floating stage and a Central Square, which is the end of the historic axis and is "suspended" over the southern embankment.

3. Yacht Harbour: The yacht harbour consists of five parallel piers, each 120 meters. The piers provide the moorings of this port for recreational boats, designed to face the tidal current and protected from the southeastern storms by the extension of Brazil Avenue, which simultaneously provides a pedestrian viewpoint and port breakwater.

4. Southern Triangle: The southern triangle establishes the vehicular and pedestrian access to the park from the south. The Southern Square is located continuous with the Forestier prow, which was recently restored. The circle defines in this area the large bulrush and flamingo lagoon, which is based on the pre-existing shape to define a vast void of circular form, facing and contrasting with the solid labyrinth of the chinampas and free relaxation areas.

5. Sport Areas: On the extension of the southern side of Brazil Avenue, and acting as an arrow shaped buffer between the recreation park and the reserve area, a sector with fields and grounds for multiple sport activities was arranged, placed with a north-south orientation. Two open-air parking lots provide for the needs of the sector, the reserve and the protection area.

6. Area for Protection of Natural Species: Land located between the southern border and the sport areas are destined to house the animal and vegetation reserve area. This area, with restricted access, will house wildlife species, and will be used for scientific study and its educational value for primary and secondary schools. Foreseeing high rates of visitors, two accesses were established, to channel the public pedestrian circulation with the use of two elevated trails, of a curved shape. Six observation posts were located there, provided with telescopes. From these posts, ramps descend to the natural land, providing access for guided visits, with restricted access, and guided by specialised staff.

7. Western Front of the Costanera Sur: This front was design as a complement to the border developed by Forestier, which was recently restored and improved. It combines the coastal defence through the use of ramps and platforms to reach water level. For defending the embankments, classic protection of road engineering was used, combining the use of a superficial steel mesh with a broken stone covering. Horizontal and vertical planes define its street furniture, constructed in white precast concrete, with strong geometric and abstract lines, while its dimensions suggest that the bench looks like a bed and the railing a table. The lighting of this sector, developed with artefacts which are incorporated in these elements, will raise its value with flush floor lights, were street furniture results in ghost style shadows suspended in space.

Landscaping

The planting of trees will use vernacular species, where the disposition will denote its man-made character as an artificial and deliberately planned product. It will respond to strict geometric patterns, building up large-scale planes and volumes of vegetation. With these aims, the species will be used as series, promoting the effects that arise from repetition and visual grouping rather than the emphasis on particular examples. The development of large clumps of colours and continuous lines of species, classified by its flowering colour, its foliage pattern, the permanence or changing of leaves, etc. Dense groups suggest a full mass, vast empty extensions will contrast with them, clear spring foliages will stand out against the perishing dark foliage, etc. Five mayor plantations will be developed to coincide with important sectors of the project, with totally differentiated characteristics: the chinampas labyrinth, the northeastern riverfront, the sport sector, the amphitheatre and the boulevards.

1. Chinampas Labyrinth: In the present sector, characterised by an orthogonal grid of channels, the planting defines a cylindrical volume, striped by the flowers of its tree species (blue jacarandas, red chivatos, yellow tipas and pink lapachos). The dense volume shaped by these species, becomes "excavated" to lodge a labyrinth trail, complemented with squares, which cuts across the strict forest grid in an unplanned manner.

2. Sport Sector: Over a curved layout, defined by various dense curtains of alamos (perennial foliage), which acts as a background, lines of alamos will stand out (seasonal foliage), and show in this way the seasonal changes in appearance: the white filigree of the naked trunks in winter, the clear green spring foliage or the golden red of autumn.

3. Amphitheatre: Only grass types will be planted to strengthen the large central void. Pure shaped gigantic flowerpots (circles, triangles and squares) will be placed in front of the pedestrian square, each of them with a single ornamental specie: red achiras, yellow and blue lirios, blue agapanthus. Agricultural species such as linen, wheat, sunflower, purple alfalfa, etc., will be planted in large extensions, suggesting the "painting" from the foreign pampas.

4. Boulevards: its three basic landscaping components have been differentiated, according to the different roles, which they play in the creation of the park landscape.

- *Northeast Costanera*: successions of parallel curtain shapes, formed by willow trees, define "screens" facing the river. Between them, dense groups of ceibos stand, in a free and unplanned manner.

- *Circus Boulevard*: its landscape has been differentiated through the planting of four rows of pink ´palo borrachos´ which follow its boundary, defining a perimeter curtain facing the labyrinth cylinder, the central amphitheatre and the bulrush lagoon.

- *Brazil Boulevard*: only flowers were planted in its central planting bed. This way, the sport sector will benefit from the strengthening of its landscape, which defines its southeastern limit, and links the boulevard with the triangle spaces.

Landscaped Buildings

Five buildings of this type will be placed at different points of the circuit, to supply in the demand for parking, shops, sanitary facilities, etc. A large accessible roof, covered in grass, define these buildings with the elementary shapes of sloping earth banks. Beneath them, parking places and shops are located, which define its streetfront, complemented by wide galleries. The development of these with the use of longitudinal volumes emphasises the basic circulation layout (Access and South Costanera, avenue from the port and Brazil Avenue).

Bicycle Circuit, Pedestrian Trails and Squares

A bicycle scheme was designed that allows for the free development of an infinite web of routes through the different areas of the park. With the development of pedestrian trails, parallel to the bicycle ones, a group of resting and viewing squares will be provided. Children's play areas will be arranged in them, and will be classified for different ages and types (water, air, fire, land and trees) and the necessary furniture for its equipment (drinking stands, rubbish bins, seats, bicycle parking, etc.).

Two Yellow Light Prisms

Located on both project diagonals, two "perfect yellow light prisms" will be arranged, which literally recreate the description Le Corbusier made of his tower project in Cité des Affaires de Buenos Aires (1929). Square shaped, sixty meters wide and two hundred meters high, two of these volumes will be defined by Laser rays facing the river, paying homage to both city foundations, to Garay´s decision to "Open doors to the land" and to all the imageries that the River Plate suggests throughout the history of the city.

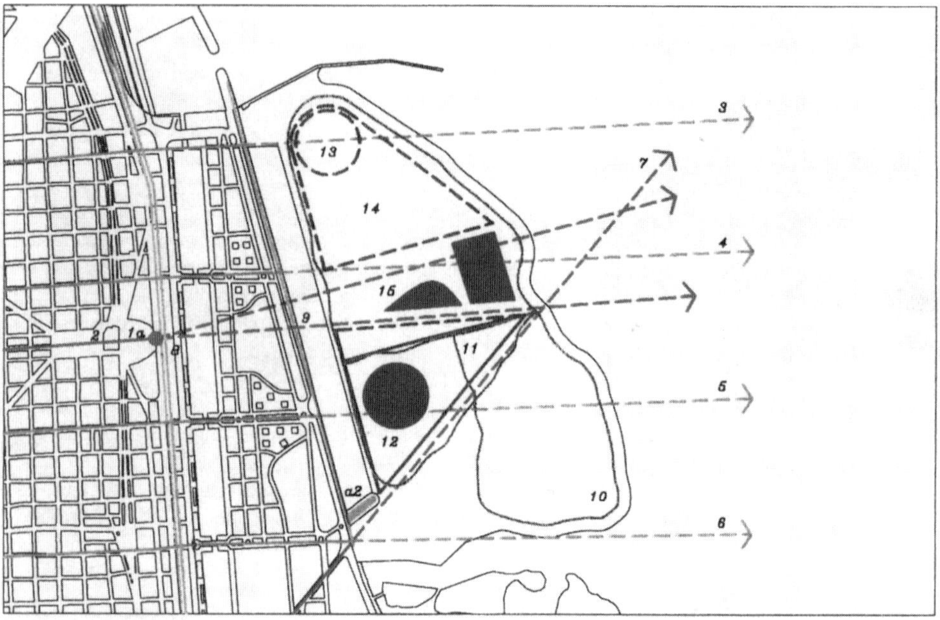

Structural Pattern own elaboration(2000)

6. Conclusions

6.1 Sequence Followed by Project

The Iceberg.

Given the importance the project fulfils in the current research, a final reflection at the end of this work is necessary. We could compare the whole project with an iceberg, with Hemingway's permission, who compared a novel with this floating mass. With an iceberg, only a small percentage of its actual volume is visible, which deceptively crops out of the water, while the underwater mass which triples its size remains invisible. The sight of the iceberg's floating mass suggests the existence of the hidden mass, but doesn't report the exact confirmation of what floats underwater, and can only give us a clue of the approximate estimated size. The same happens with the project. In its case, the visible part is established by the graphical and written documentation, which intends to transmit and explain the project. To reveal the mystery of the invisible block, which validates it and provides sustenance, we should start with the analysis of the layered composition, taking the project of this research as a particular case study.

At the centre we encounter, as the ice core of the iceberg, all the research and projects developed by the author, and additionally the conclusion that he extracted from them. This accumulation confirms his personal convictions referring to architecture and urbanism, and constitutes the genetic memory of the project. Continuing with the metaphor, we could state that a second ice layer wraps the core, which includes research and work published in recent years by the same author, related, by theme or location, with the subject of this research and its influence in the selection of the case study. Further out we find a third skin, established by the scientific knowledge produced specifically for the development of this particular work, and those inherent in the act of development, strongly associated with the development of the test project carried out. And finally, the last layer that is being built, these conclusions are a result of looking back at the work carried out in the last three years.

To carry out this reflection in relation to the line of thought and development of the project, I have used as basic material a selection of successive drafts of these works, successively enumerated in a strict chronological order. They were grouped in four main blocks, which define three partial phases of the preview project and its final solution. The different features and principal concerns, which characterise them, are pointed out, as well as their contribution to the final solution.

Initial Approximations (schemes 1 to 8)

At this stage, the structural guidelines of the Central Area were selected, extending them over the eastern corridor area, where their geometry was established. Also, an attempt to structure the ensemble establishing a vehicular circuit of precise extent (240 meters as maximum pedestrian distance to the vehicle grid), modifying the landfill, partially destroying its contentious embankment to bring the river close to the city. The distinguishing common feature of schemes at this stage is the search of a new spatial form and logical articulation which reconcile:

- functional considerations (the role of the different component parts and the inclusion of the different elements of the program, analysis of geographic conditions for the layout of a sport harbour, an amphitheatre and a reserve area),
- formal and significant considerations (the need to articulate different parts, to extend the urban axis across the project) and

- constructive considerations (landfill stage execution, partial breaking of the contentious embankment without interfering with the stability of previously filled areas).

In the first attempts (schemes 1 and 2) the area was treated as the passive receiver of the city's main structural axes: the parallel circulation of avenues in the east-west direction and the diagonal direction of Brazil Avenue, which defined the public's massive entry point into the area. These penetration axes accessed the area through the laying of multiple bridges over Costanera Sur, resulting in a random and independent road structure from the morphological variations established by the modification of the land-water axis. From the beginning, the extension of Brazil Avenue limited the Natural Reserve areas of the public park. In further attempts (schemes 3 and 4), a balanced "external" direction was conceived with the site's own potential, seeking a functional and formal structure which match them, paying particular attention to new spatial forms defined by the tentative water-ground axes. With the objective of preserving the existing Costanera Sur promenade, vehicular access in the northern and southern points were restricted. The Mayo Avenue axis determined the location of the break in the embankment and an aligned succession of formal events. The new shape of the land also defined a basic zoning and suggested the establishment of articulations between the three principal spatial components. Appearing suddenly in scheme 3, is a proposal for the Reserve area, fairly close to the definitive one.

Further on (schemes 5 to 8), the search focused in the functional location related to the new aquatic border. The definitive location of a sport harbour was established with climatic orientation and protection conditions in mind (scheme 5), later the pedestrian bridge over the urban axis (scheme 7), meeting their actual location in a civic plaza, parking place and an amphitheatre. With respect to the vehicular circuit, after the first two random attempts, the search to establish a closed circuit with two related diagonals rapidly began, with a design regularity very close to the definitive solution. At this stage the project simultaneously considered different aspects, apparently independent, which correspond with general functional objectives, meaningful and constructive, searching for formal configurations and coherent laws which relate them and merge them within a significant structure. Plan schemes were used as an exclusion tool, due to the large spatial extension of the projects, the relationship sought with the urban grid and a profound pursuit to find a "geographic" scale solution, to provide its own support.

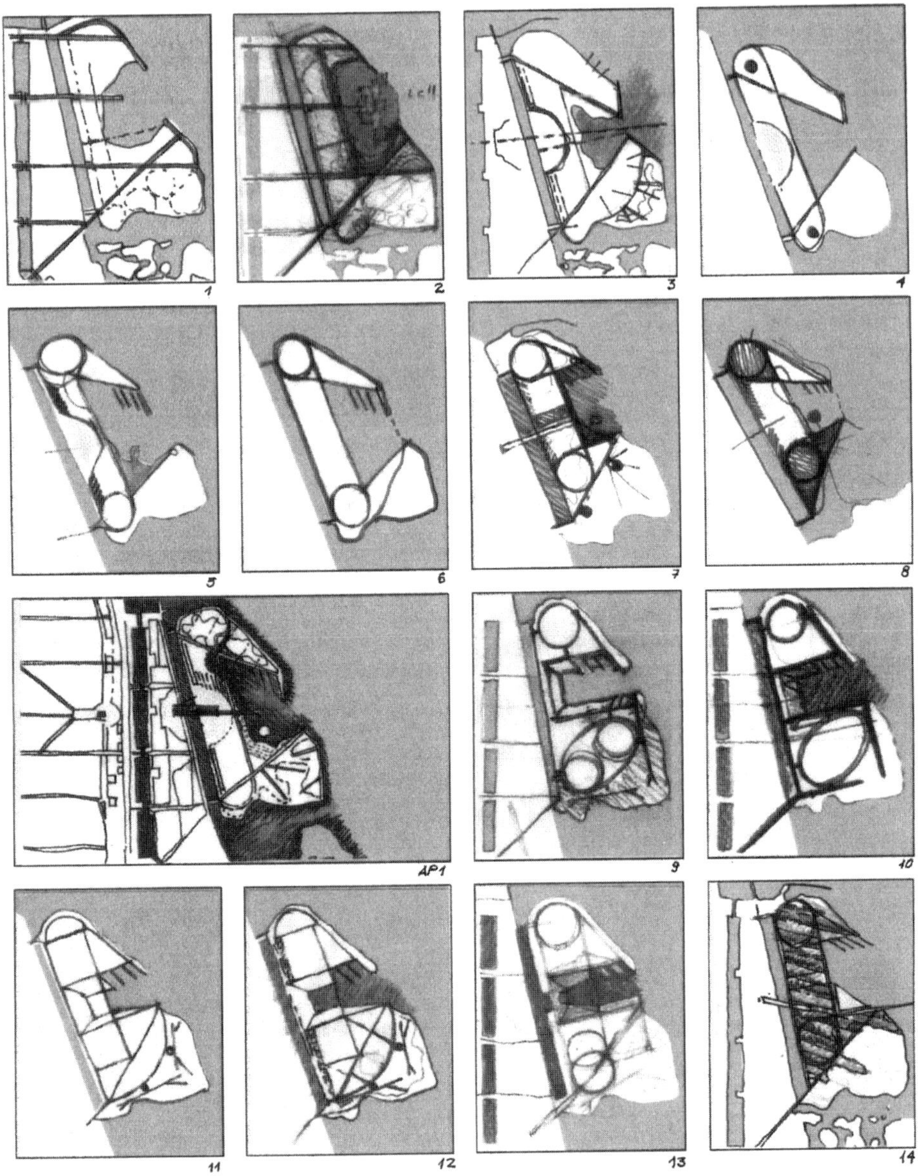

Draft Project Formulation, AP1, own elaboration (2000)

Draft Project Formulation (AP1 and AP2)

From the definitions adopted in the preceded schemes, two detailed draft projects were developed. The former (AP 1) was rapidly discarded, as it's axial emphasis turned out to be excessive and unbalanced within the project. Nevertheless, partial contributions were retained in further proposals, such as the rows of willows screening the river shore and a pedestrian trail, which connects the Reserve "tubes".

The second attempt (AP2) established the initial approximation to the final project. In a definitive manner, the elements of the program appear, such as the proposal for the pedestrian intersection at a separate level for the central stretch of the Motorway, while spatial guidelines are given for different components. Two gentle slopes, containing the aquatic insertion, define the civic heart in its crossing with the "circular" vehicular circuit. For the first time tree planting was proposed to define stripes of colour provided by flowering trees, a solution maintained until the final project.

With regard to the design tools used at this stage, sketches of the general plan appear rather than schemes, while cross-sections are needed to solve the pedestrian crossing of the motorway, as well as general perspectives showing an urban "attitude" and partial perspectives for the triangular shaped amphitheatre, and in AP2, a list of the guidelines which preceded its realisation and determined its later evaluation. At this stage a general fulfilment of the initial objectives were verified, although the excessive structural interruption of the embankments (the border as well as the transverse support), statically compromised the landfill. The definition of the water-ground axis required new adjustments, which appeared incompatible with many of the linked decisions already adopted.

New Searches (schemes 9 to 14)

The new water-ground axis solution lead to a reformation of every aspect involved, since keeping the central embankment played a predominant role, which became compromised by AP2. A more selective orthogonal penetration was chosen, the circle was broken and new circulation circuits were proposed. First using circles and ovals (schemes 9 and 10), with an evident lack of connection between the basic northern and southern sectors, later trying to improve the linked relation through the use of an orthogonal grid (11 and 12), which was combined with large arches over the Reserve and recognise a certain relationship with the "circus". In 13, the return to this circulation circuit was accepted and in 14 the tree rays were adopted for the orientation of the urban axis.

This stage is characterised, very briefly and intensively, with certain apparent confusion, attached to new searches attempting to conciliate the new land-water geometry and the vehicular grid of the project. The development of this search shows, nevertheless, that it actually worked out as a common test, and a profound confirmation of certain preceding decisions, adding certain additional contributions, such us the integration of the amphitheatre with the huge aquatic penetration, joining the softness of the arch to reduce the intrusion of the diagonal direction of Brazil Avenue, creating simultaneously a space which will soften the experience of the park and the Natural Reserve, suitable to lodge a sport area, parking and a double access to the Reserve. Other contributions at this stage determined the definitive direction of the vegetation rays as well as linking the amphitheatre and port geometries.

The Final Project

New site visits allowed the flood areas and the contention embankments to be located with greater precision. In spite of this, a new aquatic perforation was designed with the aim of conciliating the geometries of the urban axis and the central embankments.

An existing lagoon, of an approximate circular shape, defined the southern extreme of the "circle". From these considerations the AP3 and AP4 draft projects were formulated, and finally, the final project, with its graphic and written documentation in which we can find, if we search for them, contributions from previous stages. Taking into account the whole graphic unit, we can extract conclusions over the methodological particularities of the design process.

6.2 Conclusions about the Project

Methodological Particularities

The analysis methodology of Urban Planning is objective, can be programmed and transparent, similar to climbing one step at a time. It disassembles a problem in parts, it analyses it and extracts conclusions, which encourages future questioning. Every step of scientific research, therefore, is exhibited in a rigorous order; showing them in this way gives an indication of the consistency of the method. Faced with the consistent successive steps of scientific research, we should point out that the paths followed by the project and the partial advance stages are generally not shown, as its final objective is to establish documentation which will allow the fulfilment of a building or to confront an hypothesis, as in the case of this work.

Looking at the draft projects, they generally appear partially obscure, difficult to see and incomprehensible, as the design process constitutes a succession of progressive synthesis, more ample and inclusive each time, of advances and retreats, which exceeds the logical programming and are strongly based in the empirical. It is like climbing the same staircase using a capricious combination of jumps, forwards and backwards. However, analysing the process of its successive stages of advance, we have established that it develops a specific internal logic, whose consistency and rigor are verified in the final results of the project and in the correlation which they keep with the chosen guidelines established at the beginning of the design process.

Stages of Advance

The rational objectives, the strict evaluation process of the partial stages and the profound convictions of the designer guided the project's winding road. Seen after several visits, its apparent roughness and surprises turn out to be detours and reasonable appearances, possessing an internal logic which include even the most unexpected developments. The designer doesn't know in advance the results which may arise at the finish line, as these become a happy combination of conscious searches and hazardous discoveries, which only occur to those who go through the difficult challenge of the design process.

In this case, the project development took place with the increasing incorporation of a dominant theme of problems, which possessed a relatively minor importance in previous approximations or had not been considered before. The resolution of new problems unavoidably included the successes obtained in previous stages to continue the progress of the project. At a certain moment, the solution of these problems became incompatible with the preceding formalisations and "shuffling the deck" was necessary to attempt a new synthesis along new lines.

In the park project, the determination of the structural patterns, which impinge on the project structure, the incorporation of the internal site potential was followed, the establishment of an internal vehicular distribution circuit, a new land–water front definition, the zoning of the final project, intermediate evaluations, regressions to the starting point, new searches and successive discoveries until it reached a different formulation of the preceding sketch stages, the final decision on a wall, a pavement or a flower.

In the motorway project, although the selection of layout and profile followed in general the objective trail exclusively determined by the research, the resolution of a pedestrian crossing in the central stretch was not excluded from the obscure side of the park process project, nor from the hazardous discoveries. Exploring the possibilities of excavating Plaza Colón to cross the motorway, the chance of exploring the city's archaeological strata arose, which we were not looking for. In this way, at each step the project developer rectified the meander of the project track developing multiple successive approximations and evaluations in the light of the general guidelines previously adopted. Comparing the results with other alternatives reconciled the apparent incompatibilities and built an internal mass of successes, which today establish an appreciable part of the sunken iceberg.

Results and Tools

The dominant problem in each particular project imposes internal rules, which affect the resolution process and the selection of the tools needed. These also shaped the results, as their performance in the design process is not neutral and suggests a strict drift committed to its use, as happens in the case of drawing. In the same manner as the "thought" develops its conceptual categories by means of the language medium, the project develops through the means of graphs and models, which substitute and "represent" with models the real situation, which they are not.

The selection of the suitable tools and a conscious management of their limitations result in determining factors for the results to be obtained. Each selection was conditioned by the intrinsic problem approach as well as the experience of the project designer in its management and its specific intentions. In this way, the critical role played by the plan in its early stages of the solution of the Reserve Park, becomes justified by the extension and the scale of the intervention. In plan, the riverside alteration was decided, the project zoning and the functional articulation of its shape. Also, the internal circulation of the vehicular circuit was developed, while the project's dominant linkage with the urban structure was studied.

Further on, however, other tools become necessary, such as aerial perspectives, cross-sections and frontal views, to refine with extreme precision these linkages, in order to develop the project's partial components and provide spatial and constructive meaning. The plan of the Motorway played a secondary role, as the layout was defined exclusively by the research. On the contrary, the layout location within the reserve and the cross-section solution of the central crossing played an important role from the beginning until the final definition, as the success of the chosen solution depended on them. In this case, the project aimed to demonstrate that the most obvious solution was also the best one.

Methodological Limits and Validity

The approaches followed while designing were determined by strong inter-linked factors, whose results are difficult to separate from the author's subjectivity and are determined by:

- His genetic memory, tied to his praxis as researcher and designer, combining rational conclusions, empirical elements, ideological–cultural positions, aesthetic and formal, an open field which I define as personal convictions

- Rational foundations which arise from the conclusions of this research
- Internal determinants, which arise from the design process and are linked by the suggestions and discoveries provoked by the use of their tools

With different circumstantial actors, the methodology followed by the project could have reached different tracks and tools, also valid as a theoretical model if the results were based and verified from the beginning with a consistent conceptual rigor. Therefore, this study will not re-establish the corresponding transformations of the design process as universal categories, nor will it assert the absolute transparency of them. It states the possession of its own methodology and logic, simultaneously fostered by universal progress and objectives of the design discipline, by objective problems, which tend to be solved by means of research and by subjective components tied to the designer's experience, his own conviction and goals.

Scientific Value of its Results

It also asserts that the project's results can be evaluated with objectivity and can be used as proof at the time of verifying specific scientific objectives. To achieve this evaluation, the project documents, which are visible components of the iceberg, will be enough for the first instance. Its consistence and size will inevitably show up the existence of a much bigger sunken block with the same consistence. On this particular case, the most significant intermediate products were also analysed on the basis of establishing a theoretical model as the particular combination from the achieved research and project. To indulge in the existing relations between both knowledge fields, to specify methodological differences and adopt the evidence of the mutual enrichment that can be obtain by combined practices. To recognise, finally, that which constitutes the iceberg's sunken mass of the projects, partially resulting opaque, mysterious and inextricable, becomes undetachable from the design act itself. It does however give objective support and motivates the production of chained results, until it crystallises in a final synthesis.

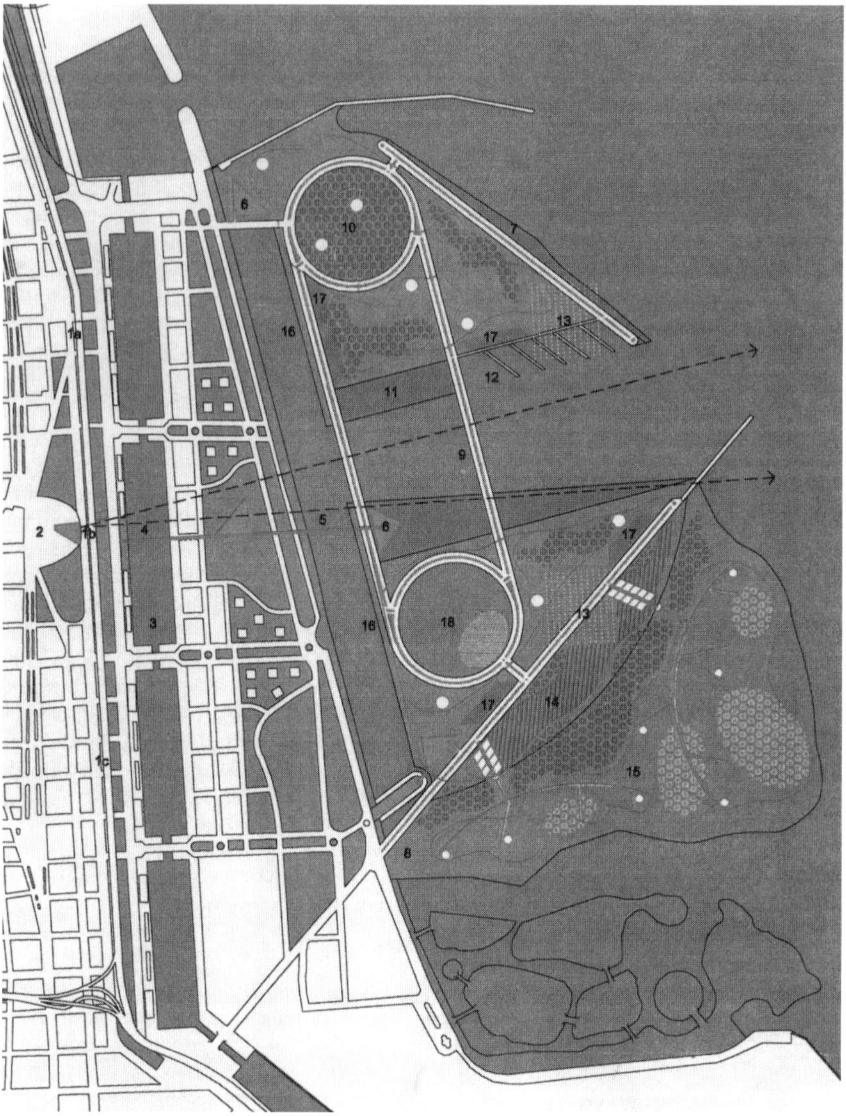

Final Project,own elaboration (2001).

6.3 Final Conclusions

Hypothesis Confrontation

Having carried out the research as well as the project proof, the performance of the initial hypotheses should be verified in the light of the results achieved by the development of the work carried out. The first general hypothesis said: "In the process of urban transformation motivated by the new inclusion of countries in the global markets, new design concepts can help to preserve the social life and the environment and enhance urban life quality".

New concepts stated by the current research at a general level, proved in the particular case of Buenos Aires Riverside, demonstrate the accuracy of this hypothesis. These referred to the privileged role which should be performed by public spaces in the urban renewal task, the ordering role as a composition element which should be performed by transport infrastructure within the urban scenery and the new relationships which could be established by the city with its landscape if it positively takes responsibility for the general well-being of the harbour transformation process outperformed around the world.

The third and fourth stated hypothesis were inevitably linked, and referred to the study case. The third one was: "The relationship between the Central Area of Buenos Aires and the River Plate can reach a final positive solution with the development of current projects, naturally articulating productive and recreational activities of the bank with the heart of the city". And the fourth: " For the fulfilment of this possibility, project and current operation co-ordination within an integrated and dynamic structural vision represents an exclusive condition, which balances the sectoral needs of each operation with its incidence within the urban structure".

Both answers received a favourable response and were established in the Design Proposal. The fourth hypothesis also possesses general validity. It opposes the fragmented vision, which has been at the forefront of recent Urban Planning. It proposes a return to an integral vision of cities and territory, inserting the analysis and formulation of proposals and renewal projects within the structural parameters, which define the singularity of each case. This is the only way in which a vital transformation action can be elaborated, within the continuous process of each urban and territorial construction.

Purposely, the verification of the second hypothesis was left to the end, as it is referred to the use of the project as a planning tool. The hypothesis was formulated in the following manner: "For the synthesis and element concretion, the project can establish as a simulation, reflection and inspiration model to handle political decisions, to state precise programs and decide from different alternatives concrete urban situations".

The research demonstrated the multiple roles the project performed and could perform to encourage decisions in the planning field. From the formulation of the general organisation of the regional space guidelines to the 'thick lines', hardly sketched, which modify preceding conceptual approximations. Also, the analysis of its use as a verification tool in the 'kitchen' of a Plan and its demonstration role of the general objectives which encourage the Plan to make it work, in the case of grand strategic projects or specifically selected fragments of a project, until reaching the comparison of alternative projects.

The role of the project to encourage the urban imaginary established in the legend of the city was demonstrated and the new roles assumed by the project in the global market era in the specific case of the Riverside of Buenos Aires were analysed. On another hand, the project was used as a verification tool of a scientific research, considering therefore that this hypothesis was amply demonstrated.

The Relationship between Project and Analysis in Urban Planning

The current work exposes a peculiar feedback between Research and Project in Urban Planning, and its methodology combines both tools. The research process about both practices and their feedback, in this case, exceeded the temporal limited boundaries of academic work, embracing previous concerns of the author, which were channelled in research and projects developed over the last ten years.

The chosen methodology allowed the characterisation of the process of urban transformations within the present context, related to the specific case of Buenos Aires, to detect the 'urban callings' with respect to the use of the riverside, to analyse the current city transformation process and the principal operations which integrate them, to study the urban structure and place the particular fragment under study and the developments formulated there. Also, to analyse the project interaction and to verify their coherence regarding the urban callings and the structural behaviour, verifying all analysis conclusions with a validation project

The validation project, therefore, couldn't been carried out without previous research. Its making also allowed the proof of the analysis starting hypothesis and its partial conclusions, contributing greater reality to them. In any other way, some research conclusions could have resulted in unverifiable abstractions. Reciprocally, the existence of previous research, allowed the establishment of a critical evaluation system, which results were essential for the rigorous project development, verifying the relationship of the partial progress with the directing guidelines adopted as starting points for its development.

The research justified the project, but this didn't translate directly into conclusions from the scientific language to the specific form of expression, an impossible task as the architectural language has its own specific character and doesn't transmit literary messages. A building can suggest rationality in the whole context of its multiple aspects; it is impossible though to transmit "The method discourse" through the architectural language.

Architecture and urbanism have, as its primary aim, the definition of utilitarian boundaries to house human activities. Due to its physical character, buildings and cities also transmit ideas linked to spaces and uses, materials, land occupation, services and infrastructures, proportions and relations established between components, etc. That is to say, urban and architectural ideas, which can be expressed in a physical manner. They can suggest and emphasise, also in a physical manner, critical opinions about some of the problems, such as the relationship between the city and its landscape, the role of infrastructure in today's city, the dominant cultural evaluation of the program, the linkage or separation of different uses, the favouring of certain components to the detriment of other established values, shapes which house them, the use of the materials which define them, the relationship between those uses, shapes and materials, etc. These project suggestions can lead to an adjustment and/or reformulation of previously stated objectives of the analysis, as the current work has verified. The specific solution of the crossing corridor leads to new significant potentialities related to the urban past, while they try to solve a tightly functional problem.

Universal Validity of the Methodology

Therefore, the universal validity of a methodology is stated, which, as in this case, combines analysis and project in different stages of Urban Planning. Research has demonstrated that both tools interact, and the combined usage is inescapable. It contributes concrete solutions to the resolution of specific urban problems, proving the real extent of general planning management and suggesting new guidelines for the development of urban policies.

Sources

With regard to the sources concerned it should be pointed out that collecting information is an important task. The consistence of the conclusions of the analysis and the project that verifies them depends on the accuracy and the update of this information.

There should be an exhaustive collection of precedents, consulting as many primary sources as possible. A crooked line of a sketch over an old sailing chart or a drawing over a travel ticket can reveal, sometimes, more than ten history books. Most of this information is found in national or international files where it can be consulted systematically, but as an important part of it is in different places such as personal or professional files, its collection could be difficult. With regards to the collecting of renewed information and present data, both are in different locations, private and official. As a consequence, there might be a situation where opposite versions or partially or intentionally changed information should be compared. In this situation the more trustworthy information, according to the criteria of the researcher, should be selected. This fact places the position of the researcher as a critic against the facts.

The base information can change during the development of the work, so it is recommended to be aware of this aspect during the entire project. Drastic changes during the formulation of policies and priorities are common in countries without consistent planning and it could happen that they influence the development of the work.

Each state of the work will demand specific requirements of information and a specific approach. In order to address this, specialised literature on the different themes such as urbanism, history, philosophy, anthropology, geography, economy, specific roles, etc, should be consulted in updated versions.

Material from other sources that relates to a shared urban legend or other cultural approaches to the problem studied should be consulted as well, such as painting collections, strictly literary works, films, songs, objects of use, clothes, etc. From these considerations, the possible sources to do this kind of work are stated.

1. The chosen problem and its present context

- Literature on philosophy, economy, sociology, arts and journalistic information to characterise the chosen problem, and to set it within the present context as well as to define a theoretical frame of reference to create concepts.
- Literature on architecture and urban planning to study the present urban evolution.
- Literature on epistemology to structure the work.

2. The vocation of a city in its evolution and structure

- Historic, iconographic, and cartographic files to detect and to analyse the calls of the named city.
- Literature on urbanism, architecture, history and archaeology to study the evolution of the urban structure and to put it in context.

- Professional and institutional files to list the plans and projects for the study area, in spite of the fact that they have been implemented or not, or if they have been built or not. Many of these non-realised projects have contributed to the constitution of an urban legend.
- Cultural manifestations that describe the evolution of that legend, such as literary essays, travel diaries, poems, songs, plays, films, journalistic articles, paintings, drawings, carves, objects of dairy use, etc.

3. Current changes in the city and its relation with the manifested vocations
- Official geographic cartography ranging from regional to supra-national territories.
- Urban cartography, relief maps and webs of services of the study area.
- Official plans, projects and norms ranging from urban, metropolitan, regional and international territories that fall into the stated operations for the same area.
- Private plans and projects for the area and its adjoining zone of influence. Interviews with investors, operators and key informers
- Official census and statistic studies, measures, quantities and trustworthy studies referring to structural problems verified for the sector as well as assessment from specialists for specific problems.

4. Validation Project
- Making of the project base documentation with the information obtained in 3.
- At the same time, the project might require the consultation of new specialists (soils, resistant structures, botany, transport, specific functional problems, etc.)

References

AAVV (Ed. Burgess Rod, Carmona Marisa, Kolstee Paul). "The Challenge of Sustainable Cities", London and New Jersey, 1997

Arendt Hannah. "The Human Condition", Chicago, 1950

Arrese Alvaro. "Manual de Proyecto Anti Recetario Básico", FADU UBA, Ediciones Previas, Buenos Aires, 1993

Berger John. "The Success and Failure of Picasso", London, 1965

Bunge Mario. Borges y Einstein o la Fantasía en Arte y Ciencia, en "Mente y Sociedad", Alianza Editorial, Madrid, 1989

Gobierno de la Ciudad de Buenos Aires. "Plan Urbano Ambiental", Buenos Aires, GCBA,2000

Echeverría Rafael. "El Lenguaje", La Nación, Buenos Aires, 2001-09-01

Lakatos Iakis "La Metodología de la Investigación Científica", Alianza Editorial, Madrid, 1993

Le Corbusier. "Précisions", Les Imprimmeries Lainé, Chartres, 1929

Valéry Paul. "Introduction au Méthode de Léonard de Vinci (Avec des Notes de 1930)", Gallimard, Paris, 1953

Romero, José Luis. "Latinoamérica Las Ciudades y las Ideas", Siglo XXI, Buenos Aires, 1976

Sassen Saskia. "Cities in a World Economy", Pine Forge Press, Thousand Oaks, 1994

Saer Juan José. " El Río sin Orillas Tratado Imaginario",Alianza Singular, Buenos Aires, 1994

Suárez Odilia. " Planes y Códigos para Buenos Aires", EUDEBA, Buenos Aires, 1986

Suárez Odilia. "El Territorio Argentino", UGYCAMBA, FADU UBA, Buenos Aires, 1999

Torres Horacio. "El Mapa Social de Buenos Aires 1940-1990", Serie Difusión FADU UBA, Buenos Aires 1992

Touraine Alain. "¿Podremos Vivir Juntos?", Fondo de Cultura Económica, México, 1998

9

The Square as Urban Element:

Comparative Analysis of Public Space in different Morphological Zones in Santiago and Cordoba.[37]

Diego Sepulveda

Abstract

This paper identifies similar morphological zones in two Southern cities of Latin America (Santiago in Chile and Cordoba in Argentine) in terms of the spatial transformation process that have taken place in the cities over the centuries. This identification of morphological zones is necessary in order to analyse the potential of the Public Square to create synergies and to affect development in different areas of the city. This paper explains the methodology used to identify and describe the different homogenous areas in terms of historical, economic and social development influencing the formation of morphologic patterns in the two case-cities. The main idea is to identify the transformation process of the different morphologies that constitute the city, recognising the existence of particular differences in terms of its historical and social context, the location, accessibility, the urban morphology and the specific built environment where the square is located. As the square is considered an element for urban restructuring and a basic element of the urban system, the square is studied at different levels in terms of its contribution to the urban fabric. Therefore it is considered necessary to study the spatial relationship between the square and the transformation of morphology as well as how citizens experience it, use it and determine its function. We believe that there is a relationship between the vitality of the place, the sense of place and the quality of the square that influence the transformation potential of the square.

I – The Places and the City: The Idea of Morphologic Zones

In the light that urban form is the product of historical actions, and that spaces and objects are the interrelated elements that compromise the basic constituents of urban form, the spatial context of urban form, grounded in the spatial behaviour of human beings in the urban environment, should be the prime focus of morphological research.

There is enough evidence that cities are not homogeneous wholes but are organic entities historically defined, formed by different places and sub-cultures with different social, spatial, economic and ecological potential for transformation and resistance to change. There is growing support that spatial fragmentation and formation of centralities of social groups, ethnicities and subcultures can be seen as an opportunity to change

37 This paper is part of a chapter of my research dealing with Public Space as an Urban Renewal Element

rather than to constrain further development. The issue is to recognise the elements that historically have constituted the basis of the particular spatial and social context in order to discover its continuity, transformation and vitality potential. For many the built environment is the connection between analysis of the morphologic structure and the identification of the historic context[38].

The importance of the spatial context is also related to the analysis of place, the built environment and its relation with building. "Loss of spatial context is even harder to retrieve than loss of building elements. This is one reason why spaces within the built environment and their relationship with buildings should be a more important concern of urban morphology than buildings alone" (Kyung Chan Lee[39])

Continuity requires that the processes of change and development that have driven the formation of each context in the city, be allowed to strengthen and vitalise the positive elements and to eliminate or repeal those negative ones that detract from a place. Recognising the importance of context is not about copying architectural elements such as the style or detailing of adjacent buildings. "Context is about analysing the urban characteristics of the site and the wider area, understanding the process of the area's historic development, and designing new development for the specific site in question". (Kim, K.J. 1998[40]).

According to Aldo Rossi, the city is a man-made object in which we can perceive differences between the past and the present, through the continued existence of past urban physical forms and structures. This difference makes us realise the fact that "the past is being experienced now". These thoughts lead to the concept of permanency of structural elements as "a past that we are still experiencing" (Rossi, 1982).

In line with this of argument we can say that Public Spaces are structural elements in the city, with their own meaning. "A public space contrary to buildings is a temporal bounded concept. Public spaces show and represent the values of each historical period in time. It represents its aspiration and culture"(Conzen 1998).

These two concepts are intrinsically contained in the definition of the homogeneous areas of the two cities.

II - Development Strategies and the Formation of Morphological zones

Both cities, Santiago and Cordoba have similar origins and have experienced similar processes of development that impacted on the transformation of the city. In a previous publication[41], I have described the changing economic, social and political strategies followed by these countries to address international changes. In both countries, it was possible to identify similar development strategies that influenced the creation of singular historical/morphological zones and that have affected the construction and transformation of the city. Certain economical, social and cultural elements impacted on urban areas in different periods, and of particular importance is the way in which urban theories, urban morphologies and building elements have been exported for other

38 Samona Giuseppe, Conforto Cina.` Il dibattito architettonico in Italia 1945-1975,Bulzoni, Roma 1977.

39 Kyung C. L. "How we view cities" at (www.odin.let.rug.nl/isuf/urbm/vpts0199.html)

40 Kim, K-J New form, classical problem: Pseudo-public residential redevelopment in Seoul: in Built environment 24 pages 234-259.

41 Diego Sepulveda (2000) From Plaza de Armas to the Shopping Mall, in Globalisation, Urban Form and Governance. .Alfa-Ibis 1 Proceedings International Conference. DUP Science.

countries and translated, experienced, lived and assimilated in another context and place. Each period in time has also produced different solutions with regards to the various urban needs that exist simultaneously.

The pressure for constant modernisation and the limited resources characteristic of these societies are expressed in a complex process influencing the transformation of the city and society. The exodus and abandonment of some areas, the renewal and consolidation of others, the changing identities with place, the growing need for new housing environments, and a constant extension of the city has all been expressed in the formation of the urban morphology.

Important in the historical determination of urban space has been the permanent evolution and penetration of the capitalist system to all sectors of society affecting the relationship between the state, the market and the community with important connotation to the urban morphologies that constitute the city. These different periods can be expressed through iso-morphological lines over the entire city, identifying the structure of the urban morphology in historical terms and the development and evolution of particular typologies.

The following chart presents the different time periods identified for the Chilean and Argentinean cases and the urban processes developed in each period, which was the topic of previous research. The chart also identifies the corresponding morphological zones. In a second step, the main processes affecting each area today have been identified. For methodological reasons the various processes that simultaneously affect the morphology have been selected and reduced to the process which represent most clearly the transformation process in each period. In this way we have selected the process of: Renewal, Consolidation, Development Gentrification and Re-functioning.

III – Definition of the Morphological Zones and the Current City Processes

Urban transformation and the choose of five processes.

	City Processes	Morphological Zones	Current Processes
1500- 1900 Colonial period Republican period	• foundational city	Historic Centre (1CBD)	Renewal
1900- 1930 Liberal period	• compact city (traditional)	First residential ring 1RR	
1930- 1960 Modernization period	• first counter urbanisation • social housing developments	2 CBD 2 RR Middle income	Consolidation
1960- 1970 Socialdistribution period	• Social interest housing • illegal settlements • urban renewal areas	3RR (Periphery) Middle income 3RR (Periphery) Low inc Renewal First Ring	Development
1970- 1990 Neoliberal period	• gentrification • new public housing schemes • gated communities	Renewal of 2CBD 4RR 4RR	Gentrification
1990- 2000 Globalisationand sustainable city	• re-functioning areas	Renewal and Infillings	Re-functioning

In this Chart it is clear that the city from 1500 to 1900, that is representative of colonial and republican periods, is still expressed in the Historic Centre of the city. This centre, despite drastic transformations and a long period of downgrading and obsolescence, has recovered again as a CBD and residential area.

The legacy of the liberal period (1900-1930) which introduced the compact city around the historical centre constituted the First Residential Ring of the city. Both morphologic zones are experiencing a significant process of **Urban Renewal**.

The influence of the Modernisation period (1930-1960), whose economic component is the internally oriented industrialisation and import substitution model, and the spatial implications of the urban theories with sectoral connotations (CIAM, ecologist school, F.L.Wright and others), contributed to two processes:

- Firstly, the exodus of the middle and high income groups from the city centre and the development of a new centrality what has today become a second CBD (2CBD);
- Secondly, the large social housing development of subsidised flats and houses for low-middle income groups located on the city fringe, constitute the Second Residential Ring (2RR).

These areas today are undergoing a process of **Urban Consolidation**.

In both cities a similar period of social and political distribution can be identified in the 60s and early 70s. This brought new ideas regarding development strategies and urban policy, since a greater support was given to industrial and infrastructure development. The growing housing problem was an issue of public policy and a reduction of housing standards took place in order to meet the demand of the growing low-income population. Large developments of social housing was built on the fringes of the city, and significant actions of occupation of land with illegal settlement followed, constituting a Third Residential Ring (3RR). At the same time the need to renew large downgraded areas in the First Residential Ring resulted in a process of urban renewal. The first actions constituted large-scale renewal development processes, which were later followed by more sensible small-scale renewal. For the purpose of this research, the areas in the process of **Urban Development,** which are those of the lower income sectors, with housing development over the past 20 to 30 years were chosen.

The orthodox neo-liberal period, that characterised countries such as Chile and Argentina between 1970 and 1990 produced significant transformations in the urban structure. The more important processes are:

- First the gentrification of the areas of the Second CBD, through the return of the high-income population from the fringe to the new globalised central areas in vertical condominiums. This has significantly changed the image of the city, creating new life-style and aspirations.
- Second the reaction of the private sector to the housing demand of the popular sector in the form of high-density development on the fringe of the city (Fourth Residential Ring). In the case of Santiago this consists of about of 300.000 units, one third of Santiago's population, just in this period.
- The third process is the formation of 'gated communities', mainly for high and middle income groups.

For this period I have chosen the **Process of Gentrification** since the process imposed itself and has impacted on urban demands and the use of resources for the rest of the city.

New democratic forces drive the current period in both cities. After decades of deregulation there is a return to public policies. These facts and the new phenomena produced by de-materialisation of space, has resulted in the viability of urban planning for dealing with democratic and sustainable values to be reconsidered. The differences and diversity of the various part of the city, its cultures, histories and meanings are recognised, as is the need to treat the city as a whole and public space as a system. In this context I have chosen the **Process of Renewal and Infill** since there is a need to connect fragments, to improve accessibility, to revitalise the different centralities and to intervene in the various contexts according to their own organic, users and spatial elements.

The next step involves the identification of one case study for the five chosen urban processes in the two cities.

The identification of one square as case study for each city representing the five chosen urban processes

IV - The defined Morphologies, the Context and the selection of Squares

Santiago and Cordoba have a simple foundational core. They did not have the magnificence of the historic centre and legacy of the viceroy such as Lima and Quito. The foundational core of these two cities had a similar scale as that of Buenos Aires, Caracas, Montevideo, and Asuncion. During colonial times they were merely small villages.

Only from the XIX century important and progressive changes in all aspects of social life occurred. This is reflected, in the building typologies and in the mode of transformation of the urban morphology and the central area urban tissue. Later both cities developed different forms and were differentiated by the fact that Santiago is a capital city and Cordoba a secondary city of a polarised system of cities. The planning practice over the following decades and the action of market forces defined unique differences in the buildings, the morphology of the different areas and in public spaces.

In order to present the various squares chosen for the empirical research, firstly a summary is given of the context in which each development period affected the formation of the morphological zone and which is the situation today. The location of each square can be seen in figures 1 and 2.

Period One. The Colonial, Republican and Liberal Period: General Context.

Since their foundation, the Spanish grid of Santiago and Cordoba did not experience any important development until the end of the XIX century. It is only **from 1880 to 1930**, that these cities consolidated their urban morphology, under the explicit ideas of European and North-American urban theories, (the Monumentalism of Haussman, the hygienic movement, the Garden City movement). These areas constituted the "compact city" and today the neighbourhoods are identified as the 'traditional neighbourhoods".

1. ***Type 1. Santiago, Compact City: Santiago Poniente.***

- This area represents the "traditional neighborhoods of Santiago". It is a peculiar introverted sub-division of the typical "Spanish blocks" done according to the European influence of the time. Other Municipalities similar to Santiago Poniente are Quinta Normal, Estacion Central, Lo Prado, San Miguel, and Macul.
- From this type the **Plaza Brasil** has been chosen as representative for empirical research.

2. Type 1. Cordoba, Alto Alberdi

- It is a sub-centre in the central-west area of the city and part of the first ring extension of the 1920's. The typology is mixed with housing, commerce and services and contains high-rise buildings and low-rise extroverted residential houses, in raw and continuous façade from the beginning of the century.
- From this type the **Plaza Alberdi** (Geronimo del Barco) has been chosen as representative for empirical research.

Period 2. The Modernisation Period: General Context

From **1930 until 1960**, the influence of 'modernism' and the sectoral explanations of urban transformation and the predominance of morphological aspects in urban planning prevailed. In this period both cities experienced an important demographic growth due to industrialisation. A rapid development of the transport system, the expansion of the automobile (city rings and highways) and the general application of zoning (CIAM ideas) took place. It represented the end of the compact city system. A new relationship between the Public and the Private domain developed and the consolidation of different morphological areas in the city according to a centre-periphery relation occurred. Public space was recognised as an important element in the "new scientific functionalist urbanism". Two simultaneous processes took place: firstly, counter-urbanisation towards the Second CBD (2CBD); and secondly social housing developments in the Second Residential Ring (2RR).

1. Type 2, Santiago. 2 CBD: Providencia.

- This area represents the second extension of the original structure and is the natural extension of the Alameda corridor. It represents the "garden city" extension and the closed and rigid repetition of Spanish blocks is forgotten. It developed as high income residential in the 1920 and later rapidly changed function to mixed offices, commerce, banking and high-rise residential, today presenting the highest density pattern of the city. The Municipalities that are similar to Providencia are Nunoa, Vitacura, and Las Condes. Low-rise densities and suburban high-income groups of Santiago Orient are Lo Barnechea and La Reina.
- From this type the **Parque Ines de Suarez** has been chosen as representative for empirical research.

2. Type 2, Cordoba. Arguello Neighbourhood.

- This area is in the northwest of the city, in the peripheral area and beyond the outer ring avenue. It is part of the second ring extension, develop according to the "city beautiful" codes and has become the entrance of an axial structure. It is a suburban typology based on lots of about 2000m^2 with detached villa residences for middle to high-income residents.

- From this type the **Plaza Novillo Saravia** has been chosen as representative for empirical research.

Period 3 - The Social Distribution Period: General Context

This period is from 1960 to the beginning of the 70s. The 60s represent an important transitional period with the predominance of social-structural explanations to urban planning. The building sector took a leading role in the economy, radical demolition and central area renewal took place and high-rise buildings were erected. The need for supporting sectors for national economic growth (industry) determined the diversification of housing production according to purchasing power (Reduction of housing standards). It signalled the start of massive construction of 'social housing' on the periphery. In the beginning of the 70s European ideas (van Eijk, Habraken) introduced approaches to urban renewal at small scale contributing to change the large-scale central area renewal. Today the urban morphologies created during this period have different manifestations responding to their location in the city. The morphology of the third residential rings following a process of 'urban development.' was chosen. These areas are a mix between old low-income neighbourhood with 'social housing' of relative good quality and large areas where illegal settlements have been transformed in formal settlements. Related to the origin of these neighbourhoods, these areas have more community cohesion and social movements and people participation than in other low-income areas.

1. *Type 3, Santiago. Lo Espejo.*

- It represents the lower income areas developed around the 40s with social housing developments of different types. They are mainly developed according to CIAM principles and present strong urban norms to achieve efficiency in the use of public infrastructure and land. It also contains areas with rural development. In these poor municipalities programs for public space development are being implemented. Municipalities similar to these are in the South, La Pintana, La Granja, San Ramon, La Cisterna, Lo Espejo, Pedro Aguirre Cerda and towards the north, old industrial areas such as Renca, Conchali, Independencia.San Joaquin.
- From this type the **Plaza La Estrella** has been chosen as representative for empirical research.

2. *Type 3, Cordoba. Arguello Norte neighbourhood.*

- This is in the northwest of the city in the peripheral area beyond the outer ring avenue. It is a social housing development of the 70's, IPV Bo. (84-89 Coronel Moldes project). It consist of detached houses of 36 to 42m^2 on lots of 200m^2. It is located in an informally built periphery outside the consolidated urban frame in a low-density context.
- From this type the **Plaza 22 de Abril** has been chosen as representative for empirical research.

Period 4. The Neo-Liberal Period

From 1973 to 1990, within the context of neo-liberalism, Chile and Argentina experienced a significant transformation in the urban and morphology structure. Free-market forces contributed to subordinate urban morphology to single architecture. Both the high-income suburbs and the low-income periphery experienced processes of disconnection and segregation in relation to the compact core. The product is that architecture carries an important scenic presence independent from the context, it is shown as a monument in the already confuse urban landscape. There is a significant growth of social polarisation and spatial fragmentation. In both cases eviction of illegal settlements from central areas to the periphery took place during the authoritarian regimes. Cities became the locus of growth, and therefore there was no control over urban growth and a high priority was placed on the improvement of urban productivity and transport system arising under the new condition of privatisation and liberalisation of urban markets.

1. Type 4. Santiago, Barrio El Golf.

- This is an area that renewal changed from a garden city model to high-rise buildings for high-income groups. The square has been renewed and the complete area improved with a connection to a commercial street. The main structural element is a Church that defines the centre of the square. The square consists of a big open space surrounded by high buildings.
- From this type the **Plaza El Golf** has been chosen as representative for empirical research.

2. Type 4. Cordoba, Bajo Palermo neighbourhood.

- It is an area located in the northwestern central zone of the city. It is an extension of the city done in the 50's, following zoning ideas. The neighborhood consists of one floor-detached houses, on lots of 600m^2. It is a low-density middle-income area experiencing gentrification. The park was a former informal settlement, transformed into an open park, surrounded by a bicycle and a jogging route.
- From this type the **Plaza de las Rosas** has been chosen as representative for empirical research.

Period 5. The Globalisation Period

From 1990 – 2000, the return to democracy has underpinned a new developing period. The 90s are characterised by the consolidation of the two countries in the global economy producing significant changes in the productive and financial activities with corresponding changes in community and social relations. The market economy has changed the life-style, family model and consumption patterns, and considerable changes in mobility, accessibility and connectivity in relation to the polycentric conformation of both cities have occurred. Poverty has decreased in absolute terms while social polarisation has increase significantly (de Mattos 2001, Cepal 1998) and new types of urban fragmentation has taken place. Both countries have arrived to a phase of demographic and economic transition, which is represented in the built environment. The urban population comprises about 90% of the total population, the population growth is around 1.2% and both countries have medium-sized GDPs. This fact has necessitated the re-functioning of important areas of the city which have become obsolete, in order to transform the city and open new opportunities in the international context. The economic situation of Argentina has been worsening from the Asiatic crisis in 1996, while structural conditions in Chile has made it possible to overcome the crisis. This situation has resulted in different types of processes in the two countries with regards to public space management.

1. Type 5 Santiago, Santiago Centro.

- It is part of a renewal area resulting in the transformation of a former railway station into a cultural centre on the riverfront and surrounded by the City park. In the square is a metro station and the surroundings form an important commercial node in the city context. It is also consider a symbolic square.
- From this type the **Plaza Estacion Mapocho** has been chosen as representative for empirical research.

2. Type 5. Cordoba, General Paz neighbourhood.

- It is a sub centre located in the central east area of the city. It is currently an urban renewal area. It was formerly a railway station neighborhood. This area is part of the first extension of the city at the beginning of the XX century. Part of the old railway station has been converted into a service area with a museum and a shopping mall; it also has a low-rise extroverted compact neighborhood with continuous façades with mixed use for low and middle-income groups and low density.
- From this type the **Parque Jose Maria Paz** has been chosen as representative for empirical research.

V - Location of the Selected Squares in the Two Cities

Santiago:

4. Plaza Brasil, Santiago Centro
5. Parque Ines de Suarez, Second Residential Ring
6. Plaza La Estrella, Third Residential Ring
7. Plaza El Golf, Renewal Second CBD
8. Plaza Estacion Mapocho, Renewal & Infill of Central Area[42]

42 Image source: "Los anillos de suburbanizacion Continua "in Greene, Margarita "Santiago de un proceso acelerado de crecimiento a uno de trasformaciones" Instituto de Estudios de Postgrado e Investigacion, Facultad de Arquitectura y Estudios Urbanos. Pontificia Universidad Catolica de Chile.2001.

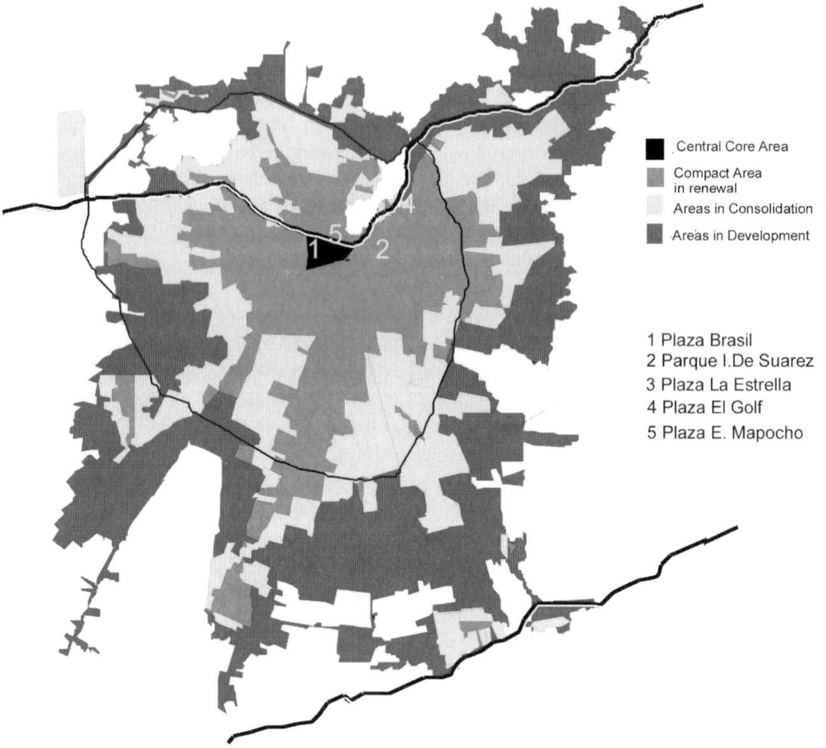

Figure 1. Map of Santiago

Cordoba:

1. -Plaza Geronimo Del Barco, Alto Alberdi Central Area,
2. -Plaza Novillo Saravia, Arguello
3. -Plaza 22 de Abril, Arguello Norte
4. -Plaza Cerro las Rosas. Cerro las Rosas
5. -Parque Jose Maria Paz. General Paz[43]

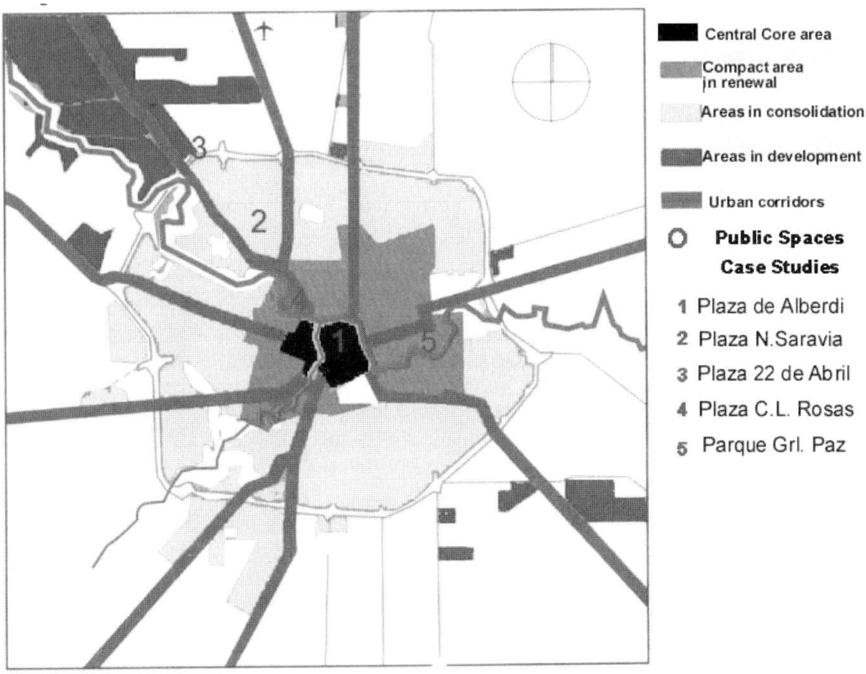

Figure 2. Map of Cordoba

43 Image source: "Sintesis de la estructura urbana".Iros,Guillermo in"Desarrollo Urbano Reflexiones y Acciones"
Editorial Municipal de la ciudad de Cordoba, June 1991.

VI - The Formulation of Preliminary Hypothesis regarding the Change for each Urban Process

Process	Hypothesis
Renewal **Plaza Brasil** Plaza Alberdi	When level of vitality and renewal processes are high, the sense of place can be strengthened by public space renewal. The question is in to what extend this sense of place can address formal and land use improvements without losing identity
Consolidation **Parque I. De Suarez** Plaza N. Sarabia	In middle income developments located in areas with high levels of vitality which underwent rapid consolidation the question is if public space development is possible to rise the sense of place to maintain the process.
Development **Plaza La Estrella** Plaza 22 de Abril	In low income areas with little sense of place, endogenous forces (public or private) are needed to induce community-building. The potential of public space is to create activity node, densification and multi-functionality
Gentrification **Plaza El Golf** Plaza C.Las Rosas	In areas of vertical gentrification with good connectivity and closed security, public space matter as an element of interaction and encounter but of a general system
Re-functioning **Plaza E. Mapocho** Parque Gral. Paz	In areas of obsolescence the public space can become a city-wide landmark and the motor of the processes of re-functioning

Conclusions

The validity of the preliminary hypothesises should be investigated in the two cities and as a question in itself. We believe here that there is a relationship between the vitality of the place, the sense of place and the quality of the square that influence the transformation potential of the square and the neighbourhood. We believe that the city is not socially homogenous and consequently different values co-exist in the urban context, that ethically make the idea of the existence of a 'good urban form' impossible since the urban form affects the different sectors of society in different ways.

Here I recognise two things: First that if the city is fragmented and a complex entity, there is a need for research into the parts that constituted the city and each part evaluated according to the values of the different communities and collective users that will directly be involved in the local transformation process. In this sense it is necessary to analyse how for instance a square is used and experienced from the point of view of **the spatial quality** in relation to the community involved.

Secondly, there are aspects of the city that override the domain of the fragments, and must be analysed at a higher level, such as the **vitality** of the place underpinned by mobility, accessibility and land uses and the **sense of place** that is underpinned by the memories, tradition and experiences of the built environment.

The formulation of the criteria of analysis at the different scales of the city and the fragments will be a matter of discussion in the next chapter, followed by the empirical verifications at the different levels.

References

Arefi, Mayhar. Non-Place and Placelessness as Narrative of Loss: Rethinking the Notion of Place, Journal of Urban Design, vol. No. 2, 1999, pages 179-194.

Arrese, Alvaro. Espacios Públicos de Buenos Aires, In Reflexiones. Espacios Públicos. Editorial de la Facultad de Arquitectura de la Universidad de Buenos Aires, FDU, UBA.1995.

Brail, R. K. Chapin, F.S. Activity Patterns of Urban Residents. In Environment and Behaviour, Vol.5 N0 2,1973.pages 163.

Belkhatir, Aziz: La gestion de Espaces Naturels Urbains. Voiron: Edition de La Letter du Cadre Territorial, Paris 1994.

Borja, Jordi. Ciudadanía y Espacio Público. In: Ciutat real, cuitat ideal. Significat I funcio a l'espai urba modern. Barcelona: Centre de Cultura contemporania de Barcelona.1998.

Borja Jordi, Manuel Castells. Local & Global Management of Cities in the Information Age. United Nations Centre for Human Settlements-Habitat/London: Earthcan Publications Ltd.1997.

Broadbent, Geoffrey. Emerging Urban Design Concepts. Van Nostraat, 1990.

Brotchie, John. Batty, Mike. Blakely, Ed. Hall, Peter y Newton, Peter. Cities in Competition. Longman Australia, Melbourne.1995.

Carmona, Drewe, Rosemann, Van Duin, Globalisation Urban Form & Governance 2. DUP Science, Delft.2000.

Castells, Manuel. Espacios Públicos en la Sociedad Internacional. In: Ciutat real, cuitat Ideal. Significat I funcio a l'espai urba modern. Barcelona: Centre de Cultura contemporania de Barcelona.1998.

Foglia, María Elena ED. La Cuadricula en el Desarrollo de la Ciudad Hispanoamericana. El Caso de Córdoba 1573-1810.Editorial del Instituto Del Ambiente Humano, Facultad de Arquitectura Y Urbanismo Universidad Nacional de Córdoba, Córdoba, Argentina 1987.

Foglia, María Elena. Goytia, Noemi, Los Procesos de Modernización en Córdoba. Editorial de la Facultad de Arquitectura y Urbanismo, Universidad Nacional de Córdoba 1989.

Gehl, Jan. Gemzoe, Lars. Public Space Public Life. Royal Danish Academy of Fine Arts. Copenhagen 1996

Gehl, Jan. New City Spaces. Copenhagen Danish Architectural Press 2000.

Iros, Guillermo. Desarrollo Urbano Reflexiones y Acciones. Editorial Municipal de la Ciudad de Córdoba, Córdoba Argentina 1994.

Kostof, Spiro. The City Shaped. Thames and Hudson.London.1991.

Lang, Jon. Urban Design, The American Experience. Van Nostrand Reinhold. New York.1994.

Kreukel, A.M.J.,W.G.M. Salet Ed. Debating Institutions and Cities. CIP-Gegevens KB, Den Haag, The Netherlands 1992.

Kyung Chang. Lee. (1999) How We View Cities? . In "Discussion of Topical Issues in Urban Morphology at: (www.odin.let.rug.nl?isuf/urbm/vpts0199.html).

León, Sergio. Conceptos Sobre Espacio Público, Gestión de Proyectos y Lógica Social: Reflexiones sobre la Experiencia Chilena. Revista: Latinoamericana de Estudios Urbanos Regionales (EURE), Santiago: Instituto de Estudios Urbanos, Pontificia Universidad Católica de Chile, vol. XXIV, No.71.1997.

Minvu. -http: www.minvu.cl-

Mop. Plan Maestro de la Edificación Pública del Centro de Santiago, Resumen Ejecutivo. Dirección de Arquitectura, Ministerio de Obras Publicas, Santiago de Chile 1999.

Necoechea, Andrés. Uso Social de Seis Plazas de Santiago, Tesis para optar al grado de magister, Editorial de la Facultad de Arquitectura y Bellas Artes, Instituto de Estudios Urbanos, Pontificia Universidad Católica de Chile 1984.

Palominos, N. Uso del Espacio Público en La Plaza de Armas de Santiago. In Taller 7, Sección Greene, Segundo Semestre 2000,Una Segunda Mirada A Santiago Centro, Pontificia Universidad Católica de Chile, 2000

Roca, Miguel Angel. De La Ciudad Contemporánea a la Arquitectura del Territorio. Eudecor Córdoba 1997.

Rojas, E. Old Cities, New Assets. Preserving Latin America's Urban Heritage. Inter-American Development Bank, Washington D.C. 1999.

Romero, José Luis. Latinoamérica las Ciudades y las Ideas. Siglo Veintiuno Editores, México D.F., 1976

Rosas, J. Partición de La Manzana. Como se Modernizo Santiago de Chile. In revista UR No3, pages 28-38. 1985.

Rossi, Aldo. La Arquitectura de La Ciudad. MIT Press, 1985.

Roberts, M. en Place and Space in the Networked City, Journal of Urban Design, vol.4. No.1, 1999, pages 54-55

Secretaria de Desarrollo Urbano. Córdoba Ciudad en Desarrollo. Municipalidad de Córdoba 1991/1999.Cordoba 1999.

Sepulveda, Diego. From The Plaza de Armas to the Shopping Mall in Carmona, Drewe, Rosemann, Van Duin. Globalisation Urban Form & Governance. DUP Science, Delft.2000.

10

The Urban Culture in the Southern Peruvian Andes. The Links with the History.

Americo Villegas Ormachea

In the Southern Peruvian Andes, apart from the perceived physical continuities between the historical urban structure and their present counterparts, there is in our opinion, a singular cultural continuity, which is materialised through the type of social development of the urban and architectural structures of the Andean cities. This development is based on the form in which urban structures have survived through time and particularly the way in which the urban scene constitutes the indispensable physical and symbolic support for the development of social and religious ritual activities over the centuries. Thereby, the continuity of this urban culture is established in direct relation to the survived forms and through it, the survival of the cultural contents of the traditional or historical urban structure.

The studies about the pre-Hispanic and colonial urbanism in term of the relationship between culture and city form, are seldom related to the Peruvian Andean, and when this happens, they do not develop the issue with specificity. Nevertheless some important matters have been advanced from which theoretical reflections and synthesis can be done which can lead us to an interpretative approach.

It is necessary to identify the determinant elements of social behaviour related to the built environment, or in other words, it is worth to identify what kind of relations survive between contemporary city form and the colonial societies and what are the contemporary consequences of this relation.

The Southern Peruvian Andean areas, until the 70s, exhibited the latest manifestations of the colonial spatial organisation based on agriculture and mining. The current urban system is characterised by new hierarchies and functional roles, resulting from a tertiary-based economy including international tourism, specialised agriculture and an emerging trade opened to the international market. Therefore we are facing a completely new context in terms of transformation, with new spatial processes, urban expansion and public space transformation. The social and cultural changes are directly influenced by the historically or traditionally based habitat (defining in this way local idiosyncrasies) and have developed very strong actions against the urban transformation of the consolidated frame. Here we will argue, that in those places where these physical and cultural condition are non-existent, or there is no heritage of the past, these transformations have no limits, neither does institutional or tradition-based regulations exist.

The purpose of this chapter is therefore, to find in the history, the resistance roots or on the contrary, the opportunities for change generated in the Southern Peruvian Andean settlements. For this purpose it is necessary to identify the links between the Hispanic colonial urban forms and the autochthonous spatial and urban structures, because we believe that the Spanish settlements were highly influenced by the social and natural realities of the particular contexts in where they were established. A systematisation of these links gives a framework to perform analysis and theoretical explanations. To achieve this it is necessary to examine certain main ideas.

The Spanish society that carried out the conquest belonged to the Spain that was victorious against the Moors. It is the Spain that accomplished the re-conquest of its own territory after eight centuries of Muslim domination. Apart from the natural practical priority to recover the geographic Iberian space, the Spanish recovered not only the concrete space within its cities, infrastructure and natural resources, but also rebuilt the cultural space as container of their symbols and memory.

This explains the destruction or radical transformation of every Muslim object that could impeach this goal in terms of symbolic architecture and urbanism. Only fully functional objects were spared this process. The Spanish Christian enterprise of the X century had in this way a mission to accomplish: to recover the economical and confessional space.

Evidently the Spanish re-conquest exercise, also meant in many cases the 'remake' of urban reality, which consisted of making profit from the basic infrastructure and in the reuse of domestic elements. This in fact was meant to assume the occupation of an inherited territory strongly structured physically and culturally.

Although Spain found a vast region in America, with a rationalised occupation of territory in terms of how nature was transformed, resources use and habitats built, it can be stated that the Spanish conquest of America constituted a very different challenge. Its objective was to productively occupy a vast territory compared to the European geographical scale. This goal obviously needed the location and functional definition of settlements, which later became fully integrated systems through the colonial economy, and experienced its influence until only a few decades ago.

The cultural continuities of many internal regions inherited from this economic restructuring process have permitted the development of the core of societies with traditional culture. It is only because of the modernisation period and development strategies of the XX century (in the 60s), that it has been possible to enter the common space of globalisation in the last ten years.

In this framework, the historical elements that can be considered as 'bridges' on the path between the formal and cultural dimension of the cities resulting from the traditional culture towards the development of the contemporary city in the Southern Andes of Peru, will constitute the main objective of this research.

The Spanish Occupation

The Spanish had a number of logistics and priorities in the occupation of the American territory. In the Caribbean, the first territory of conquest, the defensive logic and the seeking for security became a priority in the face of the unknown. The location near the sea and the relative mobility of the first settlements, all of them built in wood illustrates this preoccupation. This manner of occupation of the Caribbean islands remained from 1492 until 1508.

Later, the lack of significant military resistance on the island and the discovery of the continent, induces a definitive urbanisation located on the economically most important places of the islands taking in consideration military objectives, and the need to support the occupation of the continental lands.

After having overcome the difficulties of the first years, cities were built as a formal extension of Spanish urban culture. They reflected the traditional Iberian regional influences as well as the latest technological and stylistic considerations. This translated into the urban pattern of the Spanish settlements built before the defeat of the Moors, such as Santa Fe (a city-camp built by the catholic kings in front of Granada, planned with the clear influence of the roman orthogonal castrum) or the influence of the Italian renaissance materialised by the rediscovery of the work of Vitruvius, etc. No consideration was given to specific local conditions. The Caribbean is a direct part of Spain, and it is a direct reflection of its architecture and urbanism (Gutierrez R. 1983.13).

Having achieved the conquest and occupation of Central American continental territories (Mexico, Guatemala, Panama etc) the Spanish urbanisation in the new world established new typological elements, underpinned by the economic, social and military context. These typological elements became important in the definition of the future types of urban occupation and the land uses in the central and hierarchical areas of the colonial South American city. Some of them are the following:

- The foundation of cities as wealth concentration agents, as centres for the geographical and military control of the territory and the indigenous population, and finally the seat of the evangelical mission;
- Indigenous population concentration policies in controlled settlements related to taxes, evangelisation and security.
- From an urban point of view, the foundational layout of the settlements.
- From a formal point of view, the incorporation of the 'atriums' and 'pozas', as functional spaces for massive evangelisation and ritual acts.
- The substitution or elimination of formal symbolic structures where they existed.
- In terms of the geographic-spatial management, the defence strategies based in the morphology of the site, the control of indigenous areas and productive zones as well as the protection of the commercial routes and accessibility to the sea in order to built harbours, were the main factors.

The Central America city, is in this way the result of the particular local conditions and the renovated Vitruvian urban canons and Spanish tradition.

Some authors have pointed out the role of the church in this period, since religious buildings were established in very isolated locations, hostile and not economically attractive locations, but nearer to the indigenous population whose evangelisation was an imperative (Markman 1997,119). Many of these very remote places were chosen in order to build monastic settlements. Because there were communities with pagan rituals, it required the destruction of existing symbols and their and substitution by Christian symbols. This modality was be frequently applied in South America under the same circumstances.

The Spanish urbanisation heritage in the Peruvian territory, specifically in the Andean area, is different to the Central America and Caribbean process, due principally to two main factors:

- Firstly, the presence of a culture with autonomous development and significant achievements in the fields of the management of the natural resources and in the social administration of its economy. The quality of the agriculture, the animal husbandry practised [44], the hydraulic works, and the construction of an infrastructural base at a continental scale demonstrate this. In term of social achievements this culture is well known because of its community systems based on reciprocity and organised community work.

- Secondly, the presence of exploitable wealth in a space with dimensions never seen before, strongly divided in three natural regions and consequently difficult to exploit and to guarantee the communication and the security of the urban settlements.

The Spanish considered these two characteristics without taking into account the possibility of further developing the efficient existing productive organisation, which they partially destroyed. Faced with the magnitude of the territory and their limited resources, they gave exclusive priority to mining in well known productive places using the availability of local labour, whose brutal exploitation coupled with epidemics caused a catastrophical reduction of the population [45].

The urbanisation strategy in the Inca space was consequently a specific one, and established around four main priorities:

- Direct control and exploitation of the productive agricultural areas (cultivated land, labour force) as in the cases of the northern coast and tempered valleys in the mountains regions.
- Control of economic routes (for example the road between Lima and Cusco, which defined the foundation of Huamanga).
- Administrative and archdiocese's seats to control and to evangelise the areas with a high density of native population (the case of Ayaviri, in the Altiplano-Puno region).
- Establishment or re-establishment of settlements linked to mining activity (Juli, Potosi, Huancavelica etc).

The Spanish urbanisation in Peru started under these conditions in the north coast with the establishment of San Miguel de Piura City (1532), assuring in this way a direct connection with the Caribbean area. Later came the central-south 'sierra' region (mountains region), which constituted the main political and administrative region, with Cusco as the capital of the Inca's empire being 're-established' by the Spanish in 1534. Finally the southern part of the Inca territory, known as the 'Altiplano' and Alto Peru, with Juli and Potosi as the main settlements linked directly with the mining activity and trade and therefore the principal initial concentration centres of labour in terms of 'encomiendas'.

The Inca territory before the Spanish arrival, was a territory widely articulated by a road system, storage complexes, and physical structures for agriculture production

---

44 D. Noble Cook, in a study (1981) about the de-population of America in the colonial period, based in the relation between the extension of the agricultural frontiers and the number of people to feed, calculate the Tawantinsuyo population in 1520 - before the Spanish arrival to the Inca land- between 12 and 15 millions, while the data for the 1620 is only 600,000 native people.

45There is a number of evidences including physical structures, that the Inca culture was capable to develop a high technology level regarding the different sectors of human activity, which goes from the agricultural experimental activities until the construction of great stone channels for rivers, or unique techniques for the conservation of food until the control and complementary production in different ecological levels.

(terraces, channels, rivers protections etc.). The southern area of the Andes in Peru, the object of knowledge of this thesis, concentrated the most important productive structures, because it was the first area dominated by the Incas. Therefore it is the most populated area exerting the higher pressures on the natural environment. The Spanish colony evidently was establish in this territory with high yield potential, relying on its military superiority and on strategic alliances with the local population (Quechua and Aymarás) and to those traditional enemies of the Inca empire (the Chancas). The weaker situation of the Incas explains why the colonial cities in this region do not have defensive walls.

From this last case it is necessary to highlight the role of the 'reducciones' policy, by which Spanish planning forced the native population, since 1572, to concentrated in small towns to facilitate taxation and evangelisation. These settlements were located in the hinterland of the Spanish cities or near to the mining exploitations. The layout of these settlements was the strict orthogonal pattern or the native transformed pattern. They constitute the basis of rural settlements (half-caste) until today, as it is demonstrated in the cases of Chucuito, Acora, Ilave, Juli, Pomata, Zepita and Yunguyo, all of them placed in the surrounding the Titi-caca Lake in the province of Puno. .

In short, in urban terms and during the first periods of territorial occupation the colony was settled in the region mainly on old productive areas and later under the evangelisation and trading-administration criteria of the Spanish settlements. At the end of the XVII century the colonial system was fully established, and its functional pattern lasted until later in XX century. In this way the colonial space that substituted the Tawantinsuyu's one, in function to match the European needs, replaced the local factors that integrated the territory with new functional economic activities. These new activities were linked to the empowered mining axis between Huancavelica and Potosi, building the most important economic-territorial corridor of south America during the XVI, XVII and XVIII centuries. For some researchers the Spanish colonial space in South America was defined by the sub-regional economies structured along the mining axe Huancavelica-Potosi and secondly by the political measures to preserve the spatial unity of the entire colony (Assadourian, Bonilla et alt.1980).

The strong economic dynamics of the mining internal market, included the far regions of the viceroy, specialising in local production: cattle and textiles from Tucuman and Buenos Aires, wine and cattle from Chile, yerba mate from Paraguay and textiles from Quito (Assadourian et alt 1980). A significant source on the economic and social reality of this period (at the beginning of XVII century) remarks that while Potosi and the Andean mining settlement had 150,000 inhabitants, Madrid the capital of the most important empire in west had 105,000 inhabitants (Macera P. 1985 B).If these elements explain the origin of urban settlements in the South Andean region of Peru, they also matter at the urban scale, since they are linked to a number of reasons that explains the formal decisions of religious architecture monumentalism in the region.

To achieved spatial ordering the Incas used the 'ceque' system, which is a complex set of imaginary lines that starting from Cusco - the 'world's navel' - would organise the space and location of the settlements and the 'huacas' (sacred sites and objects) in relation to the natural world. On a local scale the settlements were organised in (Hurin = lower, Hanan= upper) (Rostworowski 1988). The hurin-hanan criterion that encapsulated concepts of gender and hierarchy, structured most of the human settlements in the Inca territory (Macera,1985A). Hereby, the natural space and built habitat are not devoid of ideological content. The spaces in the built environment have roles and sacred hierarchy. The 'huaca' is a physical entity that concentrates divinities. The city of Cusco is a huaca in itself, a totem city, a sacred city. It has 340 ritual sites and its ground becomes a ritual object (Macera, 1985 A). The Spanish realised this fact and their reaction took place at the ideological field. This was done in a similar way as during the Spanish re-conquest, during which urban and architectural symbolic elements were identified, destroyed or substituted by architectural typologies with high symbolic contents like churches, convents, civil palaces or public 'plazas'. This systemic substitution of symbolic and sacred forms, sought to physically demonstrate the superiority of one religion and culture above another, but through doing this, the Spanish manifested the perpetuation of the site's sacred character, in another words, the site's status did not change. This issue is probably one of the explanations why the native population accepted the new religion. It can be understood as a sort of initial cross breeding (miscegenation), that later became the basis of so called 'syncretism' ('sincretizacion') of the Andean culture.

On the other hand, the monument, is one of the favourite arguments of the Spanish urban language, and used as an expression of the dominant culture, in terms of political power and religious ideology. There is a plausible explanation for the monumentalism development in Spanish America and especially in Peru and Bolivia. Both centres concentrate the mining wealth, and through this the 'criollos' (Spanish people born in America) took the local economic power. According to some authors, the founding of a city was the occasion to demonstrate, through the construction of the church, the buildings, the squares and palaces, the need of modernity and independence in relation to the central powers using anachronistic synthesis of styles that in Europe remained as theoretical propositions. An example is the atrium of San Francisco in Quito (XVI century), Bramante's theoretical propositions which was built in Equator through Serlio's works. Paradoxically the different architectural styles were used with an anachronistic mixture: Italian renaissance and Spanish 'plateresco' in facades and gothic for the vaults and arches, 'mudejar' for the coat of arms etc. (Gutierrez R. 1983).

In this process of a building a 'criollo' (halfcaste) habitat, not everything was characterised by inconsistency and contradiction; the practical urbanism was meant to unite two common aspects of the two cultures: the use of public open spaces for religious activities and secondly the validation of a single hierarchical main 'plaza', which was multifunctional until its normalisation by the 'Indes Ordinance Law' in 1573.For the Inca culture, space had a deep religious connotation. The Andean geomorphology so rich in physic-spatial experiences and linked to a strong idiosyncratic nature through the presence of high mountains, glaciers, tempered valleys and roaring rivers, necessarily had to shape its people mentality and create gods and divinities bonded with those elements. The earth is the mother 'mama pacha', the mountains and rivers are gods (apus) and the sun the supreme divinity. The particular Inca architecture, which is strongly linked to the natural environment, enables the participation of the site's physical elements, since it allows the protagonism of the contextual space. Machu Picchiu citadel and Pisaq are good examples.

In the Inca settlements the main open public space, is generally the ritual one, therefore religious and sacred. The presence of the 'usnu' (ritual terrace) confirms the fact, but religion is also a state affair, the Inca (the king) is the son of the supreme god. In that sense, the 'plaza' in the Inca culture is a ritual space but at the same time political and military.

On the other hand, the Spanish ritual space, which surrounds the church is also a sacred place, the 'campo santo' (saint place). In this context, the 'atrium with pozas' is an American development, which from Mexico to Chile has been deployed with success in the urban programs of colonial urbanism, since the great susceptibility of native population towards the sacred. It is the external space used for mass evangelisation. The market square incorporate a 'criollo' use of the main square, leaving behind the exclusive official uses of the two recommended plazas: the 'cabildo' and the church square. Therefore the single square becomes a new place for social links and encounters which is rapidly incorporated by the local culture adding new functions for commerce and trade. For the native population the new plaza is also an unknown space for socialisation and not only the place to trade animals, tools and labour force.We can identify two main native influences related to the concept of urban habitat and its consequences in colonial city construction.

The first native influence is related to the direct appropriation of the Inca settlements and productive structure (agricultural mainly), which was preserved from destruction and modified or directly used in Spanish settlement. This is the reason behind using the original structures of Cusco, the capital city of Inca culture. Another clear example is Yucay, located in the Vilcanota valley, where the new settlement was planned considering the layout of the agricultural infrastructure (monumental terraces and channels) and aimed to control corn production. Final examples are the multitude of small settlements built above the 'reducciones' structures resulting from the Spanish settlement policy (1572).

The second native influence is the need to build religious architectural typologies in the predetermined sites of the original location of the 'huacas' the pagan meaningful places, in order to eliminate their influence.

With regards to the formal and the typological principle, it is necessary to argue that in colonial Peru three types of paradigmatic cities existed, which could be considered as synthesis of the local cultural mixture: Lima, the 'Spanish' city, Arequipa the 'criolla' and Cusco the 'mestiza', (Gutierrez R; 1983). This affirmation effectively represents approximately what happened in the colonial territory, in a number of settlements that reflect these types, obviously pointing out their differences regarding scale and functional hierarchies.

Despite the fact that Lima is founded on top of a pre-existing human settlement, it did not influence the classical orthogonal pattern (1535). The main square, the 'plaza', is the hierarchical element around which buildings of political and religious power (cathedral and cabildo palace) are situated, followed by the residences of the nobility. The rest corresponds to the urban environments of the Spanish and Creoles. The periphery has mixed uses and is related to domestic life and city security. The architecture itself corresponds to a city defined as the capital of the Spanish kingdom in America (viceroy). However the city followed a process of typological adaptation, finding its own architectural language generating particular housing typologies until the end of XIX century. Imposing palaces and mansions with exuberant closed balconies and closed Andalusian and Moorish patios characterises the urban image of colonial Lima.

With regards to Arequipa, it is effectively the local reflection of a Creole population that was influenced by the natural environment and local materials. Ii is built completely with aschlar masonry and from the formal point of view is a Spanish version of the Andean city. It repeats the orthogonal pattern and uses volcanic stones to build a singular architecture. The peculiar typology that is generated takes into consideration the geological precariousness of the site. Founded in 1540 very near to a volcano, the buildings posses corpulent walls, not very high (two levels only) very often with vaults as roofs which give a strong character to the city. Arequipa is one of the most important examples of a local creation of architectural decorative styles, which includes the local animal and vegetal species parallel to classical Spanish 'plateresco' style.

Finally Cusco, which is the last case in our theoretical subject, is the result of forced cultural mixing with regards to both the architecture of buildings and the final definition of its urban layout. It is strongly influenced by the restructuring of the Inca's aristocratic city (central area of the Inca's city). The Spanish grid only modifies the streets and the blocks, when this layout does not coincide with the need for land distribution between the conquerors.

However the construction of the Spanish city (1534), means in fact the destruction of the Inca city, since the destruction of the original urban morphology, the demolition of the 'huacas', of the symbolic buildings and the occupation of the ritual spaces, in fact means the disappearance of the structure which supported the symbolic meaning of the sacred city. This sacred meaning was the character which made the Inca city the centre of the universe. Despite this, the result of the construction of the Spanish city has made the co-existence of two cultures possible, the so-called 'mestiza', a non ending place of iconic combat, of ideological and parallel readings and of unexpected syncretism. In Cusco the singular monuments of the two cultures seem to dispute their right to the eternity.

The Urban Experience of Inca Culture

The territory occupation during the Inca culture has limitations in the use of the conventional meaning of the 'urban' concept. There are few settlements, which could reach somehow the features that characterise urban life, and in other hand, the formal ideas (the physical materialisation) of 'urban' in the occidental culture conception. There is undoubtedly not always a coincidence in its application to the local (native) settlements.

The 'urban' inca settlements, have generally a character linked to worship of local divinities, around them remained scattered in the territory, tens of 'proto-urban' settlements or small villages, which characteristic are not to have themselves a physical organisation that could be identify with the physical concept of an urban structure:

- lack of clear roads pattern
- lack of public spaces for social uses (markets, plazas etc.)
- lack of a land occupation density that enables community and a morphological organisation referred to a functional specification.

This allows a definition of the Inca settlements near to a concept of urban form essentially dedicated to veneration around the 'huacas', ceremonial centres and service buildings connected with some streets organising the circulation and related to the natural and agricultural space. A ceremonial centre is considered hierarchically; it is a meeting and ritual place, is the most important space connected to an inhabited space. It is the sacred "place" linked to the geographical and natural location, it is a sacred entity itself. The citadel of Machu Picchu is a complete example of this kind of settlement.

Figure 1 **Machupichu** (partial view)

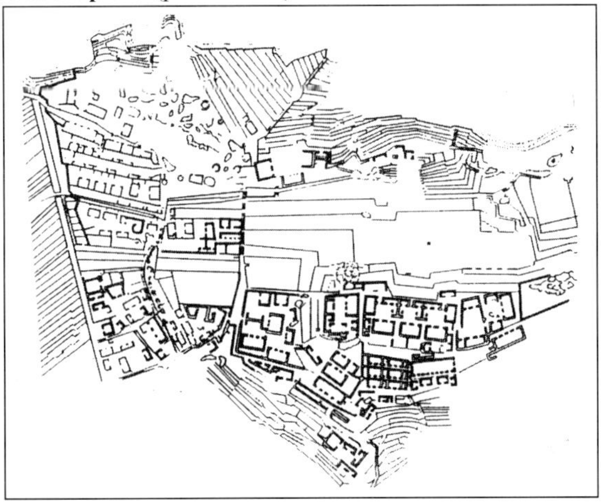

Regarding the residential settlements themselves, these are constituted by tens of small houses built of stone, burn bricks, wood and straw. Organised around patios called "canchas", they form rural developments without a recognisable geometric definition except in singular cases of local functional hierarchies, according to the topographic conditions and natural conditions. Their locations are linked to the accessibility to the communal agricultural lands. The physical relations with ceremonial centres are established through roads and food-depots ("colcas").

The Inca culture did not develop urban structures as physical and non-physical organisations with internal functions as a city concept related to its particular economic and social system. Cusco (fig.2) and Huanuco Pampa (fig 3) are probably the only settlements assimilated to a "city" concept by the morphological and functional organisation and also their population, despite of the high territorial management and the rational use of resources related to agricultural development and canalisation of watercourses. However this fact has not impeded the planned management of human settlements with specific functions, not necessarily for housing, but with characteristics which easily remember the formal organisation of western urbanisation.

The lack of morphological structures with western urban characteristics, does not mean that these were unknown by the Inca culture, due to the recognition of the urban experience from former cultures in Peruvian territory, which were dominated and assimilated, such as the Huari culture -with the settlements of Wiracochapampa in the north and Pikillacta (fig. 4) 35 km far from Cusco - and the Chimu culture -with its extarordinary Chan Chan city, in the northern coast. On the other side, the worship centres probably had as antecedents the main Tiawanaku site "Puerta del Sol" in Bolivia and the "Chavin de Huantar" centre from the Chavin culture, in the central mountain range of Peru.

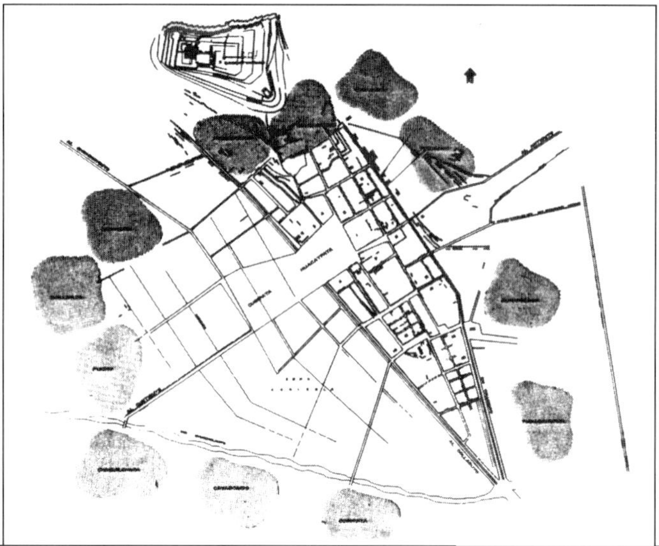

Figure. 2

"Imperial Cusco" plan 1535. It shows the location of peripheral districts

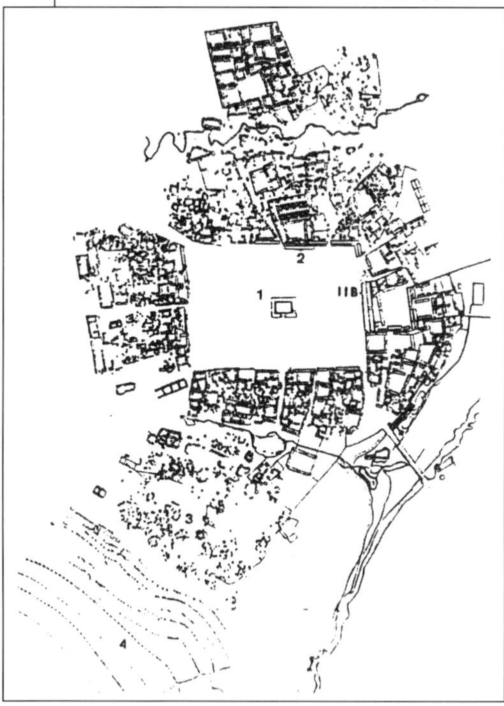

Figure 3. (Left) Huanuco Pampa. Source Morris and Thompson Plan.

Figure 4. Pikillacta. Source E. Harth Terre Plan.

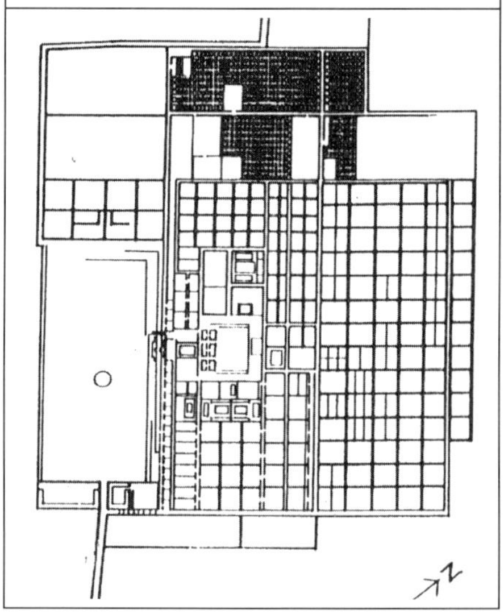

Although the Incas did not continue experiencing the planning of cities, they used this kind of organisation in lower scale at places like Wari or Chimu, and in specific cases such as militar settlements at important valleys or roads and the centres for communal management and storage of food, army and clothes ("Nieve-Nieve" in the Lurin valley and "Incawasi" in the Cañete valley, both of them near by Lima). This means a selective use of this kind of typology according to certain circunstances. This allows us to establish a parallel with the selective and hierarchical use of the stone technology in building related to the typology and rank position, setting substantive differences in terms of architecture.

The Inca urban experience thereby was not generated or structured by the progressive process of correspondence to the economic and social system. Despite of the geographic extension and environmental variations of territory, production and distribution were submitted to a rigorous central authority and management under the known conditions of reciprocity and prevention which makes the singularity of the Inca political, economic and social regime. In these conditions, the capitalist and western city did not have the reason of existing.

Therefore that there was a sort of freedom in the creative process of space and urban form. The concepts and ideologies conditioned the settlement structures and forms. The generation of urban morphology in the Inca period obeys in a parallel way to two more rationalised criteria (symbolic and practical uses) or more elaborated than the Spanish city. The Inca settlement goes further from the orthogonal pattern, a typology well known and used according to the topographic relief opposed to the overlapped Spanish application. There are archaeological remains of urban structures with radial pattern (Incawasi-Cañete valley, Chucuito-Puno), trapezoidal form (Ollantaytambo), zoomorphic (Cusco), or organic (Machu Picchu, completly adapted to the topographic and enviromental situation). The substantial formal differences between the more or less contemporary Inca settlements would prove these ideas.

Regarding the production of the urban form in terms of constructive density, therefore the residential capacity, the Inca settlement is rather lower than the Spanish one except in Cusco, with 100 to 150 thousand inhabitants according the Spanish chronicles. Some authors argue that most of them did not have more than hundreds inhabitants (Hyslop, 1990), which shows clearly the rural nature of native population of Tawantinsuyo (the so-called Inca territory), with around 10 millions of inhabitants.

A last example of an urban organisation that summarised all the potentialities of the Inca habitat has been embodied in the Ollantaytambo citadel. Even though it was built by the end of the autonomous period, and that some studies suggest that has some Spanish influences - such as the opened water channels for consumption (most of them with stone channels underground), (Pineda J. 1998), the typological definitions of housing, their disposition and modular character within the blocks (canchas), and the architectural style and technology, assure the local origin. Another great significant experience with substantial morphological differences, is the case of the already described Huanuco Pampa, where the main role has been charged to the monumental "plaza" and its ritual "usnu"

References

Agurto Calvo S. La Traza Urbana de la Ciudad Inca. Unesco- INC. Lima 1979.

Assadourian S, Bonilla H, Mitre A, Tristan Platt. Mineria y espacio economico en los Andes. siglos XVI-XX. IEP. Lima 1980.

Barbichon Guy. Espaces partagés: variation et variété des cultures. En Espaces et sociétés. L□harmattan. Paris 1991.

De Solano Francisco, Ville et geostrategie espagnole en Amerique au cours du XVIII siecle; en L□Amerique Espagnole a l□epoque des lumieres. CNRS; Paris 1987.

De Solano Francisco, Política de concentración de la población indígena (1500-1800). En Asentamientos urbanos y organización socioproductiva en la historia de América Latina. SIAP, Buenos Aires 1977.

De Azevedo Paulo. Cusco, continuidad y cambio. Unesco. Lima 1982.

Di Meo Guy. Geografía sociale et territoires. Nathan Universite. Paris 1998.

Fuksas Maximilien, La relation entre monumentalisme de la peripherie et le monumentalisme dans le langage traditional. Fin d'un langage. En Ville, Projets, forme simbolique, pouvoir. Mardaga. Bruselas 1987.

Flores Ochoa Jorge A. and Tomoeda Hirosayu, El Qosqo antropologia de la ciudad. CEAC. Cusco 1992.

Freitag Michel, Architecture et societé. De. Saint Martin. Montreal 1992

Gasparini, Margolies. Arquitectura Inka. Universidad central de Venezuela. Caracas 1977.

Gonzales de Olarte et Alt. La lenta modernizacion de la economia campesina. IEP. Lima 1987.

Golte Jurgen, La racionalidad de la organizacion andina. IEP. Lima 1980.

Gutiérrez Ramón, Arquitectura y Urbanismo en Iberoamérica. Manuales Arte Cátedra. Madrid 1983.

Gutiérrez Ramón, Esteras Cristina, Alejandro Malaga. El valle del Colca. Cinco siglos de arquitectura y urbanismo. Libros de Hispanoamérica.

Glave L. Estructura agraria y vida rural en una región Andina: Ollantaytambo siglos XVI-XIX. Centro Bartolomé de las Casas. Cusco 1983.

Hyslop John, Inka settlement planning. University of Texas press. Texas 1990.

Lorandi Ana Maria, El servicio personal como agente de desestructuracion en el Tucuman colonial.En Revista Andina. N□ 1 , Cusco 1988.

Macera Pablo, Historia del Peru. Epoca prehispanica. Lima 1985.

Macera Pablo, Historia del Peru. La Colonia. Lima 1985.

Pineda José, Planeamiento Inca. Arquitectura y paisaje. En revista Arquinka N□ 9 Lima, 1996.

Noble David Cook. Demographic collapse: Indian Peru. Cambridge University press. New York 1981

Rostworowski María. Historia del Tawantinsuyo. Instituto de Estudios Peruanos. Lima 1988.

Rowe John H. La arqueología del Cusco como historia cultural. IEP, Lima .

Tamayo Herrera Jose. Historia social del Cusco Republicano. Universo. Lima 1981.

Williams C. Arquitectura y urbanismo en el antiguo Perú. En Historia del Perú, Mejía Baca. Lima 1981.

11

The Effects of Social Housing and Market–Oriented Developments on the Urban Form

Cecilia Marengo

Introduction

There has been a considerable amount of research about the process of urban expansion in developing countries and many studies since the early Fifties has been concerned into try to guide urbanization according to some social, economic and environmental objectives. However the current urban expansion in countries with very high rate of urbanization and low demographic growth need a particular research related to the type of cities we want and the type of particular regulations which are possible and desirable to guide the process in one or other direction. In other words whether current urban policy is effective to reduce the negative externalities derived from the expansion process.

ECLAC (1998) data point out that Argentina, Venezuela, Chile and Uruguay are the countries with the highest percentage of urban population in South America. Estimates for Argentina indicate that 90.6% of the population will be urbanized in the year 2005[46]. The demographic situation in intermediate cities of these countries presents similar trends that in the large agglomerations. In Cordoba City the demographic growth has been reduced from 2,6% to 1,6% in the last ten years. ECLA indicates that there have been a growth in large Metropolitan areas, and a relative increase in cities with more than 1 million inhabitants during the '90s. For many researchers this growth is related to the effect of structural adjustment policies, which have brought an increases on social polarization. Also the changes in household formation, the movements of activities related with globalisation and to the changes in lifestyle of the population are all component of the persistence in the extension of the city. In this research we will admit that the changes are also encouraged by the location of social housing programs in the periphery, the type of social housing delivery system oriented to the supply-side, and the metropolitan growth is also encouraged by the spread of gated communities in the suburbs.

In this paper we will adress two issues: first we will present the evidences of this situation in the case of Cordoba City, and secondly we will establish some general questions related to the future research on the effect of this process in the Urban Form.

46 46Secretaría de CEPAL. De la urbanización acelerada a la consolidación de los asentamientos humanos en América Latina y el Caribe: el espacio regional. Santiago de Chile 25 al 27 de octubre de 2000, pg. 11

1. Housing Delivery System and the Changing Periphery in Cordoba during the 90s

In the last decade, the rapid and intensive processes of urban growth in Cordoba city, reveal the effect of significant transformations in the form of dwelling production and residential location. Different types of residential developments can be identified in the urban periphery: real estate developments, social housing (for subsidised sectors), housing developments (for sectors with some payment capacity), housing built through cooperatives with private funds and irregular settlements (illegal). In this analysis we will be concern with two different form of planned housing production:

- the real-estate developments addressed to high-income sectors and
- the social housing developments addressed to subsidised sectors

It attempts to reveal the intensified phenomenon of socio-spatial segmentation through three main dimensions of analysis, spatial, social and economic.

1.1. Real Estate Developments (gated communities)

Since 1991, real estate has developed a new model of urbanization identified locally as "countries" (because many of them are located in the countryside) or gated neighborhoods. Their facilities are: controlled access, permanent security, exclusivity and a homogeneous social level. The proposals can be classified in different types, among them: special urbanization (countries), gated neighborhoods, and gated neighborhoods that include housing units. (Table 1)

Table 1: Main Dimensions of Real Estate Developments in the Metropolitan Region of Cordoba (1987-2000).

		Cordoba City	**Metropolitan area only**
Interventions	**29 urbanizations**	**20**	**9**
New urbanized area	**1,563.92 (hectares)**	(941,92 hectares)	(622 hectares)
Types	Countries	665.32	148
	Gated neighborhoods	261.9	474
	Gated Neighborhoods with house	14.7	----
Quantity of lots	**7,938**		
Type	Countries	2,240	467
	Gated neighborhoods	3,160	1,848
	Gated Neighborhoods with house	223	-------
Representation according to size			
Less than 50 plots	(7) 24,13 %		
Between 50-100 plots	(3) 10,36%		
Between 100-150 plots	(5) 17,24 %		
More than 150 plots	(14) 48,27%		
Urban Location	Northwest	(15) 51,72%	(8) 27,58%
	Northeast	(-)	
	Southwest	(3) 10,34%	(1) 3,47%
79,30% to the Northwest side	Southeast	(2) 6,89%	

Source: Own elaboration, report carried out in the course of the research

In the 90s period 29 new urban areas were developed, which consists of 7,938 plots. In terms of urban expansion it represents 941,92 hectares that were urbanized within the city, representing the 5.37% of the total urbanized area of Cordoba city (in 1999) and 622 urbanized hectares in the metropolitan area.

The Types

The differences among these interventions lie in the dimensions and type of social and recreational facilities they offer, which constitutes the main indicator of segmentation in the new residential model. A great diversity is observed in terms of sporting activities as well as the amount of open green areas provided. The differences are also visible through the analyses of the maintenance costs each proposal has and the value of the plots in the real estate market.

As an example, the highest segments in the social pyramid are those countries that have golf courts, clubhouse, swimming pool and another specific spaces for sport activities. In these cases, the monthly cost of maintenance is around U$S360 and the value of the plots in the real estate market fluctuate between US$70,000 to 90,000.

The base of the pyramid focussed on middle-income sectors includes gated neighborhoods that only share permanent security costs and the maintenance of open green spaces. In these cases, the monthly cost falls to U$S80 and the value of the plots in the real-estate market is around U$S15,000 to 36,000 depending on their size.

Urban Planning Regulations

In terms of urban-planning regulations, countries and gated neighborhoods have to comply with different norms. The main differences are related to the dimensions of open areas and to the property of collective-use spaces. In the case of countries, the minimum area devoted to recreational use is 30% of the total plot area, while in the case of gated neighborhoods the minimum required is 15%. In the first case, common areas are under public domain and its exclusive use is given to the entity that administers the development. The local government reserves the prerogative to retract the exclusive use right and is able to open those spaces to public use in case the administration fails to maintain them. Given the magnitude of the interventions, the reservation of green areas has a significant importance in the urban context. In the case of gated neighborhoods the streets and green areas are under public domain. For this reason, the controlled perimeter and access entrance means a transgression to urban planning regulations.

Location

Analyzing the urban-regulations, it is noted that the only restriction imposed on the placing of special residential areas (countries) within the city limits is the existence of activities incompatible with, noxious or dangerous to the residential use. That is to say that these types of interventions are allowed to locate in urban or rural areas as long as they do not form a barrier to the normal growth of the urban grid or interfere with the main road system, or with the connections between urban sectors, or in the stormwater drainage. Another condition is to preserve the environmental qualities (landscape) of the place, although this aspect is one of the fundamental variables that condition the success of this type of interventions. (Figure 1)

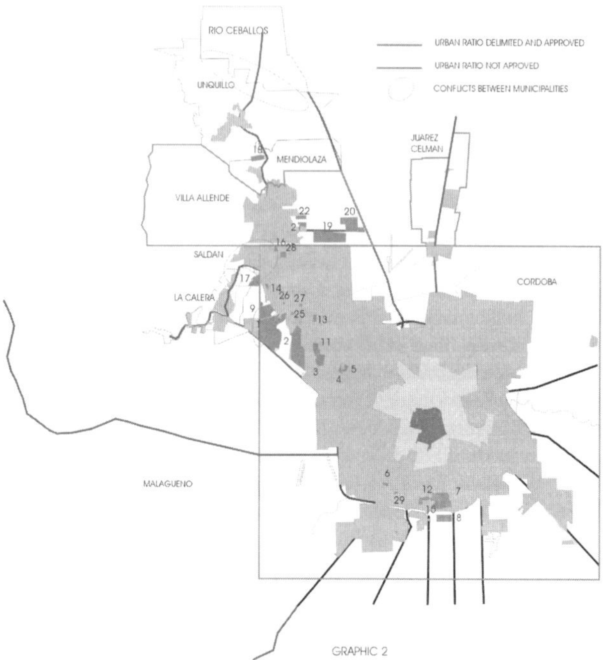

Figure 1
Real Estate Developments and Urban Ratios
Metropolitan Area of Cordoba

It is worth mentioning that in such an extensive territory under local administration (512 km2) the absence of restrictions in terms of locality reveals a new characteristic in the suburban growth pattern. The availability of services and infrastructure has a secondary importance; the fundamental variable is urban and metropolitan road accessibility.

Gated neighborhoods, on the contrary, have to adjust to urban regulations and are not allowed to locate outside urbanized limits.

When comparing their localities with the designated areas for future expansion, as well as with vacant areas within the urban form (estimated in 25.61% of the urban land) it is clear that in most cases they do not consolidate vacant spaces within the urban structure neither are they located in sectors of future expansion. (Figure 1) The model of gated urbanization follows strategic conditions in terms of accessibility and landscape qualities

From this perspective, the real estate development for high-income sectors reveals selective patterns of location and a preference for the location in the northwestern sector of the city and metropolitan area, consolidating the tendency of expansion of high-income sectors on this development axis.

In general terms, urban expansion is materialized through the selective localization of private investments in the metropolitan space according to the attractiveness that certain areas present. Among them we can mention: accessibility conditions, natural landscape, proximity to peripheral service centers.

The contiguity characteristic of the metropolitan expansion of the '80s gives way to a heterogeneous pattern of growth according to the location of private investments. Some city sectors are favored while others –with decreasing attractiveness- are left aside in terms of private investments. This situation tends to introduce distortion and imbalances among urban sectors and is not included in urban planning regulations.

Size

Urban regulations fix a maximum area to be urbanized, trying to decrease the impact related to the scale of the interventions (50 hectares outside the city ring and 15 hectares inside it), however, it is noted that this condition is not an exclusive parameter. The pressure of private investment makes this condition flexible and real estate developments have registered interventions of more than 100 hectares inside and outside the city ring.

Taking the number of plots of each intervention into account, the proposals registered a wide variety of options, although in general it is evident that in more than 48,27% of cases consist of more than 150 plots.

In the case of countries, the minimum plot is 1,500m² (outside the city ring) and 1.000m² (inside the city limit) according to the urban regulations. The average plot size is 1,478m² (it varies from 1,000m² to 2,500m²). In gated neighborhoods, it depends on the characteristics of the urban area (the minimum is 300m²). The average plot size is 910m² (it varies from 400m² to 3,000m²).

In both cases, developments that include more plots are located in the edge zones due to the availability of rural segments, whose market value and location in the urban system makes them potentially viable for new real estate developments.

The Investment

Table 2: Investment of Real Estate Developments in the Metropolitan Region of Cordoba (1987-2000)

Location	**Type**	**Investment** (estimated) (In million U$ Dollars)	**Percentage sold** (%)	**Occupation percentage** (%)
Córdoba City	Countries	156.68	**71.16%**	**55.23%**
	Gated neighborhoods	96.388	22.78%	12.78%
	Gated Neighborhoods with house (units)	----		
Metropolitan Area	Countries	38.4	50.51%	14.80%
	Gated neighborhoods	76.12	44.64%	14.88%
Total		**367.58**	**43.86%**	**25.39%**

Own elaboration. Source: report carried out in the course of the research

These interventions represent around US$368 million of private investments[47] (between 1991 to 2000) with a total number of 7,938 plots in the metropolitan area. Comparing the investments estimated in the commercial and service sector, road infrastructure, or public works developed by the local government in this period[48], it is

47 The estimation of private investment is based on the average of the market prices of the different proposals, according to the information provided by the developers during April 2001. The market price for m2 in each proposal varies according to the consolidation level of each neighborhood. It refers only to the plot value and it does not include the value of the houses since these data is not available.

48 Marengo, Cecilia (2001)

noted that the real estate market developments had a significant impact on the local economy and accompany the economic expansion that took place during this period.

The magnitude of the phenomenon of new suburban gated urbanization is evident when observing that in terms of quantity of plots they represent 23.24% of the total number of plots, when taking into account all planned interventions located in the city periphery.

In his analysis of restructuring processes that take place in the metropolitan areas of Latin America, De Mattos[49] points out that economic liberalisation has opened the way for the implementation of a strictly capitalist logic in the production and reproduction of metropolitan space since it allows for de-regulated operations of two types of social strategies: real estate business and family strategies. The most solvent sector and also the most vulnerable have contributed to intensify sub-urbanization.

Regarding the consolidation of the supply, it is important to point out that 43.86% of the total real estate supply is sold. In the case of countries located in Cordoba City, it is noted that 3 huge developments absorb 60.4% of the supply, with high levels of consolidation constituting wealthy enclaves.[50]

In these cases, it can be seen as an increase in market plot values that in some cases are 120% higher than the initial market value. (The local newspaper mentions: "In Las Delicias we (it refers to the developer) pay 150,000 Dollars for 160 hectares –rural land- and today it is the value of a single plot. The houses built are around 200 million dollars, so when you add it up its is possible to deduce the importance of the real estate sector and the investments that were carried out in the city in this period."[51])

The success of these real-estate operations result in a diversified enlarged spectrum of proposals addressed to middle-income social-sectors. In these cases, the value of the plots, which depends on the urban locality and the consolidation level, varies between US$25 to 80 per square meter.

A comparative analysis of these two demand sectors reveals that the higher-income segment is saturated, while the middle-income segment registers an oversupply. In the first case, 71,16% of the plots are sold and 55,23% of them are permanently occupied. In the second case, a wide development of interventions is detected in the metropolitan area registering 44.64% of plots sold over the 22.78% that is registered in Cordoba City. However, when analyzing the current values of occupation in both cases they are relatively lower.

This shift to new suburban neighborhoods tends to impact negatively on the urban renewal process in traditional neighborhoods in the city. Regarding the effects of the expansion in the city and in small towns in the metropolitan area, some questions arise when we analyze this incipient tendency (observing that, at the moment, real occupation values are significantly inferior to those of sold plots) because it can be foreseen that this phenomenon will consolidate completely as well as continue expanding.

In the context of the neo-liberal policy, the developments of real estate market raise doubts about local governments' capacity to guide the expansion processes in such a way as to avoid segregation and imbalances among urban sectors. In the framework of this new phenomenon, the great diversity of proposals and the magnitude of private

49 De Mattos, C. (1998 b) p.746

50 The local newspaper mentions that in Cordoba city ABC1 social segment represents the 12% of the population (estimated in 44,000 households) whose average incomes varies around U$ 5,300. It represents the 51% of the total income of the city. Source La Voz del Interior, August 12, 2001

51 Source: local newspaper, La Voz del Interior, October 15, 2000

investment lead to an investigation of the incumbencies local governments assume in their territory.

1.2. Legal Instruments of Territorial Planning: An Unresolved Topic

In 1987 and in accordance with decentralization policies, the Provincial Constitution that recognizes the political, economic, administrative, financial and institutional autonomy of local governments was sanctioned. It also states that the municipal territorial jurisdiction includes the area to benefit from municipal service provision. Likewise, local governments are in charge of delimitating the urban area on condition that the municipal limits do not overlap with the departmental jurisdiction

In 1991, the Municipal Constitution was sanctioned that established that the municipal region will include the area where services are completely or partially provided by the municipality (urban area) and the area designated for future expansion (rural activities). It is important to mention that in some cases the boundaries between municipalities are not continuous, the general situation is that a municipality borders a territory that is under provincial jurisdiction (rural use).

Ten years after the sanction of the Law, many Municipalities have not yet delimited the territory under their jurisdiction. (As an example, the northwestern side of the metropolitan area of Cordoba demonstrates the following situation: Cordoba, Villa Allende and Juarez Celman have delimited the municipal region. Other towns, such as La Calera, Malagueño, Malvinas Argentinas, only have a zoning plan of the urban area - they have not approved their urban regions yet. Lastly, Saldán, Unquillo, Mendiolaza, do not even have a plan of the urban layout. (Figure 2).

It is clear that decentralization policies have an unequal impact on the different towns of the metropolitan area of Cordoba. Small towns lacking technical support or political capacity are incapable to solve a complex issue; such as it is the layout of the urban regions.

On the other hand, the lack of definition in the urban territorial boundaries opens up the possibility for private developments to locate outside the areas under municipal administration, that is to say, in rural areas under provincial jurisdiction where the controls and requirements are less strict. This does not only disable the municipalities to capture that demand but also shift to changes in land use (land for agricultural activities can be turn into land for urban activities)

As a consequence of adjustment policies and the privatisation of services that were once the State's responsibility, the restrictions on service extensions are now dependent on the economic possibilities of a demand that is able to afford them.

A project under way at the moment by the Provincial Government aims at allowing municipalities to assume their responsibility over urban and rural areas, so that the borders between municipalities are joining in all the cases. This initiative would provide instruments of territorial planning and an integrated vision of the urban expansion processes.

Private urbanization that developed in a context of partial approaches facilitate competition between towns and favors urban expansion. The differences that are expressed in the metropolitan area (as to mention: the non-existence of common urban regulation, differences between urban land values as well as the changes in the traditional roles of cities -from tourism to dormitory cities-) are variables that need to be analyzed thoroughly while this tendency consolidates.

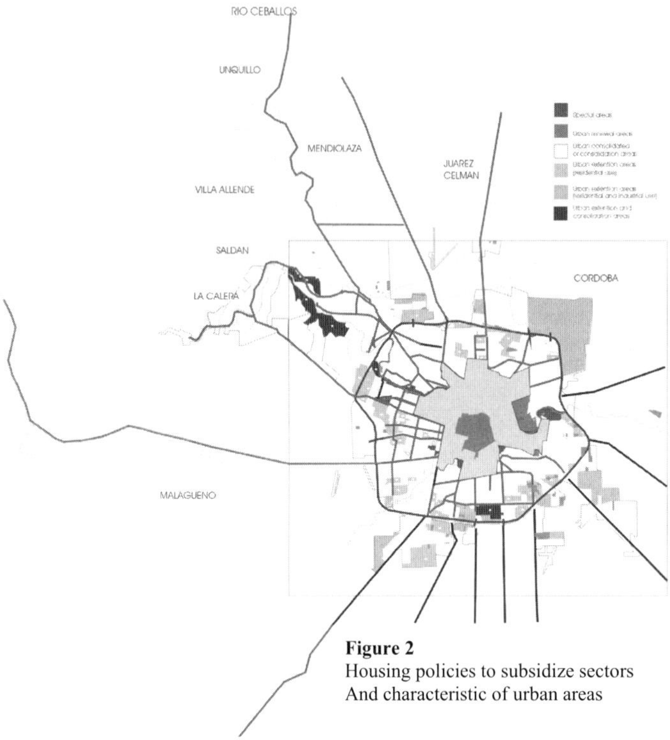

Figure 2
Housing policies to subsidize sectors
And characteristic of urban areas

The challenges in metropolitan Cordoba refer to an integrated planning which would take into account the diversity of situations present in a context where this type of interventions shows a tendency to consolidate.

2. Housing Policies for Subsidized Sectors

Urban growth, social polarization and urban fragmentation are expressed in the urban structure not only through the development of the real-estate market but also through government intervention that provide affordable housing to disadvantaged groups.

During the period 1987-2000, 7,447 housing units were built under the prevailing typology consisting of single house in ownership, resulting in a low-density extensive pattern of occupation on the urban periphery.

This pattern of lower initial cost –mainly because land values in the periphery are affordable for the vulnerable sector- has elicited criticism in public planning (contributing to urban expansion and demanding infrastructure and urban facility provision) and has also resulted in social costs. Lower-income sectors relocated at the city borders have to confront unemployment; unaffordable transport costs, loss of labor networks, and their possibilities to access to health and education have been reduced.[52]

Social housing development for the subsidized sectors constitutes the opposite type of intervention to challenge in the analysis.

This perspective is interesting for two reasons

It constitutes an innovative experience of partnership between the Government, CBOs and NGOs focused on social sectors living under the poverty line and that live in slums or have critical housing situations. [53]

– In the context of the accentuated social polarization in the last decade, the local government had to adapt regulations in order to make infrastructure requirements more flexible, and, in so doing, allow for housing provision addressed to vulnerable social groups organized in cooperatives.

2.1 Some considerations on the experience of partnership housing policy

Since 1991, important transformations were produced in housing policy in Argentina, led by the decentralization of the resources, the diversification of the programs, growing consensus on the need to improve efficiency and effectiveness as well as the incorporation of new social actors in project implementation projects. Between 1992 and 1999, an innovative experience in the political organizational field as well as in the social-political field was developed in Cordoba, named "Mesa de Concertación de Políticas Sociales" (MCPS which means a Negotiating Table where Social Policies are agreed upon by different actors)

Basically, the mechanism was the following: the beneficiaries through their social organisations (CBOs) and with the technical support of NGOs presented to government their demands for improvements in their living conditions. The participants of this experience stated that the consensus and the negotiation facilitated the agreement of a social policy articulating different actors' interests and overcoming clientelism in the implementation of social policy to vulnerable sectors.

The constitutive agreement for the formalization of the partnership process was the setting up of a budget, which was to be provided by the State. The decision-making on the funds was to be based on programs of action and priorities presented by the CBOs representatives. The community leaders state that the developed projects demonstrated the validity of organizational work, and its achievements are a demonstration of the capacity of the poor sectors to improve their housing conditions.

The importance of this experience emerges when analyzing the projects and the amount of funds that were provided by the government. As an example, in the period 1992-1995 they managed to obtain 10% of the total funds the government devoted to Social Policies. These funds operated as an Open Fund of Social Investment.

It is important to mention that the projects were mainly centered in Housing (including land access, community facilities, building housing units, infrastructure provision, technical support), while others dealt with issues such as health, nutritional

52 Marengo, Cecilia (1999)

53 Among the reasons that contribute to poverty expansion is to mention the evolution of the activity level that affects labour markets and the changes in the sectoral and occupational composition of employment. Recession caused the destruction of workstations in the industrial sector that were replaced by less stable and worse remunerated employment in construction, trade and personal services, characterized by its high informality and low remuneration. Source: Bolsa de Comercio de Córdoba, p. 370.

emergency, housing improvement, training activities for youngsters, generation of temporary employment, among others.

2.2 Intervention Description

Table 3. Housing Devoted to Subsidized Sectors.

In the period, 76 projects were built and in most of the cases they constituted less than 100 units. (Figure 2)

In terms of urban expansion they represent 1,48% of the urbanized area. Regarding the financing sources, 61,84% of interventions was financed with provincial funds (Ministry of Social Development) while in 30,26% of the cases the funds came from municipal resources. The Provincial government financed the land and housing, while the local government provided the infrastructure.

Over the last period, a new program type is noted (Program P17) which incorporates the national government's resources to support housing construction and technical assistance. The production is defined as mixed, since it is carried out by the beneficiaries themselves (as a temporary employment which benefits the community) and in collaboration with companies in those items with more constructive complexity. (Typologies vary between 2 bedrooms of 40m^2 and 3 bedrooms of 60m^2. In this case the final cost is estimated in US$10,000)

A different situation, although addressing the same type of demand, represents the development done completely by the Local government. In these cases, the housing policy is a result of the necessity to relocate population because the land is affected by the construction of public works. Since 1997 a higher level of interrelationship between the local authorities and community leaders can be found aiming at negotiating the relocation of the people as well as the programs to be implemented. Perhaps the most significant contribution of the local government and the agreement achieved in the MCPS to housing policy implementation were the changes in urban regulations in order to facilitate the access to housing programs.

Interventions (1987 – 2000)	**76 housing plans**	
Quantity of lots / housing units	**7,447 units**	
New Urbanized area	**259.40 hectares**	
Modality	Ministry of Social Development	(47) 61.84%
(According to funds provided)	Municipality of Cordoba	(23) 30.26
	Other. Without data	(6) 7.9%
Representation according to size	Less than 50 units	**(29) 38.15%**
	50-100 units	**(25) 32.89%**
	100 -150 units	(12) 15.79%
	More than 150 units	(10) 13.17%
Urban location	Northwest city sector	20.72%

	Northeast city sector	22.36%
	Southeast city sector	**39.68%**
	Southwest city sector	17.24%

Own elaboration based on data of the Municipality of Cordoba

Some Considerations on the Urbanization Conditions

The urban planning norms, which are used at present, were sanctioned in 1985. Their central goal was to avoid the expansion by means of planned interventions in areas lacking infrastructure. They also aimed at encouraging the use of the existing infrastructure, avoiding speculative excesses and urban expansion toward rural or industrial areas. (Then as a consequence of the speculative expansion that developed in the period of import substitution –'50s to the '80s- many urban sectors lacked minimum infrastructure and social facilities.)

In an attempt to regulate urban growth, the norms promoted the occupation of serviced vacant land and obliged the developers to provide infrastructure (or to extend it when necessary). The most significant features of the regulations emphasize the need to preserve the vial layout avoiding the interruption of the urban grid in urbanized areas, to reserve 15% of the plot area for green spaces and facilities and to yield the responsibility for infrastructure provision to the developer (water provision, electricity, public lighting, planting of streets, pavement, stormwater drainage and sewage networks). It is important to mention that the local government assumes the maintenance costs.

With regards to urban-planning characteristics, the occupation type is regulated for the central, intermediate and peripheral areas of the city. In this last case, which is the most heterogeneous, areas of different character are identified: consolidated, in the process of consolidation, for extension, in the process of extension and consolidation, and for extension but compatible with industrial localities.

It is important to add that the regulation encourages the placing of housing proposals of low and medium densities in the urban borders, aiming at consolidating the city borders and to optimizing infrastructure provision.

In analyzing housing schemes for subsidized groups, most schemes in the extended areas of the city follow a small parceling pattern (that is to say 160m^2 for individual dwellings and a minimum plot size of 250m^2) resulting in situations of relatively small parceling in peripheral urban extensions.

After 10 years of this policy implementation this occupation type allows for the identification of the peripheral urban sectors urbanized as a result of the housing policy implementation (evident in the northeast and southeast border). Contrary to the situation observed in other Latin American cities, the periphery of Cordoba is not characterized by the localization of slums but by housing policy implementation.

Variables to Understand these Occupation Types

Doubtlessly, land value is the main variable in housing policy location in the urban borders. The city periphery offers wide fractions for urbanization with low land-value in the market, which because of its low initial cost, constitute an accessible offer for organized poor sectors.

However, this aspect is closely related to other features. Among them I mention the following:

1 – The characteristics of social housing policy in Argentina. As Yujnovsky[54] points out, social housing policy was centered on the concept of lack of housing stock, and in consequence, on the necessity of building new dwellings, which is to say that homes with housing demands is turned into new units. This situation has resulted in the prevalence of one type of dwelling answer: house in private ownership, the construction of new dwellings is more prevalent than any other type of policy

2 – The cost structure in public production of housing. Lumi[55] who investigates public housing production costs (particularly FONAVI) in Argentina has checked that the incidence of land value varies between 2.5% to 25% of the total investment, depending on urban locality and density. In the case of housing policies implemented in Cordoba, the percentage of land on the final investment accepted by public institutions is estimated in 10%.

3 - The pattern of low-density single housing units. In general terms, subsidized housing has very low densities (between 50 to 75 inhabitants per hectare), which increases the incidence of land values on the total investment. This could explain the localization in city-border sectors where land values are very low. They oscillate between US$5 to 15 per m^2, consequently, the plot value is estimated at US$800 to US$2,400 (for 160m^2) and US$1,000 to US$3,000 (for 200m^2).

It is evident that land value has a central significance, however, other variables demand an exhaustive analysis. Although public organizations establish maximum land value according to the final investment, they do not estimate the social costs that are derived from the localization of low-income population in the urban borders, neither the operative costs of maintenance of an extensive and low-density urban structure that this model contributes to materialize.

Final Comments

These two types of interventions (new private developments – social housing for subsidized sectors) account for contrasting situations in the context of urban expansion processes. The differences among them are summarized as follows:

1. Conditioning Guidelines on Localization

Countries are allowed to settle down in any part of the city territory as long as they do not interfere with the vial main system, while urbanization for subsidized sectors should be located within urbanized areas.

Given the importance of private investment in the residential market, it is worth thinking about whether the dichotomy between urban areas and rural areas (not urbanized) are still valid or if a new explanatory framework is needed in which the urban regulations answer to the complexity of territorial restructuring processes derived from private investments.

2. Location Variables

In the case of countries, location variables are centered in regional and metropolitan accessibility while in other case these variables are conditioned by land-value. In the first case, the limits for private expansion pattern is imposed by the capacity to afford infrastructure costs in a private form, while in social housing developments, the responsibility for guaranteeing infrastructure and service supplies is assumed by the local administration.

[54]54 Yujnovsky, O. (1984)

55 Lumi, S. (1989)

3. Urban Characteristic of Expansion Areas

In the case of new private developments a selective logic (based on the attractiveness of the place) is noted while housing policy assumes the urban characteristic defined by urban regulations (expansion areas, or consolidation areas, among others)

4. Impact of These Interventions

When analyzing the impact in terms of urbanized area, it is noted that new private developments reach 5,37% of the total urbanized area and include 5,623 lots while housing policy for subsidized sectors reach 1,48% of the urbanized area and include 7,447 lots. A high-income level corresponds with a larger section of the urbanized area.

When analyzing the impact on the territory, housing policy is only centered in the consolidation of peripheral sectors and do not intervene in intermediate or central city areas, while gated neighborhoods develop from the periphery toward the metropolitan area. In this case, the main challenge is the integrated planning of the metropolitan area in an effort to avoid territorial fragmentation.

Both types of interventions accentuate the processes of urban expansion. The analysis has identified the following preliminary effects:

1 – The analysis of the social dimension: is reveals increasing **segregation**. Urban expansion follows a segregated pattern. When analyzing the urban localization of the interventions, expansion areas are characterized by a homogeneous demand. High-income sectors are consolidating the tendency of development to the northwestern city-border, while low-income sectors are located toward the periphery in general and preferably on the southeastern border. The massive concentration of homogeneous demand increases segregation, urban violence and insecurity.

2 – The analysis of the economic dimension: is reveals growing **imbalances** among urban sectors. These types of interventions exemplify unequal situations in terms of the possibilities to afford services and urban equipment. Countries assumed, in a private way infrastructure extension and maintenance costs, while housing policy has to assume them with public funds. Consequently, the effects on the urban system are very different; the private expansion does not have direct costs on the urban system; public expansion implies costs, (in terms of extension and maintenance) which stress the strong dichotomies.

3 – The analysis of the territorial dimension: is reveal the shift from a pattern of continuous expansion to a pattern of **selective** expansion. Private capital intervenes in new areas of interest, constituting urban segments or fragments, sometimes like "new cities" within the city, or outside its limits.

In the context of these processes, housing policy also operates selectively (they only solve the imperatives of their own intervention and do not contemplate the effects on the urban system). They do not attenuate the negative effects of the expansion instead they accentuate them. In consequence, urban territory expresses favored and disfavored sectors as well as polarized areas observing strong imbalances among them. The fragmentation introduces disfunctionalities and undermines the possibilities to achieve sustainable growth.

The contrast in the urban territory becomes worse; a new social geography is becoming evident with the increment of poverty in strong contrast with the increase of wealth in higher-consumption sectors. Housing policy - analyzed through different types of interventions and their localization in the periphery of the city is a valid case study for the analysis of the processes of social polarization and space fragmentation that took place in the last period.

The dimensions of analysis of this problem are centered in the main challenges that urban development has to face in the Latin American cities: growing levels of social segregation, search for more efficiency in the urban dynamics that facilitates sustainable development, an efficiency in service provision as well as the quality of public space.

Taking this perspective of analysis there are some questions on the possible effects of this incipient processes of social polarization and imbalances among urban sectors. Are local governments able to implement urban policies to assist the imbalances? Is urban policy functional to the logic of private investment? Is it possible to overcome the lack of articulation between housing policy and urban policy?

Facing this new segregated city it is necessary to think about the evolution of the pattern and future scenarios for urban development. The new spaces of anodyne, excluded, violent and insecure city, demand active policies to preserve the cohesion of the territory, to guarantee sustainable development and to assist the social and spatial imbalances. These questions outline the evident necessity of building new explanatory frameworks in urban theory and local governments' capacities to intervene and to attenuate the effects of expansion.

Preliminary Questions to Proceed with the Analysis on the Effect of Residential Peripheral Developments and the Urban Form

This research is focused on the following questions:

What are the effects of suburban expansion on the existing city?

In the context of deep-seated changes in macro economic policy, structural adjustment, privatisation and concessioning of public services and the deregulation and decentralization that started in Argentina in the 90's, the interventions in the urban area shows evidence of a process of increasing social imbalance.

The spatial restructuring processes derived from the location of large investment (public and private) in the city structure have brought about a central issue: *whether urban planning, focusing on the development of the economic potential of the cit as a wholwy, is loosing sight of the social and spatial dimensions and in this way, is contributing to accentuate the processes of fragmentation and urban segregation.* The possibilities to achieve a more integrated urban development are related to the capacities that local governments have to negotiate between the interest of private investments and the collective interests of the citizens, that is to say, to guarantee appropriate levels in the infrastructure and services provision and to achieve a balanced urban growth.

Are public policies effective in their attempt to reduce the internal imbalances that expansion generates in the urban system?

After a decade, it seems that public policies -aiming to attract investment to the city area- have not succeeded in guiding balanced urban development and in addressing the social imbalances that the expansion produces.

In the context of political decentralization, one of the constraints to implement urban policy measures is the weak political capacity of the local government to direct urban development strategies according to the internal nature of the urban system. Another restriction is the lack of effective planning instruments to facilitate the implementation of coordinated actions between different cities to address urban expansion in the metropolitan area.

As stated by De Mattos 'as a consequence of the advances in restructuring and globalisation, territory production has been essentially in the hands of private capital acting basically in accordance with the guidelines of a scarcely regulated market'. (De Mattos1998: 58)

Sectors that are either favored or not by public and private investments, undermines the possibilities of economic prosperity and sustainable growth, bringing forward the question whether urban policy is effective to reduce the negative externalities derived from the expansion process.

What is the relationship between expansion and urban fragmentation?

The transformations registered in the urban system are influenced by macroeconomic pressures but also by changes in local forces adapting to this pressures. Amongst other is the change in the housing delivery system and the private and public production of residential areas. Apparently an accentuation of social exclusion, segregation and spatial fragmentation has occurred in certain expanded city areas. The emergence of private citadels[56] as well as the increase of impoverished areas and slums is noted as new housing development are built.

Rusk[57] in his attempt to explain the phenomenon of the peripheral growth and inner city decay that take place in North American cities has devised the concept of Cities without Suburbs. The central question he presents is: "Could the city defend itself against the circle of outward growth and inner abandonment by capturing its share of new growth?"

This idea is based on the Elasticity of cities, that is to say, the capacity to grow within their own administrative boundaries and to retain growth within these boundaries[58] either through expansion (elastic outward) or through concentration and increasing densities (elastic upward). An elastic city is able to contain the growth inside its own administrative limits or to maintain those limits even through expansion.

Rusk demonstrates that there is a correlation between the degree of social integration and economic prosperity in the metropolitan area as a whole,[59] *"Areas with a high segregation factor and wide income disparities between the central city and the suburbs are less economically successful"* .

Rosemann[60] points to three ideas that Rusk mentioned, which I find important to review in the framework of this work. These are:

- That idea of the elastic city to capture growth
- The need of a unified government (between the city and the suburbs) to promote integration and to achieve economic success.
- Cities without Suburbs is the concept of future urban development that facilitates integration, sustainable growth and no fiscal imbalances between the city and suburbs.

It is worth questioning at this stage if this theory, proposed in developed countries could be applied to Latin American cities, where the urban form is characterized by sprawl with widespread patterns of very low-density, an inefficient system of transport a

56 Marcuse (2000) p.4 explains citadels as exclusive enclaves for high-income sectors.
57 Rusk is mentioned by Rosemann, J. (1999) p.37
58 Rusk (1999) p.10
59 Rosemann J. (1999) p.36.
60 Roseman J. (1999) p.44

lack of integrated system of centralities, low income per capita, and a general impoverishment of the population.

Two central questions are whether the concept of elastic cities, devised for developed societies, could be applied in developing countries to achieve a more integrated urban form, or, on the contrary, if this concept can lead to accentuate fragmentation and to increase the costs of maintenance of an urban structure characterized by a low-density, incomplete occupation pattern, diseconomies in the urban dynamics, in a context of general impoverishment of the population.

In this sense, a preliminary hypothesis is that urban expansion is undermining the possibility of an integrated, efficient and balanced urban system, which is contrary to the current aims of strategic urban planning to pursue urban productivity.

Urban growth decreases the efficiency in the use of existing urban infrastructure involving increasing costs to preserve the functional dynamics of the whole city, it also has differential effects with regards to the possibilities of affordable urban extension. Higher-income sectors are moving to the suburbs in response to new proposals of the market, lower-income sectors are also located on the city periphery but the effects the expansion has on them seems to be quite different. The intermediate areas of the city are experiencing a process of de-investment and in some cases deterioration.

The restructuring process that takes place in the territory, as a consequence of structural adjustments and the logic of capitalism, works under a selective pattern of location. Contrary to the previous pattern, which retained continuity with the urban form, the current tendency in the real state development is the selective localization of private investments in the metropolitan area in places that offer comparative advantages, often without continuity with the existing urban layout.

This logic that chooses and excludes certain places in the territory according to their attractiveness (accessibility, environmental qualities, socio-economic conditions, and the availability of urban land, amongst others) contributes not only to increase urban growth but also to emphasize fragmentation and segregation of residential areas.

Social housing policy tends to emphasize urban expansion through the building of residential areas on the edges. The pattern of low density and extensive occupation that has lower initial cost –mainly land-value in the periphery- has been critiqued in public planning because of the lacking of infrastructure and urban facilities. Many important research has been done about the social costs that low-income sectors relocated in the borders are unable to carry (unemployment, unaffordable transport costs, loss of social and labor networks, difficulties to access to education, health, recreation, amongst others).

The phenomenon of **segregated suburban expansion**, that seems in conflict with the achievement of an integrated urban form, is the result of both, public and private intervention on the city structure.

Urban expansion implies specific investments in infrastructure extension and increasing maintenance costs, depending on the agents involved. To an extent this process becomes polarizes in the territory, and loses the balance of the urban structure and the possibilities for a sustainable urban system decreases. (In the sense that some city sectors that capture private/public investments are revalued while others are relegated in the process, devalued and impoverished)

According to the hypothesis previously mentioned the dimensions of analysis are centered in social, economic and spatial aspects; to investigate the effects that balanced/unbalanced growth produces on the area. Social effects of expansion are related to the degree of segregation and economic effects are related to the differences in terms of economic prosperity derived from expansion.

References

Burgess R., Carmona M., Kolstee T. (1997) *The challenge of sustainable cities. Neoliberalism and urban strategies in developing countries.* London, Zed Books

CEPAL. *De la urbanización acelerada a la consolidación de los asentamientos humanos en América Latina y el Caribe: el espacio regional.* Santiago de Chile 25 al 27 de octubre de 2000, 99 p.

Ciccolella, Pablo, (1999) "Globalización y dualización en la Región metropolitana de Buenos Aires. Grandes inversiones y reestructuración socioterritorial en los años 90"en *Revista EURE*, Vol XXV, Diciembre, Nro 76

De Mattos C., et alt. (1998a) *Globalización y territorio Impactos y perspectivas.* Pontificia Universidad Católica de Chile, Instituto de Estudios Urbanos, Fondo de cultura económica.

De Mattos C., (1998b) "Reestructuración crecimiento y expansión metropolitana en las economías emergentes latinoamericanas" en *Economía Sociedad y territorio,* Vol I, munero 4, p 723-754

Lumi, Susana. "Capítulo II Hacia una política habitacional" en Isuani E. Et alt., *Estado democrático y política social* I Edición Buenos Aires, Eudeba 1989, 264 p.

Marcuse and van Kempen, (2000) "Introduction" in Globalizing *Cities. A new spatial order?* Oxford, Blackwell, p 1-22

Marengo, Cecilia (1999) "Las políticas habitacionales y otras de impacto social en Córdoba" Estudio de caso: la relocalización de la Villa El Pocito. Beca CONICET (mimeo)

Marengo, Cecilia (2001) "Urbanizaciones privadas en el marco de los procesos de reestructuración metropolitana. El caso de Córdoba, Argentina" en *Globalización, Forma urbana y Gobernabilidad* Serie 4 Red Alfa - Ibis (en prensa)

Pradilla Cobos, Emilio, "Regiones o territorios, totalidad y fragmentos: reflexiones críticas sobre el estado de la teoría regional urbana" en *Revista EURE*, Vol..XXII Abril 1997 Nº 68. p. 45-56

Rosemann, J. (1999) "Lessons from America, Cities without suburbs" in *Planning Metropolis. Urban growth and social patterns.* Amsterdam, Deltametropool, p.34-47

Rusk, David, (1999) "Urban growth. Conversations on urban policy: the USA and the Netherlands" in *Planning Metropolis. Urban growth and social patterns.* Amsterdam, Deltametropool, p.7-32

Yujnovsky, O., (1984) *Claves políticas del problema habitacional en Argentina*, Grupo Editor Latinoamericano

Part III

Urban Governance

12

The Urban-Spatial Transformation of Quito and Guidelines for Its Spatial Planning

Diego Carrión M.

1. Urban-Spatial Transformations in Quito: Main Issues

During the period 1990-2000, Quito and its metropolitan region have experienced severe urban-spatial transformations. A new urban-regional layout has emerged during the nineties in Quito and in its metropolitan region. The new pattern shows, on the one hand, a process of consolidation of the main urban area and, on the other hand, the emergence of dispersed and scattered residential developments in the nearby valleys. At the same time, massive capital-intensive agriculture for export has appeared in these valleys. Changes have occurred because of urban deterioration, the presence of 'modern activities', the increase in poverty and informal employment, the extension of urban infrastructure, and changes in land use regulations.

Economic and social policies carried out by the State during the nineties, in the context of the so-called 'modernisation', have caused an acute process of social exclusion of wide segments of the population. In Quito, poverty levels have increased during these years enhancing marginality, unemployment, and social differences. Urban-spatial transformations that occurred in the period 1990-2000 have contributed to reinforce a kind of dualism, due to which two overlapping cities coexist: the formal and modern city; the informal and backward city.

The non-existence of a collective city project has led to spatial disintegration and deterioration of the urban image of the city given that urban agents have operated without any policy guidelines and/or controls. The deterioration of traditional areas – especially in of the Historic Centre- the scattered housing development and the inconvenient location of commerce, services and industry are clear examples of such processes.

2. Policy and Planning Guidelines for Spatial Development

2.1. Point of Departure: Society and Space

Space as a factor of development

Space is the intrinsic basis and resource for the existence of a society. It is from the human and physical dimensions of an area that development takes shape. Space is an accumulation of interdependent phenomena: scope of individual and collective identities (acts, conceptions and imageries); land (surface land and subsoil), air and water;

landscape and vital reference; availability of renewable and non-renewable natural resources. It also constitutes the spatial, temporal, and cultural condition of multiple, concurrent and recursive dimensions. It represents one of the key factors for the integral development of society. In the case of the Metropolitan District of Quito (MDQ), the diversity of identities, skills and competencies of its inhabitants, and the geographical and environmental diversity that characterises its territory, are sources of enormous richness and potential.

Therefore, a development project for the metropolitan region has to rely on its people and its territory. From this perspective, the question of space should be seen and treated as an opportunity for:

a) strengthening processes of international, national and regional integration;
b) developing links with the economical, political and technological environment of the modern world;
c) achieving prosperity and assuring an equitable and just distribution of material and non-material resources.

Ecuador is experiencing a serious economic and governance crisis, shortage of resources, fractured social tissue and deep-seated inequalities. The MDQ is part of such national context. Therefore, the municipal government should assume the task of anticipating the future in order to contribute to the reversal of these trends.

Current Context

During the last decade, changes in the international context have modified the socio-economic organisation of countries and cities of Latin America. Among these, it is worth noting the unexpected and changing conditions in which the labour market operate; the impact of the reordering of the world economy; the increasing inclusion of capital and technology in certain sectors of production; the diversification of exports- with emphasis in non-traditional products- and technological improvements in telecommunications and in transport systems.

The new world reality increasingly demands more constant shifts of the economy and a reorientation of the role of major cities. Progressive urban development needs to make use of the processes of integration, supported by the comparative and competitive advantages of each agglomeration and its hinterland. This context imposes a great challenge to the MDQ, which necessitates the adoption of new policies and projects in order to meet contemporary developmental requirements in a globalised world.

Quito is one of two major development poles of the country, together with Guayaquil. From a positive perspective, it means a series of advantages that could well be of benefit to for the future of the region and of the country. The MDQ is an area of economic and social regional development, enhanced by a process of integration of neighbouring parroquias, cantons, and provinces. The consolidation of the Quito region will come about once it complies with a set of competitive conditions oriented towards social development: adequate infrastructure (communications, energy, water), high education and health standards, job opportunities, and good governance. The concept of region implies necessarily a territorial substratum; therefore, it is necessary to establish long-term policy strategies that take into account its own environmental capacities, economic specificities, and social and cultural richness. In doing so, the Quito region will directly benefit and will contribute to the nation's development.

Vision for the Year 2020

By the year 2020, the Metropolitan District of Quito will be an urban and spatially modern complex, with approximately 3.300.000 inhabitants, consolidated as an Andean metropolis, developed on the basis of principles, policies and strategies of sustainable development, in accordance with its strength derived from its status as the capital of Ecuador. It will have a strong, competitive, diversified, and integrated economy linked to national and international markets, and will be a node of international importance in the country, due to its historical and cultural dimensions and for its geo-strategic position.

Quito will keep and expand its current position as Metropolitan District and its role as Capital of the country. It will actively and irreversibly assume new functions, responsibilities and resources as an a Local Government that will promote, manage and regulate local development in order to guarantee adequate living conditions for all citizens and to enhance competitiveness for production and service activities.

In the future it is seen Metropolitan District, integrated with the rest of the country as a generating axis of nationality, an ordered space, with welfare and solidarity for all. It will be of excellent environmental and esthetical quality; with historical and natural areas protected, preserved, and used with equity; secured from natural and human risks; with autonomous and efficient management capacity; governable and democratic for a united society with identity and self-esteem.

In order to achieve this vision for Quito within the near future, it is necessary to establish some overall guidelines for spatial management for a twenty years time period, from a social-technical position, and with a methodological progressive-strategic vision of development.

2.2. Policy Premises and Strategic Guidelines for a Spatial Development Plan for the MDQ

The re-configuration of the spatial structure of the Metropolitan District of Quito should be oriented towards its role as a modern metropolitan centre with strong regional influence. It should stimulate productivity, procure environmental sustainability, improve the quality of life and strengthen governance in physical and functional terms, as well as in political and administrative ambits. These broad policies should characterise the whole of the General Spatial Development Plan (PGDT).

Premises for Spatial Management Policies

Spatial management policies for the MDQ should be based upon the following premises.

- The Municipality has the responsibility of directing, regulating and controlling spatial development within the MDQ, in order to ensure democratic sense, equity, and sustainability.
- The Municipality should act as regulator, facilitator, and stimulator of actions geared towards the achievement of individual and collective welfare for the whole of the territory of the MDQ.
- The Municipality should also establish clear rules and adequate frameworks of action for the market to ensure that it contributes to the objectives of equity, unity and of fulfilment of the potential of the MDQ. Overcoming regional and local instability and inequality, and the enhancement of development are collective tasks that require consensus, co-ordination, and complementary actions over the whole range of

strengths and skills of both public sector and civil society. The unique spatial quality forms an emporium of cultural richness (material and non-material) that require concerted actions in order to improve its capacity and to overcome its weaknesses in stimulating local development from a new perspective and for bettering the quality of life of all its residents.

These policy premises for spatial management are the points of departure for stimulating processes of transformation in order to address the problems of the District. Institutions, mechanisms, and practices should be adequate in order to generate the necessary transformation for achieving the great ideals of change in the District.

Strategic Objectives

Planning objectives are meant to ensure the achievement of the development perspective and vision stated in the strategic definitions of the "Plan de Desarrollo Integral Quito Siglo XXI". These objectives are related to those central issues that the MDQ will have to address in the near future in order to overcome problems and to set up a positive development platform: overcoming socio-spatial instability; strengthening the development conditions of Quito; stimulating social and economic development, rescuing cultural identity; assuring the existence of a governance system based on the deepening of democracy and the improvement of management efficiency, and maintaining sustainable use of natural resources.

Methodological Guidelines of the PGDT

From a methodological point of view, the PGDT should be based on notions of continuity, generality, spatial integration, functional integration, developing structuring and flagship operations, flexibility, temporality.

Strategic Guidelines of the PGDT

In terms of strategic guidelines, the plan should be: anticipatory, systematic, a plan for influencing the organisation of space, a plan for developing areas for the construction of identity and citizenship, a plan for equitable spatial development, a plan for enhancing the linkage to external environs and to reaffirm competitiveness.

The Metropolitan Government for Spatial Management

The new organisation and spatial development of the MDQ implies enhancement of a process of correlation between the District's space and the regional and national environment, for attaining the integration of physical, economical, political, and cultural diversity at the regional and local levels. A process of development of this nature presupposes the existence of a Metropolitan Government being proactive, efficient, and conciliatory.

3. Spatial Planning Proposals

3.1. General Land Classification

It is proposed that the PGDT should define three general land use groupings: urban land, proposed urban land, and non-urban land. This classification responds to a criterion of current land characteristics, potential and vocational uses, and to land use restrictions due to environmental sustainability, given that it constitutes a fundamental resource for economic and social development for the future.

3.2. Population Distribution

The total MDQ population estimated for the year 2020 is 3.300.000 inhabitants. Considering a risk factor of 10% for planning purposes, the metropolitan population by 2020 may be approximately 3.630.000 inhabitants (3.410.000 inhabitants in urban and in proposed urban areas and 220.000 inhabitants in non-urban areas).

Population in Urban and in Proposed Urban Areas

In the MDQ there are heterogeneous spatial structures, that are changeable and with specific dynamics of economic, ecological, and physical characteristics. In urban land areas and in proposed urban areas, four processes of occupation and urban development can be identified: consolidated, under consolidation, under incorporation, and under conservation/protection. These processes and land development capacity allow the establishment of the real potential of building and densification of population. This exercise allows the determination of population distribution in order to guarantee environmental, functional, safe, and sustainable development of the District. It is estimated that the current urban area of the city of Quito will accommodate 2.260.000 inhabitants by the year 2020. Land development in other urban areas and in proposed urban areas, could house 1.150.000 inhabitants by the year 2020.

Population in the Non-Urban Area

Non-urban areas of the Metropolitan District of Quito include 19 parroquias. These settlements are considered to have a moderate rate of population growth. It is estimated that by the year 2020 these areas will support a total population of 220.000 inhabitants. Population distribution is compatible with the conservation of its land uses for traditional and for export agriculture, cattle, and ecological tourism.

3.3. A Spatial Model Based on a System of Centralities

Proposed spatial structure of the MDQ. The spatial structure proposed for the MDQ, is based on four components: multi-centrality of the territory, fundamental urban macro-centrality, environmental sustainability, and decentralisation.

System of Centralities

In order to enhance even development over space in the MDQ, a system of centralities based in the demography, geography, and history of the District is suggested. The system of centralities is meant to reinforce the macro-centrality role of the city (Quito), the consolidation of local urban centralities in the periphery and in rural territories of the MDQ, and to have a de-concentrated management system for improving efficiency and citizen participation.

Consolidation of the Metropolitan Macro-Centrality

In order to revert current expansion tendencies and to consolidate the metropolitan macro-centrality it is necessary to design a new city project for Quito, based on the existing city in accordance with new realities and future needs. It should consider improvement of urban efficiency, revitalisation of the urban image and the enhancement of Quito as Capital of the country and as a regional centre. The new city project is intended to reinforce the macro-centrality via interventions in representative and symbolic elements; the integration of expansion areas; the adequate use of under-utilised and abandoned structures and land; allocation of complementary roles to the different areas of the city; and strengthening the central role of the city for the whole of the MDQ. This set of actions should take into account tendencies, existing infrastructure, main activities, potential and weaknesses.

Consolidation of the metropolitan macro-centrality requires the existence of efficient systems of: communication, transport, and mobility; public spaces and green areas; and urban facilities, services and infrastructure. These systems should be linked to land uses and to the built environment.

Consolidation of a System of Sub-Centres in the Urban Periphery

In order to consolidate a system of centralities in the Metropolitan Area it is proposed to strengthen existing human settlements that have been historical nodes in their respective areas of influence in the nearby valleys of Quito (Tumbaco, Los Chillos and Pomasqui). Given current dispersed urbanisation trends in these valleys it is necessary to protect irrational land occupation; reinforce residential and industrial potential; concentrate provision of infrastructures and facilities thereby minimising costs; raise the quality of urbanisation; spatially and functionally integrate the territory; and protect the natural environment. Additionally, it is important for economic and social purposes to enhance traditional community and identity values through creating symbolic projects.

Consolidation of Metropolitan and Regional Agro-Productive Centres

In terms of the spatial organisation of the MDQ, it is important to consolidate the agro-productive role of several areas. The MDQ has a great economic potential in agrarian production for local consumption and for exports. From this perspective, it is necessary to stimulate agricultural productive processes through adequate communication facilities and credit and technical assistance. In the agropolitan region, it is important to assure social and economic development and sustainability of natural resources in accordance with the spatial structure of the MDQ. Therefore, there is a need to rationalise land use zoning and regulations based on the potential of natural resources and economic and social sustainability.

Creation of Management Centralities

In a complementary form to the consolidation of the system of centralities, it is necessary to create an efficient administrative management system based on de-concentration and decentralisation. The municipal administrative structure should be directly related with the spatial zoning and with the system of centralities in order to guarantee a better institutional relationship with community needs and to support social participation in planning, budgeting and monitoring.

3.4.Spatial Development through Key Metropolitan Projects

One of the key issues in order to overcome past tendencies of *post factum* spatial development and to assure the implementation of the Plan is to place *in site* a series of major infrastructural developments and facilities conceived to fix the desired model of spatial configuration and development. These projects could be carried out either directly by the Municipality or other governmental institutions, or by the private sector. These major projects are: productive and infrastructure projects, water provision and sanitation, roads and transport system, environmental and green space, historical centre, urban renewal and rehabilitation, and projects for the consolidation of centralities.

3.5. Plan Implementation and Management

The implementation process of the Plan presupposes an institutional involvement of the Municipality in five subsequent steps: debate, approval, dissemination, implementation and management, and monitoring and evaluation.

3. Concluding Remarks

Quito and its metropolitan area are facing critical challenges. Ecuador's economy has been under a dollarisation scheme since the year 2000, that implies a high dependency on exports. Quito, due to its historical background, has based its economy in State investments and employment, and in production for the internal market. These structures are exhausted. The QMD has to move towards a new setting, in which productivity and competitiveness stimulate public and private investment, creating business opportunities and jobs.

The General Spatial Development Plan is one of the key instruments meant to develop a set of strategic conditions to establish a new environment in order to enhance economic potential and to improve living conditions. The 2000-2020 Plan for the QMD incorporates rational land use and the implementation of large infrastructure and urban projects together with facilities for productive and consumption activities, under sustainability premises, as the basis for increasing competitive conditions oriented in the direction of social development.

References

- MDMQ-DGP, 1995. La Transición a Distrito Metropolitano de Quito. Quito.
- MDMQ-DGP, 1996 a. Régimen Distrital del Suelo. Propuesta. Quito.
- MDMQ-DGP 1996 b. El Mercado del Suelo en Quito. Quito.
- MDMQ-DGP, 2001. Plan General de Desarrollo Territorial. Quito.

13

Urban Policies in the South Cone:

An Analytical Approach to the cases of La Plata, Rosario and Santiago de Chile.

Maria J. Bazan Lopes

Presentation

This paper is referred to a PhD proposal about the relationship between urban spatial planning and housing policies in terms of convergence towards the sustainability of urban structure under territorial restructuring and globalisation trends, considering 3 city-cases in the South Cone of Latin America (La Plata, Rosario and Santiago de Chile). The study is currently in progress in the Housing and Urban Renewal Sector, Faculty of Architecture, TU Delft.

The main aim of this piece of work is to present the analysis of urban planning in the cases along the XX century. It is necessary to highlight that it is not our intention to compare the 3 cases. Further on, seeking upon the historical backgrounds from the national context -in terms of the development models adopted, the position of these cities in national and regional urban systems, the social structure, the political performances and the institutional development- to the local scenario –the economic basis, the social profile and demands, the local government role in the sectoral policies taken, the territorial and environmental conditions, and even the configuration of urban structure-, it is far too clear that the diverging characters of the cases avoid any methodological attempt in a comparative sense.

The analysis focuses on some crucial factors in the relationship between urban planning and housing policies related to the theoretical concepts; the institutional frameworks considering the national, provincial and local levers and the state model implemented; the specific performances based on the most significant examples whether the convergence or not of the sectoral policies under study; and the demographic change related to the urban structure.

The Context

The import substitution and industrialisation model of the economies in Latin America induced the increasing migrations from the rural areas to the urban centres since the late 30s with a declining trend in the mid-60s. As the main concentration of capital investments, employment and social opportunities were located in the capital cities, this population trend enhanced notoriously their weight in the domestic economies. In late 40s, it started to be evident that cities were not capable to receive such an important migration flow and emerged the so-called “villas miseria” in Argentina and “callampas” in Chile along the urban periphery, expanding the urbanised area totally lack of basic infrastructure provision, urban equipment and services.

Even when high GNP growth rates exceeded population growth rates in early 70s, the promised urbanisation and industrialisation benefits failed to materialise for a large proportion of population deteriorating living conditions, lowering employment opportunities and increasing income inequalities. Simultaneously developed countries started to shift industrial low aggregated value and labour intensive production to developing countries in search for cheap and unorganised labour force. The master plans have devised a vast technical and rational instruments, but could not meet the socio-economic and political needs and urbanising dynamics, whilst the job creation in industrial and services sectors had not enough absorption capacity to reach the pace. Slums and shantytowns continued proliferating while conventional housing was impossible to access for extended beneficiaries despite the subsidies, and therefore, housing shortage kept on increasing.

In the South Cone along the 80s, there was a dramatic slow-down in rates of economic growth associated with restricted demand conditions and a general decline in living standards and worsening rates and levels of unemployment, poverty and inequality particularly in cities. The urban systems were reorganised by a sort of homogenising urbanisation process enhancing the historical primacy of national capital cities -in economic, social and political terms- as highly- industrialised and specialised metropolitan areas, while the dynamism of a large group of middle cities -in terms of economic growth and population trends- decreased to a far secondary level, unable to place in the new context (Fadda Cori 1996).

The most accelerated urbanising rates in Latin America in the 90s belonged to the South Cone. The exponential urbanising curve in Latin America shows that urban population of 69 millions inhabitants in 1950 (41,32% of regional total population) increased to 391 millions in 2000 (75,34%), and in 2030 urban population will be 604 millions of inhabitants (83,20%) (Prats 2000). Argentina has a national urban population over 85% of total inhabitants (INDEC 1991), due to the stabilisation of the urbanisation process since the 70s given the low levels in natural growth rates and urban migration rates (Varpñarsky 1994). Meanwhile Chile has a more than 75% of its national population living in cities (Mac Donald et al 2000), due to the economic policies over the last 20 years and the liberation of land controls which accelerated the metropolisation trends (Gross Fuentes 1989).

The Institutional Framework of Urban Policies

The institutional system affects and shapes the urban spatial planning and housing policies in terms of policy-thinking, decision-making and implementation. This is a main factor in the analysis of the city-cases considering that some are regulated under a federal system (La Plata and Rosario) and a unitary system (Santiago).

Argentina has been organised as a federal system which implies that the provinces have the political power to define its own institutions, between them the local government regime. Beyond this, the formalisation of the regional level concerning to urban or regional planning represented always a political problem given the need of a power balance between the different institutional levels evolved by the addition of a new lever in the political structure. And it is far from a straightforward consequence of decentralisation process started in the past decade.

Traditionally urban planning in Argentina was a question mainly preserved to local government regulated by specific municipal codes, while the provinces are usually attached to land planning laws. Since the 60s, the municipalities have specific urban offices according to the requirement of master plans from the modernist approach and underpinned to the regionalisation and development poles proposed by national development systems. In the 80s, only the border provinces have specific development plans and offices and the national planning system disappears from the political agenda. After the state reform (started in 1991 and consolidated in 1994), the role of local government has been strengthened focusing on urban planning underpinned to the local economic growth and development.

Since the 40s, when housing policy got relevance in the political agenda at national level, has been an important shape of the government performances. The 40s and early 50s are characterised by housing policies addressed to improve the life quality of mid-urban classes underpinned to the substitutive industrialisation economic model, changing the urban development trends in middle and big cities along the country through large housing schemes in periphery with facilities. In the 70s after a slow-down performance of the housing policies in the 60s, the sectoral policies were strengthened by a centralised structure in terms of decision-making and execution and remaining up to the present. Although the political relevance of housing has been diminishing in the last decades in domestic and international agendas, it has been reduced remaining as part of social agenda at national and provincial levels, often without any presence in the local government's actions.

Chile is structured under a unitary system which means that the political decision-making is mainly concentrated in the central level. The traditional political structure is ordered (from top-down) in national, regional and communal level, being elective the national president and the local government but the head of the regional government (stablished in the 1980s) determined directly by the president. This administrative structure was enhanced by the new law of regional governments and the deepening of the municipalisation process in a renovated political environment.

Urban planning and housing policies were developed through a centralised structure, the Minister of Housing an Urbanism (MINVU) since the 60s in parallel offices. In the 90s, the new political situation contributed to decentralise urban planning in order to strengthen the commitment of local levels. There are 4 levels of planning practice: the national level in order to devise the national development policy; the regional level refers to the regional plan; the communal or municipal level -as the lowest- concerned with the local plans focusing on urban structure; and between the provincial and the communal, the "inter-communal" level is pointed out specifically to urban areas which embrace more than one communal jurisdiction, in order to link and articulate the local plans in a regulator plan. Although each planning level must consider the restrictions and possibilities given in the upper plan, there is no legal attachment in between. In the case of the "inter-communal" plan, there is no legal commitment to underpin the local plans to its lines.

Housing policies were always conscious about the historical demands of poor sectors in Chile as an important difference with the Argentine performance. In the 60s, the explosive location of the "callampas" (poor settlements) in the urban peripheries stressed the need of giving responses through large developments up to the early 70s. In the next decade, there was a main statement which subordinated the other actions in urban development: "the land is not a scarce resource", and therefore peripheries were sprawled out by private housing schemes and land developments according to the market orientation of domestic economy. The unique housing system devised in the 80s, has been perfected permanently regarding the improvement of the sectoral market functioning, and on the other side, the centralised character of the subsidy programs for the poor. At the regional level, there is only the delegation of the National Ministry of Housing and Urbanism (MINVU) in the Regional Service of Housing and Urbanism (SERVIU), which defines the local actions and specific subsidy programs for poor and lately on upgrade of poor neighbourhoods.

The City Planning

Although many similarities in economic development and planning practices along this century, South Cone's cities presented great differences in terms of urban structure depending on the historical legate, the role of cities in the accumulation process, the economic basis, and the nature of political processes. Regarding to this, the city-cases could be analysed in terms of similarities, differences and particularities of the instruments applied in urban planning. Without considering any possibility of comparison, the evolution of the ideas behind could be divided in the "beautiful city" model (the end of XIX century up to the 20s); a transitional period when the market dominated the urban scene and the modernist ideas started to be considered (up to the 50s); the modernist city (the 60s); the technical order of the city (the 70s up to the 80s); and the strategic approach (the 90s and nowadays).

The "beautiful city" model took some ideas from the "garden city" developed by Howard in England giving an spatial order to the urban functions and smoothing the transition from city to rural areas, in combination with the monumentality in the Paris renewal during the administration of Baron Haussman in 1850s to emphasise the city through a grid of avenues, parks and relevant buildings. These ideas structured the remaining Spanish colonial "chess-board" grid pattern considering the symbolic power of a modern city. The local bourgeoisie based on the agricultural economy, needs to enrich the urban environment to recreate the new ideals of "order and progress" enhanced in an incipient national society. In this line, we can consider the foundation of La Plata (1882) as the new provincial capital city; the Boulevard Plan of Rosario (1911) to ornament big avenues and parks to link the bourgeois residential neighbourhoods with the centre; and the plan of B. Vicuña Mackenna for Santiago (1878).

During the first decades of the XX century, the market demands dominated the urban growth by reproducing the Spanish grid remaining the concentric urban model, while the increasing demands of the new urban activities located along the road system in a transition from an agricultural export economy to a import substitution-and-industrialisation economy. New neighbourhoods emerged around the new industrial locations along the railroad system and later commercial centres. The city has a double structure: the concentric model for the residential use and the street network for the urban activities. Some plans considered this problematic in urban structure and intended to reorganise the city in formal and functional terms by defining areas and organising the new extensions. In the case of La Plata, the combination of the regular land subdivision pattern, the functional differentiation and scale of urban spaces and the popular housing typology (the "casa chorizo"), has made feasible the reproduction of the urban fabric by market with no major interventions to organise the urban development. The plan of Guido, Farengo y Della Paolera in Rosario (1935) intended to reorganise the railroad system inside the city but had no institutional support, on the other side little towns emerged around the train stations and the port. In Santiago the plan of K. Brunner (developed between 1924 and 1939) with institutional support from the National Government, worked on urban morphology in order to upgrade and give unity to the whole metropolitan area (the "Great Santiago").

In the 60s, urban planning was guided by fundamental questions addressed on social transformations and large problems in city. The Marxist theory analysed the impact of the monopolist capitalism in state and urban social movements. The structuralism replaced traditional studies from human ecology of the Chicago School and the economical point of view, considering physical-spatial phenomena as the non-perfect reflex of social processes in works of H. Lefebvre and M. Castells. On the other side, some studies started to explain the configuration of urban systems through the "dependency theory" (Prebisch 1964) as the effect of the "world imperialism, economic dependency and elite domination". The ECLAC uphold that national economic development was related to the implementation of regional planning systems modernising cities as "development poles" towards a social and economic redistribution and the consolidation of internal market. In line with this approach, a group of professionals from different disciplines devised for the microrregion of La Plata the URBIS Plan (1961) considering the "development pole" concepts and the functional specialisation of the urban centres. In Rosario, the Regulator Plan (1967) structured the city from the mobility systems (the port, the railroad system and the street system ranked). The Inter-communal Regulator Plan of Santiago (1960) considered the spatial models of modernism and the catholic French school with G. Bardet proposing the creation of a coordinating planning organism for the metropolitan area, the decentralisation of activities and services, and urban growth controls regarding the renewal of the central city. The ideas developed in the Modernism were carefully considered in the region through the master plans. The defined zoning, the separation of the 4 main functions of city, the high-densed housing typologies and the relevance of local activities to support the actions, were considered in physical proposals linked to a long-run vision about the city trends and the national scenario –characterised by the increasing rise-up of population, the industrialisation and a slow but continuous economic growth. These considerations and the lack of a political and operational tools, threatened the implementation with partial results.

In the 70s, the urban and regional theories in the region moved in the "local-regional-global" dichotomy, vanishing the regional planning as a possible intervention scale related to the non-democratic context. Meanwhile urban policies emphasised the clearance of urban slums and the "sites and services" programs in peripheries. A more practical and operational vision tinged the urban planning in the region, turning the scope into the city itself to limit and order the urban sprawl. The instruments considered were zoning, precised land controls on new developments and detailed building codes based on a technical understanding of spatial structure, strengthening the spatial and functional centrality of the urban structure. On the contrary, the application of this instruments accelerated the conversion of rural land into urban areas by private sector and large housing schemes in peripheries, and restricted more the access of the poor to land through the formal market. In La Plata, it is relevant a new normative focused on land use (1978) considering the city isolated from its microregion which facilitated the pyramidal shape of the city. The "Great Rosario" Plan (1972) from an inter-municipal entity, elaborated a metropolitan development scheme to devise communal plans and structural projects focusing on an integrated transport system. On the contrary to this scope, the Plan of Urban Upgrade Corporation (CORMU) in Santiago (1975) was framed by the territorial development beyond the national frontiers through transport and urban corridors and defined sub-systems by complexity and functioning; later on the land liberalisation (1979) in the metropolitan area activated the real estate market in peripheral and rural areas, doubling the urban extension in the metropolitan area in only 20 years.

The modernising urban policies could not reach the initial goals to update urban structures based on the implementation of land use patterns. The master plans were too comprehensive in goals which contemplated social and spatial equity, concentrated on spatial and land issues, expensive in resources, time-consuming in preparation, and with a wide weakness in the articulation between plan-making and decision-making. The planning system was highly centralised with rigid bureaucracies, weak technical coordination, a top-down planning fashion, local interests and communities excluded and poorly articulated with urban development forces. Moreover, modernist design and planning conceptions were alien to the common people as radical, utopian and voluntary, going against the spirit and values embodied in the existent city. On the other side, policy attempts to restrict squatting and clear slums became increasingly unviable politically resisted by increasing urban social movements. From these experiences, a new urban structure arose in line with demands shaped by the accelerated the pace of metropolisation; the transformation of spatial structure from a mono-concentric into a non-articulated polycentric model; the increasing social segregation and stratification with increasing levels of violence and insecurity; the shortage in urban facilities and infrastructure supply; the impoverishment of middle income groups due to the inelasticity of labour markets under restructuring process; and the environmental crisis due to the non-renewal of natural resources.

The increasing critique of Welfare state policies and Marxist theories driven by the neo-liberalism, has enhanced market as the new distributive system in the 80s. The “urban-regional” interphase was analysed through the local government role, sectoral studies, the starting decentralisation and the civil participation but showed also the increasing ‘academy-policy’ dichotomy. Innercity functions have been reorganised towards the global markets demands and urban space has been fragmented due to the increasing social polarisation in a complex structure. In line with this, urban policies have become restructuring policies considering the demands of new technologies, infrastructure and public services in search of competitive advantages through the offer of business centre locations; specific projects on public space and urban infrastructure as part of decentralisation of city functions; the recreation of symbolic centrality through culture, leisure and the enhancement of local identity; the diminish of social polarisation by “solidarity networks”; the holistic consideration of the environmental dimension; and the articulation of different participative arenas in decision-making.

In the 90s, more important than production of physical results was the device of political, institutional and managerial changes. The plans focus on the relevance of upgrading urban structure towards the new global demands opening the scope of intervention to the microregional and the metropolitan scale in territorial planning. La Plata developed a set of programs (Re-foundation of the Capital Microregion in 1994, administrative decentralisation in 1996, Local Strategic Plan in 1998, Participative Municipal Budget in 1999, and the new land use code in 2001) in order to consolidate its economic and political position as a south node of the metropolitan area of Buenos Aires related to the road system and the port. The Strategic Plan of Rosario (PER) considers specially the bi-oceanic urban corridor “Santiago-Sao Paulo” related to the port, the cereal production oriented to exportation, the river-road projected to Asunción

("Hidrovía") and the formal articulation of the metropolitan area; the PER is complemented by other instruments (Decentralisation Program from 1996 and the updating of the Director Plan in 2001) which emphasises the decentralisation of city government and a wide set of infrastructure projects. Santiago has been positioned as the linkage of the South Cone to the Pacific and the Asian markets (the Regional Development Strategy of 1990, Regional Plan on Urban Development in 1992 and the Metropolitan or Inter-communal Regulator Plan of 1994); the metropolitan region has been restructured in a poly-nuclear structure by the creation of relevant public spaces and the implementation of environmental actions (supported by the Environmental Sustainable Territorial Planning Project –OTAS- since 1998).

Bibliography

Banco Mundial (1994) Vivienda. Un entorno propicio para el mercado habitacional. Con suplementos técnicos, Documento de Política del Banco Mundial, Washington, 1ra. Edición en español.

Boisier S. (1998) "Post-scriptum sobre desarrollo regional: Modelos reales y modelos mentales", Revista EURE Vol XXIV N.72, Septiembre 1998, Santiago de Chile.

Borja J, Perdigo J, Palomar Llovet M, Botella M & Castells M (1987) Organización y descentralización municipal, Buenos Aires (Arg), Col. Urbanismo y Administracion Local, EUDEBA.

Burgess R. and Carmona M. (2000) "Urban renewal and development strategies", in: Carmona M. (ed.) (2000) Reader 2000, D4 Module, Bouwkunde, TU-Delft.

Clichevsky N, Herzer H, Pirez P & Satterwhaite D (1990) Construcción y administración de la ciudad latinoamericana, Buenos Aires, IIED-AL, Grupo Editor Latinoamericano.

Coraggio J L (1999) "Competir por el capital o competir por la gente? Sentidos alternativos de la planificación estratégica metropolitana », in UNIVERSIDAD

Etchegaray A, Giraldo F, Mejia J & Mac Donald (1997) Las reformas sociales en acción: Vivienda, Santiago de Chile, Serie Politicas Sociales No 20, ECLAC, UUNN.

Fernández Guell J.M. (1997) Planificación estratégica de ciudades, Gustavo Gili Ed., Barcelona.

Gilbert A. (1993) "Third World cities: The changing national settlement system", in: Carmona M. (ed.) (2000) Reader 2000, D4 Module, Bouwkunde, TU-Delft.

Hall P. (1996) Cities of Tomorrow – History of Urbanism in the XX Century.

Hintze S. (Org.) (1996) Políticas sociales - Contribución al debate teórico-metodológico, Programa Especial de Investigación sobre Estado y Políticas Públicas N°11, Colección CEA-CBC, Sec. De Ciencia y Técnica, UBA, BA.

Kliksberg B & Sulbrandt (1999) "America Latina: Una región en riesgo – Pobreza, inequidad e institucionalidad social", Banco Mundial, mimeo.

Kullock D. (1999) Urbanismo y Ciudad, Maestría en Planificación Urbana y Regional, Eudeba, Bs. As.

Mac Donald J & Simioni D (2000) Urban Consensus. Contributions from the Latin American and the Caribbean Regional Plans of Action on Human Settlements, Serie Medio Ambiente y Desarrollo No21, Santiago de Chile, ECLAC, June.

Municipalidad De La Plata (1999) Bases Estratégicas para el Desarrollo Sustentable de La Plata, Documento Final del Proceso Participativo, La Plata.

Municipalidad De Rosario (1997) La ciudad de Rosario – Los alcances de una gestión descentralizada – La delimitación de distritos, Programa de Descentralización y Modernización, Secretaria General, Rosario.

Pradilla Cobos E. (1997) "Regiones o territories, totalidad o fragmentos: Reflexiones críticas sobre el estado de la teoría regional y urbana", Revista EURE Vol. XXII N.68, Abril 1997, Santiago de Chile.

Provincia De Buenos Aires (1996) Planificación estratégica urbana y territorial – Herramientas de politicas publicas municipales – Seminario Internacional de Gobierno para Intendentes, Subsecretaria de Asuntos Municipales y Fundación Bonaerense de Ciencias de la Administración, La Plata.

Raposo I M (1998) "Rosario y el desafío the liderar las transformaciones urbanas", in Seminar on Urban Research: The New Millennium and the Urban Issue, Gino Germani Institute, University of Buenos Aires.

Ravella O (2001) Orígenes, presente y futuro de la planificación urbano regional, Editorial de la Universidad Nacional de La Plata, La Plata.

Rusk D (1999) "Segregation and Sprawl: The Region's Principal Challenges", in www.lcmoc.org/Drspeech.htm

Universidad Nacional De La Plata and Instituto De Estudios De Administracion Local (1983) La Plata Ciudad Nueva Ciudad Antigua – Historia, forma y estructura de un espacio urbano singular, Madrid.

Vanderschueren F, Wegelin E & Wekwete K (1996) Policy Programme Options for Urban Poverty Reduction – A Framework for Action at the Municipal Level,

Van Kempen R. and Marcuse P. (1997) "A new spatial order in the cities?", in: Carmona M. (ed.) (2000) Reader 2000, D4 Module, Bouwkunde, TU-Delft.

Vapñarsky C (1994) "Crecimiento urbano diferencial y migraciones en la Argentina: Cambios de tendencias desde 1970", en Fernández Wagner R comp. (1994) Urbanización y Vivienda – Aportes al estado de la cuestión, CETyV, Facultad de Arquitectura Urbanismo y Diseño, Universidad Nacional de Mar Del Plata.

14

A Decade of Proposals and Debates around the Management of the Retiro Project. Buenos Aires 1991/2001

Beatriz Cuenya

Introduction

This article aims to reconstruct the unfinished, unwritten and largely unknown history of the Retiro Project, the largest urban rehabilitation scheme of the city. The objective of the project is to redevelop the strategic area of Retiro as the most important transportation node of the country (railways, harbor and buses), the extension of the central administrative district, a high cost residential area, a set of public parks and a precarious settlement (villa miseria) called *villa 31.* With a population of 12 thousand people in 2000, it is the oldest in the city and has a long history of resistance to evictions.

This huge undertaking aimed to refurbish the terminal stations of trains and in this way to release some 130ha of land which will be destined to new uses: a modern public transport center, commercial buildings and high standard residential areas, convention and cultural centers, international level hotels and vast green areas. In other words, the Retiro Project strives for the development of a new front for the city of Buenos Aires and in this way to become competitive at regional and international levels.

In this sense, the RP is, undoubtedly, a good example of the new paradigm of urban development, which emerges in large cities of the world in times of globalization: the creation of new centralities in fragments of the old city. By means of urban operations that involve massive investments, those areas that previously were considered marginal are being reconstituted as central and modern areas, efficient and functional, capable of attracting and housing the internationalized sector of the economy and its local support platform. The brand-new territorial complexes with their facilities of advanced communications, high class hotels, housing, commercial malls and luxury offices, carefully designed by renowned architects contribute to change the shape of the city and to conform what has been called the second-generation metropolis, i.e. the city of latest modernism.

Recent urban literature has pointed out three undesired impacts in the pattern of transformation of the city.

- The key role of large private investors associated with international holdings whose decisions of how and where to invest are consistently out of governments' control.
- Privatization of public space, gentrification and social polarization in the region since investment concentrate in certain places and tend to expel groups of former residents

and

- Weakening of tools for comprehensive planning while privileging the design of the city by pieces or fragments.

In the case of the Retiro Project, the ultimate impacts are still uncertain. However, almost 11 years of proposals and debates around its implementation are a clear example of how a certain realm of local interests, in a specific political, institutional and socio-cultural context, constitute key aspects for explaining the direction and changes of gear. Founded with a clear real estate logic, a limited urban design proposal, a bad solution for transportation and a social arrangement based on exclusion, a proposal was submitted which was supposed to provide an integrative response to all of these dimension from a more strategic point of view. This partial solution may constitute a challenge to the consequences that are associated with globalization, to its investment patterns and to its ideology of privatism.

In this sense, RP may be seen as a scenario in which a set of public and private players, with diverse and contradictory interests are confronting their opinions and proposals and have taken decisions, established agreements, enacted conflicts and fights geared towards their own views of the project and also associated to realms of power and authority on the city.

From the point of view of public administration, the Retiro Project is the main stem of the relation between national forces and the government of the city, the latter being clearly affected in the mid-period under analysis, when the city acquired juridical autonomy.

In short, the history of the RP has been complex and has presented many aspects, among which, private and public, regulation and market, conflict and control, physical configuration and social composition have interacted in a continuous way.

This paper tries to show these aspects by means of an analysis that is descriptive and follows the chronological order of the decisions and actions undertaken around this project. All information stems from an intensive investigation of journalistic sources, national and municipal legislation (laws, decrees and ordinances) official documents on the project when available (a good part of the data is unavailable) and interviews with officials and other key actors involved in the subject. My thanks to all of them for having helped me to reconstruct the intricate progress of this project.

I - First Project for the Retiro Area, Conflicts on the Management Scene and first Debate around the Real Estate Logic present in the Project. 1991 - 1995

1. Background

1.1. Privatization of Railway Services and Subsidy Funds for the Concessionaires.

The project of urban redevelopment of the Retiro area emerged as an initiative of the National Government, with a background which was not urban at all, but essentially economic and financial, as it is was necessary to obtain resources in order to pay the necessary subsidies to the concessionaires of passenger train services in the Metropolitan area of Buenos Aires. This obligation was contracted by virtue of the privatization of railways in the frame of the State Reform.

In order to do so, the National Government approved (by means of Decree 1143/91) the creation of a Fund which might capture resources derived from real estate and other goods which were being left unused by the concession and rationalization of those services. Furthermore, it authorized the Ministry of Economy and Public Works and Services (Ministerio de Obras y Servicios Públicos), together with the Municipality of Buenos Aires (the authority that had to implement the decree) to attend to this purpose by a) meeting a presentation of proposals for urban development and the corresponding offer for their implementation, and b) to engage the assistance of experts on the subject.

While economic motives were not explicitly declared in the document of the Retiro Project that was elaborated and presented in 1993, they can be clearly identified in the before-mentioned decree, which directed the preliminary actions undertaken by the National Government in this area. Later, the interest and the urgency for selling and exploiting these areas were evident in the recurrent pressure which the Government exercised all along the unraveling of this project in order to initiate it.

1.2. First Study of Feasibility of Real Estate Development: a Forgotten Report Filed

In May 1991, the Argentine Government asked a Canadian consulting agency, Canac International INC[61] to make a preliminary study on the situation of the railways in the Retiro Area. This study had to be ready in three months, since Argentine authorities wanted to call for a swift international offer in order to develop the properties under consideration. This document, produced by Canadian consultants and their local associates was the first stage of further, more detailed analysis which were undertaken on the assets of FEMESA[62] and of Ferrocarriles Argentinos (well-known as the Retiro Complex) at that moment to be ordered and classified. The purpose of this study was to find out what properties of the railways in the Retiro area would remain vacant for further private development. In this, the identification of any special physical condition that might be considered an obstacle to real estate development had to be included.[63]

This study mentions "recent announcements" on the part of Port authorities, together with the city of Buenos Aires about the release of considerable properties for private development, mainly offices, hotels, a shopping center and exclusive condominiums. Furthermore, this report quotes previous studies of 5 or 6 years earlier. Three of them focused on the improvement of existing facilities, without taking into account the use of property for private redevelopment.[64] However, the work done by Ferrocarriles Argentinos, best known as that of "the 80 meters" was concentrated on a piece of land parallel to Avenida Libertador. Their conclusion was that it seemed practical to relocate

---

61 Consultants linked to Canadian railways, with experience in railway rationalization in cities such as Montreal, Toronto, and others.

62 FEMESA is a company created in the early 90s to operate all the independent suburban train services from Ferrocarriles Argentinos.

63 Taking into account this demand, it is interesting to realize that in the section "Description of existing facilities", the study makes detailed reference to existing assets, but does not mention the existence of villa 31.

64 A Study undertaken by Spanish consultants was dedicated to a reorganization of all facilities in the Retiro complex. Another study by FA dealt with the consolidation of interurban and suburban trains between lines FC Mitre and FC San Martin. The latter was an extension of certain recommendations done by the Spanish consultants. In addition, Soviet consultants were engaged to study the electrification of FC San Martin, including the provision of electric locomotives.

and/or abandon buildings and rails in the area, thus liberating some 3ha for redevelopment. Which means that the idea of commercially exploiting the released land had been already explored (Canac International INC. 1991).

The Canac International paper pointed to the need to undertake studies in more depth. It also advanced the conclusion that a portion of land of about 100ha could be separated from the railways in order to be redeveloped, leaving to the train a strip of some 100 meters between the railway station of FC Mitre and FC Belgrano in which the whole Retiro Complex could be developed. They recommended the consolidation of the interurban and suburban trains from the FC San Martin to the FC Mitre, keeping FC Belgrano aside due to its narrow gauge.

This conclusion appeared very reasonable in the eyes of the Argentine transportation experts. "This was an obvious conclusion which any team of Argentine engineers with expertise on the subject of transportation would have arrived at. There is a very run-down station (FC San Martin), another magnificent one (FC Mitre) and a third one, smaller but in good shape (FC Belgrano) that due to its narrow gauge is not fit to be touched. In short, that all the trains of the San Martin railways could be moved to the Mitre Station; that an urban development could be envisaged on the land overlooking Avenida Libertador; and that the area released by the San Martin railways was fit for something that could be defined later on." (Interview)

In spite of the reasonable conclusions and recommendations, the Argentine Government decided to support the idea that ample resources could be obtained by the development of enormous areas without endangering the operation of railways. As a consequence, they continued to take measures to put the Project underway.

1.3. Authorization for Selling Land in the Retiro Area and Prefiguration of a Management Model with Centralization of Decisions in a National Agency

In April, 1992, Decree 602 was issued in which the National Executive transferred to a Commission for Selling State Property[65] all the buildings pertaining to the National Government, to the Argentine Railways, to Metropolitan Railways and the General Administration of Ports located in the Retiro area[66]. In the outline of the decree, it was clearly expressed that significant benefits with regard to the urbanization of this area, were to be expected: "Given the importance of real estate values in the properties which surround this area, an adequate management of urbanization and later commercialization of buildings involved in said area, will result in obtaining of important revenues for the National State."

The relevance of this decree lies not only in that it authorizes to sell the land and exploit the buildings, but also in that it defined the way in which the decisions in this area would have to be managed. It preshaped a model of urban management, with centralization of key decisions in the national agency: A Commission for Selling State Property. This Commission expressly received the authorization that were inherent to the Ministry of Economy together with the Municipality of Buenos Aires according to the former Decree 1143/91.

---

65 This Commission was created by means of Decree 2137/91 and later became the Undersecretary for the Administration of Assets, then ONABE (National Agency of State Assets) and finally ENABIEF. These were the entities which took charge of the functions originally destined to this commission.

66 The defined area encompasses more than 200 Hectares and is limited by the street Salguero in the NW, Rio de la Plata to the N and E; the rails of Ferrocarril Mitre, Avenida del Libertador and Avenida E Madero to the SW and W and the extension of Avenida Coórdoba to the South.

The Commission was endowed with the following tasks: a) engage the necessary studies for the outline of an urban development master plan and the study of necessary facilities to facilitate real estate investment in the area; b) to determine what buildings had to be assigned to the harbor and railways and what others should be released in order to be sold or given in concessions for residential, commercial, recreation or green spaces use, c) to find a consistency of needs for all the sectors involved and allow for the design of an urban plan with the participation of the Municipality.

The Commission also received "power to propose to competent authorities of the municipality the urban zoning they considered most adequate after finishing the corresponding studies and negotiate necessary changes." It also received, of course, the power to "sell, make concessions, give in total or partial lease all buildings which are a property of the National Government, Metropolitan Argentine Railways and the General Administration of Ports, once they are listed and approved by the competent authority." Finally, it had the power to declare the retraction of all concessions and/or leases granted in the area which could possibly endanger the outline of a city plan. (Decree 602/92)

2. Essentials of the first project for the Retiro Area: radical change with respect to the preliminary study

Towards mid-1992, the National Government, with the support of the World Bank and the United Nations Program for Development (UNDP) launched an offer to present expert knowledge for studying the Retiro area, after which they decided to engage the same firm that had undertaken the previous report, i.e. Canac International[67]. With this firm, others also participated: CN Real Estate and IBI Group of Canada and the local enterprises Technical Consultants Federico Camba and Associates, Lorenzo Escurra Medrano SA and Daniel Badens and Associates as real estate dealers. The total value of this contract was nearly a million dollars.

After a few days, the foreign consultants defined the project's alternatives. The speed with which this stage was finished and the lack of interest shown by the experts in maintaining conversations with the Argentine professionals designated as local counterparts (in the facilities area) show the existence of preconceived ideas. Expectations that the Canadian consultants would propose "a good study", in view of their former experience and the ample resources now available, were proved wrong. These studies went directly to the key objective of the National Government: a maximization of land to be released from railway use on the stretch close to Avenida Libertador.

As a consequence, this proposal implied a radical change with respect to the railway solution suggested in the first study. Instead of consolidating the trains from the San Martin to the FC Mitre, they proposed the opposite: to unify the terminal passenger stations in the area occupied by the stations of the San Martin and Belgrano lines, while liberating the FC Mitre for commercial and public use. This proposal assumes moving the train terminals to the North (towards the bus terminal) and recycling the FC Mitre terminal and the release of 93ha for real estate development. With this, the Government hoped to collect some 300 million dollars of which 90 million would have to be invested in new facilities. This area comprises approximately 50% of the one defined by Decree 602/92.

67 In the competition, two other European consultants had participated who were linked to the real estate branches of the French and British railways.

In September, 1993, the Retiro Area Project was presented with that name to the public, in an official presentation at the main headquarters of the National Bank (Banco de la Nacion). The speeches were made by the President of the Nation himself (Carlos Menem) and by his Minister of Economy (Domingo Cavallo) before an audience of officials and businessmen.

3. Critical Views of the Project

From the moment of its presentation, the Retiro Project received a great amount of critical reviews with regard to two basic questions. On the one hand, the purely real estate interests this project seemed to represent which were expressed in a very narrow urban design conception of the proposal. On the other, the lack of consultation, during the creation of the project, with local professionals and the city's authorities who know about decision-making and urban policies.

3.1. The View of the Journalist Media

From the beginning, newspapers characterized this proposal as a real estate mega project. Clarin, the newspaper with largest circulation in the country, spread the news under the title "The Retiro train station is moved in order to subdivide 93ha" and summarized it in the following way:

> The Retiro Area Project is the new plan announced by the Minister of Economy Domingo Cavallo. The idea is to move the railway station: it will be moved, together with the bus terminal to where the San Martin and Belgrano terminals are located now. Railway lines will change places towards the river. Part of this project will also be the subdivision of 93ha currently occupied by the railway lines; half of it will be sold to private compnaies and with this money works will be undertaken which will initially cost 90 million dollars (*Clarin, September 16, 1993*)

Another newspaper, Pagina 12, put the title "Retiro for Sale with a capital S: the Government sells 93ha in the most expensive part of Buenos Aires" and continues with the following text:

> (...) The government has discovered a new box with the family jewels, since the most valuable ones have been sold (it refers to the privatization of public service enterprises). (...) The preliminary study, with a budget of 900.000 dollars loaned by the World Bank, was conducted by the Canadian Canac International, with the participation of local firms. This area will be divided from North to South into four regions: a residential, low-density one, another institutional one, yet another residential medium-density one and finally, a medium density residential and for office area. For the stretch of 12ha without railway lines bordering Libertador which will be the first one to be sold, it is known that there are several chains of luxury hotels interested in them, among others the Ritz-Carlton and the Mirage. This location will continue the luxury chain initiated with the nearby Hyatt and Caesar's *(Diario Pagina 12, September 16, 1993).*

3.2. The View of the Experts

The well-known urban planner Odilia Suarez offered three main objections to the official project:

> I have three objections. First, the degradation of a high-density residential area such as Barrio Norte, under the pretence of developing some 700.000 square meters more or less 50% of what is today the central business district. The project would

only dismember this center overlapping the administrative with the high-prestige residential area.

Secondly, there will be more traffic jams and movement of vehicles in an already saturated area (...) If we add more offices and a large shopping center we will face a disaster equivalent to the one we would have if we were to move a train station and a bus terminal to Plaza de Mayo (...) It is not true either that new green spaces will be gained since in the plans that were presented there are no others than the existent ones, except for a small fringe bordering the railwayline.

Third, the agony of the port of Buenos Aires. There are no projects for the harbor. They are not telling us where to go with the containers which are at this point crowding areas of the Belgrano railways and the Southern Coastal area. Instead of reducing the space for entering the harbor, one should improve the gate to train freight (...) Expansion of the city's center should be made towards Puerto Madero and Constitucion. Later, they can build condominiums and even a hotel, if they want to do so", *(Pagina 12, September 23, 1993)*

On the other hand, the famous architect Clorindo Testa criticized the project very harshly, emphasizing the lack of consultation with local professionals and the limited outlook of the proposal.

By hiring Canadian consultants the professional councils who have ethic tribunals, were disregarded. This happens when the Government points with his hand, when there is no consensus and of course, a suspicion remains." (Pagina 12, September 23, 1993)

This project could be evaluated with the lowest grade by any professor of any School of architecture. They dare to mark as green spaces certain parts that are beneath the highways. The lack of culture of the authorities is unbelievable since they seem not to realize the enormous danger underlying the subdivision of the city" *(Clarin Arquitectura, September 25, 1993)*

Severe comments were expressed also by the urban historian Adrian Gorelik:

Exactly as in Puerto Madero where luxury apartments and offices are not needed, but nevertheless are being built, in Retiro the public powers show their theory that the only thing which must guide the development of the city is the real estate logic. Retiro is the manifestation of a Government that gives up any task of urban or social compensation and regards the city as the exclusive realm for private businesses... *(Diario Pagina 12, Suplemento Futuro, September 25, 1993)*

3.3. The Stance of the Central Society of Architects (SCA)

In September 1993, the SCA released a strong critical view, pointing out that:

The National Government insists on its role as simple realtor, acting with an urban shortsightedness and a highly speculative spirit in such a way that the first stage of the project will most probably be the only one to be accomplished. It consists of the release for sale of 12ha facing Avenida del Libertador, from Callao to Retiro in order to destine this land for high-density offices *(FOT=7)*.

Furthermore, the SCA enumerated a set of undesirable impacts and finally demanded the participation of technical agencies of the city and the professional associations in the treatment of this subject.

4. Conflicts on the Management Scene

4.1. Opposition of the Municipal Council to the Retiro project

The Municipal Executive and the city councilors demanded participation in the Retiro project. Although the largest part of the area in question belong to the National State, the municipality has the power to dictate those policies which govern the use of urban spaces. Thus, if the project is not disputed by the municipal executive it still has to be approved by the Municipal Council (legislative power)[68], While the Mayor of the city (Saul Bouer) was still an official designated by the Nation's President, a fact that ensured the agreement with the national initiative, in the Municipal Council the various political groupings were represented and a strong presence of opposition parties. Debates and discussion of the project were treated twice in this manner:

a) In September, 1993, opposition tried, without success, to freeze the Retiro Project. The strategy of the main opposition group (Union Civica Radical) was to promote an ordinance in which Retiro would have become an area for Future Urbanization. In that way it would have been impossible to do any work without agreements between the Government, the associations of architects and urban planners and the non-governmental organizations. It also meant that anything to be built on the premises would have to be enforced through an ordinance. For the radical legislators the project presented "resembled more a subdivision". The project also encountered opposition in other parties such as the Federal, the Socialist Unity and the Democratic Left. The socialists demanded a park development, that is to say, one exclusively intended for green spaces.[69] (*Clarin, September 25, 1993*)

b) In October 1993, the Municipal Council barred the Government's Retiro Project. After several delays the MC finally destined the FU (Future Urbanization) for the 93ha of the Retiro Area Project (Ordinance Nr.47.190/93). This means that to whatever purpose this land may be destined, the Council will have to discuss its zoning, i.e. each modification will have to be done with an ordinance.[70]

4.2. Measures to Soften the Conflict and Put the Project Underway

In order to avoid a worsening of the conflict, the National Government decided to summon the professional associations of architects and engineers to hear their opinions and discuss the matter. While the Argentine Center of Engineers (CAI) declined the offer[71], the Central society of Architects accepted the invitation. In December 1993 an agreement was signed between the Argentine Railways, the Municipality and the SCA with the goal of having an opinion on the Project and outline new criteria with consensus which would overcome the other objections.

---

68 The allocation of land uses in the city is a right inherent to the MC, enforced by the Municipal Organic Law since 1972.

69 The discussion of the project took place in a special session that lasted from the afternoon of Thursday, September 23, to the early hours of Friday, the 24th. In spite of the unipersonal benches, the radicalism could not block the Nation's Executive project. They needed 31 votes in order to change the proposal into an ordinance, but they managed only to gather 30 votes. The session of the Council that had to deal with the controversial issue was postponed for October 7.

70 Actually, 90% of the land was already UF, with the exception of two strips: one near to the harbor, which is U10 (permits, among other things to build offices, museums, supermakets and radio and TV stations) and other on the opposite side on Libertador (between Callao and Cerrito) which has special regulations.

71 What this entity estimated was that the analysis of the urban issues around Retiro should not be limited to a study of 94 Hectares and even so, these studies could not be undertaken with the required speed.

After a few months of work, in October 1994, the SCA produced the first report (Urban Considerations on the Retiro Project) in which they warned about many odd aspects which could be improved. [72]

Box 1. The SCA defined its position in "Urban Considerations over the Retiro Project"

The team of the SCA said that they considered the initiative of improving railway operations "valid and stimulating", as well as the idea of articulating with the city those areas that might be released from railway or harbor usages. However, they stressed "the serious lack of definitions and omissions in the studies that establish the Terms of Reference for the proposals" and "the lack of a management structure in agreement with the nature of the problem."

The study proposed a new approach for changing and readjusting the project. It suggested giving priority to the refurbishing of railways and the harbor in a stage prior to the urban transformation. The basis of the proposal maintains that "the main benefits in the remodeling of the Retiro area should be centered on the improvement of productive efforts which the country undertakes in order to relate commercially and competitively to the world." It does not mention, nor suggest anything about villa 31. However, it recommends to "evaluate in a sanctioned way the results and functional, environmental, railway and urban consequences in general of the transformation operations, over the optimization of economic ends and the balance of financial flows" *(SCA, 1994, Urban Considerations...)*

4.3. Haste and New Decree of the National Government to Urbanize the Retiro Area

Before the SCA could finish their assessment on the Retiro Area Project and formally deliver their reports, the National Government announced in May 1994, to the press that by end of the year they would call an international public competition to develop proposals for the Retiro Project.

The urgency in calling for this competition had a dual motivation. The first one was that two of the railways operating in Retiro were already in private hands and the third one would be so in July. "The enterprises will have to know what the Government wants to do with these lands" declared Matias Ordonez (head of the Undersecretary of Assets Administration) who also added that specifications for the competition would emerge from the study outlined by the SCA that had changed the original project.

The second reason of importance that rushed the Retiro Project was the need of the National Government to anticipate the change of authorities in the city of Buenos Aires. For the first time in 100 years, the next year Buenos Aires would become autonomous, which meant that officials would not be named by the Nation's President, but be elected by the citizens. The future authorities might eventually be opposed to the RP.

Together with this urgency, in October 1994, by means of Decree 1737/94, the President of the Nation ordained the redevelopment of 120ha in the Retiro area, limited by the streets Libertador, Salguero, Costanera and Ramos Mejia. The Decree stipulated

72 The working team was integrated by Architects Julio Keselman and Heriberto Allende in the general survey, Odilia Suarez as coordinator, Luis Ainstein, Carlos Lebrero and Alberto Varas. (Lebrero, Carlos, 1995).

that in 4 months ideas had to be presented in order to urbanize the area, by means of a competition of ideas. It indicated that on the basis of the selected ideas, Ferrocarriles Argentinos would have to elaborate the urban development project of the sector, which in turn would have to be submitted to the Municipality for approval.

4.4. The Mayor of the City Backs Up the Decree: the Wall on Libertador is Demolished and Villa 31 is Partially Evicted

The Mayor of the city of Buenos Aires (Jorge Dominguez) accompanied the presidential decree with two measures of highly symbolic significance and strong political impact. The first one was the demolition of the wall extending on Avenida del Libertador from the street of Suipacha to the Callao Avenue. The second was the eviction by force of a portion of villa 31 located on the site of the extension of highway 9 de Julio.Villa 31, as well as all the other slums in the Federal Capital, had been subject to a new municipal policy towards these settlements (beginnings in the early 80s) which consisted of settling and integrating their inhabitants within the urban and social network. The National Program Arraigo that was in charge of taking the necessary actions in this slum that had settled mainly on national lands, had proposed to the dwellers to be relocated in other neighborhoods of the city, so as to clean the site which soon would be required for the future highway and the Retiro Project. The unsuccessful negotiations with the organizations and the refusal of neighbors to be evicted provoked the end of the proposals formulated by Arraigo and their retreat from the area. Another failure was the second round of negotiations led by the Municipality who proposed to the slum dwellers three options in order to facilitate their relocation[73]. In June 1995, in face of the urgency to enact the eviction, Mayor Dominguez resorted to force and with the help of bulldozers destroyed 35 slum dwellings. Months later, by means of decree 110/96 officials were allowed to resort to public force in order to evict people and goods located on the other side of highway 9 de Julio.

4.5. Protests and New Discussion

- The protest of villa 31 in the face of eviction

Nine catholic priests and others from different denominations started a hunger strike to oppose the decree of Mayor Dominguez that allowed the violent eviction of the slum. Many artists and public personalities coming from the cultural and political realms expressed their solidarity with the affected slum dwellers.

Festivals, press conferences and various protests were organized which had ample coverage in the media. After a week the Archbishop of Buenos Aires came to the slum in order to oversee the fasting priests. In spite of the accusations of the authorities that the clergymen had made political use of the conflict, at long last President Menem commanded the mayor to stop compulsive evictions and to make peace with the slum dwellers (Cravino,1998)[74].

---

[73] The three options contemplated by ordinance 47.665/94 were a) a subsidy of US$ 12.000 for returning them to their places of origin, b) a credit of US$ 25.000 for buying a dwelling, and c) access to new housing built by the State. Many families who had opted for the subsidy returned again to the slum after a certain time and also new inhabitants continued to pour into the zone.

[74] In October, 2000, about 12.000 people lived in villa 31 according to a census undertaken by the CMV and the secretary of Social Promotion of the Municipality. Source: Catenazzi

Sector of the slum	Dwellings	Families	Persons
Villa 31	1991	2791	9130
Villa 31 bis	970	1164	256
Total	2961	3955	12386

- Opposition of legislators to Decree 1737

The city's legislators reacted mainly against the presidential decree which ordered the redevelopment of the Retiro area, since it bypassed any participation of the Municipal Council and ignored the ordinance of one year before. By means of this ordinance of the Municipal Council there was a decision of Future Urbanization of the zone and in this way, any project that did not take into account the integration of this area with the rest of the city, was dispelled. Some councilors also attended the complaints around villa 31. The head of the radical assembly in the MC (Carlos Louzan) argued that the project would influence future generations of citizens [75].

The socialist Norberto La Porta said that "this new presidential encumbrance, making our rights his own, more than a planned project seems to be a real estate speculation." He denied that the proportions for green spaces were 65% and the rest for buildings. He also maintained that 35% was destined to private areas, the same for public spaces and the rest for streets and sidewalks. Abel Fatala, on his part, raised the proposal of the Frente Grande party to destine the neighborhood for social housing. He said that to continue the Catalinas Complex to the North would imbalance the center of the city and to change the design of railways would be a drawback rather than a progress.The proposal of Frente Grande had been presented and discussed in what was called the First Meeting of the Retiro Area: another city is possible, a seminar which had taken place a few months before (July, 1994) in the annex building of the Nation's House of Representatives. It included a proposal to settle villa 31 in that area

- Critical view of the SCA

The SCA also made public its critical view about the presidential decree and the demolition of the wall bordering Avenida Libertador, although passing no judgement on the subject of slum 31 and without slamming the door on a future participation in an eventual competition of ideas. In a note, signed by its chief, Arch. Julio Keselman, the SCA stressed that the main merit of the Retiro project was not "to change the face of the urban front but by demolishing an ugly wall bordering Libertador, which hides a platform for train movements."

That "the main benefits should concentrate on the improvement of operationality in view of the efforts the country is taking in order to relate commercially and competitively to the world". His approach meant -according to the studies undertaken by the SCA- setting a priority for the redevelopment of the harbor instead of real estate development. It should facilitate the movement of freight with origin or destination in the Port of Buenos Aires for all arrivals by train as well as by trucks. Thus, a previous stage to any urban transformation, should be that freight carried by railways obtain direct access to the harbor by the wide gauge. Again, freight by trucks should be channeled all along the highways (9 de julio and La Plata-Buenos Aires) with the result and the enormous benefit of suppressing a great part of truck traffic in the city.

Afterwards, the SCA left a door open for future participation: "Although we maintain that government and planning of the city should be left to the institutional channels and not to a decree, the SCA supports the political energy which aims at planning the operations of train hauling in Retiro. This should be oriented according to

---

[75] On the following month, in November, 1994, the radical bench of the MC presented an alternative project for the Retiro area. The president of the radical bench, Alberto Louzan, explained to the press that the project was shown as an alternative to the other one presented by the party in power and in order to open a debate with the people of the city of Buenos Aires "so that it should be finally elaborated by the coming authorities elected by the people."

the urban priorities which our city requires, among which we would include 'a posteriori' the urbanization of those areas released from railway usage." (*SCA, Note Nr.404, Buenos Aires, October 14, 1994)*

4.6. Achieving an Agreement: Calling for a National Competition of Ideas

After many moves and countermoves, on March 1995, a second agreement between the SCA and the Argentine Railways with the Municipality of the City of Buenos Aires, was signed. Its goal was to organize a National Competition of Ideas for the urban development of the Retiro zone. The SCA was requested to organize this competition by outlining the baseline beforehand, a task that should have been completed in 45 days. Newspapers covered these events and also gathered the opinion of the main actors involved: of those in favor as well as those who were critical. The newspaper Clarin published in its Architecture Section the following information:

Mr Keselman, president of the SCA stressed the importance of this event. "It cost us long months of discussions and disputes, but what became clear is that Retiro requires a substantial change. It is necessary to rationalize the railways, as well as the access to the port, both have been waiting a long time for a solution."

Mr Matias Ordonez welcomed the decision taken by the National Government to stimulate joint action of this organization and the Municipality of Buenos Aires, thus allowing for a better use of State property. Also Mayor Jorge Dominguez agreed with Keselman in that it was the best way to find a planned solution for this area.

Together with these declarations, a note signed by architect and urban planner Claude Della Paolera was published, pointing at two key questions of urban management which the Retiro Project might possibly overlook: a) the possible encroachment of the scarce green areas available in the city and the need to create certain mechanisms to avoid this and b) the importance of discussing a city plan which would allow for new ideas about urban policies in the long range without immobilizing the city.

II - National Competition of Ideas, New Retiro Project and Second Debate geared to the Solution of Transportation 1996-1999

5. Baselines, the National Contest of Ideas and the Winning Proposal

5.1. Approval of the Baselines for the Contest in the Area

Instead of 45 days, the elaboration of Terms of Reference for calling a National Competition of Ideas took more than one year. On March 12, 1996, they were approved by the Argentine Railways and the Executive of the Municipality of Buenos Aires. The Terms of Reference pointed at an important new rethinking of the original project for various reasons. In the first place, it established in an explicit way that the Retiro project was not to be conceived as a real estate speculation. Therefore, a series of changes with respect to the official project were introduced trying to establish three main questions: 1) the railway linkage of Retiro with the Port, 2) the extension of the green area in the North continuing the 3 de Febrero park along Libertador and 3) the change in uses of buildings allowed for private investment that now would not permit office buildings as the original project suggested. With the latter, it was avoided that this area would constitute an attraction of activities from the central district, a fact that would have produced its decay, since the natural alleys of expansion have to be Catalinas, Plaza Roma and Puerto Madero (Terms of Reference for the Competition, 1996). In the second place, the Terms of Reference established three stages for the project's development and the sequence tried to ensure that railways were envisaged before the urban planning:

First stage: railway management of connection between port and trains. Also a linkage between this and the Buenos Aires-La Plata highway.

Second stage: release from railway use of some 18 blocks facing Avenida del Libertador from Avenue Ramos Mejia to Avenue Callao. This stage is included the construction of a transfer point (train to bus) in the area of the FC San Martin terminal.

Third stage: release of another 57 blocks for urbanization, construction of a new unified terminal, incorporating the transfer point and the recycling of the Retiro-Mitre station. In the third place, regarding the sector for urbanization, the Terms of Reference ensured that the better part of this surface is destined for public spaces and green areas. 65% of the surface was destined for public use (streets, sidewalks and green spaces) while the remaining 35% could be subdivided and sold to the private sector, including specifications about use and building codes. Of the land to be sold, 40% had to be destined for housing and the other 60% to other uses such as luxury hotels, commercial facilities, cultural buildings, nurseries and primary schools.

Box 2. Sixteen Ideas for the Retiro Area (second and third stages)

- Multifunctional Center: high-density complex with private development for public access. Includes stores, hotel, apartment-hotel, studios, office facilities, communication facilities.
- Residential urban mesh separated from Av Libertador by a green corridor of medium height
- High density front: on the crossroad with highway 9 de Julio a platform is proposed with the same height as the highway and two buildings for various hotel complexes
- Green corridor: with a width of 50m, it will be the prolongation of already existent city parks
- Street structure: elimination of the high-speed route after Callao, and maintenance of the by-pass on Avenida del Libertador in order to protect the new neighborhood from rapid transit
- The new public park: will unify the existing parks with new areas for public use
- Urban front and park: line of buildings marking the new limit of the city with the river
- Landscaped boulevard (third stage) which connects with the present outline of Avenida Madero up to Salguero
- Cultural park: buildings with ample site for exhibitions, museums and cultural organizations
- A low and green site: low buildings with space for servicing the new housing in the area which, in the final stage, will encompass a neighborhood of between 8 and 10 thousand inhabitants
- A low-density neighborhood: completion of existing Barrio Parque.
- Underground transfer point: for passengers of intermodal distribution connected to the western sidewalk (before crossing) Avenida del Libertador upto the new unified station of railways, undergound at depths of 5 and 9 meters
- Bus station: located across the railway station (+1.20m) with pedestrian access from the transfer point (-2.50 meters). Center for supplies that will contribute to finance it.
- Premetro and underground: light train with a terminal in Retiro and arrival at Av. Brasil-Costanera Sur to serve the new areas on the limits of the central district (Retiro-Nueva Catalinas-Puerto Madero-Ecological Reservation-Southern Coastal area-Sports

City of Boca Juniors).Includes a transfer station with underground of Line C
• Underground: enlargement of Line C up to the new railway station and eventual lengthening under Avenida Pueyrredon
• Environment and conservation: refurbishing of terminal stations Mitre and Belgrano (second and third stages). Recycling of railways building. New center of supplies connected to the node
(SCA, Revista de Arquitectura Nr.184, January, 1997)

. In spite of this very positive orientation, the Terms of Reference did not question the solution for railway transportation designed by the official project (regarding functional and territorial zoning of train terminals) and did not make any references to the existence of villa 31 and the need to find a solution for thousands of inhabitants located in that area during several decades. Rather, it was presumed that the Municipality would move the slums to another part since its location on the land destined for a linkage node between highway and streets would provoke serious circulatory and environmental problems in the area.

5.2 The Contest

The National Competition of Ideas was called on April 22, 1996, and deadline for delivering projects was established for the 24th of July 1996. At this time the city of Buenos Aires was already autonomous. Some 100 sheets of specifications were sold and 48 proposals were submitted. The jury, presided by the new Mayor for the autonomous city (Dr. Fernando de la Rua) announced that the winners were members of the workshop Miguel Baudizzone, Jorge Lestard, Alberto Varas, architects. On October 30, 1996, President Carlos Menem and De la Rua shared the stage at the White Room of the Casa Rosada in order to deliver the prizes.

Official declarations to the press showed the new direction the project had chosen, in face of critical views from all over. President Menem said: "There is no real estate business. What we want is a more beautiful city". De la Rua on his part declared that "The winning proposal overcomes the excessive level of occupation which was forthcoming in the first project where more attention was given to the revenues gathered by selling these lands, than to urban planning. Now there are more benefits for the people who will have access and expansions with a balanced proposal for the city" *(Pagina 12, October 31, 1996).*

6. The Silent March of the Project under the Administration of the City's Autonomous Government

6.1. Adjustments to the Winning Proposal

In August, 1997, an agreement was signed between the National Committee for the Management of Railway Assets (ENABIEF) and the architecture workshop of Baudizzone-Lestard-Varas, who had won the Competition of Ideas, in order to elaborate the final project. The winning project did not show the detailed level required by the government of the city in order to be approved. At this stage (from August to December 1997) the government of the city appointed an ad-hoc advisory committee to follow-up and maintain continuous meetings with the designers and the members of Enabief.[76](16)

---

76 The Commission, under the presidency of Rodriguez Giavarini did not study only the Retiro Project, but all of the railway lands which would change uses due to a dismissal of freight platforms of the railways. It

The preliminary sketch -proceedings which contained a folder with more than 50 plans at various scales and two volumes with a project for standards- was presented by ENABIEF to the Secretary for Planning, on December 29, 1997, so that authorities might comment on the subject. That same month of December, Project Retiro received the support from the Chief Executive of the city's Government, Fernando de la Rua, who announced the formation of a new mixed committee with members of the city's and nation's governments that would deal with the control of the process until the call of an auction bidding estimated to take place the following year. With this decision, the final stage of the procedures, that is, the official approval of the preliminary urban sketch and the city standards for the Retiro Project should have started. Steps to be followed were the following: The City Planning Secretary was appointed to elaborate a relocation project. Later, the initiative should have been transferred as a legislative bill to the new city's legislature for approval. Then they would have issued an ordinance to call an auction bidding for the construction of the site. According to this outline, the deadlines to keep the project underway would finally depend on the political rhythms of the Legislature. However, the project never reached this government instance.

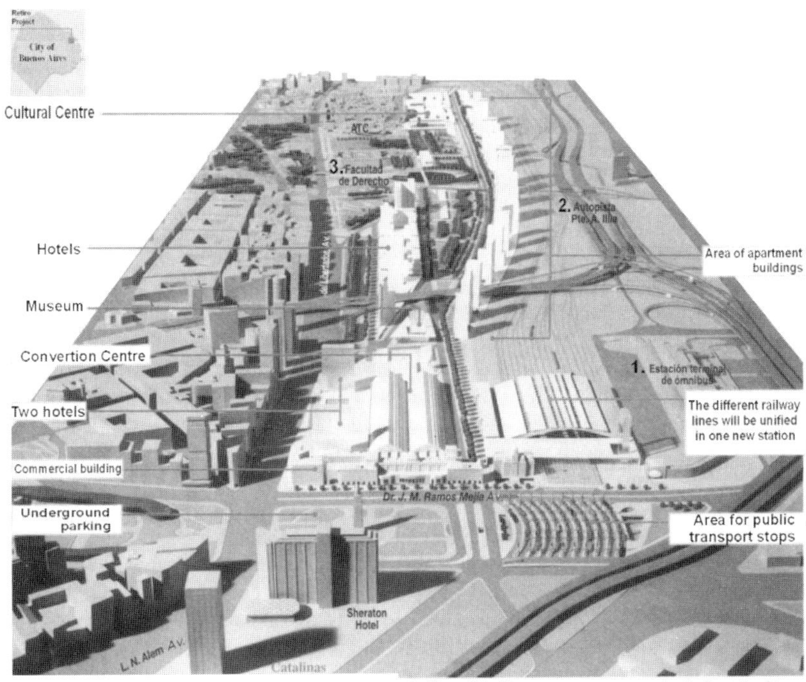

Source: La Nacion magazine

1. Bus Station
2. Pte. A. Illia Highway
3. School of Law

Figure 1. The Winning Proposal

---

dealt with 10 areas which encompass some 120ha and constitute the only urban reserve of the city of Buenos Aires. The Enabief was interested in determining whether the percentages of 35% for private uses and 65% for public uses -established in the case of the Retiro project- should be kept for all the other areas.

6.2. Recommendations of the Advisory Council for City Planning CAPU

A year after having received the proceedings, on August 14, 1998, the Advisory Council for City Planning CAPU produced a statement on the Retiro project[77]. The evaluation of the minutes of the CAPU presented to the Executive of the City's Government formulated the following recommendations:

a) To approve the urban design and corresponding zoning of the second stage and send them to the city's Legislature.
b) To approve the general city plan for the third stage in order to submit to investors with a spectrum of foresight in the immediate environment (No urban standards to be approved yet).
c) Foresee (in the second stage) the necessary work to improve the area of transportation transfer in its functional as well as spatial aspects.
d) To stipulate expressly, by means of certain standards, the obligation to proceed until the termination of the first stage (trains) to ensure accessibility and proper functioning of the Port of Buenos Aires, prior to the beginning of the second stage.
e) To fix expressly, by means of standards, the obligation to build and transfer to the city's domain the totality of public spaces corresponding to stages 2 and 3, before proceeding to sell the land on each of them.
f) To constitute management authorities in the area in which the National and City governments should participate, previous to the enforcement of the second stage urban standards.

Recommendation (d) has a crucial importance since it aimed to avoid the elimination of other stages of the project, as was agreed, and to secure the execution of the so-called railway stage which consisted in the moving of the freight railway lines (which at this point lies parallel to Avenida Libertador) to allow for direct access to the Port. The second stage permitted the release of land bordering Avenida Libertador right up to Avenida Pueyrredon. The third stage meant a transfer of rail towards the river (from FC Mitre to FC San Martin) and the release of another stretch of land on Libertador and the recycling of stations from the FC Belgrano and FC Mitre.

The idea of eliminating these stages in the outline of the Retiro Project had been proposed several times by the members of ENABIEF in the mixed Nation-City Committee, with the justification that certain capital investors were interested in investing in the totality of land and not in doing so in parts. However, the CAPU was very strict in following the stages as well as with the percentages (35%/65%) allotted to private as well as public uses and the urban standards of FOS and FOT designed only for the second stage. The CAPU maintained that the debate over stage three had not been completed. That it required, therefore, a new round of deliberation, after which a proposal on standards for these areas could be outlined. Actually, while the first two stages presented no objections, the moving of stations Mitre and Belgrano towards the river resulted in a controversial subject which had not been sufficiently analyzed or solved.

---

77 Proceedings on the Evaluation of a Preliminary Urban Project in the Retiro Area directed by the Secretary of Urban Planning Arq. Garcia Espil and the Undersecretary of Urban Planning Roberto Converti. Councilors signing the proceedings: Arq. Heriberto Allende, Arq. Mario Linder, Arq. Jorge Iribarne, Dr. Raul Navas and Ing. Olga Vicente.

6.3. The Government of the City finally sketches a "possible" Bill that never arrived at the Legislature

Eight months later, on April 12, 1999, CAPU presented the Government's Executive with a new Complementary Report on the Evaluation of the Preliminary Urban Project of the Retiro Area (outlined after analyzing "the last reports of the project under reference") in which two alternatives were presented with respect to the continuation of the proceedings. They meant to ensure that the first stage corresponding to the railway redevelopment is executed before selling and zoning the land released from railway use.[78]

- Before submitting the Master Plan and the standards for the second stage to the Legislature in the form of a bill, it is necessary to obtain from the corresponding areas of the National Government a commitment that the railway access to the Port of Buenos Aires will be built (according to attached criteria
- Propose a Bill for the Legislature, which contemplates aforementioned conditions as a previous step to the enforcement of zoning regulations.
- The possible Bill included, among others, the following key aspects:
- Approval of a Master Plan of urban development for areas released from railway use in the Retiro area
- This master Plan should not be enforce until:
  a) The National Government has constructed the railway access to the Port of Buenos Aires
  b) The National and City governments have created an agency for Urban Development according to the Master Plan
- No authorization to sell any land within the area regulated by the Master Plan and not until the following prerequisites are accomplished:
  a) the construction of facilities, streets and public spaces in the sector to be sold and no surety over their construction in the future
  b) the tools for delivering to public jurisdiction of the City those spaces destined to streets and other public spaces.

(Government of the City of Buenos Aires, Draft of a Proposed Law, included in "Evaluation of the Preliminary Urban Project of the Retiro Area. Complementary Report" February 11, 1999).

This project never reached the city's legislature. The proceedings were filed during the rest of the De la Rua administration and by the person who succeeded him in the post (Olivera) when the former had access to the Presidency of the Republic after the victory of the Alliance (a coalition of Parties) that brought him into power in December, 1999.

The reasons why the Project Retiro was stopped in the city's Executive government are not found explicitly anywhere. People who were interviewed said they ignored the fact, although they mentioned the existence of certain influences that made the approval of the project highly improbable if the main lines outlined at the time were pursued.

To the already mentioned critical views and opposition to the project, two other types of criticisms against the Retiro Project should be added. Both were of a different order and even contradictory in their intention as could be verified by their public manifestation. The first were harsh critics coming from certain sectors related to transportation engineering, who doubted precisely "the transportation solution" involved

78 To state that "the evaluation process has been delayed in time due to the complexity of the issues and the need to agree with the designers and the ENABIEF on joint solutions to various partial aspects which emerged during the study of the important documents here presented."

in the Retiro project. The second one was a strong lobby of private investors interested in buying and developing the land in the area.

7. Project Retiro receives New Critical Reviews from Sectors Specialized in Transportation Engineering

7.1. Critical Review and Alternative Proposal from ATEC-Engineering Consultants

It is on this subject -solving transportation- that the Retiro Project received a violent attack. This happened due to the entrance on the scene of another actor: ATEC-Engineering Consultants whose head is Eng. Larocca, a man who says that he is representing the technical views of an ample group of engineers and experts on the subject of transportation.[79]

In September 1998, this group met in the Annex of the House of Representatives, with the aim of expressing their views with respect to the Retiro Project and to be heard by the representatives. This purpose was not fulfilled because in spite of their being invited, nobody assisted. All the speakers were against Project Retiro.

In a document entitled Strategic and Functional Planning of Retiro (s/f) the engineering advisors of ATEC explained a number of well-based critiques and corresponding alternative proposals which will be summarized in the next paragraph.

- *Critical review of the Retiro project*

One first critical aspect, is the proposal for a new station on the west side of the existing precarious terminal of the San Martin line, by inactivating the Mitre station, a fact which involves:

- a very high cost, as much for the new station as for the reconstruction of 8 main railway lines of circulation and their facilities on something like 4 kilometers
- economic and functional damage due to loss of transportation capacity during the period in which these complex changes are being built
- removal from the passenger terminal of "origin and destination" of trips (in the area comprised by Catalinas-Plaza San Martin-Northern part of the central district) so that 23.000 passengers who circulated daily through Retiro will have to walk 300 meters more
- inadequate resolution of the railway connection with the underground (used daily by some 75.000 passengers) by abolishing the only station in good shape linked to Line C (which reaches the Mitre terminal)

On the other hand, this document warns that the project did not exhibit a rigorous cost-benefit analysis in order to prove that the moving of the terminals render economic benefits to the total project of a value that would compensate the cost of these gigantic works.

The second aspect, which deserved a strong opposition, is the false pretension of taking advantage of the real estate value of one of the most valuable reservations of the

[79] The ATEC consultants had been partners with the architecture workshop of Antonini, who won the fifth prize in the Competition of Ideas. The proposal for the Retiro Project presented by Antonini consisted in maintaining the Mitre Station in its actual position, but building it underground, a fact which did not conform to the bases established by the Competition. Ing. Larocca continued developing this idea because he was convinced that it was the best from a point of view of solving the transportation problems in the area.

city in order to achieve short range revenues for the "daily cash" of public finances. The strategic value of these lands for the community is not compensated by actual revenues of a scarce amount.

Finally, the approach of the project with respect to the Port is not considered valid since it was conceived before the concession of terminals in Puerto Nuevo, which have produced a incisive transformation in the development of the harbor.

(Extracted from ATEC Strategic and functional planning of Retiro)

- *The Proposal*

The main strategy of the ATEC proposal is to optimize the railway usage of the Mitre station by also including also the movements of trains from the FC San Martin (the terminal to be located in the available space close to the Mitre platforms on the side of Avenida Libertador) and keeping the Belgrano terminal in service.

The opinion of ATEC and the efforts made by their members to change the path of the Retiro Project for a better solution of the transportation problem were not attended in a first instance, but yielded its fruits sometime later, as shall be seen.

7.2. Objections and Suggestions contained in the Urban Environment Plan

Objections to the solution of transportation were also included in the Urban Environment Plan of the City of Buenos Aires in the chapter on transportation and urban circulation (1999). The Plan, outlined by Engineers Daniel Batalla and Roberto Nasta objected to the fact that road solution of the Retiro project only encompassed a restricted area and did not take into account the linkages and repercussions in neighboring zones, particularly the central district, the Port and the Northern area.

By marking the impossibility of an adequate solution to the complex node of transportation in the area if the influence and interconnections of the traffic generated in the remaining urban and regional areas was not taken into account, the document suggested:

a) to contemplate jointly the projects and solutions proposed by the various agencies with jurisdiction on the area (Coastal High-way, Bus Terminal, Port of Buenos Aires, River Station, Railway and Public Transport Terminals).
b) To facilitate coordination between local and sectoral authorities of transportation in order to outline a transportation and traffic policy by defining priorities. These suggestions were apparently taken into account in the following reformulation of the project.

8. Offensive of Private Investors to get the Retiro Project Underway

In the context of a vacuum of actions and official announcements in the course of the Retiro Project -a silence which lasted for several months- private investors started lobbying in order to renew the works in the Retiro zone. At first, towards May, 1999, a group of firms controlled by the financier George Soros started a lobby for buying and investing in the land around the Retiro area. Under the title "Soros wants to own Retiro for 1000 million pesos" the newspaper Clarin published an article in its Economy Section announcing the following:

> Before the city's Legislature had approved the zoning of the area and called for an international competition, IRSA had already started to move. It contacted two of the local giants: the Techint group and the cement factory of Loma Negra, i.e. the main

constructing enterprise and the leader in the cement business. Besides, it included the Mortgage Bank (which owns funds from Soros) with the idea of financing the acquisition of 6000 dwellings planned to be built in the area. The technical team of the Mortgage Bank made a detailed study of the project. Apparently it adjusted to the winning proposal of the Competition of Ideas.

Later on, it was known that the group headed by Eduardo Elsztain (Soros BHN) had tempted the real estate branch of the Spanish Bilbao Vizcaya-Argentaria Bank. But other Spanish firms had also studied this juicy business (Clarin, Economia, May 26, 1999).

Probably due to strong lobbies in the government of the city, it was decided not to continue with the Retiro project. It was detained until new events initiated a third stage in its development.

III - Third Proposal for Retiro, more Management Conflicts and New Polemics around the Relocation of Villa 31

9. The New National Authorities Announce a Change in the Direction of the Retiro Project: The Retiro-Harbor Project of the Puerto-Madero Corporation 2000-2001

9.1.Announcement of the Minister of Utilities and Facilities

One year after the Alliance was set in power of the Nation's Government, the new Minister of Utilities and Facilities of the Nation, Nicolas Gallo[80](20) publicly presented in August, 2000, his Plan for Urban Development and Central Logistics Area for the zone of Retiro and the Port, calling for private capital to invest some 2000 million dollars. The redevelopment of the Retiro area was announced as a 10-year plan which would follow the mode adopted in Puerto Madero. The interest of the Puerto Madero Corporation to lead this project seemed to be the force which drove the reactivation of the subject[81]. The President of the Corporation at that time was Architect Converti, who had acted as undersecretary in the Government of the city, before occupying this new post. All this goes to show that the Minister as well as Converti were acquainted with the Retiro project.

This Plan started to be called Retiro-Harbor (or Retiro-Harbor Project) since it meant essentially the actualization of Project Retiro with a new approach. According to the announcement of Minister Gallo to the press, the new project was similar to the first one in that its main objective was to modernize and optimize the railways, harbor and transportation services, as well as to urbanize the land on Avenida Libertador. However, the new proposal included some substantial changes with respect to the former outline, among which the following have to be stressed:[82]

a) Maintenance of the Mitre station under present usage. Instead of moving the railway platforms and concentrating them in one station close to the bus terminal with the intention of releasing a great surface of land to sell, the new project

80 Previous to being Minister, Nicolas Gallo had been an official in the City of Buenos Aires while Fernando de la Rua was the Nation's President.

81 The Old Puerto Madero Corporation is a mixed society in which the board of directors is representing the Nation and the City in equal parts.

82 According to information submitted by the newspapers Clarin (August 31, 2000), La Nacion, Suplemento de Arquitectura (August 31, 2000) and Cronista Comercial (September the 1st., 2000).

recommended moving the rails in the opposite direction, as was suggested by the ATEC consultants.

b) Extension of the reference zone, by incorporating the port area (and a corresponding modernization of the harbor system) and the definition of the so-called Coastal Highway which links La Plata to Buenos Aires. By extending over Puerto Madero it joins the highway that passes through Retiro.
c) The construction of 40.000 dwellings in the zone
d) The intention of entrusting the old Puerto Madero Corporation with the technical elaboration and management of the new project

9.2. Disagreements with the City's Government

Despite the fact that the National Government and the City of Buenos Aires were in the hands of the same political party -the Alliance- Minister Gallo and the authorities of the City's Government had some disagreements with respect to the announcements of the Retiro-Harbor Project. Issues under conflict had to do essentially with the following questions:

1) The lack of participation of the City's Government in the elaboration of the new project
2) Suspicions that this enterprise again would hide a basically real estate business
3) Disagreements with respect to residential development and the outline foreseen for the so-called coastal highway
4) The attitude towards villa 31.

Part of these disagreements can be explained by the confusion provoked by the National government's inability to provide a formal project. Its extent was only known through public declarations of officials who were in favor or against the project and the secret existence of a new plan for the area.

According to information submitted to the press, Minister Gallo's announcement caused surprise in the City's Government. The Secretary of Planning (E.Garcia Espil) said he knew nothing about the project although he agreed to a change of the railway proposal: "The city believes that the railway core should be in the FC Mitre station. From there on, the project will have to be discussed. I am amazed at the announcement of the location of 200 thousand inhabitants in that area, which is contrary to the projects of the city to unclog the central district".

On his part, the new Chief of Government (Anibal Ibarra) reacted by saying that he was interested in developing the Southern part of the city. With these ideas in mind, the standards had been changed in order to allow the construction of housing in the South. Also, the fact that the coastal highway would pass "at equal level" with the frontage of Puerto Madero caused a firm critical reaction on the part of Ibarra who pointed out that "This highway passing in front of the Puerto Madero docks will be an insurmountable barrier between Buenos Aires and this urbanization. The best alternative would be to build it underground. We agree with the National Government to the need for a highway, but not at street level."

Finally, with respect to villa 31, Ibarra took a decision, which he made public: to relocate the slum on the same site. Thus, he disclaimed the Minister Gallo's insinuation that the slum had to be evicted by the Government of the City and in turn opened a new discussion over the Retiro project, which still continues and will be commented further on.

The controversial issues were clearly expressed in a Bill elaborated by the Legislative Power of the Government of the city. Its purpose was to request from the Executive of the city the following information with regard to the so-called 'Retiro-Harbor' Project:

a) What differences were there between the Retiro Project which was the goal of the Competition of Ideas in the year 1996 and the new 'Retiro-Harbor' project issued by the National Executive for the Executive of the city
b) Whether the new real estate and urban 'Retiro-Harbor' Project contemplates the construction of 40.000 dwellings on the land released in that area
c) Whether the new 'Retiro-Harbor' project foresees the extension or refurbishing of the Port of Buenos Aires with the participation of the General Administration of Ports S.E. at present to be abolished. If the answer is affirmative, whether legal advice had been requested to turn over the harbor to the city and to create a 'Society for the Administration of the Port of Buenos Aires'.
d) Whether the agency or executive unit of the project 'Retiro-Harbor' has foreseen to what extent, if any, the government of the city will participate (Article 1).

The basis for this Bill -a definitely eloquent one- points at the anxiety of the legislators that the new Retiro-Harbor Project would show once more its real estate profile.

> Motivation of the present Bill is the anxiety of neighbours of a new launching of Menem's old real estate project called 'Retiro Project' which under the cover of optimizing harbor and railway facilities hid real estate businesses of hotels and office buildings in that zone. The building of megaconstructions in the port area or in front of the river, generally linked to realtors and without due participation of the City's Government has become a real insult to the city's autonomy (...). Lastly, we would especially like to stress that the undertaking of a real estate megaproject in the zone of the Retiro-Harbor (which according to the National Executive would house more that 40.000 dwellings) expressly contradicts the policies of urban as well as economic promotion and development of the long-delayed improvement of the Southern part of our city" (*Parliamentary Document 3049d00*)

9.3. The Debate around Villa 31

The political decision of the Chief of Government of the city with respect to the relocation of villa 31 in the area of Retiro was technically argued by the Secretary of Planning by means of two central reasons: the need for an adequate solution to the transportation node and the importance of developing policies of social inclusion. In an article published by the newspaper La Nacion, under the title "Villa 31: to urbanize or to look the other way", the Secretary Garcia Espil developed his points of view.

1. The location of villa 31 on the site where the access to the harbor should be constructed, remains an obstacle and delays the undertaking of work for a highway, initiated 23 years ago. These works would allow a better movement of trucks coming and going to the harbor, as well as buses that arrive and issue from the long distance bus terminal. At present, the latter have to use adjacent streets and avenues provoking traffic jams and bringing about economic losses to the city
2. In the past half century, the city has lacked plans and projects for the Retiro slums due to old-fashioned prejudices that segregate cities in zones for the rich and for the poor. "It is time to incorporate the slums into the urban life and develop inclusion policies, so that all inhabitants may share the services and ways of life that the city

has to offer."

The urban solutions outlined by the city's authorities consist of "...transforming this sector of the city: by removing the sand depots, opening up a avenue -a green boulevard with trees- in order to join the promenades of the Northern Coast with Puerto Madero, open-up streets, build facilities and utilities, and housing, and give an option to the present inhabitants of squatter zones to buy with subsidized credits as other sectors of the population (no more neighbourhoods with high-rise buildings like in Fort Apache, nor ghettoes for a single social sector) and integrate this zone into the urban mesh and the life of the city. (Diario La Nacion, 2001).

In opposition to the integrated character, from an urban and social point of view, other voices were being heard from certain professionals who stressed the functional incompatibility between housing and other functions essentially linked to transportation, as well as the lawlessness of handing out lands to illegal occupants.

9.4. Strategic Framework for Agreements

Foregoing disagreements and issues still under debate, there might possibly be some main points of agreement between the national government, the government of the city and other agencies operative in the area, for example:

- The new framework of the Retiro Project from a more strategic perspective together with the planning of the harbor, the coastal highway and villa 31 and the reurbanization of the area while searching to integrate the different points of view and interests involved in the area. This extended view had been already contemplated by the Urban Environment Plan of the City's Government.
- The reformulation of a series of aspects that were previously questioned in the solution of transportation.[83]
- The intention to hand the management of the Project to the Puerto Madero corporation which appears to have been a successful example in urban as well as in managerial terms.[84]. This being a mixed enterprise whose shareholders belong to the Government of the City of Buenos Aires and the National State, a better coordination of decisions would be achieved with regard to the project, by overcoming the continuing conflicts between both jurisdictions.

83 Stations Mitre and Belgrano would be retained; trains from the San Martin would leave their run-down station and move to the Mitre; in the place of the San Martin station the center of transfer for urban buses would be located; large extensions for activities supporting the bus terminal were foreseen; a linkage with Puerto Madero had been outlined; the station of underground Libe H would be placed at the side of the Mitre Station and similar location was meant for the station of Line E. These positive aspects were pointed out by Ing. Larocca who showed his satisfaction with the new course taken by Project Retiro, in accordance to the proposals submitted by ATEC consultants (El Cronista, Wednesday, March 28, 2001.

84 The experience of Puerto Madero meant recovery for the State, of lands historically destined to the harbor and to industrial uses belonging to the General Port Administration. Rehabilitation was large in scale and in visibility.

Table 1. Players that participated in the management, proposals design and debates related to Retiro Project. 1991 –2001

PUBLIC SECTOR	
National level	
President of the Nation	Presenta y avala el the first Retiro Project
Ministry of Economy: Comisión Venta Inmuebles Fiscales, Subsecretaría de Administración de Bienes, ENABIEF y ONABE	A cargo de vender, concesionar, permutar o arrendar los predios de Retiro, desarrollar un Plan Maestro de urbanización para el área.
National Secretary of Transports	Emite opinión sobre el Poyecto
General Port Administration	Responsable del Plan Director del Puerto. Participa en el Proyecto Retiro-Puerto
Arraigo Programe	Propone plan para la villa 31
OCRABA In charge of the control of the Buenos Aires Network Entrance Routes Concessionaires	Participa en el Proyecto como encargado de la gestión de la Autopista Ribereña
Local level	
Mayor Chief of Government of the City	Debe aprobar el Proyecto presentado por el organismo nacional y elevarlo a la legislatura de la Ciudad
Urban Planning Secretary and Advisory Council for City Planning CAPU	Evalúa la propuesta del organismo nacional, dicta las normas urbanísticas para el área, formula recomendaciones
Housing Municipal Office Social Management	A cargo de la villa 31 y su relación con el proyecto Retiro. Elabora propuestas habitacionales y sociales
Municipal Council (legislative power)	Encargado de aprobar las normas urbanísticas para el área de Retiro y convertirlas en ordenanza
Mixed Organizations Nation-City	
Ad-hoc Mixed organizations	Encargada de seguimiento del Proyecto
Corporación Antiguo Puerto Madero	Elabora el nuevo Proyecto Retiro-Puerto Potencial encargado de su futura gestión
PRIVATE SECTOR	
CANAC Internacional INC And local partners	A cargo de primer estudio de factibilidad para el área.(1991) y autora del primer Proyecto Retiro (1993)
World Bank and UNDP	Apoyo para concurso de antecedentes que culmina en la contratación de la firma Canac.
Central Society of Architects	Organiza un Concurso nacional de Ideas para el área Retiro. Elabora las bases de dicho Concurso.
Architectural offices	Participan en el Concurso nacional de Ideas para el desarrollo urbanístico del área de Retiro
Estudio Baudizzone-Lestard-Varas arqs.	Gana el primer Premio en el concurso de Ideas. Elabora la nueva versión del proyecto Retiro-Puerto
Fine Arts National Academy	Se opone a que obras se realicen con la venta de las tierras. Propone áreas verdes en las hectáreas desafectadas del uso ferroviario.
ATEC. Engineering consultants	Cuestiona el proyecto Retiro, espacialmente en su Solución del transporte y elabora una propuesta alternativa. Incide en la reformulación del Proyecto
IRSA	Grupo empresarial interesado en efectuar inversiones en el área. Realiza una propuesta
REPSOL	Empresa dueña de uno de los terrenos propuestos para áreas de viviendas sociales

COVIARES	Concesionario contratado para realizar la autopista ribereña
COMUNITARY SECTOR	
Community-based organizations	Negocia la permanencia de la villa 31y sus alternativas
NGO	Elaboran propuestas para la vlla 31 y acompañan sus protestas
Churches	Acompañan los reclamos de los habitantes de la villa 31

Final Comments

The emergence and development of the Retiro Project has been indicative of a complex process involving successive adjustments in basic views, objectives and components. Created with an exclusively real estate logic, a limited urban proposal, a bad solution for transportation and a social context based on exclusion, it derived into another proposal which meant to give a comprehensive response to all of these dimensions from a more strategic point of view.

This result, for the time being, may constitute a challenge to the consequences, which are generally associated with large urban enterprises in the age of globalization, with its selective investment patterns and its exclusively private ideology.

In the history of the project a set of state policies, and private and community actions interlinked in such a way that it is difficult to establish with a certain precision in what proportion the change of course observed in the project can be assigned to one or the other. However, two questions seem to be evident:

a) Different sectors of civil society have shown great interest in the significant issues of the city and also an important capacity for action, a fact that has made a basic difference in the course of the project under study.
b) The institutional autonomy acquired by the Government of the City has allowed it to adopt an institutional role of more leadership in spite of the great difficulties involved in the shared management of city and nation.

The challenge involved in this new integrated and strategic direction of the project is now to prevent that it remains reduced to a small group of public officials and developers, isolating the management process from the influence of the local society

References

- *Legal Texts*

Decreto 1143/91 Poder Ejecutivo Nacional "Reforma del Estado" 14/691

Decreto 602/92 Poder Ejecutivo Nacional "Inmuebles" 8/4/92

Decreto 1737 /94. Poder Ejecutivo Nacional

Ordenanza N° 47.190 Aféctase y desaféctase distritos en el CPU.Boletín Municipal de la Ciudad de Buenos Aires N° 19.716

Ordenanza 47.665/94

- *Official Documents*

Canac International INC. 1991. "Proposed Property Redevelopment for Retiro Railway Complex Buenos Aires, Argentina." August (Mimeo)

Gobierno de la Ciudad de Buenos Aires. 1998. Informe del Consejo Asesor de Planeamiento Urbano. "Evaluación del Anteproyecto Urbano para el Area Retiro", Buenos Aires, Agosto

Gobierno de la Ciudad de Buenos Aires 1999. "Evaluación Anteproyecto Urbano para el Area Retiro". Informe Complementario, Buenos Aires, Febrero.

Plan Urbano Ambiental. 1999. Buenos Aires.

Ferrocarriles Argentinos, Municipalidad de la Ciudad de Buenos Aires (Entes promotores), Sociedad Central de Arquitectos (Organizadora). 1996. *Concurso Area Retiro. Bases de Consulta*, Buenos Aires

Poder Ejecutivo Nacional, Ministerio de Economía. 1993. *Proyecto Retiro. Optimización del Transporte y Recuperación Urbana. Plan de Racionalización Ferroviaria y Desarrollo Urbano del Area Terminal de Retiro, Buenos Aires*., Buenos Aires

- *Other documents*

Arqa.com Archivos. Proyecto Area Retiro: Introducción, El contexto del Proyecto Retiro Aspectos operativos y mecanismos de gestión

Atec, Ingenieros Consultores. (S/f) *Ordenamiento estratégico y funcional de Retiro*, Buenos Aires

Catenazzi, Andrea. 2001. "La villa 31 en el Proyecto Retiro" (mimeo)

Cravino, Cristina. 1998. Gestión municipal y movimiento villero entre 1989 y 1996., INAP

Sociedad Central de Arquitectos. 1994. "La SCA ante una nueva etapa del Proyecto Retiro", Nota Nº 404, Buenos Aires, Octubre.

FADU. S/f. "La FADU ante el Proyecto Retiro", Proyecto de Nota.

Frente Grande, Comisión de Ecología y Medio Ambiente. 1994. *Primer Encuentro Area Retiro: Otra ciudad es posible*, Cámara de Diputados de la Nación, Buenos Aires 11 de julio.

Lebrero, Carlos. 1995. "La gestión urbana y el área de Retiro", en Revista de la SCA, Nº 175, Buenos Aires, mayo-junio

- *Information from Journals*

Diarios La Nación, Clarín, Cronista Comercial, Página 12.

- *Interviews*

Lic. Luan Gutierrez. Ex sacerdote en la villa 31

Arq. Nestor Jifetz. Aseror Movimiento de Villas y Barrios Carenciados

Arq. Jorge García. Subgerente en la Comisión Municipal de la Vivienda. Area Social

Arq. David Kullock. Asesor del Gobierno de la Ciudad en al CAPU

Arq. Heriberto Allende. Asesor del Gobierno de la Ciudad en el CAPU

Arq. Olga Vicente. Asesora del Gobierno de la ciudad en el CAPU

Arq. Jorge Lembo. Gerente en la Comisión Municipal de la Vivienda. Gobierno de la Ciudad

Ing. Juan Pablo Martinez. Ingenieros Consultores

Arq. Juan Carlos Angelomé (Asesor Corporación Puerto Madero)

Arq. Andrea Catenazzi (ex-Asesora en la Corporación Puerto Madero)

Arq. Alberto Varas (Ganador Concurso de Ideas Proyecto Retiro)

15

Development of Centralities or Real Estate Market? A Research into Strategic Planning

Preliminary Hypothesis from the Case of Cordoba City.

Ana Falú

Abstract

This paper presents a preliminary hypothesis on the research into Strategic Planning and the feasibility for restructuring cities through creation or development of centralities in intermediate cities in Latin America[85]. In this paper we want to strengthen the significance of the subject given that strategic planning has develop side by side with structural adjustment. The resulting macroeconomic and institutional transformations framed a new logic in city planning and urban management on the city of Cordoba. The opening to the external markets, the financial policy of "convertibility"[86] and the new attribution of local authorities by which they has been empowered to deal directly with global entities, has create new actors and new instruments for decision making and implementation of sectoral policies and actions in the city. In this new context the institutional power have shift from the central entities to local authorities and the responsible of negotiation and the implementation of new mechanism are the local governments. Significant has been the empowerment of Buenos Aires, Córdoba and Rosario's local authorities in the negotiation regarding foreign direct investments, privatisation of assets, concessions and deregulations of infrastructure and urban utilities, land uses and strategic urban projects. The traditional aspiration of restructuring the city through development of centralities seems to be hindered by market opportunities enhancing the concentration of real estate in particular locations. This paper present a first approach to the study, it framed the object of knowledge, and provides preliminary hypothesis and a methodological scheme of successive verifications in the different scales and sectors on which the problem is embedded.

85 The city of Córdoba population is of 1.250.000 inhabitants. It is the second city of the country following Buenos Aires, the capital city of 13 million.inhabitants.

86 During the last government and after the period of high inflation of the country it was installed the "convertibility" stabilizing the argentinian peso = one USA dollar.

The Historical and Institutional Frame of Strategic Urban Planning in Cordoba

Two issues in the study of Latin American urban planning must be highlighted that has form a continuity through the different development period along the run of the XX century. The first is the permanent transference of regional planning instruments, urban theories and urban strategies developed in advanced western countries and applied in the different territorial, social and political context. (Carmona and Burgess, 2001,)[87] and second has been the application of spatial theories, under the conception that structures and spatial processes are independent of the social dimension and therefore subjected to the existence of autonomous spatial laws (Sabatini 1997).

When analysing how it has been treated the issue of urban growth and urban restructuring in Cordoba, we have found that there has not been an exeption. During the whole XX century and specially after the Second World War, it is possible to identify similar trends in spatial planning as those express formerly. There has been a continuous idea that the control of urban growth could be possible through establishing plans and land regulations.

A special question, which will reiterate through time is the idea that mononuclearity, - the expression of the application of the spanish grid layout -, could be overcome through making possible the functional articulation of activity poles in the urban system. The idea of decentralisation and articulation of development poles, centralities, multinodal systems until ideas about the network-city has along the years became an important thinking in the planning and restructuring of the city of Cordoba.

The idea in this paper is to make a review of the planning instrument and to identify the main links between theories and urban restructuring tools. From this review is possible to conclude in some preliminary hypothesis related to the feasibility of focalisation urban development in specific location within a general development strategy of the city.

Historical Review

In fact the first extension plan of the colonial city of Cordoba is done in 1927 and it represents the first intention to correct the monocuclear tendecy of the city. The plan seek to integrate the Spanish grid system of the original city layout to the impressing natural environment of the Sierras, enhancing the creation of sustainable (sub) centres in the frame of the garden city ideas.

Following Ramos [88], the institutionalisation of urban planning practices started with the authorisation for the formulation of the first Direct Plan (Plan Regulador) for the city of Cordoba in 1954, considering an agreement between the technical offices of the Ministry of Public Works and the Municipality (Ordering 4307).

---

87 Carmona and Burgess (2001) in Strategic Planning and Urban Projects. In the chapter about Urban Renewal Policies in Developing Countries. A Historic Review. DUP Sciences .Delft

88 Ramos, Jose Luis, "Planificación Urbana y Regional", FAU, third edition, October 1991.

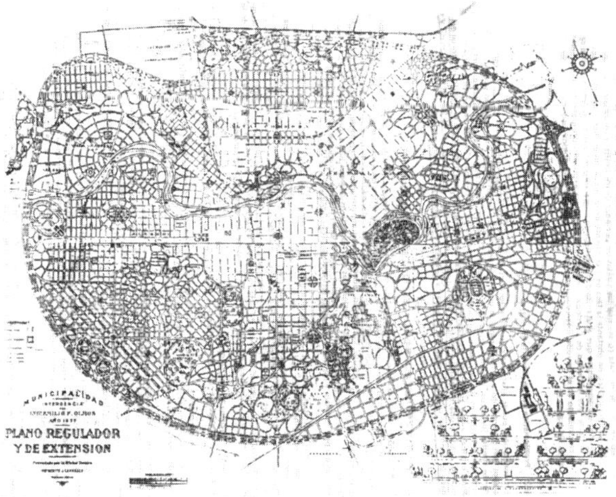

Figura 4. Plano regulador de extensión 1927

Figure 1.Cordoba Map 1927 *Source Ramos*

Several studies are made in this period to answer to the huge transformation ocurred during the two decades of industrialisation and urbanization. Especially was the concern with public works shortages to meet the new requirements.

The most important outcomes are the design of principal civil works and hydraulic studies such as the peripheral-ring, the sanitation of the "Cañada"[89], and the definition of special areas as for the airport and cemetery. Commission where form to deal with the New Building Ordering, the conservation of the historic centre, the definition of the location of the University Campus, etc. Most of the studies and proposal of this time, followed English oriented theories and urban design incorporating important green areas as barriers for the extension of the city.

The Plan 1954 is based on ideas of regional articulation with development poles. From the point of view of the proposed physical model, three main principles were stated:

- Recognition of the difficulties brought about by the mono-centric growth, and therefore the need to create multifunctional polarised centres, whilst urban growth control;
- The growth along preferential access (radial axes) for development. Definition of development axes in relation to the structuring elements (main road system, railway, social equipment).
- The ennvironmental concern was expressed in the creation of green reserve areas.
- From social point of view the model was oriented to meet basic needs

Several institutional changes due to the militar coupe d'etat of 1955 -which meant the end of the peronist government - occurred, making possible the recognition of the Metropolitan level as necessary for dealing with urban development and with the

89 Crick crossing the central area of the city.

ordering of the city. Although the economic weaknesses of the period, some studies were done, particularly the study on the historical center, as well as industrial and transport system. In 1968 is created the APU (Asesoría de Planeamiento Urbano/ Urban Planning Advisorship Office, Law 5465), and the theories of regional development poles as those supported by Kuklinski 1972, Friedman 1967 were applied to studies on the city system. Planning in this decade is considered as to provide some general long-term visions of city form, in which specific urban problems are identified as barrier to attain it. The Metropolitan area was defined in term of the area of influence, accessibility, articulations and flows.

The separation of administrative tasks (income and outcomes of municipal expenditures) and urban controlling task (zoning, specific project regulation) was maintained within a general department of urban planning. In this decade the urbanisation process is accelerated and there is the urgent need to define technically how urban growth should be control. In particular the location of industrial zones, the functional role of the outer-ring, the definitions of zoning, the conservation of the historic centre and the planning of human settlements, which appears as key problem of urban planning of the time. In 1968 it is recognised the need of functional delimitation of responsibilities and attributions, following the existent ideas of the time on 'development poles' and 'system of cities' (Plandemet 1981:57).

In 1973 in the frame of the prevalent ideas of the time both technical based and social-functional oriented studies based on zoning and neighbourhood units ideas where introduced.

Tentative Diagnosis of Physical Development for the city.

From 1973 there is an important turning point in which planning studies are made available to public in general and to the political sector in particular. The transport studies, the same as in most large cities of Latin.America started to be technically improved, informatized and managerialise an adquired a significant role in city planning. This is to say, studies where developed in order to apply efficiency features such as cost-benefits to road and rail systems. Accent is given to the relationship between production and consumption and to the distribution of goods and services. The transport studies propose to involve accesibility to areas, traffic and transit congestion including pedestrianisation ideas in the historic centre.

During this decade some advanced is done in the human settlement studies and practices, particularly between 1973-76, in spite of the former military system (1966-73) and the coup d'etat that takes place in 76. In general the 70s advanced in technical proposition to the city under dualistic believes of the importance of public control to guarantee the conflicts occasioned by market forces liberalisation. During the period the still prevaling welfare state policies approach are tensioned with at the same time the enhancing of private property values and the role of private capitals to construct the city. (see maps of road system, 1974, city centre).

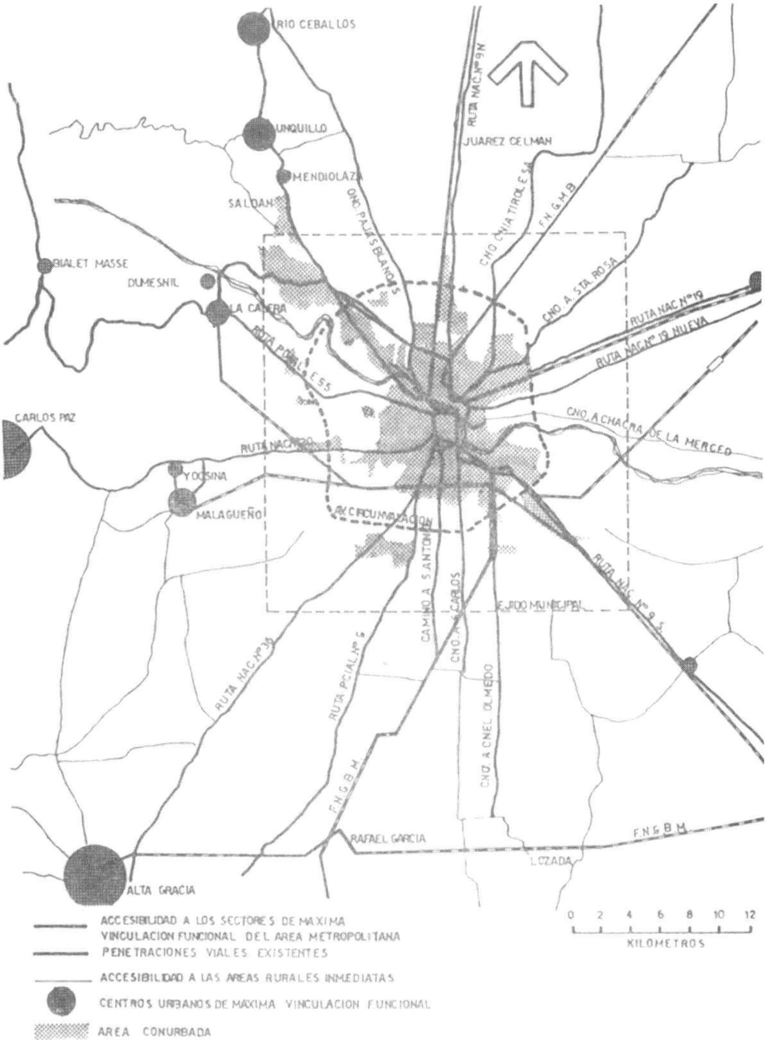

Source: Municipality of Córdoba. 1973

Figure 2. City of Córdoba, Principal Road System.

Metropolisation and the social and economic situation of the 80s are very much responsible for the new and more 'technical position' regarding city planning and policy making. The almost three decades of 'rational planning' implemented under a period of economic growth and welfare which was coming to an end, and the city face an allarming situation of poverty and shortages of public utilities in general. Several urban centres have been affected by the influence of Cordoba's overwhelming growth (eg San

Vicente), while others centres have formed axes strengthening relationships with the central agglomeration. The consolidation of industrialisation and touristical activities nearby the Sierras, the development of certain mining activities, the improvement of road system, the initiation of massive -public- transportation system and later the rapid growth of private automobile contributed to expand the city, and was necessary to think the city and the territory on another way. Ideas about hirerarchy and systematisation of urban centres appeared, parallel with a strong commitment with the environment and ecologic zones. The aptitude and comparative advantage of each microregion will be important for the regional and urban planning of Cordoba agglomeration. Especially the study of not nenovable resources and the protection of hydrographical basin are becaming principal components of the Plandemet-2000 diagnostic at metropolitan level and the protection of the landscape and riverfront at urban level (Plandemet 1981: 123-133).

Plandemet is based also on the believe that urban centres' role is to supply services, therefore more than facilitating productive activity, the city planning should answer to the need of social reproduction and to the organization of the 'collective means'. It is assumed that within the city structure, the various urban centres must maintain a close functional relationship among them, and it should be aim to attain a continuous tissue of activities, assigning to the transport system the role of materializing the flows of goods, persons and services. A 'system of centralities' should be created with particular hierarchy and urban planning should be oriented to solve the specific problem arised among them.

However was recognised the deep problems that hinder the city of Cordoba the possibility to became a polynuclear system with smooth flux of goods, persons and services enhancing accessibility to activity place and social and economic mobility. The Plandemet attributes the main constraints to achieve a functional integrated polynuclear structure to precisely the persistance of the mononuclear and radial orientation of Cordoba's agglomeration and the strong tendency towards polarisation in a regional context.[90]

The second problem that negatively attempts against polynuclearity at a regional scale is the structure of manufactured production, with little integration amongst them and little reinvestments in the region, at the moment 94% of the production is concentrated in the city of Córdoba. The scale factor is also another constrain for the expansion of the market since is related to the behaviour of market forces at national level. These accentuate the uneven distribution of opportunities between poor centres and the great dynamism of others. The sort of productive activity for the internal market (building industry, and activities related to tourism) do not generate a reinvestment process that unable the expansion and diversification of activities and the reduction of the high vulnerability product of the lack of diversification. (Plandemet 81)

At the level of urban structure Plandemet considers the low density of residential settlements, the mono functional character of residential zones, inadequate use of land and urban services and the exaggerated existence of speculative 'empty' land as the main cause of urban inefficiency, that strikes against polynuclearity. It argues for the consequences of diminish the level of rentability of public investments that in last instance accentuates monocentrality.

---

90 Cordoba is at regional scale, an important centre of economic, cultural and administrative activities. In 1980 it concentrates the 45% of the provintial population, prognosis to the year 2000 did advanced that the population would grew to 57%. (Plandemet p 158)

Several proposals offer the Plandemet to achieve a system of urban centres in Cordoba:
- First is the creation of location advantage for new industries and productive activities.
- Second is the discouragement of location of industries oriented at a critical mass in order to avoid a short life and possible fluctuation.
- Third is the re-location of industries and activities that produce negative externalities.

Plandemet also propose the need of significant investments in socio-cultural functions and to improve service infrastructure in the urban centres in function of a hierarchical order. It also supports the creation of peripheral located alternatives in order to supply secondary centres along the ring. It support the elaboration of norms for urban ordering that enhance site values and opportunities (e.g. central area, traditional neighbourhoods, peripheral neighbourhoods, sub-centres) and able to respect and/or orient the demographic trends. Also it supports the use of empty and derelict land within the urban structure according to their functions and zoning regulations. It also proposes to increase taxation in speculative empty land, especially of those lands that hinder the extension of infrastructure and municipal services efficiently. Plandemet propose the consolidation of inter-urban sub-centres in order to reduce daily population mobility. It comprehends the urban subcentres consolidated, such as: Alta Cordoba; General Paz; San Vicente; Maipu; the roadcross Ave. Velez Sarsfield-Santa Gracia Road; the national road N^0 20; Alberdi and Alto Alberdi; San Martin; Cerro la Rosas; Boulevard Monsenor Pablo Cabrera and Boulevard Los Granaderos. Eleven subcentres located in the consolidated neighbourhoods of the city. Most of them corresponding with the so-called "Pueblos de Córdoba" (Córdoba Towns).

During the Eighties Argentina has fully entered to neoliberalism and has opened the economy to external markets. In the Nineties it started a second phase of development known as the phase of 'social adjustments'. Social inequalities and unemployment has grown alarmingly and the period of economic and finantial adjustments was already completed.

The period from 1995-2001 is one characterised by a new financial crisis of unexpected conseuences, insofar it is linked to global financial forces. In fact the few years of rapid economic growth has come to an end and a new constitutional and economic crisis started in the mid 90s and will revert the expectation of the Strategic Plan for the City of Cordoba (PEC).

Cordoba's metropolitan region experienced new social-urban transformations. Spatial and social polarisation is made more evident, and the social fragmentation more marked. There is the flow of important industries to Buenos Aires, started to be developed the phenomena of gated community in the suburbs 'the countries', the car industries suffer significantly, the PYMES (small and medium industries) collapses and capital investments in general flows away. The presence of 'modern activities' and services develop together with the increase of poverty and informal employment grew. Finally the risk country indicator score dramatically: Argentina is located in the first place, there is a generalised lack of political confidence.

In this context the Strategic Plan of Cordoba is launched (1994). The strategic plan understood Cordoba inserted in a national and regional-continental strategic position in respect to the MERCOSUR (the regional bloc market was structured in 1995). According to the PEC the polarization of Buenos Aires and the enlargement of the area of influence have grew significantly, en Cordoba in spite of its economic strength, reduce its population rate from 2.16% in the decade 1970-1980 to 1.64% in the decade 1980-1991

(PEC,1996). In 1991 the population of Buenos Aires metropolitan region is 10.887.000 and the population of Cordoba metropolitan is 1.200.000. The economic vitality of the region remains in the manufacturing sector, which is able to resist and to reconvert although the pressures from great Buenos Aires. The secondary sector contributes with 25% of the GNP while the primary sector the 23% and the tertiary the 52%. The manufacturing sector represent and important part of the provincial production. Only 3 of the total branches represent more than the 2/3 part of the GDP. These are the basic metallic industries and manufacturing of metallic industries (specially the car production), the non-metallic product (as cement) and the food sector. The 50% of the national car production are done in Cordoba. The car production grew from almost 100 millions US dollar from 1990 to 450 million US dollar in 1994.

Provincial Manufacture sector 1994	Number of enterprises	%100	Working population	%100
Total Provincial	5.422	100	80.930	100
Food, drinks and tobacco	2.349	43.3	26.486	32,7
Non metallic minerals	269	5.0	5.296	6,5
Basic industries specially car production	1,357	25,0	31,844	39,3

Source:Ministry of Commerce. PEC 1996

Although the diversified economic base and tendencies towards specialisation a need to increase foreign investments attraction, as well as diversification and technologic and managerial modernization is recognized necessary.

The thinking about polynuclearity is now seen in a more pragmatic way, and this is to seen because centralities are not a preocupation expressed particularly by the local technicians and professionals, but what can be observed, is the change on the planning conception according the changes of political perspective of the power sector linked to the city government. The PEC develop a number of principles and instruments which need to be analysed through the study of the implementation in the city.

The New Principles and Planning Instruments

The Strategic Plan of the city of Cordoba (PEC) is meant to be an holistic project addressed to inter-sectoral objectives oriented towards development. The Plan is a structure framework consisting of proposals for medium and long-term action, accompanied by a mechanism for short-term micro planning. The main characteristic of the PEC are:

- It aims to improve traditional planning and meant to be closer to reality, resources and social actors.
- It define urban objectives from the existing social dynamic.
- It develops a permanent relationship between objectives, strategies, projects and impacts .
- It recognises the need for the converging of interests between public and private actors in all phases of plan making and implementation.
- Concrete results can be measured in the short term and that actions identify resources needed.
- It aims to take advantage of existing opportunities to create new opportunities for the future.

- Strategic Planning brings together public and private efforts and initiatives to create a new city consciousness.

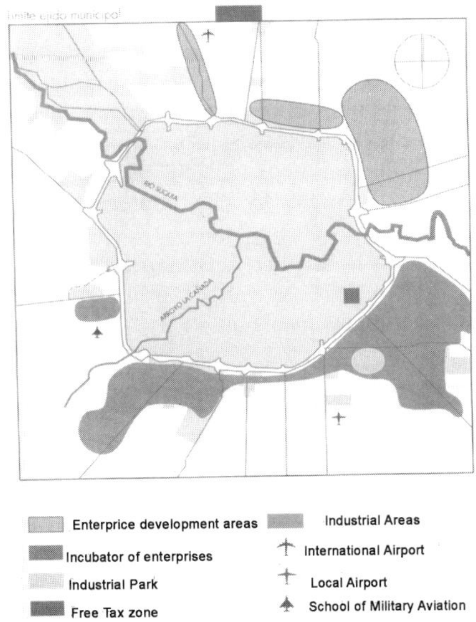

Figure 3.
Development of New Spaces for the Economic Diversity of the City
Source PEC Municipality of Córdoba

The Figure 3 shows PEC proposition regarding the new space for the economic diversity of the city of Cordoba

The PEC also recognises the existence of three spatial zones. First the Central area of about 170 Spanish blocks, of high density, which coincide with the historic centre. Secondly, the intermediate area, which corresponds to the traditional residential area around and concentrically to the central area. And third a peripheral suburban area consolidated during the last 40 years, the low-density area, containing both low-income as high-income residential zones.

The weakness of Cordoba's city structure according to the PEC is the persistence of the mononuclear and radial structure of the city, with and extended suburban periphery which creates a number of negative externalities. Those externalities are: the excessive concentration of activities in the central area, the high grows rhythm of the suburban periphery with excessive urban costs, the high social and physical fragmentation, a significant increase of private cars, which grew from about 250.000 units in 1990 to about 340.000 in 1995. This fact is aggravated with the critical public transport of the city, with insufficient response in terms of supply and demand as well as a critical policy in respect to the natural environment. Finally is to mention the persistence of the lack of coordination between public entities.

Concerning the urban structure transformations the PEC considers that decisions regarding the densification and consolidation of the periphery and urban renewal and refunctioning of city-centres, need to be integrated and based on comprehensive studies about land use, accessibility and transportation changes. There is a recognition of existing links between environmental objectives and the need to enhance the economic and functional vitality of the central areas, the peripheral nodes and the growth of the city.

The political discourse of the PEC is to enhance financial and managerial modernisation of municipal entities, and to improve decision-making through planning, information and citizen participation. The first two fronts, planning and information, aim to cope with complexity through urban management rationalisation, thereby enhancing efficiency in the allocation of resources and through the creation of instruments to improve technical and financial management according to politically rationalised objectives, supported by the strategic processes of analysis, implementation and evaluation.

The third front, citizen participation, was to be a political instrument for municipal modernisation, and for planning through programmes of decentralisation and the development of the local authority.

The PEC aim at the "descentralisation" of civil and social activities, which is to say the organic deconcentration of activities of the Municipality of Córdoba was concretized in the construction of the CPC..

The CPCs are more than a center of deconcentration in terms of facilitating the performing of citizens civic responsibilities (taxes, public services payment, marriages, among others), but also cultural and social gathering activities. The materialization of the CPC included spaces for multiple purposes, auditorium, theater, as well as public libraries. The CPC are opened from 8 to 20 hs and they have increased their activity from 1999 to 2000 in around 60% of public demand.[91]

Complementary to this organic deconcentration concretized in the CPCs, the city of Córdoba materializedthe functional diversification and services supply in the old "centralities" system of the city, the consolidated sub-centers of San Vicente, Alta Córdoba and General Paz, "Cultural Centers".

In short, the Strategic Planning for the city of Córdoba PEC (1994) position:

- Aims to transform Cordoba in a modern, sustainable, equitable and competitive city.
- It enhances liberalisation and the need to attract investments on new modern sector including service, tourism and industrial diversification
- Recognises the weakness of the radial and mononuclear structure of the city, and the existence of three spatial zones related to city consolidation
- It looks for the opportunities of regional integration.
- It takes advantages from the decentralisation process and the Municipal Reform.
- It enhances urban transformation through decentralisation and the construction of Centres of Popular Participation - CPC

91 CEDIN, *Radiografía de Córdoba.*Julio 2001.

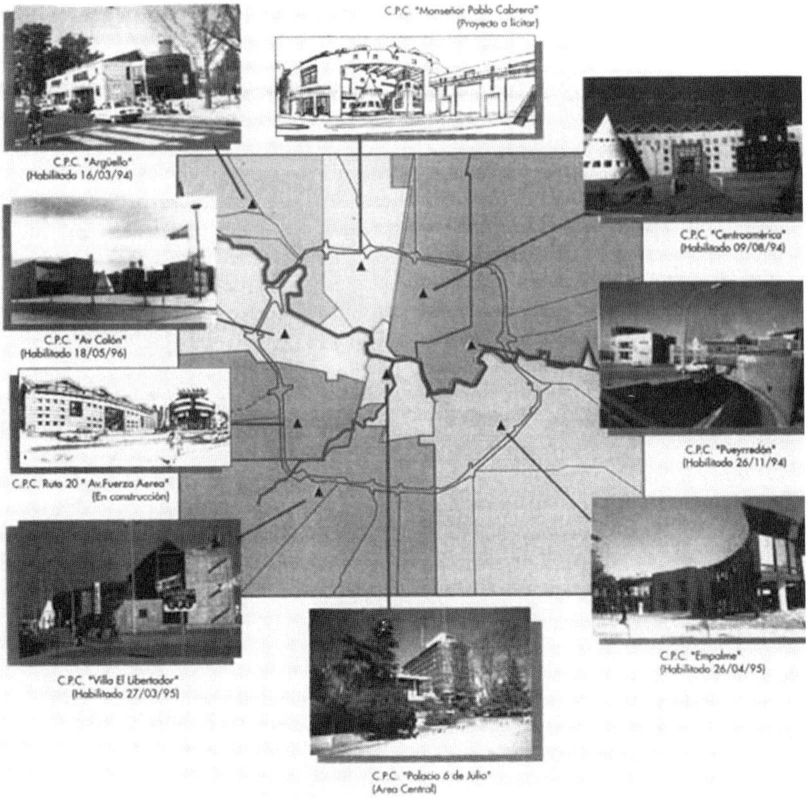

Source PEC Municipality of Córdoba

Figure 4. Location of the CPC

The urban Transformation is based on the decentralization process initiated with the functioning of the centers of popular participation (CPC)

The New Development Context and the System of Centralities.

In order to analyse the feasibility of System of centralities, this study has selected a case study and has performed some preliminary gathering of empirical evidences.

Since the first planning instruments, the city of Córdoba was concerned about the danger of monocentrality, this preoccupation was reinforced in the period of import substitution, and the planning proposals were oriented by the desire for institutional decentralization and polinuclearity. The different planning instruments (EDEOU – Plandemet, among others) were implemented with more or less success according to the political period and city management capacities. Even with different political regimes, the decentralization and polinuclearity were issues of strong interests, not only in the discourse but in some well known project implementation as the CPC during the late 90s.

The process of "deconcentration with centralisation" (de Mattos 1999) the spatial characterization of the new spatial model of globalisation and neoliberalism, is being accelerated by the generalisation in the use of the private car and the new consumption habits of the elite. New urban corridors have expanded the city towards peripheral gated communities taking with them the high income recreational, commercial and high tech services activities. Simultaneously large mega-projects are being negotiated by central and local governments in the framework of a focalised strategy for investment based on public/private partnerships. They mainly consist of malls for the high income sectors and hyper markets (Makro, Carrefour,) for the medium and low income sectors. The city is becoming increasingly polarised - with mega projects conveniently located on the urban corridors or nearby them; the historical centre of the city is loosing its hegemonic role with only the financial sector and the traditional retail sectors remaining , and there are large downgraded residential areas of pauperised populations. (Falú 2000) [92]

In term of social context the period is characterised a deepening of poverty conditions and social polarisation. In the low-income areas of the city poverty has growth significantly. In the total country urban poverty represent 7,4 millions people of a total population of 34.8 millions inhabitants (Permanent Survey of Household) and earns U$S 2.2 per day per capita. The official data defines the "poverty level" in U$S4.1 per day per capita. The national polarisation is evident when compare that in Cordoba, where population registers much more degradation with U$S1.7 per day per capita, even lower than the critical situation of the Metropolitan Area of Buenos Aires which reaches a U$S1.9 per capita/ per day. [93]

Hypothesis

Considering this new context, the main hypothesis leading this research is that, revitalisation strategies based on urban intensification policies in central city areas are valid in societies with a high degree of economic and social homogeneity. In socially heterogeneous societies they can lead to social and spatial segregation rather than increased social diversity and interaction.

It is argued that urban operations would have a number of positive impacts on the revitalisation of the area of implementation, including increased dynamism, the development of a rapid process of densification and the consolidation of a tertiary urban sector (employment generation). Given the strong social and territorial evidences, in the case of negative response to the former inquiries, the emerging questions are related to which would be the possible tools, norms and/ or strategies to fulfil the proposed strategies and objectives.

This research wants to verify which is the contribution of these type of project implementation for the city as a whole and particularly in the self area of intervention, does it creates multiplying effects of urban renovation?

Which is the effectiveness of these interventions to improve urban productivity?

To develop consistent evidence on the main hypothesis, a case study research is on going focusing in one significant megaproject in a central part of the city, in the periphery of the historic centre. This project gathers a number of traditional strategies

---

92 Falú, Ana, URBAN POLICIES REVIEW. The Opportunities and Limitations of Urban Revitalisation strategy: *A case study analysis,* in Carmona et al, Alfa IBIS No 2. Delft Press, 2000.

93 Bolsa de Comercio de Córdoba e Instituto de Investigaciones Económicas, *El Balance de la Economía Argentina en 2000*: pp366-68.

and processes - as well as new ones -, related to urban renovation, resulting in a number of complex issues involved as:

- Identification of potential areas for urban development that have conditions for attracting investments and at the same time, to promote revitalisation to depressed city areas;
- Intensification of land use, with positive externalities generation.
- Eradication of squatters (illegal settlements relocated on the urban periphery).
- Reinforcement, of the sector under study, of the Spanish city grid structure with the opening of new roads and the creation of accessibility to the sector and connexions at city scale.
- New urban land use regulations and zoning flexibility (increase of densities).
- Production of negative externalities, like traffic jams, noises pollution, as the most evident.
- The generation of a process of urban land speculation, therefore stock of "speculative land".
- The construction of a great closed mall, with a program of around 150.000m2, including a five stars hotel, a cinema complex, convention centre facilities, public services, and the moll itself.

The interest in this contribution is to review the physical impact and to analyse the land use regulations, increase of density, land uses, new infrastructure (traffic nodes, new city corridor), increase of traffic congestion and pollution

The Site Opportunities

The site is a vacant area nearby the historical centre. It is located on the top of a steep slope. It is a "natural" barrier, selected for creating a new sub centre to revitalise the sector. An illegal settlements is located in sector B. which must be evicted

The plot has about 12 ha. is located in a consolidated middle-class sector. It is a connecting-area between the historical centre and the most dynamic growth axe of the city: a high-income area. The University Hospital as well as other important services are located in the sector as well the Ave. Colon, the main city axe and to the north of the plot a garden city neighbourhood and to the south a depressed sector.

The objective of this project for the local authorities is to improve the urban productivity as a whole and to revitalise the sector in particular. Therefore a long-term investment program has been done with infrastructure delivery, consisting in a new urban corridor and traffic node and the development of a multifunctional activity centre.

A new land regulation has been established for the development of a new urban centrality and for facilitating the attraction of national and foreign investors.

Important components arouse from this public private partnership has been the importance to the architectonic image, and well-known Architectural firms has been invited.

Secondary hypothesis are in preparation, however it is anticipated that data gathering and empirical verification are being directed to verify a number of question that we have stated in an earlier phase and which is in elaboration. These are the following.

- At national level, there are an amount of information necessary to be gathered to analyse investments opportunities. Besides the questions on country risks variables, there is information related to the amount of FDI investments in real estate and it relation to the size of the urban economy and to the physical extension of the city. Amount of ITC connections in relation to primary agglomeration. Level (quantity and quality) of technical and social infrastructure. The hypothesis that could be able to be established here is: *Hitherto large headquarters of international firms have not been located in secondary cities in L.A.*

- Study on urban vitality, nature and intensity of accessibility improvements. Accessibility advantages and mobility (including O&D information of trips). Property taxes, comparative analysis of market pricing of the city and of the surrounding in particular. Here we can anticipate the hypothesis that: *Large retail- centers (malls) in inner city areas seek car-based accessibility advantages based on corridors, and produce very few multipliers that lead to economic and physical revitalization of surrounding areas.*

- Surveys to entrepreneurs about opportunities of investments and choices. Here we can anticipate the hypothesis that: In the absence of proactive public policies, market forces associated with malls do not encourage upgrading and urban development by themselves.
- Studies in nuisance level (traffic congestion, noise, air pollution, visual pollution) and changes in the market pricing of housing can lead to results oriented to the generation of externalities and level of maintenance of surrounding properties. It can lead to hypothesis such as: *Sub-centres can generate negative externalities which affect surrounding areas and other centres elsewhere.*

- Studies on the compatibility of land use, and newly created direct and indirect employment and the relation with accessibility and mobility (question 2) *can lead to studies on residential upgrading potentials. It can be advanced the following hypothesis:*

a) The greater the diversity of community, civic and services functions in the sub-centres the better the opportunities there will be for residential development and/or improvement.
b) The positive externalities of a sub-centre in term of labour and capital are not necessarily locally based.

- Studies on coverage of infrastructure, incomes, public investments in the city and the real estate survey in main rapid developing corridors and considering periods with market forces liberalisation, changes in zonning regulation and system of centralities (quantification and calification of centralities) can study the relation between public investments and income sectors. The question that can be poses here is: Accessibility improvements are generally undertaken by public investment which have been oriented towards areas with high levels of consumption rather than towards deprived urban areas.

References

Bolsa de Comercio de Córdoba e Instituto de Investigaciones Económicas, *El Balance de la Economía Argentina en 2000*: pp366-68.

Burgess y Carmona "Urban Renewal Policies in Developing Countries" Delft University Press 2000.

Carmona, Burgess (2001) ". Strategic Planning & Urban Projects" Responses to Globalisation from 15 Cities, Forthcoming Delft University Press. 2001.

Diagnóstico Tentativo y Alternativas de Desarrollo Físico para la Ciudad de Córdoba, Municipalidad de Córdoba, Argentina. 1973.

EDOU, Esquema de Ordenamiento Urbano, Municipalidad de Córdoba, Argentina. 1978.

Falú, Ana, *"Conceptual Framework for the Assessment of Strategic Urban Planning in Córdoba, Argentina"*, en Carmona & Rosemann, "Globalization, Urban Form and Governance", No 2 First International Conference Proceedings. Delft University Press. 2000.

Falú, Ana, *"Local and Global. The new paradigm of the postmodern city"*, en Carmona, Drewe, Rosemann, Van Duin, "Globalization, Urban Form and Governance", No 1 First International Conference Proceedings. Delft University Press. 2000.

PEC Plan Estratégico para la Ciudad de Córdoba , Municipalidad de Córdoba, Argentina, 1994.

Friedmann,J. (1986) Planificación en Latino America: de la ilusión tecnocratica a la democracia abierta. Revista EURE, Vol 13, N.37.

Friedmann,J. (1966) . Hyperurbanization and national Development in Chile: some hypotheses. Urban Affairs Quartely, June

Kuklinsky (1972) Ponencia al Seminario Ilpes-Siap. Buenos Aires

PLANDEMET, Municipalidad de Córdoba, Argentina. 1981.

Ramos, Jose Luis, "Planificación Urbana y Regional", FAU- UNC, Tercera Edición , Octubre 1991, Córdoba, Argentina.

Valenzuela. J. (1997) Urban Decay and Local Management Strategies for the Metropolitan Centre: The Experience of the Municipality of Santiago, Chile. In Latin American Regional Development In an Era of Transition. The Challenge of Decentralization, Privatization and Globalization. UN Centre for Regional Development. Nagoya, Japan.

16

Socio-Economic Impacts on Urban Public Space: A Case in Downtown San Miguel De Tucuman, Argentina

Raul di Lullo, Ana Kantarovsky

Abstract

In this paper some of the consequences that investment decisions in private spaces have on urban public space (UPS) are discussed. After defining UPS as a multi-value collective asset its potential for development in the perspective of a sound governance scheme is acknowledged. Under the hypothesis that selective private investments do establish conditions that largely influence and set trends for UPS development a case study in the innermost part of downtown San Miguel de Tucuman is presented, the traditional CBD referred to locally as the *'microcentro'*. The evidence collected shows how two commercial streets, a few hundred meters apart from each other, constitute two contrasting worlds as a result of the development options induced by their respective private investment strategies. The paper concludes with some reflections about the need of reviewing present urban management attitudes in search of better governance alternatives, where UPS development strategies could play an important role in generating a safer stance in front of globalisation forces.

Introduction

This short paper pursues to discuss some of the consequences produced on the urban public space (UPS) by investment decisions in private spaces. It is a first approach to a complex topic we are starting to work on and will be a research subject for years to come. A recurrent problem is worth mentioning from the outset. Trustworthy data is difficult to collect due to the reluctance of the involved actors to release economic and financial information about their activities, as much as to the lack of systematic and updated records together with the extent of informal arrangements in the local commercial activities. Consequently, in this primary research stage an overall empirical method has been adopted. By reading the dynamics of change in the study area over the last decade in largely phenomenological terms the construction of a first database is pursued, making use of both pre-existing and ad-hoc surveys, which allow us to make some inferences from a few discernible variables:

- Changes in localised activities (primary function, occupancy / vacancy)
- Visible morphological aspects (architectural features, estimated building age, present

status –under construction / demolition- state of repair)
- Trading activity and type of products offered.
- Origin of investment (local / national / international)

On the other hand, key-informants and a number of other sources have been consulted such as real estate agents specialised in the study area, newspaper articles, and informal interviews to shop owners and employees. We also resorted to our own memory and our experience of the city.

Studying the case of the *microcentro* in San Miguel de Tucumán we start to collect preliminary evidence in order to build up pertinent knowledge along time about local development mechanisms, aiming to contribute to a gradual transformation of decision-making models and to the formulation of concrete and realistic project proposals.

Some Definitions and Points of Departure

Urban landscape is closely associated to structural transformation processes. In the informational society of growing globalisation, processes of production, distribution and management are generating deep transformations across socio-cultural, economic, environmental and spatial aspects. The effects vary from city to city, imposing conditions and characteristics according to their respective history, development level, culture and institutions.

We conceive of urban public space as a multi-value entity (morphological, functional, social, cultural, political, economical, environmental), as a collective asset with a historical memory (not as nobody's land), and as a source of opportunities for a great variety of human activities and civic life. We see it also as an effective vehicle to help to achieve a better urban quality of life and competitiveness, not only in a strictly economic sense but in terms of social and cultural enjoyment as well. It is in such perspective that we envisage the potentiality of UPS as a true resource for strategic development in cities (Di Lullo 1998).

On the other hand we realise the intimate link between public and private spaces. Both realms are physically adjacent and influence each other in every sense, be it morphological, functional, economic, or communicational. Thus, we acknowledge the forces which interventions in the public space can release in order to achieve a positive synergy with private initiatives, provided that they are guided by principles of integrity and 'good governance'. Both are considered essential to conducive urban management and the latter refers to relationships between the state and civil society based upon credibility and legitimacy ensured by mutual responsibility, transparency, responsiveness and real participation (McCarney et al. 1995). In a similar way we realise the negative effects of decisions taken in the name of exclusively sectoral interests and detached from the aforementioned conditions or in a context of low enforcement capacities. Unfortunately, in our direct experience this is the most familiar scenario.

In line with these definitions, we set forward the working hypothesis that the spatial selectivity of investments in the private realm do establish conditions that largely influence and set trends that characterise the development of urban public space, not only in economic but also in morphological-functional, socio-cultural and environmental terms.

The *'Microcentro'* in Downtown San Miguel De Tucumán

1. Relevant background data

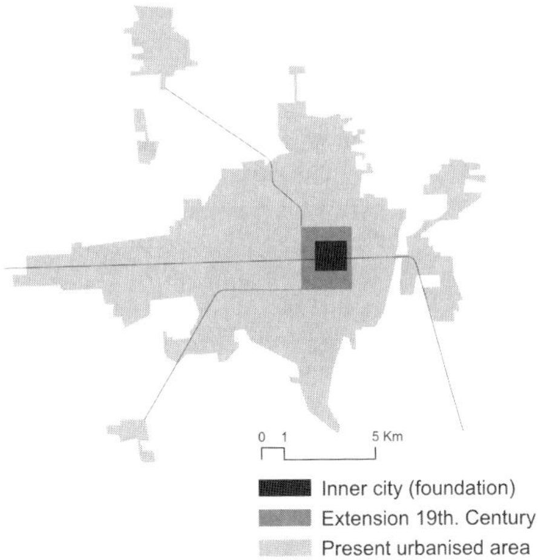

The city of Tucumán is today an urban agglomeration of 6 municipalities and 10 rural communes encompassing a territory of 867 km2, so-called Greater San Miguel de Tucuman (GSMT) or Metropolitan Area. The resident population of 717.772 inh. in 1991 (INDEC 1993) is expected to reach 1 million by 2010 according to projections (Di Lullo & Giobellina 1996). A recent socio-economic survey reveals that 30% of that population suffers from 'unfulfilled basic needs' (or NBI in the local statistical jargon) 94, ranking as the fourth poorest urban conglomerate in the country.

After its foundation in 1565 and once moved to its present location in 1685, the city grew from the original settlement of 9 x 9 blocks to the 19th century expansion of 14 x 18 blocks in 1900. Both layouts keep recognisable features in the urban fabric today. From then on the city expanded well beyond, consistently following the original grid pattern through a combined model of concentric and linear growth with the successive dominance of the E-W axis from the 50's and the N-S axis from the 70's. The *microcentro* takes up approximately 30 blocks within the foundational city.

2. Characteristics of the 'microcentro'

From the morphological and functional points of view the *microcentro* shares its basic characteristics with the inner areas of most of the Argentine intermediate cities: a relatively small area with a large concentration of commercial, finance, institutional and leisure activities. It is a real enclave within an originally residential fabric featuring narrow streets and sidewalks, a very recognisable environment in the oldest part of the city which still functions as its most important centre, if not its only one widely recognised as such. Both historical and present functional reasons make it a very lively place: a great variety of objects, activities and agents gather in the *microcentro*, weaving

94: EPH – Permanent Household Survey, late 2000 round.

a complex fabric of economic, socio-cultural, and political relationships –both formal and informal.

Its present physical configuration as well as its dynamics come out of a process of mostly private investments which have been characterising and consolidating different sub-zones along time, becoming today true structuring elements for the whole area. They define with striking precision formal and visible features as much as commercial performance standards. A difference in location of just a few meters can determine not only the convenience –or inconvenience- of establishing a certain trading activity together with its corresponding architectural outlook but also the success or failure of a business initiative.

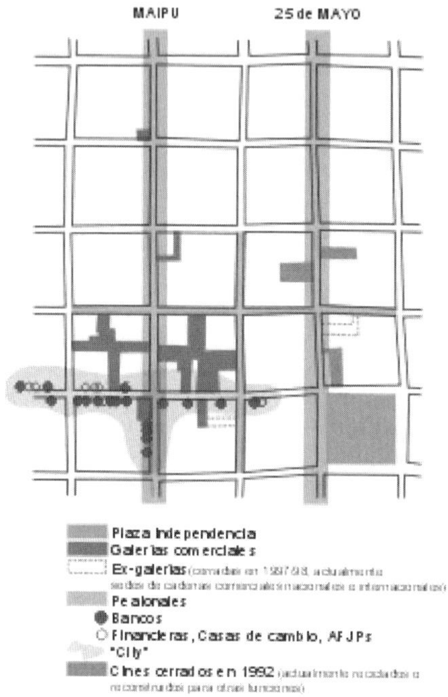

Regarding public spaces the *microcentro* can be defined in general terms as a small group of intensely commercial streets (4 running N-S and 6 in the direction E-W) located in the vicinity of the central foundational plaza. Some of them stand out for different reasons: *24 de Setiembre* is a definite and recognisable structural E-W axis at the macro-urban scale and still acts as a major traffic collector, *Muñecas* and *Mendoza* constitute a highly distinct pedestrian precinct (the former being the largest public investment in the area dating back from the 80's), whereas *San Martín* is the seat of banking and finance-related activities. Other streets such as *25 de Mayo* and *Maipú*, running parallel at about 300 metres from each other, share the intensity of commercial activity but are set apart by deep differences in their respective development processes and responses to the effects of globalisation. They constitute our specific study object and illustrate the validity of our hypothesis.

Regarding private spaces the most salient and characterising feature of the *microcentro* is the network of shopping arcades carved out through the built-up blocks and gradually developed since *Galería Pezza* opened in 1938, followed in 1950 by *Galería La Gaceta*. After them the most significant investments concentrated in the early 60's –with the construction of 3 major ones- and during the 80's, when 5 others were added. All of them have kept their commercial significance until today, with differences stemming from their relative location in the network. The last one belonging to the third period, though, was located slightly off the centre of gravity of the *microcentro* and failed to survive as an arcade. After being shut down for a long time it has been reconverted a few years back to house the branch of a country-wide, foreign capital-owned chain selling home appliances.

The most noticeable changes that took place along the past decade produced two major effects regarding the landscape structuring elements in the *microcentro*. On the one hand there has been a remarkable refurbishment of the rather modest financial district. In fact, from harbouring a half-dozen of mostly public banks until the late 80's it became at present the seat for around 20 banks –all private, except one- together with some 10 offices for finance-related services (currency exchange and credit agencies, pension fund administrators, insurance companies). On the other hand a new, unprecedented sort of commercial and leisure axis came up and consolidated along *25 de Mayo* street.

3. Case study

Based on our and others' everyday experience and knowledge of the city, together with some critical considerations about the present state of affairs and the impacts of global transformations along the past decade, we selected two streets as representative cases for typical situations currently manifested in the *microcentro* :

- **25 de Mayo**: once a traditional street of movie theatres, coffee shops and institutional buildings, it has become today the business place mostly for high-end clothing and mixed catering (bars, restaurants, fast-food). A thriving teen-age street activity adds up to the more formal bustle, although it is no longer at its peak when the street used to be literally transformed into 'occupied territory' during certain weekdays. In the early 90's all 4 movie theatres which gave its imprint to the character of the area – among them 3 major ones and emblematic for movie goers- were dismantled. Two have been recycled for other purposes and the remaining ones have been demolished to give way to a recently opened 4-star hotel with associated shopping, bar, and covered parking areas. Nevertheless, a series of valuable buildings as architectural heritage still stand and serve their original purposes keeping an institutional presence in the area, such as the House of the Provincial Government, set in 19th century eclecticism, the head Post Office -a visual landmark for years with its picturesque Italian neo-gothic, devaluated at present by uncontrolled commercial signage- and the University Cultural Centre, an early 20th century exemplar of academic architecture originally built for one of the local newspapers and recycled in 1984 into its present format.
- **Maipú**: a traditional and popular commercial street in the *microcentro*, characterised by a mixed collection of trading activities but dominated by clothing, textiles, furniture and food, along with a concentration of wholesale shops. Years ago the notorious presence of shop owners of Arab and Jewish descent used to characterise the streetscape with their outwardly trading habits, but they are being challenged and

their territory disputed today by the increasing informal sector. The most significant urban landmark is the *Mercado del Norte* (Northern Market), still working according to the traditional scheme of individual stall operators inside and a ring of shops open to the streets outside. Its presence largely stresses the popular character of this busy sub-zone in the *microcentro*. The street dynamics is further accentuated by another important fact. Two blocks with a high concentration of shopping arcades happen to communicate at a central point across this street, where two of the *galerias* open in front of each other and give access to about 80% of the arcade network.

As it has already been said both streets run parallel not far away from each other and represent two different worlds, two contrasting realities set apart by just 300 metres and expressing the duality that in the last decade has reached unprecedented marks in our country. On the one hand there is the affluent *25 de Mayo*, selected by international and national firms to enter the local market setting shopping outlets directly or through franchising. Together with the best equipped pedestrian area running in between both streets under study this new commercial haven added up business investments for some 40 million U.S. dollars by April 2000, pushing rents as much as a 40% higher and setting the price of shopping window frontage at $ 1.000 to $ 1.100 per lineal metre [95]. On the other hand, there lies the semi-stagnating *Maipú*, with a substantially slower investment pace manifested in the lower relative percentage of new buildings and recent refurbishments, together with a comparatively poorer state of repair and the proliferating informal street trade fuelled by unbending recession and growing unemployment.

Taking a municipal survey conducted in 1993 as the reference base and a recent fieldwork update carried out by ourselves a quantitative comparison was made using a small group of relevant indicators postulated within the limitations emerging from the categories used in the previous survey:

Aspect explored	Postulated indicator	Values
Dynamics / Mobility	Change In Activity	• YES • NO
	Vacancy (closed off premises)	• YES • NO
Investment / Building Quality	Status	• New (< 5 years) • Recent remodelling • Demolishing or building
	State of Repair	• Good • Fair • Bad

After processing the collected data the following observations can be made. The quantification of the dynamics of change in *25 de Mayo* almost doubles the one in *Maipú* and is confirmed by the vacancy indicator (in the latter the proportion of empty units is 50% higher than in the former). Looking at investments and building quality this trend is corroborated with even more disparate values: in *25 de Mayo* the percentage of new units is almost 4 times larger whereas its recent remodelings doubles and its proportion of

95: interview to the Commercial Development Manager of Feler Real Estate Brokers, a major firm dealing with the new business environment in the area (*El Periodico, 02 APR 2000*)

buildings or demolition works is 6 times higher than the ones in *Maipú*. Being the state of repair a variable tightly related to the building age the pattern of relationships is consistent with the previous measurements: *25 de Mayo* almost trebles the proportion of units in good state of repair as compared with *Maipú* and this one in its turn features a 50% and almost 5 times more units qualifying as 'fair' and 'bad' regarding their state of repair respectively. Such values constitute a quantitative confirmation of the magnitude of qualitative differences recorded in the visual survey. On the other hand, the change of activity between commerce and services scores with similar proportions in both streets.

Those differences are also corroborated through the real estate market:

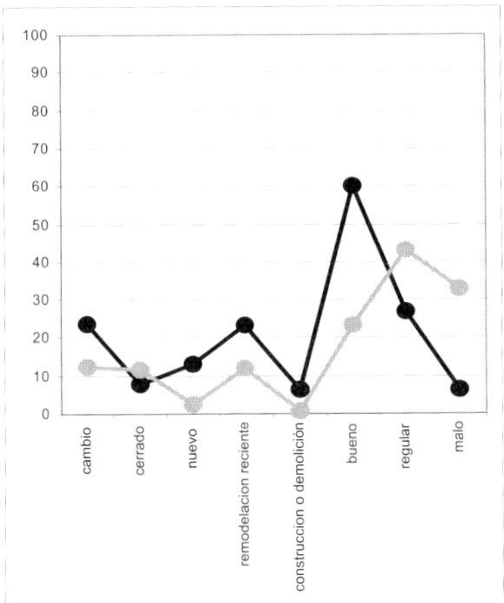

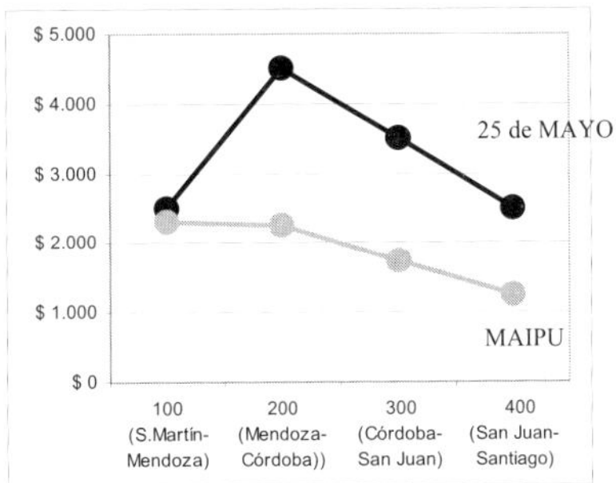

Average Rent Prices

(april 2000)

The rental value for a commercial unit in the so-called 'phenomenon 25' is approximately 0.7% to 0.8% of its property value, reaching 1% in some cases. The owner of a standard 6 x 20 meter unit in April 2000 rented it out at the prices indicated in Graph II, with a gross monthly investment return of 0.8% to 1% in front of current interest bank rates of 0.4% to 0.5% at that time. The same graph depicts how rental values vary in different blocks along both streets and the value gap between them, with *Maipú* consistently scoring at 50% of the current values in *25 de Mayo*. The only exception is the first block of the latter, where the San Francisco church is located: one of the most valued historical monuments in the city paradoxically 'devaluates' the street in real estate terms. That happens because its atrium and front stairs usually attract loitering street children and beggars, turning it into an 'unpleasant' landscape for commerce. Immediately past that block the monthly rental prices go up and in cases can reach a peak of U.S. 5000 dollars [96]. In both streets the declining tendency is clear towards the North, as a more intense residential character gradually takes over the area.

Variations in the number of units engaged in different trading activities could be recorded just for two central blocks in both streets, restriction emerging from the design of the one and only previous survey available with the necessary details (carried out in 2000):

96: information supplied by Perez Jaime Real Estate (April 2000)

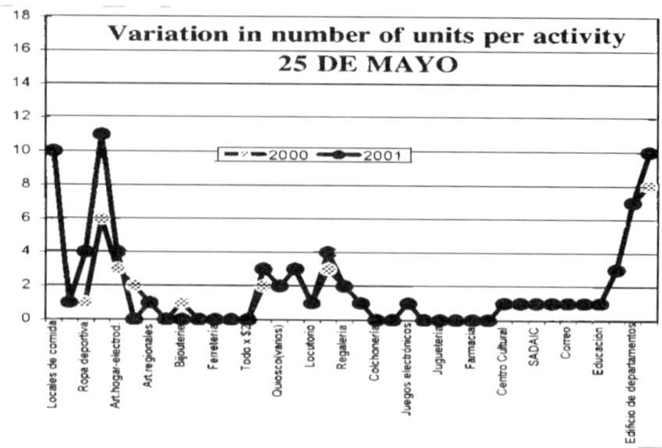

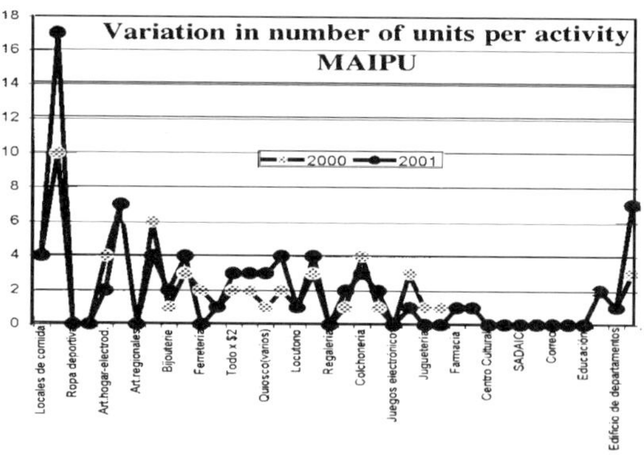

Comparing both streets in the short period of one year the relative stability of *25 de Mayo* is remarkable, where the increments are almost exclusively recorded for specific clothing-related items (such as sport gear, young collections, and shoes) at the same time that others disappear (furniture pieces and fantasy jewellery). On the contrary, *Maipú* is subject to a proliferation of increments and losses, such as clothing in general, kiosks, and parking places among the former and textiles, home appliances, tool ware, toys and flower shops among the latter.

All this would constitute at a first glance the evidence supporting the idea that *25 de Mayo* is burgeoning and consolidating, as opposed to *Maipú* where the somehow haphazard changes would be a manifestation of the prolonged and relentless recession being suffered countrywide and striking with particular severity in the province, but keeping its dynamics thanks to its popular character and to the presence of the Northern Market. The second part of the proposition seems to be a plausible explanation for the hard facts collected in our study. Yet, behind the image of apparent economic affluence in the 'phenomenon 25' many shop owners are increasingly troubled by the mounting difficulty to afford rent prices 97. Such business atmosphere may be eventually a transitory plus for investors rather than for renters but the danger of backfiring lurks behind the unsustainable mismatch between rent prices and recession.

The correlation between the economic dynamics in both cases –measured through the investments in private spaces- and their respective public space is direct. While *25 de Mayo* recycles buildings with architectural values adapting them to new market requirements...

...and erects new units with good construction quality and designs aspiring to the 'architecture-spectacle" expected to perform as a selling device,

... *Maipú* overburdens its existing structures and abuses public space with

(97): informal interviews

uncontrolled signage...

...and attracts informal street sellers who, in absence of a realistic policy to deal with the informal trade, end up aggravating pedestrian as well as vehicular circulation problems.

Illusion of First World, evidence of poverty.

Concluding Reflections

The *microcentro*, as any other part of the city must be understood as a system composed of different sets of objects (buildings, infrastructure, street furniture, vehicles), functions (commercial, leisure, financial, circulation, information activities) and agents (people –permanent and temporary 'users'- and institutions). The complexity of such a system is determined by the number and nature of their components as much as of the relationships among them. Different zones in the city may be classified according to these parameters, and the *microcentro* certainly ranks high in that 'complexity ladder'.

Every urban intervention will affect not only the sector primarily concerned but also those spatially, functionally or institutionally connected with it to a lesser or larger extent. This well-known argument is nevertheless frequently disregarded, so the insistence in preserving the principle of integrity as a *conditio sine qua non* for every intervention in the socio-physical fabric of the city will never be overabundant. This is particularly relevant in cases like the *microcentro* because of its above mentioned complexity, its economic importance (number and relative volume of commercial and financial transactions, real estate values), its attracting role for people, goods and services, and its political-cultural significance in terms of heritage values, institutional presence, and effectiveness as a stage for civic expression.

That is precisely why the *microcentro* deserves special attention during the present critical times: its symbolic contents and its economic significance can be tapped on to set in motion realistic projects to safeguard its vitality and counteract some of the negative impacts of stern globalisation. In fact, a high concentration of small and medium-scale commercial activity and local entrepreneurs, traditional sources of employment and job generation, are confronted in an unequal competition with big national and international firms operating mainly in foodstuff, home appliances and clothing with devastating effects in the local socio-economic fabric and the internal market. A regressive tax system and the lack of aggressive policies to stimulate small and medium-scale business along with the deregulated irruption of mega-stores, shopping malls and 'brand chains', make those differences even deeper and unsustainable.

Decisions made in the private realm in the absence of clear policies and effective enforcement capacities carry to the public domain their achievements and failures without the possibility of a necessary mediation in safeguard of collective interests. Only part of this problem may be regarded as emerging from the endemic scarcity of economic resources (or, rather, from their unreasonable administration) and the heavy bureaucratic and top-down tradition characterising the public sector for so long. Its roots should be rather looked for in the persistent governance crisis and in the lack of a proactive profile plaguing the state institutions. The urban public space will not become an object of efficient management unless necessary changes are introduced in the current urban management models and it is conceived of as a true resource in itself, possible to be exploited for the benefit of the overall urban quality.

References

Di Lullo (1996), *"El Espacio Público como recurso estratégico para el desarrollo urbano",* in Di Lullo & Giobellina (edit.): Hacia una Planificación estratégica del Gran San Miguel de Tucumán, nr.2. LIGHaM, FAU/UNT, Tucumán,

Di Lullo R. & Giobellina B. (1966), La Otra Ciudad: Tucumán frente al 2000, Convenio Programa Arraigo-FAU. FAU/UNT, Tucumán

INDEC (1993), Censo Ncional de población y vivienda 1991. Ministerio de Economía y Obras y Servicios Públicos. Buenos Aires

McCarney P., Halfani M., Rodriguez A. (1995), *"Towards an Understanding of Governance"*, in Stren & Kjellberg (edit.): Perspectives on the City; Centre for Urban & Community Studies, University of Toronto

17

A Study on the Sustainability of the Housing Finance System in China

Hao Hu and Jürgen Rosemann

Abstract

China adopted the socialist welfare housing system since the founding of the People's Republic of China in 1949. Urban housing reform has been a major component of China's economic reform since 1979. Nowadays, huge housing need, low affordability and oversupply of high-end commodity housing are the major concerns and the resolution of the problem heavily depends on an efficient and sustainable housing financing system. The purpose of this paper is to examine issues related to the sustainability of the Chinese housing finance framework. Based on the review of the socialist housing finance structure and the discussion of the recent housing reform policies, recommendations are made concerning the means to establish a sustainable housing finance system for China.

Introduction

Sustainable development has been and is becoming an important issue in more and more governments' agenda. The concept of sustainability was spawned by the United Nations report titled "Our common future" from the Brunlandt commission. In that report, "sustainable development" was defined as "development that meets the needs of the present without compromising the ability of future generations to meet their own needs" (United Nations, 1987). A healthy development should be economically, socially and environmentally sustainable.

An important target group of sustainable development policy is the sector of building and housing. Housing sustainability involves a wide range of issues, such as energy conservation, use of materials that does less harm to the environment, housing quality surrounding environment and financial policy. Housing finance has risen to the top of urban policy and research agenda and there is a consensus that a correctly structured finance system can deliver improved housing (Datta and Jones, 2001; Buckley, 1996; Renaud, 1999; etc.) Housing and urban development are heavily dependent on the nature of the housing finance system and the availability of credit (Zhang, 2001). The way housing is built reflects the way it is financed because methods of financing determine methods of production (Okpala, 1994). Financing issues received major attention in the policy for human settlement development (Kim, 1997).

Considering the limited space, we only discuss the financial sustainability of the urban housing system in China in this study.

A sustainable housing finance system is of the following characteristics: (1) A stable source of finance is available for housing development; (2) The housing finance system is self-evolved, that is, revenue is produced and can be reinvested for future housing development; (3) Housing is affordable and the government can keep funding the subsidy for housing for the lower-income group.

However, sustainability was not a theme of housing development in P.R. China in the first thirty years. Rather, immediate results of short-term solution were the path taken by both local and central government. Under the Chinese socialist welfare housing system, housing was solely financed by the State. The private sector was not allowed to be involved in urban housing development. This single-channel state funding could not be sustainable on economic terms (Zhang, 2001) and therefore had lots of problems. Housing shortages, insufficient investment, low rent, low efficiency, corruption and inequality were some examples. An important purpose of the urban housing reform that started in 1979 was to restructure the housing finance system.

A lot of effort has been input into investigating policies related to Chinese housing reform. In the planned economy era, all housing units were state-owned and allocated to the employees through work units. Transformation from the welfare-oriented housing system to a market-oriented one was the ultimate goal of housing reform. A very important measure was to develop commodity housing. Wang and Murie (1996) provided a system account of the key features of the process of commercialization of urban housing in China. In a later paper, Wang and Murie (1999) systematically studied the development of commercial housing in Chinese cities. They examined the scale of housing investment during the early 1990s, the development process, quality and design standards, the commercial housing market and the management of residential estates. Private housing was gradually phased out since the founding of China in 1949. However, 30 years later, privatisation of public-sector housing was set up as a priority in China's economic reform. The first shift from private to public and second reverse shift drew the attention of some researchers. Zhu et al. (2001) compared the public housing development in three countries, China, U.S. and Singapore. Wu (2001) argued that economic globalisation and marketisation, especially in the arena of housing and urban land, are becoming the key variables determining the post-reform urban development in China. In recent years, some interesting topics were also addressed in the research. Wang (2000) addressed housing reform and its impacts on the urban poor in China. The study found that although housing problems of the official urban poor have been recognized, there is no formal policy related to housing provision for the unofficial poor, i.e. the peasant workers. Li (2000) conducted a multi-level logit analysis of the housing allocation process and of tenure decisions. The results of the statistical analysis are generally in accordance with the nature of housing market segmentation and the forces governing housing allocation and consumption. Chinese housing reform is not isolated and it also attracted wide attention of international organizations. A World Bank research team investigated urban housing reform and a research report was released in 1992. The report proposed an innovative model that suggested the establishment of joint-stock housing management companies and hence separated housing provision from the responsibility of enterprises.

Although a large number of publications regarding housing reform in China have been produced, limited studies have been done on the housing finance system. Zhang (2000) investigated the restructuring of housing finance system with particular focus on the housing finance institutions and financing resources. The impact of the new finance system on housing development was also discussed. Wang (2001) evaluated the new housing finance mechanism by examining policy development and practice in Beijing. However, there is no literature undertaking a systematic analysis of the sustainability of the Chinese housing finance framework. This paper aims to fill the gap in this regard. The rest of the paper is organized as follows: immediately following this section is a review of the socialist housing finance system. This is followed by the summary of the urban housing system reform in China since 1979. The restructuring of the finance system is examined in detail and the sustainability of the new housing finance structure is discussed. The paper concludes by suggestions to secure sustainable housing finance.

China adopted the socialist welfare-oriented housing system since the founding of the People's Republic of China in 1949. The first thirty years' experiments in China in developing public housing and the socialist housing were summarized in Zhu et al. (2001) and are reviewed in this section with an emphasis on the formulation and transformation of the socialist finance system.

Public Housing in 1949 – 1978

1- Transformation of homeownership from private to public (1949 - 1966)

The socialist theory regards private ownership as a means for exploitation of labor. In order to terminate the exploitation of man, the private ownership of a resource has to be eliminated first. Therefore, socialist China started to eliminate the private housing building industry and control the private rental sector since its foundation. The Land Reform Act in 1950 abolished the land market by prohibiting land sales and renting, making it impossible for private developers to buy land and build housing. By 1956, 95% of urban land was in state ownership. Along with the socialist transformation of land ownership, a transformation of housing ownership occurred for urban residents. But the new government adopted a cautiously gradual approach to transform urban housing ownership. Both homeowners and small rental property owners were allowed to keep their own private ownership and operate legally in the real estate market during the early years. All cities and one third of the towns had completed the socialist transformation of the private rental sector by 1964. The government took the final step to transform all private rental housing to public ownership in 1966. Housing in China was no longer a commodity but an in-kind welfare benefit.

2- Slum clearance and the construction of "New Villages" (1949-1957)

The new communist government was ambitious to improve housing conditions when facing severe housing shortage and unsanitary slums. It took immediate action, launching a broad campaign to clear slums and unsanitary and unsafe housing. In the mean time, the government initiated many new public housing projects to alleviate housing shortages. New developments were often named "New Villages" or "Worker Villages" which were multi-story buildings organized in rows that formed homogenous neighborhoods. The dominant type of housing in these new villages was a mix of one- and two-bedroom units. The average floor space per unit was 30 square meters, with three or four units sharing a kitchen and a toilet (Zhu et al, 2001). The built housing units were allocated to the households as rental housing through their work units. To make rental units affordable and relieve the housing burden from urban residents, the government set up a low-rent policy. Often the rent was only about one to two per cent of the household's total expenditure.

3- Specific-project-oriented development and satellite "Factory Towns" (1958-1966)

In the late 1950s, the government adopted a development strategy oriented toward specific-projects. Essentially, it empowered various ministries in the central government to build large plants and factories throughout the country to achieve rapid economic development and industrialization. The investment for housing construction was included in the total investment of the project. However, the state or central government provided no direct housing funds to the enterprise after the initial budgets for the new "factory towns". Afterwards, work units had to raise money from their own profits to construct new housing units. Therefore, work units' capacity of producing housing is linked to their ability to generate a surplus in their economic activities. This meant those work units with better resources and economic performance could invest more money into the housing sector (Zhang, 2000).

4- Stagnation and deterioration of the housing stock (1966-1978)

By 1966 when the socialist transformation of homeownership was completed, the entire urban housing stock was in the hands of the government. There was no private sector left to develop or maintain housing. People had to wait for the allocated housing if they changed jobs or formed new households or add new members to their households and therefore need more space. But the government almost stopped taking responsibilities for urban housing in 1966 when the Cultural Revolution was launched. Urban housing construction remained a particularly low priority in the nation's economy in the subsequent years. By 1978, less than 25% of families lived in self-contained units, and the average living space per capita was only 4 square meters. The low rent policy also made it impossible to maintain housing units properly. This stagnation in housing construction and deterioration of the existing housing stock had devastating results. It is fair to say that the ideals of the 1949 revolution failed to materialize and the country was waiting for new direction (Zhu et al., 2001).

Socialist Housing Finance System

Under the socialist welfare housing system, the State was the sole supplier in terms of housing production, distribution, management and maintenance, while housing units were allocated to individual households through work units. After the transformation of homeownership from private to public, private and informal modes of housing finance were non-existent in the sector of urban housing. Housing finance virtually came solely from the State and housing construction was determined by the annual state budgetary funding. The State was responsible for housing production and provision of funds and subsidies to the local governments and work units. Maintenance fees and other expenditure relating to housing services were also subsidized by the State. The final recipients of the most state budgetary funding were either work units (occupying 90%) or local governments (occupying 10%). Individual enterprises (work units) were not allowed to invest in housing production (Wong et al., 1998). There were two types of State Owned Enterprises (SOEs): central enterprises and local enterprises. The former was directly managed by the ministries of the State Council whilst the later was under the authority of local governments below provincial level.However, the central government did not set aside special funds for housing. Rather, it was included in the central and local governments' capital construction investment funds. The government's central budget first determined a national total amount of capital construction investment funds. This total amount was distributed among local governments and central government ministries and further allocated to either work units or housing bureaus. Even though work units' housing investment was funded through central budget, it is observed that the government did not provide any funds directly to enterprises unless it was newly set up. The money for housing production of established enterprises had to be raised from their own profits. Budgetary funds meant that work units could retain a certain amount of their profits for housing investment within the approved budgetary limit by the government. Housing construction was also organized by individual work units. The socialist housing finance framework in China is depicted in Figure 1.

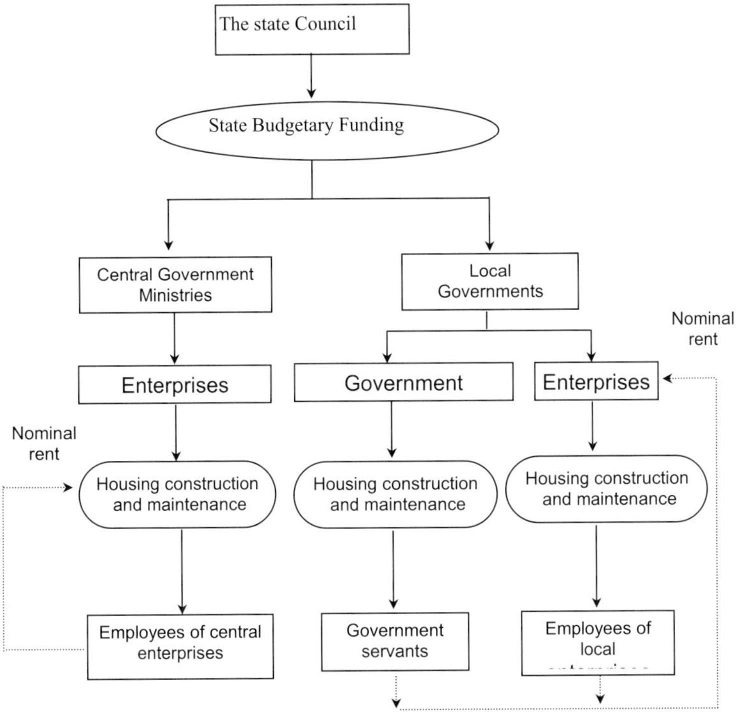

Figure1 The Socialist Housing Finance Framework in China

→ Housing investment ⇢ Repayment of investment

Single-channel state funding could not be sustainable in economic terms (Zhang 2000). The socialist ideology put excessive emphasis on heavy industries and paid insufficient attention to the development of other sectors especially the housing sector. The philosophy of the Socialist economic system is "production first and consumption second". Housing was seen as a kind of non-productive sector and thus received less priority in the national economy. Housing was neglected especially after the completion of the socialist transformation in 1956. Between 1952 and 1978, housing investment accounted for only 0.78% of the GNP. Additionally, all public-sector housing was freely distributed to the employees through work units. No deposits or other payments were required before the tenants moved in (Wang and Murie, 1996). That is, the government could not get back what had been spent on housing construction. Housing production became a drain of the State's budget (Wong et al, 1998). The more housing units were built, the more the government had to subsidize. Consequently, the state did not want to invest in housing construction when facing very high competing demands from the production sectors for state financial resources. Finally, the rent of public housing units was very low and did not even cover the maintenance costs. Urban residents only spent about 1.4% of their monthly income on rent (Kim, 1990). The burden of the subsidy kept increasing with the growing public housing stock and the rising construction cost. On the other hand, quality of the housing stock worsened because of inadequate maintenance. For example, there were still 3.65 million square meters of dangerous and simple living buildings in Shanghai in 1995 (Rosemann and Hu, 2001).

In conclusion, the socialist housing finance system is not sustainable. Various problems relating to it were identified in the literature. For example, insufficient investment, serious housing shortages, the nominally low rent policy, poor maintenance and inequality etc. (Wang and Murie, 1996; Wong et al, 1998; Zhang, 2001).

Faced with these problems, the government began to search for and experiment with new ways of housing provision since 1979 through urban housing system reform, which is summarized in the following section.

Urban Housing System Reform

China has launched a series of economic reforms since 1979. Urban housing reform is an important component of the national economic reform. Various new policies were explored to commercialize and privatize the public-sector-dominated housing system. The urban housing reform in the past two decades is divided into four stages in this paper.

1- Rapid construction and experimental privatisation of public housing (1979-1985)

The housing crisis in the late 1970s was typically represented by the serious housing shortage. The overwhelming task of the reform was consequently to build more housing units. Large amounts of investment went into housing between 1979 and 1985, and most of the construction was implemented through work units. On the other hand, private ownership of housing properties again became legally protected. The government encouraged and promoted homeownership by selling public housing units to individual households. The main policy of housing reform experimented with before 1982 was the sale of new housing units in building cost. Over 60 cities and towns all over the country have carried out the experiment by 1981. However, most cities reported a low demand for housing purchase because the price was too high, the method of payment was too inflexible and the rent for public housing was so low as to discourage house buying (Wang and Murie, 1996). The first round of experiments was formally abandoned in 1982. But the government initiated another round of experiments in four cities, i.e. Zhengzhou, Guangzhou, Siping and Shashi. The main policy was the subsidized sale of public housing, that is, the individual household, the employer and the municipality each pay one-third of the total price of the housing unit. However, the employers (work units) strongly objected to this policy for the undertaking of most of the subsidies. The policy was repealed again, halting the second attempt to privatize housing. By 1985, 10,928 square meters of public housing had been sold (Hong, 1999).

2- Failures to reform subsidized rent (1986 – 1990)

The difficulties in privatizing housing highlighted the necessity and importance of rent reform. With rent as low as 1-2 per cent of household income, tenants would never have the motivation to buy their units. Starting in 1986, experiments began in several cities to increase rent of public housing units. In particular, the pilot reform in Yaitai was very successful (Wang and Murie, 1996). In early 1988, the Chinese government announced a comprehensive housing reform plan: “Implementation Plan for a Gradual Housing System Reform in Cities and Towns”. This document marked the turning-point of housing reform from pilot tests to overall implementation in all urban areas and was the most important policy document on housing reform. One goal of this plan was to raise rent to cover all the operational costs. But wages of SOEs and public sectors were too low to afford such rents. So the government had to give out housing vouchers to offset the rent increase. But the amount of the voucher distributed should be kept within 25% of the salary.

However, rent was only one of many items on which the prices had been set too low in the central planning economy. As the economic reform continued, living expenditures increased rapidly due to price reforms. In the late 1980s a round of serious inflation swept the country. In 1988 alone, urban residents’ living expenditure index increased by 20.7% and the country faced panic purchasing (Zhu et al., 2001) Concerns over social stability and resistance from vested interest groups led the government to suspend the rent-oriented housing reform. By 1989, political unrest and a government crackdown slowed down the housing and other economic reforms.

3- Reinforcement period (1991-1994)

By 1991, both the economic and political situation had stabilized. In May 1991, Shanghai put forward a comprehensive reform plan and pushed housing reform onto the government agenda again. One important policy of Shanghai reform was to establish the Housing Provident Fund (HPF). In October 1991, the State Council announced the “Opinions on Actively and Carefully Promote Urban Housing System Reform”. It reconfirmed and updated the 1988 resolution. In detail, the plan decided to increase the rent, sell public housing units and apply a new policy for newly built housing flats. In particularly, the policy indicated funds for housing construction should be jointly undertaken by the State, the work units and individuals and it was necessary to develop a housing finance system (State Council, 1991). In 1994, the State Council issued the “Decision on Deepening the Urban Housing Reform” along with several detailed explanatory documents. The policy continued to emphasize rental reform and the sale of public housing units. Additionally, new emphasis was given to establish a public- and private-housing saving system - Housing Provident Funds and to establish an efficient housing finance system which enable both policy-oriented and commercial developments. Furthermore, the government began to pay more attention to the housing shortage problem of middle and low-income households and proposed to develop more economic and comfortable housing for those most in need.

4- New national reform period (1995-present)

In 1995, the State Council announced the "Implementation Plan for National Comfortable Housing Project". Fifty-nine cities were first selected as experimental cities to build comfortable housing for low-income households. In 1996, the State Council's Leading Team for Housing System Reform confirmed the plan of national comfortable housing construction in the following five years.

In order to accelerate the housing reform towards 2000, the State Council's Leading Team for Housing Reform and local governments held an urban housing reform conference in Shanghai in 1995 to conclude lessons drawn from the previous practices of various cities. One of the Shanghai experiences, that is, the establishment of Housing Provident Fund, was regarded as a success in the housing sector and hence was extended to other cities. There were 35 cities who launched the Provident Funds Scheme in 1995 (Wong et al, 1998). The establishment of Provident Fund was then affirmed as the major direction of housing finance reform. China State Council issued the "Ordinance of Housing Provident Funds" in March 1999. To date, most cities in China have established HPF.

New urban housing policies were introduced by the Central government in July 1998. The major changes include: to end direct housing distribution by employers and introduce housing cash subsidies; to create a diversified housing supply system with state-supported affordable commercial housing as the main form and to put in place a new housing finance system to help developers and individuals with loans and mortgages to facilitate the urban housing market. With the implementation of 1998 housing reform policy, work units gradually disappeared from the housing provision system. Instead, more and more households began to purchase commodity housing from the market.

In 1999, social rental housing for lower-income groups was advocated by the government. Meanwhile, in order to promote the development of a housing market and housing filtering, a "Provisional Management Method of the Resale of Public Housing" was announced. The government hoped to establish a multi-tier housing delivery system: The higher-income group purchases full-price commodity housing from the market; the middle and low-income group purchases subsidized economic and comfortable housing from the open market; and the lower-income households rent social rental housing provided by local municipalities.

China's main housing reform policies are summarized in Table 1. As a whole, the reform achieved very encouraging results. As indicated in Figure 2, the average living area per capita increased annually in 1980s and 1990s with the progress of urban housing reform.

Table 1 Summary of China's main housing reform policies since 1978

Year	Policies
1979	Selected cities carried out full-price housing sales. Individuals could purchase the housing units at RMB 120-150 per square meter. However, this experimental project failed due to the low wages of the people and low rents associated with welfare housing.
1984-1985	The State Council's Leading Team for Housing System Reform was set up. The basic direction of reform was to raise rent and employees' wages, and to sell public housing to the individual households at a subsidized price.
1988	The State Council announced "Implementation Plan for a Gradual Housing System Reform in Cities and Towns".
1991	The State Council announced "Opinions on Actively and Carefully Promoting Urban Housing Reform" and reconfirmed earlier objectives and policies.
1994	The State Council issued "Decision on Deepening the Urban Housing System Reform". Emphasis was given to establish housing finance system.
1995	The State Council announced the "Implementation Plan for National Comfortable Housing Project". 59 Cities and work units were selected to carry out these experimental housing projects.
1998	The State Council announced the "Opinions on Further Deepening Urban Housing System Reform and Speeding Up Housing Development". The government decided to end direct housing distribution by employers and introduce housing cash subsides.
1999	State Council issued the "Ordinance of Housing Provident Funds". HPF had to be established in all cities. The Ministry of Construction issued "Management Methods of Social Rented Housing" and "Provisional Management Methods of the Resale of Public Housing"

Restructuring of the Housing Finance System

The primary objective of the housing reform is to restructure the housing finance system (State Housing Reform Leading Group, 1994). The most serious problem of the old housing system was its unability to facilitate the inflow of funds into the housing sector and to formulate a healthy circulation of funds within the housing sector. In fact, the recent restructuring the housing finance system by the Chinese government basically concentrates on these two aspects. The detailed measures include the set up of work unit housing funds, the establishment of a Housing Provident Fund and the development of mortgaged housing loans.

- Setting up of work unit housing funds

Urban housing reform has generated several different kinds of funds that are dedicated to housing. The sources of the funds include income from house sale, rent, government approved tax allowance for housing in the enterprise sector, and budgetary allocations for housing in institutions or government departments (Wang 2001). Funds of different sources were put together as the work unit housing funds and once became the major source of finance for housing development in the first 1990s.

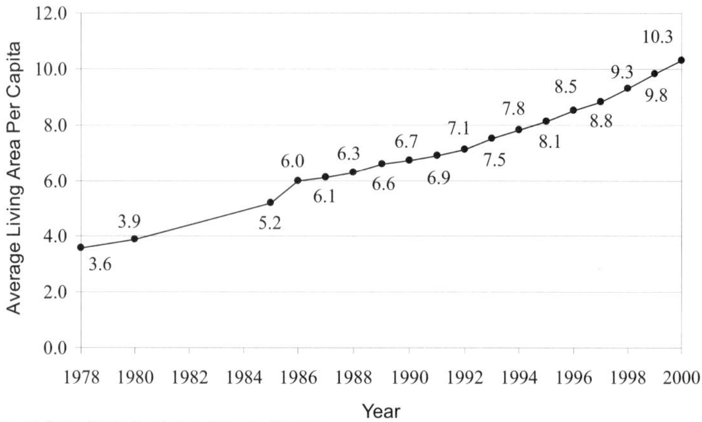

Source of data: State Statistics Bureau (2000).

Figure2. Average urban living area per capita from 1978 to 2000

With the implementation of the 1998 housing reform policy, the major function of the work unit funds was to pay the employer's contribution for employee's HPF. The government hoped to gradually reduce funds in this category and replace it with HPF so as to relieve enterprise from the housing burden.

- Establishment of Housing Provident Fund

After careful review and investigation of the Central Provident Fund scheme (CPF) of Singapore, the Shanghai municipal government proposed to establish a Housing Provident Fund (HPF) for the first time in 1991. After five years' of experimentation, provident fund policy was enacted by the Shanghai People's Congress in 1996 as the "Ordinance of Housing Provident Fund in Shanghai". The Shanghai experience was regarded as a success in establishing a new housing finance structure and hence was extended to other cities. There were 35 cities who launched the HPF scheme in 1995 (Wong et al, 1998). The establishment of Provident Fund was then affirmed as the major direction of housing finance reform. China State Council issued the "Ordinance of Provident Housing" in March 1999. To date, most cities in China have established this policy.

The HPF in China is a compulsory housing savings scheme. The purpose is to accumulate capital for housing production and consumption. The employer and employee each contribute a certain percentage of the employee's salary to the saving. The contribution is deposited monthly into a special HPF account at the China Construction Bank for each employee by the employer. The account can only be closed if the account holder has left the city, died or retired. Work units play a very important role in managing employee's HPF. They make the saving on behalf of the employees, pass information between the fund management organisations and employees, and arrange for withdrawal (Wang, 2001). A specialized organization, Housing Provident Fund Management Center, is usually set up in each city and is responsible for the daily management of the HPF. The Center is under the supervision of Housing Authority, which is also responsible for the making of relevant HPF policies.

The contribution rate varied in different cities. The central government requests that he minimum contribution rate from both employer and employee is 5%. That is, the minimum monthly saving of HPF is 10% of the employee's salary. However, cities with good economic performances are allowed to increase the rate. In 1999 it was 8% and 7% in Beijing and Shanghai respectively. Enterprises in good economic conditions are also encouraged to set up a supplement account for their employees in some cities like Shanghai. Currently, the contribution rate of the supplement account in Shanghai is between 1% and 9%.

The savings fully belong to the employees and can only be used for two purposes: (1) Short-term loan to work units, real estate developers and housing cooperatives for developing economic and comfortable housing. (2) Help individual households in home purchase, housing construction, renovation and rent payment in some cases. The account holders can withdraw their savings for housing purpose. Most importantly, they can apply for HPF loans. The highest loan per household at one time is 100 thousand yuan in Shanghai. In general, the Housing Provident Fund Scheme achieved significant success in China. Since the HPF provides a steady stream of deposits, it therefore provides a major source of housing finance for individuals and promotes the conversion of the welfare-oriented housing system into the market-oriented housing system. The employees will rely on themselves to own a house rather than depend on the state or their work unit. The housing distribution consequently shifts from the traditional physical housing distribution to monetary distribution. Housing Provident Fund plays an increasing role in the urban housing finance system. For example, by the end of 2000, the amount of HPF accumulated in Shanghai was 37.663 billion yuan. In terms of total assets, the Shanghai HPF management center has exceeded many local small banks. The HPF withdrawal for housing purchase in Shanghai in 2000 was 6.862 billion yuan, whilst the PFH mortgage loan reached 8.645 billion yuan. Together, the PFH withdrawals and loans were 15.507 billion yuan in 2000.

- Development of Mortgage Housing Loans

Since 1979, commercial bank loans have been playing an important role in stimulating housing construction. However, the loans were mainly provided for housing development and only a small amount was for housing purchase during the early stage. In 1994, mortgage banking was reintroduced to China after nearly fifty years of absence (Zhu et al, 2001). After several years of experiments, people are now becoming more comfortable with making home mortgages. The amount of the loan was as high as 70 to 80 per cent of the purchase price and the longest loan term today is 20 to 30 years. However, the scale of mortgage lending is not very significant in general (Zhu et al, 2001; Wang, 2001). By the end of June 1998, Commercial Bank's total housing loans were 264.3 billion yuan, of which only 35 billion yuan or 13% was mortgage housing loans (Han, 1999). China Construction Bank, one of the major banks that provide a mortgage service, had only issued 11,000 individual loans in Beijing by the end of 1998 (Wang, 2001).

Besides the commercial bank loan, another kind of home mortgage is HPF loan, which has been introduced above and is very popular. People usually prefer to take HPF loans than commercial bank loans because the interest rate of the former is lower and this also provides the households with the opportunity to use the deposited money in the HPF account. However, an HPF loan alone is not enough to purchase a house to most households. As a result, the third kind of home mortgage, the combined mortgage loan, which is composed of HPF and commercial bank loans, was developed in recent years.

The household gives the property rights to a specialized guarantee organization that provides guarantees for the HPF loan and the commercial loan respectively. But the HPF Management Center is the first beneficiary of the guarantee.

Chinese housing finance system has experienced two shifts since the economic reform. The state was the only source of housing funds in the time of the socialist system, which was changed in 1979 when the government encouraged work units and individuals to invest in housing development. But the emphasis was still with the work units that gained more financial and management power in the economic reform (Wang and Murie, 1996). This is the first shift. Since the late 1980s, the government gradually implemented a series of policies and the individuals were encouraged and requested to finance their own housing. Particularly, the 1998 policy terminated the direct housing provision by the work units. China is experiencing the second shift.

After efforts of two decades, a new Chinese-characteristic housing finance system with similar features to developed countries was formulated in China. It is illustrated in Figure 3.

In the new finance system, the funds for housing developers are mainly from the commercial banks. On the other hand, individual households use HPF savings, HPF mortgage loans, commercial bank mortgage loans for the purchase of commodity housing from the market. The government subsidizes the economic and affordable housing for middle- and low-income households through favorable land and tax policies.

Sustainability of Housing Finance System

A housing finance system must be sustainable. That is, the system must be self-circulated and self-evolved. The essence of building a sustainable housing finance system is to identify and properly manage the various risks involved (Diamond and Lea, 1995). We will examine the sustainability of the Chinese urban housing system by concentrating on discussing risk factors inherent in the framework depicted in Figure 3.

On the demand side, individuals will mainly rely on HPF loans and/or bank loans for housing purchase. HPF has played an increasing role in the housing finance system and is regarded as the main measure by the government in helping people own their homes. However, some problems related to HPF policy have been identified. Firstly, HPF has only a limited impact because few families have accumulated enough money in their accounts. The contribution rate in most Chinese cities is 5%, which is not significant particularly in a low wage system. On the contrary, in Singapore, both employers and employees contribute 20% of the employees' income to the CPF account and 75% of the money can be used for housing, which is enough for the down payment and monthly installments of a publicly subsidized housing flat. Secondly, the coverage of HPF is limited. Only limited enterprises have participated in the HPF in some cities. And some enterprises are in operational difficulty and therefore cannot pay HPF for their employees. Thirdly, some problems related to HPF management was also reported. In the beginning years, a great amount of the funds was lent to real estate developer and a large part was not repaid or repaid on time due to the operational difficulties of those projects. It was reported that by 1997 90% of Shanghai's provident fund had gone into luxury housing and other projects. Housing Authorities in many cities actually cannot impose effective supervision on the management of HPF.

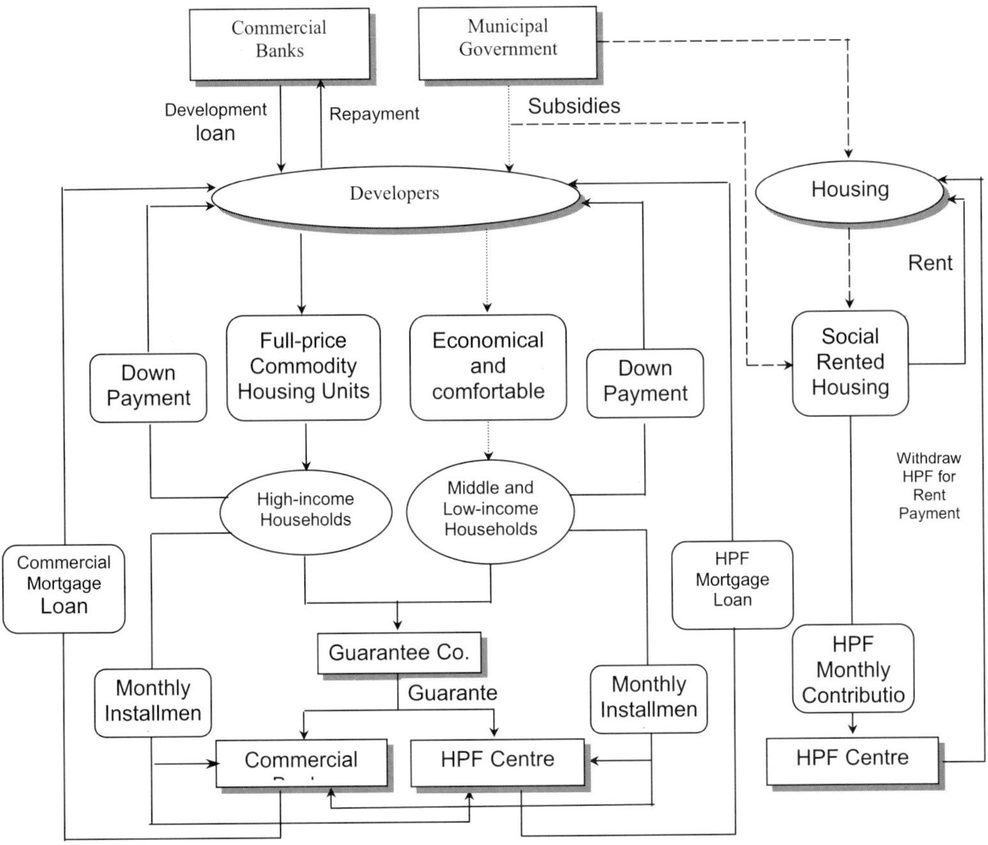

Figure 3. Current Urban Housing Finance Framework in China

Inflation is the most serious risk to the long-term commercial loan. High inflation rate increases the risk to the bank. However, the inflation rate in China in the past decade was considerably high (Figure 4). Therefore, a proper borrowing and repayment model that guarantees a real positive loan interest for the lenders is essential. On the other hand, innovative loan products should be provided to make a housing loan more affordable (Kim, 1997). For example, more frequent repayment can help households with irregular incomes. The payment schedule can be tailored to fit the borrower's income stream over time by gradually increasing monthly payments to reduce the initial burden (Kim, 1997). Figure 5 illustrates three typical kinds of mortgage repayment modes. (A) is commonly used in the Chinese bank system, whilst (B) and (C) are recommended in this study.

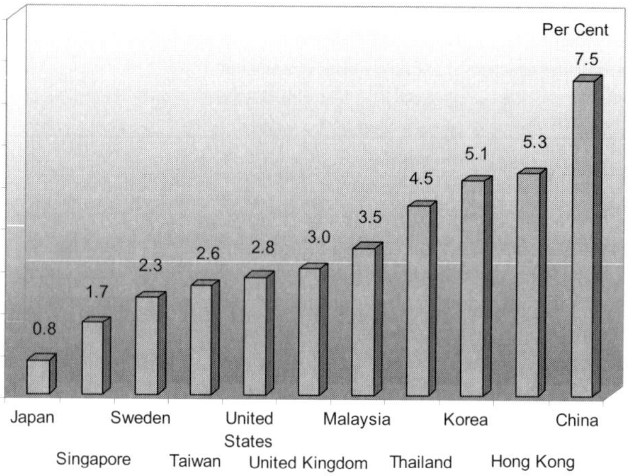

Figure 4. Inflation Rate 1990-2000

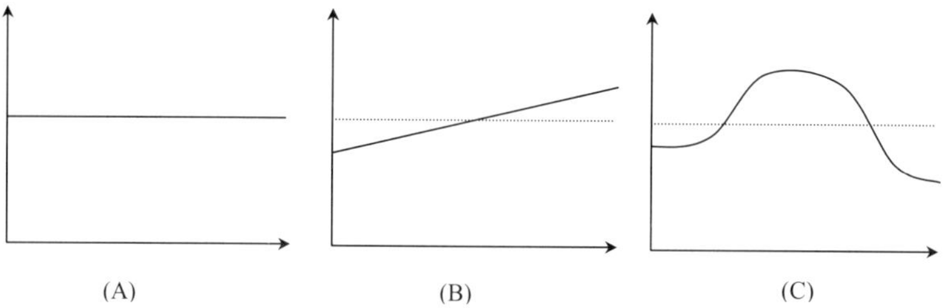

Figure 5. Modes of Mortgage Loan Repayment

When the housing sector was used as a motor to drive the deflated economy in 1998, the government started to encourage people to apply for mortgage loans and to urge the banks to issue more loans for housing consumption. Nowadays, more and more households are getting used to borrowing HPF and or commercial bank loans. However, reduction or fluctuation in income caused by job changes is becoming popular. The growing insecurity in the labor market has led to a decrease in stability and an increase in risk to the mortgage finance sector (Dudleston, 2001). It is worrying whether some households are capable of repaying these 20 to 30- year loan. For example, some mortgage borrowers are in their 40s or 50s, which impose a problem of repayment after their retirement. The risk is hidden in the early stage, but the accumulated risk will be fatal once it bursts out. Two major mechanisms, Mortgage Payment Protection Insurance and Flexible Mortgage have been identified to reduce the risks of mortgage default and repossession (Dudleston, 2001). But these kinds of products are not available in Chinese mortgage market.

On the supply side, it is crucial to establish a circulation of housing funds so as to provide sustainable finance source for the next round of investment in housing. Currently, most housing developers obtain loans from the commercial banks and get revenues through pre-selling and selling the completed housing units in the market. The housing market follows the same rule of the market economy. The products (housing) must be those demanded in the market. However, a mismatch between the demand and the supply exists in Chinese housing market. Many developers prefer to build high-end housing projects, which lead to the over-supply of luxurious housing that is not affordable to common households. In recent years, a serious housing shortage coexists with large amounts of vacant housing in China. For example, the floor area of vacant new housing reached 67.87 million sq. meters in 2000 and the stock increases at an annual rate of about 10% (Table 2). In Beijing, the survey revealed that only 15% of the market supply were offered at a price that is correspondingly affordable to almost 55% of all households (Wang and Chen, 2001). Large amounts of vacant housing result in the idleness of the investment and partially defer the inflow of more funds into the housing sector.

Table 2 Increase of Vacant New Housing Stock in China

Year	1995	1996	1997	1998	1999	2000
Vacant new housing (million sq. meters)	43	62	70	78	94	100

The lack of funds for housing construction is a big challenge in China because other economy sectors also competing for the scarce financial resources. It is estimated that housing of about 8 billion square meters in floor area amounting to the investment of $20 trillion is needed from 1998 to 2010 (Chen, 2000). Foreign investment has become an important financial source for housing development in China. The growth of foreign investment in China has been very impressive during the past two decades. Since 1993 China has become the second largest FDI recipient in the world and the single largest host country among the developing countries. China has attracted FDI of over US$ 300 billion in the last two decades. Real estate and housing are the major sectors of receiving FDI inflows into China. In terms of the accumulated FDI stock from 1983-1993, the share of the real estate was 32% (Chen, 1996). Actual foreign investment in real estate totaled US$3.8 billion in 1997. According to Construction vice-Minister Song Chunhua, more than 5,000 overseas real estate enterprises, or 20 percent of the country's total, have participated in real estate development in China (China Business Information Network, 1999). China has been putting an effort into encouraging the participation of foreign investment in infrastructure and housing sectors since 1995. However, the survey revealed that the cost of utilizing foreign funds is usually very high (Rosemann and Hu, 2001). For example, an annual return rate as high as 15% was guaranteed for foreign funds in the Shanghai Foreign-investment Domestic-sale low cost housing policy made in 1995. The high cost of the construction funds directly led to a high selling price of the housing and hence made it unaffordable to middle- and low-income households.

In order to provide housing for middle- and low-income households, the government decided to develop more economic and comfortable housing (ECH) through favorable land supply and tax treatment etc. In 1998, China built 140 million sq. meters of urban housing and 38% of which was in the category of ECH. In 1999, the completed floor area was 160 million and the ECH occupied 62%. The proportion of ECH further increased to about 70% in 2000. ECH help to alleviate the housing shortage problem, prevent speculation in the housing market and promote economic development through stimulating housing consumption of middle and low-income households. However, some problems have been revealed in the implementation of the ECH policy. For example, the developers used illegal approaches to get higher profits than the 3% level set by the government. Additionally, the price of ECH is still not affordable to most middle- and low-income households. As there is no detailed approach to determine the income of households, many high-income groups also purchase ECH flats. As such, the subsidy that is targeted for low-income groups goes to the high-income households. Although housing subsidies are quite common in the world, it is necessary to utilize them in an efficient, equitable and transparent manner because the resources of the public sector is scarce (Kim, 1997). Furthermore, the government should get back a full or partial amount of the subsidies in order to provide continuous support in the future.

Figure 6. Real GDP Annual Growth, 1990-2000

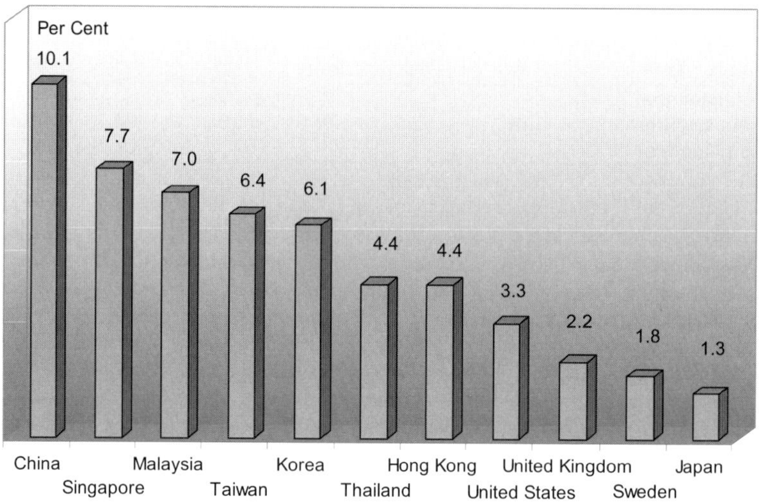

Constant economic development is the context for establishing a sustainable housing finance system. This means a constantly increasing income to each household. People can then spend more of their income on housing consumption. China, as the largest developing country, enjoyed strong economic growth in the last two decades. The Gross Domestic Product (GDP) grew at an average of 10.1 per cent per annum in real terms. This was much higher than most economies in the world (Figure 6). Family income of most urban residents has been increasing year by year. Furthermore, it is predicted that China will continue to enjoy a strong economic growth in the next 30 to 50 years. This provides an important background for establishing a sustainable housing finance system.

Concluding Remarks

This paper reviews the public housing policy in China from 1949 to 1978 and the urban housing reform in the past two decades with an emphasis on the investigation of the development of a housing finance system. The analysis shows that the public sector dominated socialist housing finance system is not sustainable. The private sector and the market were excluded from this system. Government was the sole supplier and controller in housing production, distribution and consumption. Housing was distributed freely to employees without any deposit or payment. So housing was looked as a non-productive sector and received less priority in the national economy. In addition, the rent was very low and could not even cover the maintenance costs. This unsustainable finance system deferred the inflow of funds into the housing sector and also destroyed the circulation of funds within the sector. The results were the serious shortage of housing and the deterioration of the housing stock.

Urban housing system reform has been carried out in China since 1979. After two decades' efforts, the prototype of a new housing finance system was established. A Housing Provident Fund was the major component of the new system. Households rely on HPF and/or commercial bank loans to purchase housing from the market, whilst social rental housing units for lower-income group are provided by the municipal governments. Although basic elements of the market economies like mortgage and home insurance are included, the current system is still in its infancy and is not sustainable unless those identified risk factors are properly managed.

The most effective way to secure sustainable housing finance is to develop a market-based system as an integral part of the overall financial and capital markets (Kim, 1997). It will be a slow process over a relative long period towards the establishment of a sustainable housing finance system. But the road has been paved and the future is very promising within the context of strong Chinese economic growth in the medium and long term. The following are some of our considerations and recommendations:

- The establishment of a sustainable housing finance system should be considered in a context of a growing economy. Chinese household income and consumption capacity will continue to increase steadily. Active and bold financial policies may be considered.
- More innovative mortgage products like Flexible Mortgage (Dudleston, 2001) should be provided. It is important to create new mortgage models that adapt to the income change of borrowers and reduce the charged interest.
- HPF should be used in a more creative way. Currently, the use of the HPF mainly concentrates on individual withdrawal and mortgage loan. Whilst it may also be used in a collective way. For example, HPF can provide guarantees for individuals to reduce the interest rate of commercial mortgage loans.
- The government should make different financial supporting policies for the housing needs of different income groups. The demand of the lower-income group cannot be neglected.
- The restructuring of the urban housing finance system is not isolated. Rather, it is related to the whole economic and political reforms. In particular, it is largely dependent on the reforms of the wage system and state-owned enterprises, the readjustment of the social welfare provision and the restructuring of the financial

system.

We hope to extend our studies to these issues in our next research step.

Note

(1) Foreign currency exchange rate: 1US$=8.28 Yuan.

References

Buckley, R. (1996). *Housing finance in developing countries*. New York: Macmillan.

Datta, K. and Jones, G. A. (2001) Housing and finance in developing countries: invisible issues on research and policy agendas, *Habitat International*, 25, pp. 333-357.

Diamond, D.B. and Lea, M. (1995) *Sustainable Financing for Housing: a Contribution to Habitat II*, working paper, Fannie Mae Office of Housing Research, Washington, DC.

Dudleston, A. (2001) The flexible mortgage: a risk reducing product? *Housing Studies*, 16(2), pp. 163-177.

Han, Q. (1999) The dilemma and solutions in China's housing financial system, Chinese Real Estate, 1999 (1), pp. 58-61. [in Chinese].

Hong, Y.M. (1999) Look back at China's urban housing system reform, in Chen, S.W. (ed.), *China's Urban Housing System Reform – Target, Model and Difficulties*. Beijing: Democracy and Construction Press.

Kim, J. (1990) Housing development and reforms in China, in Gil Shidlo (ed.), *Housing Policy in Developing Countries*. London: Routledge.

Kim, K.H. (1997) Housing finance and urban infrastructure finance, *Urban Studies*, 34(10), pp. 1597-1620.

Li, S.M. (2000) The housing market and tenure decisions in Chinese cities: a multivariate analysis of the case of Guangzhou, *Housing Studies*, 15(2), pp. 213-236.

Ministry of Information and the Arts (MITA) (2001) *Singapore: the Last 10 Years*. Singapore: the Ministry of Information and the Arts.

Okpala, D.C.I. (1994) Financing housing in developing countries: a review of the pitfalls and potentials in the development of formal housing finance systems, *Urban Studies*, 31(9), pp. 1581-1586.

Renaud, B. (1999). The financing of social housing in integrating financial markets: A view from developing countries, *Urban Studies*, 36(4), pp. 755-773.

Roseman, J. and Hu, H. (2001). Participation of foreign investment in Asian housing market, in *Proceedings of the 6th Annual Conference of Asian Real Estate Society*. Keio University, Tokyo, Japan.

State Councils (1988) *Opinions on Nationwide Urban Housing Reform by Stages and Groups*. Beijing: the State Councils. [in Chinese]

State Councils (1991) *Opinions on Actively and Carefully Promote Urban Housing System Reform*. Beijing: the State Councils. [in Chinese]

State Councils (1994) *Opinions on Further Deepening Urban Housing System Reform and Speeding up Housing Development*. Beijing: the State Councils. [in Chinese]

State Councils (1998) *Opinions on Nationwide Urban Housing Reform by Stages and Groups*. Beijing: the State Councils. [in Chinese].

State Statistics Bureau (2000) China Statistics Yearbook 2000. Beijing: China State Statistics Bureau.

United Nations *(1987) Our common future*, The World Commission on Environment and Development. New York: United Nations.

Wang, H. and Chen Y. (20010 Market segmentation and structural mismatch: affordability issues of housing in Beijing, China. In *Proceedings of the 6th Annual Conference of Asian Real Estate Society*. Keio University, Tokyo, Japan.

Wang, Y.P. (2000) Housing reform and its impacts on the urban poor in China, Housing Studies, 15(6), pp. 845-864.

Wang, Y.P. (2001) Urban housing reform and finance in China a case study of Beijing, *Urban Affair Review*, 36(5), pp. 620-645.

Wang, Y.P. and Murie, A. (1996) The process of commercialisation of urban housing in China, Urban Studies, 33(6), pp. 971-989.

Wang, Y.P. and Murie, A. (1999) Commercial housing development in China, Urban Studies, 36(9), pp. 1475-1494.

Wong, F.K.W., Yeung, S.C.W., Hui, E.C.M., Howes, R. and Kong, L.S.P. (1998). *A Study of Welfare Housing Development in Major Cities in China*, (Research Monograph), Hong Kong: Department of Building and Real Estate, The Hong Kong Polytechnic University.

World Bank (1992) *China: Implementation Options for Urban Housing Reform.* Washington, D.C.: The World Bank.

Wu, F.L. (1996). Changes in the structure of public housing provision in urban China. *Urban Studies*. 33(9), pp. 1601-1627.

Wu, F.L. (2001) China's recent urban development in the process of land housing marketisation and economic globalisation, Habitat International, 25, pp. 273-289.

Zhang, X.Q. (2000) The restructuring of the housing finance system in urban China, *Cities*, 17(5), pp. 339-348.

Zhu, X.D., Hu, H., Deng, L. and Huang, L. (2001) *Fifty Years of Public Housing: An International Perspective.* Working paper of Joint Centre of Housing Studies, Harvard University.

18

The Urban Water Management in Latin America

From the Theory to the Practice

José Francisco Chanez Mendia

1. Introduction

In 1992, the International Conference for water and the environment adopted the Declaration of Dublin[98]., and it will influence later almost all Latin American water constitutions. This seems to be the current tendency, the globalisation of water management via the standardisation of foundations and principles.

Two important principles:

- The participation of users
- The economical value of this resource.

Water management based on these two basis have been working since long time in Europe.

Are these principles applicable to Latin American urban centres ?

Latin America location, dimension, history, topography and inhabitants created a different natural environment, hydrological patterns, river basin dimensions, cultural differences, heterogeneous societies, democratic practices, confidence on authorities, economical resources, and degree of poverty.

The application of the Dublin Declaration in Latin American urban centres depends on carefully contextual process, and the long sustainability of the water policy, plans, programs, management and institutions, rest on this.

Objectives of this Paper

In this paper I will describe the environmental, social and economical conditions and analyse the problems present in urban centres of Latin America related to water

---

98 The International conference for Water and the Environment adopted, in January 26-31 1992, the following declaration:

1. Water is a finite, vulnerable and essential resource, which should be managed in an integrated manner.
2. Water resources development and management should be based on a participatory approach, involving all relevant stakeholders.
3. Women play a central role in the provision, management, and safeguarding of water.
4. Water has an economic value and should be recognise as an economic good, taking in to account affordability and equity criteria.

management besides make some general suggestions. The practical application of the water management needs to consider realistic policies, mechanisms and instruments, besides the legal framework.

Cities are the geographical scenarios wherein the agents, economical activities, industrial production, social relationships meet. The dynamism in this centres creates, a long of theirs histories great differences. A part of this society has access to almost all basic services, posses well economical position, are important part of the society, has enough education for facing changes, such as globalisation, are important part of the economical indicators. This group possess a particular perception of water that influences the water management.

On the other hand, there exist other important part of the population which facing difficulties for access to basic services. Poverty is another characteristic of this group, its participation into the society is neglected, its level of educations is very low and unable to face changers. This group is submerged into illegality. The illegal businesses in the streets of Latin American are the visible expression of this unknown sector. Additionally, the high trend of illegal land use and housing is evident as well.

This group has non practically participation in water management, but of course are interfering with this resources.

Questions to be Answer

The main question is: It is possible to apply the principles of the Dublin Declaration in Latin American?

What managerial arrangements are necessary for it practically application ?

Do poverty and social deterioration difficult its application?

Does the informal sector interfere to water management?

What managerial arrangements are necessary in order to apply these principles under urban centres in Latin American conditions?

The Conditions for Water Management

The characteristics of water (universality, social and economical values) and the current conditions in developing countries (poverty, social exclusion and cultural diversity) suggest the necessity of a carefully analysis about the agents, urban process, natural conditions, social reality, economical situation and legal background wherein a selected water policy and strategy will be applied. The water management has the potential for influencing the urban planning, economical development, social relationships, industrial production, and the expansion of the urban space.

Concepts and theories originated in different conditions- normally from United State and Europe- are using in order to create models for urban water management and instruments, that after will be applied in urban centres of Latin America. Do this transposition of models and instruments contribute to create problems in water management or are part of the solutions?

Consequently, alternative concepts and theories are necessary to increase and improve the understanding of the current urban water problems, and the present models in these fields.

The selected water policy must be an objective response to water problems. Laws, plans, rules, norms and institutions have to establish conditions for solving conflicts in this sector.

This require knowledge about agents, the scenario, the natural conditions, the legal background -even in related sectors-, social and economical conditions.

A coherent water policy will show the real purposes for its application. Uncertainties and contradictions will bring undesired doubts about the objectives of its utilisation.

The successful application of specific policy management depends on these considerations.

The possibilities of a successful long term application of an specific water policy, which depends on:

Social and Natural Conditions

I. Environmental.
II. Urban
III. Social.
IV. Economical.
V. Spatial and time water distribution.
VI. How these interacting

Management Arrangements

VII. Legal water background.
VIII. Institutions related to water management.
IX. Operational, control and information network.

The social and natural conditions (I – IV) describe problems and circumstances present in the country, related to the water sector and its externalities, a product of the past and present interrelation of man and the environment.

The management arrangements (V to VII) are a selected group of managerial tools, as a result of the previous analysis of social and natural current conditions (and even the former management arrangements) and carrying out of a water strategy. The objective is to establish the future "outcomes" in the water sector, that will influence the environment in a desired manner, ensure the water users and stakeholders participation, and guarantee funds for running and controlling the water network.

The effective and efficient management arrangements are the practical and objective responses to the current problems related to water resources, and prevent futures conflicts in this sector.

Coherent managerial arrangements must be done on the clear objectives of the water policy, after a previous consensus process.

The intervention of man is necessary in order to guarantee the availability of this resource for future generations. The control of this trend of water deterioration seems to be one of the principal activities for water management. The natural characteristic of water and its relationship to the environment and human beings requires a consistent and long term water management application.

The economical sustainability of water management ensures funds for preserving, operating, and developing this resource. This is a hard issue since most states are facing financial problems and general poverty reduces the possibilities for a cost recovery policy in this sector.

The social acceptability of a specific water management is related to several factors, such as; cultural, political and social. Since the Dublin declaration water management seems to be globalised, and the participation of users is a crucial activity. But, the problem is how to ensure this participation since the majority of the population are "excluded" from almost all their rights.

Water law establishes the legal background and gives legality to institutions related to water management, and also defines principles and foundations that are a guidance for rules, norms and plans for conserving, allocating and using water.

Institutions related to water management need to be constituted in favour of establishing a desired relationship between users and this essential resource. The conduct and behaviour of users depends on their "objective function " , ideas and beliefs. The clear understanding of these aspects will assist in the creation of effective institutional conditions.

The control and information network are a technical requirement, that provide essential information for water management , and establish responsibilities and procedures for running and controlling the water system.

This is one of the most important requirements and is related to the long term sustainability of the environment that will guarantee water for future generations. Its main issue is to make this condition compatible with social and economical sustainability.

The current models in urban water management need to be improved in order to response to L. A. conditions.These models have emerged in western countries, which posses stronger governments, respect to the law, different hydrological patterns, smaller river basin size, better organised cities, better access to basic services, enhance wealth distribution, less cultural diversity, more homogeneous societies, and low levels of poverty compared to L. A. countries. These tendencies have emerged in this scenario and responding to these natural, social, economic and cultural conditions.

In the case of water the Dublin Declaration plays significant role and common bases are: decentralization, water charge, user and stakeholders participation in water management, adoption of the river basin as unit for planning and intervention, state role in regulation and control trough concessions and licences, private participation in the water services provision (Lanna E. A., 2001). The influence or European countries in this field is evident such as the case of England and France. Two clearly tendencies are perceptible: private and centralised, and decentralised and participative

The Necessity of Alternative Models for Urban Water Management

The sharp and widespread crisis conscience was the initial point of the success of Barcelona Strategic Urban Planning (Vainer C., 2000). This crisis conscience is present in L.A. countries wherein the agents, scenario and water resources access are different. A diverse mosaic of sub cultures composes the population in L.A., with different perception about the city and water resources. The unequal wealth distribution increases the economical differences. The social exclusion experimented by a part of the society is product of the present social relationships and the result of the L.A. history.

The cultural diversity, social deterioration and poverty enlarge the social value of water – which is not the case of developed countries-.On the other hand, the already deteriorated water networks, the low coverage of water sanitation services, the necessity of treatment plants, and infrastructure for flood protection urgently need funds, which enlarge the economic value of this resource.

The native culture and western culture meet in Latin American creating complex social and economic conditions that seems to reach water management and spatial urban distribution, as well as the water services.

In these circumstances the water shortages is called to play significant role in the magnitude of this crisis conscience and able to generate – due to its characteristics-alternative ideologies according to these conditions.

Simpson L. and Ringskog K. in 1997, suggest, for every management programme, to succeed in long-term water management, it must be financially sustainable. Additionally, the acceptability of the water management needs to consider the cultural and societal values of water. These settlements include new aspects into the water management and even urban planning: social and cultural considerations that will reach the police, plans, laws, rules, operations and control activities in these fields.

The low efficiency and effectiveness of urban water management strategies are product of the an incomplete vision of problems, thus being product of a partial knowledge of water dimensions and its perceptions, agents and their behaviour, the urban space, and the relationships between them.

A question arises. The models have applied in urban water management consider these aspects? In cases of water abundance, social equity and no urban exclusion there is not problem. On the contrary, the urban water management need to be carefully study in cases of water shortages, limited infrastructure, bad water services, high social and economical differences, exclusion of the urban space, poverty and social deterioration.

4.1 Environmental Considerations

Due the current trend of urbanisation, cities are the geographical space wherein the effect of human beings and environmental degradation are concentrated. This relationship is difficult to study, -in 1992 Davis already mentions this problem-.

The relation of the human with the environment has origin with the life. In 1859, Charles Darwin in his great book, "On the origin of species", explains the role of the natural selection in the origin of species. A key word is: survival. In other book published in 1871 "The Descendent of Man" Darwin extend his theory for human beings. The natural selection is able to influence organic beings and to modify them in order to better adapted to natural environment. Darwin argues, there is no country wherein the native inhabitants are perfectly adapted among them and the environment. The environment is able to influence ideas, beliefs, culture, behaviours and social relationships. In 1952, Alfred Kroeber and Clyde Kluckhohn, defined: the functional part of the culture is the manner humans solve problems of adapting to the environment or living together. In 1990 Moran argues, every society has its ideas about its relationship with the environment. But, the Latin American society Latin America is composed by several sub cultures, with different perception about this resource.Davis suggest to study the following four concepts: the laws that govern the relationship, the support capacity of nature, the limits for the urban growth , the demographic transition and the urban centres economical and social sustainability.

What is the idea about this relationship in Latin American? What laws govern this relationship? A mosaic of different cultures compounds the society of Latin American urban centres, as a product of the colony time and migration. For example: Sao Paulo is a cosmopolitan city with Europeans, Arabs, Asian and African. This condition brings a complex mix of ideas about the relationship of human beings and the environment.

Another important aspect is that human beings are every time in less contact with the natural environment in the cities. The constructed environment is replacing the former one with consequent changes in the natural cycle of water.

Understanding this relationship (human beings and the environment) will be possible to introduce managerial arrangements in order to solve problems and prevent future water deterioration.

What is the support capacity of nature ? Water managers need to consider this intricate water interaction with other natural resources and prevent undesired effects from its exploitation. Water exploitation of surface sources needs to analyse its hydrological and hydraulic effects. This is related to flow, velocity, level and volume changes. Additional alterations are in sediment transport and morphology. The discharge from agriculture and industry produces the presence of new elements and micro organisms that will change the temperature and the quality conditions of the source.

In the case of groundwater exploitation the main issue is to consider its quality and quantity. The analysis of conservative contaminants and non-conservative pollutants are two activities related

to the first issue. Examination of the changes in the regime of groundwater, such as flow, direction, level of the water table and hydraulic gradients; are activities required for the second issue. The real objective of these analyses is to quantify the alterations due to water exploitation and determine how it will affect future water provision and avoid water deterioration.

What is the limit for urban growth, related to environmental considerations? The extension of the city is modifying land use. Large natural landscape has changed to urban centres, interfering with the transpiration of water and its balance. Vegetation is an important part in the water cycle, since it provides 10 % of the evaporation process. Every change in land use, such as changes in the depth of unsaturated zone, plants , permeability of the soil, topography implying a change in the water cycle.

The construction of artificial structures in rivers, lakes and even in the sea are altering the natural conditions of the environment in these places, such as reservoirs for multiple purposes and hydropower generation stations.

The high concentration of human beings in urban centres is significant in Latin America. In some regions the density reaches more than 90 %. Due to the high densities the water discharge is in constantly increasing and there is not enough treatment plants. This tendency is crating a serious stress in the current sanitation services. In some centres there exist a great uncertainty about the population growth, which is highly depend on the economical policy, employment, value of the land, industrial production and others.

The sustainability of the city is related to environmental, social and economical considerations. . Water is the element that strongly affects the environment, has a social function and through its use is possible to get economical benefits.

Some Problems

The environmental dimension is the most important component of water management. (Solanes M., 1997). The importance of its protection increases due to the increasing demand and the reduction of supply, as well as the water quality deterioration, plus the uncertainties and the externalities that strongly affect this resource.

The environment itself has no representative into water management structure, its representative appears as a stakeholder from society. Its effective presence in the whole water system depends on the environmental awareness of the population. Since this consideration the presence of ONG's plays significant role.

Long term plans are useful instruments for environmental protection. This seems to be a conflictive from the political, economical and social point of view. The common duration of a government period is between 4-6 years, and politicians are use to considering this time for their decisions. Additionally, the population thinks that long term plans are needless and useless. Political and economical uncertainties erode even more the importance of long term plans.

The adoption of long term plans requires a previous political and social consensus, otherwise the possibilities for their application is less. Short term plans are not desired, because they are not able to see the long term effects from application.

The privatisation process in the water sector is an additional problem. Concessions and permits are for around 30-40 years. During this period it will be possible to see some environmental effects, but not all, there exist others that will take more time.

Additionally, effects on air, ocean, plants and landscape will affect the water supply.

Integrated water resource management is relevant, since it requires the participation of different scientific disciplines.The magnitude of the land dimension in Latin America, (several times more than land dimensions in Europe, for example), increases the complexity of the environmental sustainabilityThe same problem is present in the division of the river basins.

Suggestions

The selected water policy must consider and recognise the environment proportions of the water resource and translate into facts of this recognition. The effective participation of the environment sector rests on the sufficient participation of its representative. The presence of this sector must be guaranteed, by law, within the whole institutional framework, such as decisions, evaluation, planning, operations and control, at all levels.

The previous consensus and awareness about the real dimension of this sector would ensure its protection. Additionally, this must be present in the principles and foundation of the law. Furthermore, permits, prohibitions and charges must be used in order to prevent water deterioration.

The access to water use must consider the restriction concerning from the environment. Water rights for using water need to consider two specific activities:

- Quantify the minimum flow in rivers, considering the biotic environment (fish and plants), and the interrelation with the level of the ground water table.
- The volume of water extraction from the groundwater, that will not over exploit and put in risk the future of the source

The current quality conditions of water sources is a limitation for licenses and permits of discharge waste water. Additionally, these must consider the type of substances, according to its process (conservative, substances subject to linear decay, and substances and even organisms subject to a high order process). In addition, the relation of concentration changes as a function of time and space is necessary in order to determine the carrying capacity of the rivers.

4.2. Urban Environment

The successful application of the water management is a crucial issue in which will depend the future of the urban centres.

Urban Centres in Latin American are experimented and intensive increment in its population. In some countries there are urban centres that hold more than 80 % of its population. For example; Sao Paulo holds more than 90 % of state population. This trend of urbanisation brings problems in water services extension. Authorities are facing problems for attend the increasing water demand and services related to.

For example, Since 1950, L.A. has experimented an intense population growth. In 1950 the population was 166.3 million of inhabitants. It increased to 359.3 million in 1980 and it is expected to reach 719.9 million of inhabitants by the year 2030.

According to Dourojeanni A., and Jouravlev A.(1997), Latin American is one of the most urbanised areas, following Europe and the United States. In 1950 urban population reached 40 % of inhabitants (68.9 million) , 73.4 % in 1995, and it is expected to be 83.2 % in 2030 (598.8 million of inhabitants)

In some cases the main part of the population is centred in few urban centres. For example, according to same authors, 53% of Guatemala's population resides in Guatemala city. San Jose holds 55 % of Costa Rica's population and Santiago 41 % of Chile's population. In 1995, 49.7 % of the total population in LA lived in 88 cities with more than 500 000 inhabitants. This number will increase to 131 cities in 2015. (United Nations, 1998).

The exclusion from urban space is a common picture in L.A. Furthermore, according to CEPAL[99], in 1997, 30 % of urban houses are living in poor conditions or 126 million of inhabitants and 10 % of urban houses are considered indigents (43 million of persons).

The continuous population and economic growth, urban poverty, trend of land occupation and land uses are causing the constant increasing water demand for drinking purposes, industrial and agricultural and others, as well as the quickly water quality deterioration. As a consequence, some cities already are facing period of serious water scarcity and pollution of their water bodies.

In LA, 79 % of the population has in house connection to the drinking water system and 52 % has connection to sewage collection system. (OPS[100], 1995). The population who has not access to water are poor inhabitants that usually have to buy water from private vendors at high prices.

Other important problem is the contamination of superficial water and groundwater product of direct discharge from households, industry and agriculture, as well as illegal human settlements close to water bodies. There is a general lack of treatment plants; according to OPS less than 10 % of sewage receives treatment. As a result, rivers and other water bodies are contaminated.

Because of the irregular urban growth the majority of the cities are facing flood problems during wet periods. The drainage and sewage collection usually have the same physical system with serious consequences on constructed and health environments.

Some Problems

The urban centres are the scenario wherein the agents meet. In this space take place the social relationship, the economical activities and political actions.

A strong relationship exists between water and urban planning (in urban centres that already are facing water shortage). The strategies in both sectors have to be functional under the specific conditions of the cities. The current models in these fields are based on

99 Economic Commission for Latin America
100 Pan American Health Organisation

concepts and theories originated from western countries, which have different natural, social, economical, and cultural conditions (normally from Europe and United States). The successful application of these models is impossible in poor countries without a careful process of adaptation to the conditions of Latin America.

The failure of the urban planning is visible under the current conditions of cities in LA. The evidence of these statements is the characteristics of disordered space growth, with segregation of basic services, and the significant economic and social differences visible in the access to urban space and services. The urban plans are insufficient for facing the social, economic and political dynamism of the cities. The administration instruments difficultly are applied, as being mechanisms of territorial planning, land use and intervention areas. The difficult regular access to the use of the land increases the indexes of illegal occupation of the urban space.

In some even more critical case it is evident even the lack of any intent of urban planning, being this assumed by sectors like transporting, basic services or housing.

One problem that contributes to the absence of urban planning is the lack information related to water and urban growth. Information related to current tendencies of population growth, densities, quantity and quality of water and wastewater are not available for policy and decision making processes. Additionally, the illegal urban access directly affects the water quality. In some countries this illegality reaches almost 50 % of inhabitants. This group is partially know because the absence of information.

Other great problem, usually underestimate, is the current tendency of international urban planning. It has indeed influenced greatly how water system is managed and the ideology of the tendencies in urban planning in Latin America, as a consequence of Globalisation.

This process started via the standardisation of norms, rules, and laws. Which in turn, established the grounds for internationalisation as well as the transposition of laws, rules, norms and institutions originated from different conditions worldwide and were logically adopted in LA. Despite the fact, that it varies according the different conditions such as place, agents and relationships it should add serious social, economic and environmental strain in urban centres.

The failure of the urban planning is visible under the current conditions of cities in LA. The evidence of these statements is the characteristics of disordered space growth, with segregation of basic services, and the significant economic and social differences visible in the access to urban space and services. The urban plans are insufficient for facing the social, economic and political dynamism of the cities. The administration instruments difficultly are applied, as being mechanisms of territorial planning, land use and intervention areas. The difficult regular access to the use of the land increases the indexes of illegal occupation of the urban space.

In some even more critical case it is evident even the lack of any intent of urban planning, being this assumed by sectors like transporting, basic services or housing. It is important to discuss the European and North American influences present during the all history of L.A. For example, Villaca (1999) mentions that firsts urban plans in Brazil were related to improving and beautifying the city (from 1875 to 1930) highly influenced by the urbanism of Versailles, Washington -planed in 1793- and Chicago. This urban planning concept was originated in the renascence period. In 1927 the Regional Survey of New York was the model called to replace the former one. The efficient city replaced the City Beautiful.

The strategic urban planning model is influenced by the experience of Barcelona, which was initiated in 1980 under urban design, and got, from the plan Barcelona 2000 (a continuation of the plan Barcelona 1992) a great dimension. It tried to establish clear goals with regard to all the improvements for the city that sought to be the vital centre of the region and Europe (Arantes O., 2000)

4.3 Social Acceptability

Cities are the principal place wherein the complex social relationships take a place. The high densities in these centres, the heterogeneous society, the cultural diversity contributes even more to this complexity. For this reason the social acceptance of water management is necessary for every water policy and strategy. This would contribute with the adherence to the water policy, strategy, objectives and rules. +

Water is essential for life, indispensable for alimentation, health and hygiene. Additionally, it is a necessity for establishing the minimum conditions for social and economical development. Every human being need this resource for surviving and is able to interfere with it (as an individual). Additionally the value of water as a social good and human interference (as a community) is more complex, and it is related to the cultural, social and economical reality of the country.

Management must be in accordance with the social, cultural and economical background. How does a people perceive water in different cultures in Latin America ? Are the social conditions in favour to selected water management ?

To define social and cultural concepts is a hard topic, and it is not the objective of this paper. The focus of the following analysis is to try to understand the ideas and conduct of humans with respect to water resources and how these will influence the acceptance and successful application of a specific water management.

Behaviour is a reflex of ideas, beliefs and values, which are established on a constant interrelation with the environment and other human beings.

Culture is the result of the complex interaction of the human beings with the environment and other human beings. Because it is learned and transmitted, it is a connection with past and how earlier inhabitants were interacted each others and with their environment. Since it is adaptive and integrated, it reflects the interaction of humans with different cultural background and even the relation of different cultures.

The Perception about Water

The perception about water has been established since time immemorial. The relationship between humans and this resource is related to the relation of men with the environment. For example: in the northern part of Europe, at the initial stage of human history and under certain climatic conditions with four clearly defined seasons; spring and summer were the "good times" in order to collect and store food and clothes for the winter. Additionally, long daylight provided light and warmth for production and trade. In this period nature supplied food, clothe, housing and transport for human being.

On the other hand the winter time was hard, daylights was short, the temperature decreased to less than 0° C, and rivers froze over.

Survival was not a day by day issue, it was a long term problem.

Environment was perceived as a "friend " in summer and spring time, and as an "enemy" in winter. From the same source people received life and death.

The population here found that nature would not always provide for their necessities, and the first ideas about long term provision took place. The storage of goods for winter was a crucial issue that would ensure life. In addition, man-made tools were necessary in order to provide optional pathways of access to essential goods. The access to natural resources needed high human participation, and it was possible to calculate the "price" of this participation.

These conditions strongly influenced the behaviour of people in these regions. For example, water management in The Netherlands is older than the nation itself. In the 13Th century people started to protect the land against flooding, to reclaim land from the sea and to control the drainage of low lying areas. This was the first form of democracy for the Dutch, as a consequence of the fight against the common enemy: water. Co-operation, consultation and commitment were conditions for survival. (Savanije, 1998)

It is evident that religion influenced culture in Europe, as well. The conviction in European tradition that human beings have been put in a position of dominance over the nature is very strong. This is based on Christian (and even Muslim) tradition. (Savanije, 1998)

The result of these influences; humans considering themselves separate from the environment. How it is possible to be part of "something" that could kill humans in winter ? Thus, the men need to dominate nature in order to survive. The concept of management is close to this settlement.

This idea influences concepts, knowledge, science, technology, development, values and conduct at this time and will influence all the word later.

In 1776, the Scotland Adam Smith wrote "The wealth of Nations" in which he described the theory of the economical growth and remarked the importance of the private property , division of work and capital.

The cultural background established at an early time plus the market economic concept contribute to the western philosophy about progress. Before the 18Th century the predominant opinion about progress was the world in decline. After this century the concept changed, due to the advance of science and technology, and the necessity of economical grow for survival started to take place in Europe. (Savanije, 1998). After all, nature was perceived such a commodity that man needed to manage and dominate in order to ensure the economical growth.

In those circumstances wherein the difference between spring and winter is not clear, the perception of the environment was different. For example, in South America in regions placed close to the equator, where few climatic changes from summer to winter exist. The temperature changes from around 30° C to 20° C in a low plateau. The amount of precipitation is maybe the most evident difference between the seasons. The duration of daylight has no significant changes, and the production activities were always possible throughout the year. Surviving in these conditions was a day by day issue, nature always provided food, clothes and home. Planning for the future was no necessary and as a result man established a friendly relationship with an environment which was the source of life.

In places close to the Andes mountains, around 3500 meters above sea level, wherein harder climatic conditions with the difference of temperature between daylight and night existing throughout all the year. To survive in these conditions was faced in different way. In Peru and Bolivia, the ancient population was concentrated close to the Titicaca lake, which created a micro-climate reducing the extreme temperature differences between daylight and night. Other important parts of the population were concentrated in closed valleys and in regions where mountains offered protection against the cold wind of the Andes. It was possible because population density permitted.

For inhabitants in these regions religion was related to nature. For example: In Inca, Maya and Colla cultures the gods were, sun, moon and land.

Of course, in these circumstances they believe that humans are part of the environment and its preservation was a condition for surviving. The concept about management is neglected.

Important activities for sustaining life in other environments, such as the storage of goods, are useless and a waste of time under these conditions. Money and capital were not necessary because they were in contact with natural products throughout the year. In these region the communal property was established.

Difference between environments generates different ideas, values, beliefs and behaviour as a response to the same objective: survival. For example the idea of wealth was different according to the place. Adam Smith wrote: When Spaniards arrived in America the first question that they asked was: Are there gold and silver in the surrounding places ?. On the other hand, Tartars in contact with the French ambassador asked: Do lambs exist in France?

These questions were related to their concept of wealth. In Europe, useful money was made from gold and silver and the quantity of its possession determined riches. For Tartars the possession of lambs, the source of meat and milk, determines wealth.

The statement of Garcia in 1983 acquires significance; every culture has a structure and posses coherence, sense and is functional for its existence.

It is important to mention the possible negatives effects of cultural transposition (with all it significance), without a context process. In a new environment rules, norms, laws, models, instruments and mechanism (useful for survival in other conditions) lose their objectives.

Latin American History

In 1492, Christopher Columbus arrived in America and the contact between two different cultures started. Values, laws, costumes, values and rules originating for surviving in different conditions were imposed. Under these new circumstances the difference between cultures became on unequal relationship, since the dominator stimulated the idea of his superiority.

Latin America is the result of this unequal conquest, with the imitation, assimilation and re- invention of ideas and institutions from Europe. (Castro J., 1998).

Do this circumstances are contributing to the current problems in Latin America ?

Most countries got their independence after French revolution and before 1850. The first years of the republic period were characterised by anarchy. The democracy today is incipient, after long military governments during 60's and 70's.

After 500 years, the society in Latin America is a complex mix and is the consequence of the current natural, social, cultural, economical environment, which is the product of past and present relationships between humans, cultures and their environments. The conditions are not unvaried, and it is possible to distinguish two kinds of countries: Uniform societies, based on populations descending from Europeans, such as the southern region (Argentina, Chile and Uruguay); and dual societies with an important native influence exist in Peru, Guatemala, Mexico and Bolivia. (Castro J., 1998)

The principal religion is Catholic which is based on Christianity. In dual societies paganism and Catholicism are mixed. The majority of the people recognise themselves as catholic, but they do not know the clearly significance of their asseverations. Religions were intentionally confused in the past. Spanners used to build "churches" on the same places where natives use to offer veneration to their gods.

Social Deterioration

The deterioration of social condition is the common issue. Violence, corruption, murders, poverty, illiteracy are the "objects" always present in this social picture, and are the visible expression of the large exclusion practised since the colony time.

In some countries, the majority of the population is excluded from their citizenship and rights established by law. They are part of the obligation, such as taxes, but their rights are not effective, such as access to education, health , justice, work, effective access to a "civilised life" and be an active part of the community, as Marshall defined. The unequal economical relationship and the "price" of citizenship, seem to ensure this exclusion.

The urban centres of Latin American present a common characteristic: the important migration from rural areas. Thousands of peasants have arrived to the cities in spite of the urban hostility. The new citizens found a wall of impenetrable of rules that exclude them from social and economic activities. (De Soto, 2000)

This absence of real citizenship takes place in civil, political and social rights.

The miss of justice seems to be a common pattern for "excludes". Jim Shultz, from The democracy Centre wrote: "Of the 1,380 men and women imprisoned here (San Sebastian, Cochabamba- Bolivia) , more than a 1,000 have no official sentence, have never had their day in court, and have no idea when they might be released". Justice seems to be a commodity.

Political rights are not effective in developing countries, even in the popular participation in the election process, their political rights are reduced to "vote emitter", because they are not effective electing authorities, this election is done in secret meetings and considering the political and economical interest of the few inhabitants who possess real citizenship. The high percentage of abstentions in an election clearly shows this problem. Additionally, in countries with a high percentage of native population, since the republic period, only 3 national authorities came from these group, the president Benito Juares in Mexico, the vice president of Bolivia Victor Hugo Cardenas, and the current president of Peru Alejandro Toledo .

Corruption and the illicit enrichment is a common problem in almost all countries in Latin America. Presidents, prefects, mayors, and other politicians are no exception. Actually, the mayor of the largest city in South America is under investigation process for illicit enrichment, as well as previous presidents of three countries are suspicious of the same crime.

Social rights are even worst, the living conditions of the majority of the population who do not have access to their rights for education, health, economical well-being, housing, a civilised life, and cultural and social inheritance.

The privation of these rights for the majority of the population creates an abysm between law dispositions and their application. Additionally, laws transposed from other backgrounds are not working in developing countries due to the under estimation of the context process considering social, cultural and economical conditions. Other laws respond to the private interest of economical groups, with much economical power. These conditions create a lack confidence in laws, regulation, rules, norms as regards the majority of the population. Frustration is generalised under this picture.

The extremely unequal relationship between few citizens and high number of "excludes" are driving these societies to an imminent collapse. The worse part is: there is not hope.

The influence of the globalisation and the neo-liberalism economy adopted by almost all countries in this continent contribute to construct capitalist societies and their concepts about progress, and establish the supremacy of the economical grow. Public founds are not enough to attend financing the accumulation of capital or financing reproduction of the work force. The elimination of subsidies in the social sector in some countries shows the tendency to finance the accumulation of capital.

Globalisation and the free market economy are contributing to this process. The fall of frontiers and the construction of new boundaries is followed by an integration process that in practice is translated to "standardisation". The standardisation process will enlarge the differences between rules and norms promulgated and their real application even more due to lack contextual process.

The new huge market needs additional capital and technology in order to face, in a competitive manner, these new conditions. For Latin America it seems to be a restriction due the generalised fragile economy. The main issue will be to obtain capital and technology via privatisation, that would contributes to diminishing the welfare state and public control over strategic sectors and basic services. International corporations with budget larger compared with the National budget, will augmenting the fragility of democracy.

This will increase the number of "the excluded", enlarge the "economical value" of citizenship.

How will all these Aspects Affect Water Management ?

Water cannot be isolated. The characteristics of this resource introduce it into the social arena. Large numbers of individuals are failing in the processes for being included into the community, and insuring water for everybody will provide possibilities to still disputing a space into a society. Citizens that are excludes from almost all their rights are not willing to be excluded from the most important one, the right to live.

The participation of water users is a essential activity on which depend the water management. This necessity come from: the natural condition of water and the current water policies in Latin America.

The natural characteristics of this resource makes every human being a user that would interfere with this resource in desired manner or damage it reducing its water quality and quantity for other users. The easy access and the cheaper cots in some Latin American countries increase the fragility of this resource.

In the second point of the declaration of The Dublin Conference it is establish the importance of the user participation in every water management. This settlement has been incorporated in almost all water laws promulgated after 1992. Since this time, water policies are based on the participation of water users and stakeholders.

Latin America today is composed by heterogeneous societies product of the colony history and the unequal wealth distribution. Urban centres are the geographical point wherein this societies share the same space.

The lack of the democracy would be a problem. The majority of the countries faced more than two decades of military governments with deficiency democratic practices.

The exclusion process and lack of confidence on authorities play additional role. The population excluded from almost all their rights are not willing to participated in any management activity. How is possible to ensure their participation ?

How does ensure the participation of users in water management?

The consensus of the policy and management of water start in the firs step of this process. Water policy must be taking into consideration the cultural and social aspects in the current country where it will be applied.

How does the population perceives water ? How does society understand this resource ? Is it the "common enemy" or is it a source of life.?.

It is necessary a clearly comprehension about the perception related to this resource. In some places it is described as a commodity. Part of the people who live in large cities and in a constant inter-relation with a capitalistic societies would be component of this perception.

In the other places, water is appreciated as part of the nature and a source for life. Normally, this conception is present in places with clear native influences or in places disconnected and isolated from large urban centres. The absence of the western values is clearly in between of this population. Normally, they are not able to face successfully in the post-modern societies, especially in the economic issue.

The groups described above are easily recognised. The problem is to recognise the perception of water in dual societies. In a mixed culture it is possible to find a combination of visions, described above, and this is the most complex case of the cultural importance in water management. The migration from rural areas to urban centres is significance. The emerging groups in urban centres are individuals with native or rural cultural influence, who were obligate to move to urban centres and to survive adopting their cultures. How do they perceives water? The mix between their inherit values and late worth (that respond the new environment conditions) produce a complex amalgamate of cultures. The majority of urban centres have this problem. The current tendency of urban centres seems to contribute to increase this problem . For example, urban population has increased from 41.4% in 1950 to 73.4 % in 1995, and according to projection it will be 83.2% in 2030, in Latin America. (United Nations, 1998)

It is essential to determine the degree of confidence on the social system. Unconfident on authorities, politician and technician is the result of these processes of exclusion and corruption. This uncertain will reach laws, rules, institutions, plans programs and water management.

In dual societies, this lack of confidence, started since the first contact between Europeans and natives. This relationship provoked a larger distance between authorities and population.

Some of consequences of the underestimation of this analysis would produce the reject of the water policy. Additionally, the citizen will deny his participation in all water management process, since the conception of the master plan to the operational management. But even worst, it will be provoked the boycott of the water management. Under this conditions the illegal accesses to water use and unpaid water bills will be a common practice.

The future participation of users and the favourable application of water management depend on the objective and exactitude of this analysis. No water management is possible with a minimum confidence of user.

Suggestions

It becomes a necessity to reach a minimum agreement on water policy that will encourage the participation of user. The consensus process will star with the conception of the policy and to conclude with the participation of the users on the running of the water system. This activity requires a institutional framework in order to define, organise and execute this participation.

The subdivision of the river basin will contribute to these objectives. The problem inside of this new division will be more homogeneous and the consensus process less difficult.

The transparency and honesty will be reflected by the consistency in the policy, institutions law, rules and norms. Transparency in all the process will enlarge the possibilities of acceptance and diminish the lack confidence on the water policy. Secret meetings and pacts are undesired. The political pragmatism use to be a problem due to the common use of "the political right sentences" which are an obstacle in the water management consensus. It is preferable honesty in the formulation of the policy with the real objectives.

The coherence of water management will be with itself and other sectors such us protection of the environment, economical growth and national objectives.

The principles and fundament of the water law must be in accordance with the remaining body of law.

The water management must be an important part of the national policy. It is not possible to construct a isolated water policy. Institutions, authorities, and managerial instruments must be clearly adherence with the general objectives of the water policy.

A coherent water management clearly will answer the question about the necessity for its application.

No laws and rules against cultural aspect. Traditional values of water such as religious and social have to be considered and no rules can be established that enter in conflict with these inherited values. Water managers use to underestimated the importance of this problem.

This requires a clearly comprehension of the culture in the place. In dual societies it requires even major attention. The mixed cultures will cause different disunite thinking and behaviour related to water.

In a context when the idea of water is a commodity, the water management is possible focussing in its economical value. Under this condition the majority of population will face the economical background in better conditions and it will increase their possibilities to access to this resource.

In the other hand, in places wherein the vision of water as a part of the nature and a source for life is present; the water management, plans, rules must consider these concept. Usually, in this circumstances the cosmos-vision and the value of the majority of commodities is different. In the extreme cases, their monetary value is neglected. Actually, there exist communities in dual societies that are not using money, and of course, they are using water. The people are dysfunctional in a market economy, and are not able to understand the value of the "metal " and "paper" called money, it is not possible to eat or to make clothes with it. In these places will be difficult to apply policy based on its economical value. The reduction of the value of water to monetary terms will be a dangerous practice, since the people perceives the value of water in different parameters. Money will exclude people from water use, according to their grade of adaptability to post-modern culture. The ethical question will be why they need to success in this culture in order to access water?

The challenge is to establish alternatives pathways to water access in order to guarantee the general right of use.

Alternative forms to water access will be possible from the analysis of the **social indicators** present in the country. Information related to poverty, basic services, education, literacy, health and housing will be a useful information in order to describe the general living conditions. The average income and the living cost will give an idea about the economical situation for the majority and their real possibilities for paying.

Percentage of unemployment and active labour force will provide information about of the stability of the population and possibility for migration. (movement of water demand). Information related to housing and its services will contribute to understand the amount of water consumption and water discharge. The conditions of the health, focusing on illness related to water, will give information related to the quality of the water and its influence in the mortality rate. All these information will provide a clear idea about the social reality in the country and the possibilities for successfully applying a specific water management. The central idea is to detect small users that are unable to pay for this resource. In urban centres it is a obligatory task.

Balanced participation of users. The participation of users with their perceptions about this resource will influence its management. Under this consideration the river basin committee plays a substantial role. The traditional division according to their activities or their objective function, are useful, but not enough in order to guarantee the equity water management The heterogeneous social mosaic need to be represented in the river basin committee and it is not possible still thinking about uniform or dual societies. The social conditions existing in third world countries wouldn't ignore the largest group of small users and the emerging groups with their identities and perception about water need a space into this committee (these are pare informal sector) . This will require a great effort related to increase information about the informal sector.

Foment and the traditional water management in places where it is possible. The absence of basic technology in most developing countries makes this possibility a real option of water management.

Deep analysis of the possible consequences of the water policy. This is a hard issue due to the uncertainties, externalities and universality of the water sector. This analysis requires, at least, the consideration of the main topics that will influence the future development of the selected water management. Long term objectives will contribute to clearly identification of the consequences of water management. Short term objectives will assist the creation of more uncertainties.

It seems that **poverty alleviation** for Latin America will be an important component of the policy that will increase the possibilities for its acceptance. The absence of this consideration will occasion the enlargement of the difference between "excludes" with "citizens", that will collapse not only a water management even the social system.

All water management needs to consider these aspects, otherwise it would fail and produce a violent reaction from the general population. The access to water becomes an initial factor of effective citizenship and possession of rights. It establish the right for existence, for being.

On the other hand, with all these information it will be possible to determine the objective function of the society that would make possible the application of a specific water policy; with appropriates laws, rules, institutions and measures; in order to obtain the desired outcomes.

4.4 Economical Sustainability

Cities are the place wherein the economical activities are concentred. A s a consequence, the long term success of the water policy depends on long term economic sustainability and it is related to two considerations: the first is the price of water, and the second is related to how much consumers are able and willing to pay.

Having economic value, water markets and water rights acquire high importance. (Solanes M., 1997).

The settlement: water as an economical good, present in the four point of the Dublin Declaration is the common principle present in almost every constitution promulgated after 1992. Even though the water markets in United States has been working for 150 years, and the Chilean water code promulgated in 1981 was based in its economic value.

The national economical policy will influence these conditions. Some countries are under the welfare state concept, based on the Keynes theory, and the participation of the state is visible in some sector such as, economical, energy, basic services and others. On the other hand, there are countries which economy is based on neo-liberalism that is the abandonee of the Keynes theory. In these countries, the role of the private sector is increasing, and the reduction of the state is perceptible.

Additionally, there exist economies that are in between. The welfare state is not complete abandonee and states are looking for an increasing participation of the private sector. In these countries the process of private participation is going via temporary concessions and permits.

The current tendency is to assume the neo-liberalism economy.

The Economical Problem of Water

The water sector requires investments in order to expand and to improve the current water network.

The economical problem in this sector, in Latin America, is related to the deficit and under pricing of water, practise for almost all countries, resulted in a massive transfer of income from marginal users to the middle and upper class consumer, and to commerce and industry. (Marvin S. and Laurie N., 1999). In conditions of economic limitations, the first that receive a reduced budget is operation and maintenance, as a consequence, the system works inadequately and provided unsafe water to peripheral users.

Throughout the 20th century, the states have found in extremely difficult to keep pace with increasing the demand for water. Domestic under investments and chronic dependence on external capital resulted in the systematic exclusion of the new users (Marvin S. and Laurie N., 1999). The economic sustainability of the water sector needs fresh capital from other sources in order to improve the current and actual conditions of the whole water network, and for enlarging the system for all uses.

The main water consumer in South American is the agricultural sector, with almost 70 % of the total demand. The crop land under irrigation is around 10 % of the total arable land, and it is associated to low-efficiency in water distribution. This sector has a great potential for expansion because only 6 % of the total land is already used.

79 % of the population is connected to drinking systems which work with considerable losses. This sector is the second largest water consumer. The population connected to sewage is around 52 %. It is estimated that only 13 % of the water discharge is treated (OPS, 1998).

Industrial activity is the third largest consumer, but 80 % of this activity is concentrate in Brazil and Argentina. The main problem related to this sector is the pollution discharge directly to surface water.

The last decade was characterised for the adoption of the neo-liberalism economical system for almost all countries in Latin America, and as a consequence the denationalisation process has been developed quickly in almost all sectors, even in public utilities. In this scenario the central problem is : to compete for the investment of capital, technology and management expertise. (World Economic Development Congress & The World Bank ,1998).

The driving force for the participation of the private investments in this sector is the feasibility for obtaining economic revenues from water management. The possibilities of transfer water to a place, time and use which will generate more profits than in the current pattern use will increase the private participation of this sector, this being possible when buyers and sellers perceive larger revenues. (Lee T. and Juravlev A.,1998)

Markets take into consideration the full cost of consumption, the elimination of subsidies, the diminished role of the state, and the increase in privatisation.

On the other hand, in third world countries the majority of the population are surviving under poverty conditions and are not able to pay for the full cost of consumption even if they are willing to pay. The Gross Development Product per capita in Latin American countries is around 10-20 % compared to developed countries and the problem becomes worse if it is considered the large unequal distribution of wealth. Additionally, a important part of the economy is moving into illegality. For example, in Cochabamba - Bolivia, the 70 % of employees is the informal sector.

Some increase in water price will affect all sectors and enlarge living costs. The price of all products will increase according to the consumption of water.

In developing countries this would have a negative repercussion on the capacity of competition of the industrial (specifically the large water users) and agricultural sectors. On the other hand, for the general population the minimum income is less than 100 $us in almost all countries in Latin America and the inflation rate is equal or more than the increase rate.

Water demand is related to all human activities from drinking, households, industry and agriculture. The average consumption of water per household is 50 m^3/year/person. In the case of industry this depend; larger users(such as iron and paper sectors), could use around500m^3/kg of production. The largest user is agriculture consumes 5000m^3/há/year , which is in some countries subsidised by the government.

The charge of water resources will affect its final price in every structure of water markets, in some cases more and in others less. It will depend on the elasticity price-demand, price-supply and price-income.

In Latin America water has a price-demand and income-demand inelastic relationship. For domestic water user groups, these elasticity values are from -0.37 to -0.597 for the price-demand, and from +0.32 to +0.784 for the income-demand relationship. For industrial sector some values of the price-demand elasticity are: -0.45 for steel in India, -0.958 chemical water use in the U K, -0.98 paper and chemical plants in the USA, -77 for petroleum in the USA , and -0.88 for steel in the USA. (Bhatia R., Cestti R. and Winpenny J., 1995)

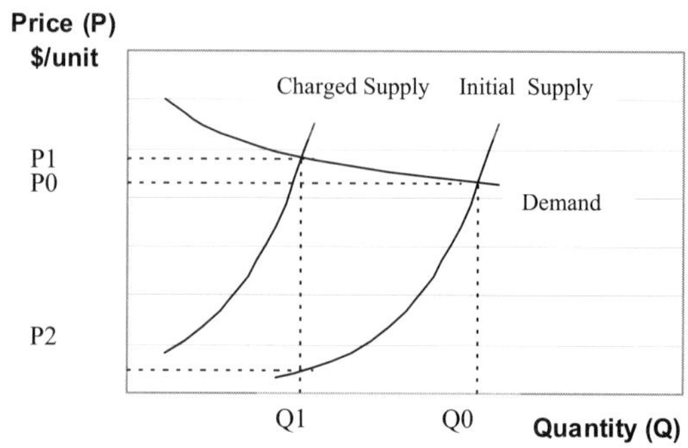

Graphic. 5.1 Water Charge in Perfect Markets.Elastic Price-Demand and Inelastic Price-Supply

According to De Souza, M. and Pires J., in the best case, a perfect market, the influence of increasing the price of water will affect the water supply company and the final consumer.The charge of water will be more reflected in its price according to how much the price-demand and price-supply elasticity are close to the perfect inelastic relationship (**E=0**). It will produce changes of the initial equilibrium point and displace the supply curve to the upper price. The magnitude of this impact will be in inverse relation to the elasticity of both curves. In an elastic price-demand and inelastic price-supply relationship, the water supply company pay the largest part in relation to final consumers. According to graph **G 5.1**, the initial supply,(no charged), and demand define the equilibrium point at (Q0, P0), after water charge, the supply curve is displaced and the new equilibrium point is at (Q1, P1). The final consumer pays the additional amount of P1-P0. The supply company refunds the additional amount P0-P2.
On the other hand, in an inelastic price-demand and elastic price-supply relationship, graph **G 5.2**, the final consumer suffers more with the charge of water. He refunds an increased value of P1- P0 which is more than P0-P2, that is the part that the supply company pays.

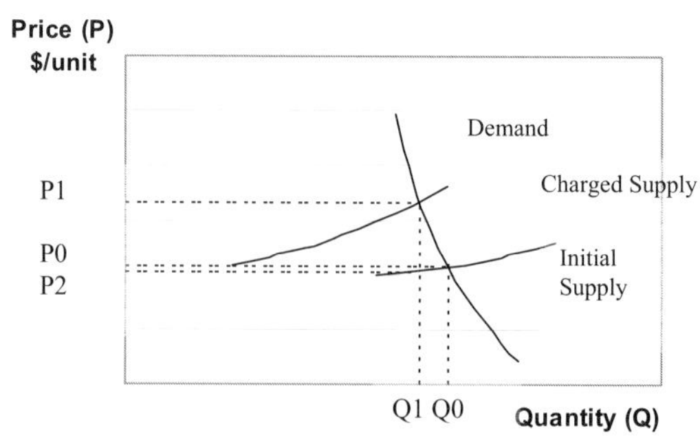

Graphic. 5.2 Water Charge in Perfect Markets Inelastic Price Demand and Elastic Price Supply

In the case of monopoly, the water supply company and the final consumer will receive the impact of the water charge. The amount is determined by the inverse elasticity of the price-demand relationship. The monopoly company, even it is maximising its benefits under these conditions, will reduce its extraordinary profits compared to the first case (no water charge).

This reduction will be depending on the elasticity of price-demand. Graph **G 5.3**, shows this relationship. Under this condition the equilibrium point is defined by the intersection between initial marginal cost and marginal revenue. The benefit obtained at this point for the water supply company is (P0-P2)*Q0 and the price for the final consumer is P0. The water charge displaces the cost curve to the upper price. The final consumer will pay an additional amount of P1-P0 and the water supply company will reduce its benefits to (P1 - P111)*Q1.

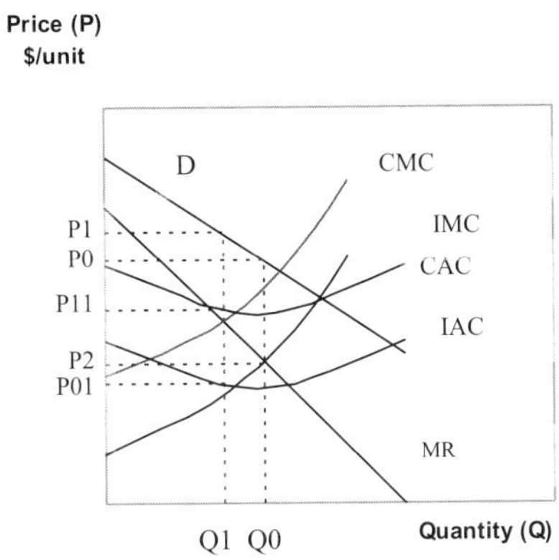

Graphic 5.3. Water Charge in Monopoly

When: CMC = Charged Marginal Cost
IMC = Initial Marginal Cost
CAC = Charged Average Cost
IAC = Initial Average Cost
MR = Marginal Revenue
D = Demand

Water markets seem to be inside the oligopoly structure, due the existence of few a largest water users. In an oligopoly situation it is not clear who will receive the largest impact, this will be according to the response of the market. Three possibilities exist, the first reaction is the organisation of water users and reproduction of the monopoly conditions. The second possibility is the existence of a leader company which defines the price and quantity. The last alternative is the free competition between users, largely dominated by the largest users.

The first and second option are close to each other, in both cases the monopoly condition is reproduced, with some differences. In the third case, the final consumer and the water supply company will receive, once again, the impact of the water charge.

Social and equity considerations are absent in the private sector. Maximisation of the rate return over the capital invested is the basic objective of privates companies and corporations.

Another problem related is the misunderstand about the economical value of water and reduce it to its financial value, and even worst to diminish it to a monetary terms, being this high influenced by post-modernism and globalisation.

The current water policy establish conditions for the participation of the private sector in water management. The majority of constitution institute water access via temporary concession and water charge. The water rights define privileges and obligations for use this resource for 30 - 40 year, according to each case, (Chile is the sole example in Latin America of permanent water rights). There exist the river basin committee and the technical water agencies, which are in charged of the planning, operation and control of the water use. Some of the responsibilities of these agencies are the economical support of water management and the control of the water rights.

The equilibrium between the interest of the private corporation and the interest of the society as a whole is the main question to be answered. The challenge is how to balance these aspects. The key issue is how to determine the water price. Under pricing and pricing above the budget of people go against the sustainability of water management. The answer is related to cost recovery, scarcity, willingness to pay, availability from other water resources, and how much the population is able to pay. This analysis must be based on economical information;(minimum income, inflation rate, increase rate). Additionally, social information will be useful, as we sow before. The economical policy of the country will influence. In countries wherein the welfare state is present, subsidies or block tariffs would be solutions. On the other hand, in neo-liberalism economies, the solution would be related to block tariffs, subsidise from government is not possible.

Under this situation, excessive increases of water price will be rejected by the general population thus generating unpaid water bills will cause the water policy to collapse.

Suggestions

- Foment users participation in control activities of water management in areas such us economical, administrative and operational, in all levels. According to the current law conditions in Latin America the lowest level is the river basin committee and its strengths come from the water law and from the effective participation of the users.

This control activity must be possible on the executive agency , responsible of the application of water policy. The legal power from law need to describe clearly its competence and its attributes.

The percentage of participation of the water users and stakeholders will be definitive in the control activity. The presence of final small users (domestic, small agriculture, fishing and riparian users) or their representative institutions would be guarantee the protection of these group of consumers. The attendance of the private sector, via industrial agriculture, industry or water corporation would ensure the protection of private investments. The number of representatives of this two large groups will determine the protection of the economical interest of final consumers or the private sector. Unbalanced participation will ensure the dominance of one group over the other.

From an economical point of view it is necessary to ensure the presence of the largest group of users whom are unable to pay in order to establish conditions for introducing the equity consideration in water management.

- The **subdivision of the river basin in smaller areas** will contribute to facilitate the control activity from users.
- **Clearly procedures in order to determine the price of water**. It is not possible to establish the economical value of water ignoring how much consumers are able to pay and how much they are willing to pay.. In some countries the welfare state is able to fund subsidies for people whom are unable to pay. But, it is necessary to analyse the long term application of this policy. The economical sustainability of the system obligate the equity consideration in the analysis of the price of water.
- **A clear and transparent contract** with well defined obligations and privileges contributes to its economical sustainability, and even to reduces costs. For example, clearly specifications related to: objectives, quality and quantity of the services, number of low income new access, new connections in defined areas and social tariff. Additionally, the amount of investments, its destination and schedule made by the concessionaire may help to a well defined contract. The regulator, control procedures and his attribution contribute to same objective.
- **Reduce costs.** A crucial issue is to diminish the current patterns of low efficiency in water systems. . The revenues from water charge need to be efficiently used in the water system and how distribute it is a crucial issue. .
- **The presence of technology** will make easier the control activities, and this seems to be a constraint in third world countries due to its absence. The traditional water management and control activities will be an real alternative in poor places.
- Promote competence in water access. **Free entrance into the water sector** is guaranteed by available public information related to the demand, supply, customers, costs, and opportunities. Information should be easy and free for the potential customer. (Lee T. and Juravlev A.,1998)

4.5 Spatial and Time Conditions.

The spatial and time water distributions have high influence in water management. It will increase or decrease the probability of successful application of the water policy. For example, water markets will be a success in places wherein the hydrological pattern shows a deficit balance between supply and demand.

Additionally, it will define the industrial, agricultural and economical development in the country.

Problems

The hydrological patterns are inconstant, changing during a certain period of time from one place to another. From this irregularity it is possible to identify two main types of variability: seasonal fluctuation and drastic occurrences such as extended droughts (Rosegrant M.W. and Binswanger H. P., 1994). Due to this erratically water distribution, it is viable to distinguish a period with abundant water, sometimes causing flood problems, and a period of scarcity.

In order to handle normal variability, or even drastic occurrences, water is stored during the wet period, but the reserve of water is able to cause ecological problems, changing the natural background of the rivers and affecting the general conditions of the environment. Another problem is distance, for water must be transported from the source to the demand at the right time, but long distances are not recommended because of the cost of infrastructure, management and the losses during transportation. On the other hand, this water acquires a high economic value during the dry period.

Additionally, shortages grow by reason of: water demand increases and supply decreases over time. The main reasons are: population growth, enlargement of consumption, expansion of the agricultural and industrial sectors, and water quality deterioration.

Since 1950, Latin American countries have grown from 166.3 million to 476.6 in 1995, and it is expect to have 719.9 million in 2030. (United Nations, 1998). A result of this high trend of population growth and quick urbanisation, is the deterioration of the water quality. There is a generalised absence of treatment plants. In fact, it is estimated that only 13 % of waste water is treated. (OPS,1998)

There is a strong connection between scarcity and the economical value of water, by reason of under this condition users are willing to pay for this resource. The development of the industry and agriculture depends on this resource.

Numerous countries are facing a growing water scarcity, for example, India's growing water shortages is occurring despite it being one of the wettest countries in the world (Agarwal A. and Narain S., 1999) and the United States, considered a wetter country, nevertheless have developed water markets in the dry South-western states. (Simpson L. Ringskog K.,1997)

In conditions of scarcity it is possible to introduce a water management using as a principal tool the charge of water.

Suggestions

The analysis of spatial and time water distribution is via hydrological information specifically; precipitation, evaporation, infiltration, capillary rise, discharge runoff, temperature, wind, groundwater flow and others. With this information it will be possible to determine the water supply in a determinate season.

Demand information related to drinking, agricultural , industrial , hydropower, recreation and others. For a clearly comprehension of the demand and its "movement" in space and time, information related to mortality rate, birth rate, immigration and emigration will be useful. Additionally, creation of industrial centres, habitat conditions, social information, national and regional development plans and other national plans will affect the demand in near future or even in long term future.

The long sustainability of water requires environmental information (minimum flow, groundwater levels, water quality indicators).

4.6 Legal Conditions

Water laws must establish rules, define authorities and firm procedures for assessing and using water. The spirit of the law must incentive a sustainable water use, and the water code must translate this intention into a consistent legal procedures. Inconsistency would generate uncertainties and misunderstandings that will create negative environment for users participation or will cause distortions in the application of the law.

It is important to mention the illegality in Latin America. The legal framework is unable to introduce into legality a thousands of poor and marginal inhabitants. The growing illegality suggests that the current laws are unable to reflect the social contracts that really exist. De Soto agues, the challenge for Latin American leaders is to crate legal framework in order to reflect the social contract existing and incorporate at least the majority of the population. This challenge reaches water managers. The legal water background is the key. The inclusion of the majority in water management will increase the probabilities for the real participation of user. In this process it is necessary to clear understanding the social contract existing in each country.

Problems

Water rights already exist in most developing countries, either by effect of the law trough charged concessions or via free primary appropriation and riparian doctrine. The private ownership of the water rights and the charge of water itself introduce this resource in the market arena. In some countries this market is regulated in other works based on the market mechanism. The marketable good in water markets is water itself or water rights. In the case of water rights that grants water ownership, the commercial good is water, and Chile is the sole example of this case in Latin America. In the other hand, most countries in South America establish water use over water rights, which do not grant water ownership.

Disputes and conflicts between the use and ownership of water use rights always seem to develop. (Simpson L. and Ringskog K., 1997). The reason are: the climate changes, economic and social uncertainties, the long time of the concessions, the doubts about of the population growth and others. Water law must be able to establish condition for solving these conflicts. It reacquires a carefully study of the problem of water and considers the interaction between different sectors. Besides this, problems such as social, economical, cultural, urban, political and others, need to be taken into account. Clear consistent water rights define privileges and obligations, which will assist in the solutions of water problems.

From a water market point of view, law have to ensure the effective ownership of water rights and the flexibility for water transferring.

The protection of the investments is via stable water rights, which need to establish privileges and obligations for their owners. In addition an important social dimension of water rights, close to its economical value, is the prevention of water accumulation, speculation , monopolies and waste (Solanes M., 1997)

Suggestions

The law have clearly define the **participation of users in control activities and their attributions** . This participation should be on all levels.

Legalise the traditional water management in places where it is possible. This became a real alternative of water management in poor regions and places where exist a high native influence.

Water rights must **define rights and obligations** between owners of water rights and from them to all society. Water markets work on water rights trading, assigning a price, for using in a limited period of time, or selling . The way how rights are defined establishes incentives in order to invest in this sector. (Lee T. and Juravlev A., 1998).

The customer needs to have a secure expectation about the benefits and costs related to water rights possession or transfer and how his rights are protected .(Colby, 1988)

The amount of water to be traded, that define the water rights, needs an accurate hydrological information (water availability is the result of water balance in the river basin.). The volumetric measure and pricing (volume/unit time) or quasi volumetric, is the right way to link water use benefit with water cost and the value of services provided.(Perry C.J., Rock M. and Seckler D.)

Allocation and uses priorities. Define under what conditions, the social value of the water is over its economical value. A clear definition of priorities avoids conflicts between users and clearly defined the water rights under extreme instances. Two examples: First, under a situation of extreme scarcity drinking purposes have the priority. Second, in an extremely poor region water should be not transferred because of its undesired effects. In both cases the interests of the whole society is above that the individual, and there is no choice.

Compensation in cases when rights are confiscated or transferred by the water authorities. The water rights must be protected from usurpation from others, including from the state. Certainly, rules and procedures for confiscation and indemnity have to established.

Effective and beneficial use of water, the central idea is looking for the best utilisation of water according to the society as a whole. The tenets of this doctrine are; avoid speculation, not use just to run the waste, the end of the use must be generally recognised and socially acceptable, not misused, reasonable use compared with other uses. (Solanes M.,1999).

Law must establish **easy water rights transfer** through selling, renting or a combination of both.

In the case of selling, water rights entitlement is transferred to the other that permits the long term use of water, and is a response for long term shortages. In this case the time duration is the remaining life time of the water rights.

Rent age of water rights is a temporal transfer of the rights which concedes the transitory use of water. The time duration is few years or even months.

A special case is when exists a contract in which water is temporarily transferred to another, and there is the possibility for a long term transfer.

4.7 Managerial Conditions

Specific institutional and management conditions are required to induce actions from users in favour of a desired interaction with this resource. For example, from a water market point of view, the institutional design determined the framework within which the private sector is prompted to invest in water development and conservation, and is not limited to water management and regulation of water related activities. (Solanes M., 1999).

The selected water management needs establish conditions for controlling and developing this resource in a sustainable manner and protect its social and economical values. The selected water management strategy,(consist in management arrangements), is an application of the water policy, after a previous consensus process. In according to Savanije, tools required for these purposes are:

- Institutional arrangements are composite of organisation establish by society, laws, procedures and customs.
- The management instruments are operational rules, economic incentives (charge), regulatory proceeding and structural measures.

Information, such as governance structure, social conditions, cultural background, economical, policy, legal framework, degree of people participation on democracy, the current water management, and others will be useful in order to determine the possible institutional arrangements and management instruments to use in water management.

Some Problems

The effective and efficient management arrangements depends on the serious analysis of the social, cultural, legal and economical background.

Water management and development are firmly related to actions of a user, which depends on the existing opportunities and is strongly interrelated to the action of the society as a whole also.

The behaviour of consumers is determined by their objectives. The water consumer elects from some specified settled alternatives, choosing the option that maximises some objective function.

Beginning with understanding these interactions, (the behaviour of users, the nature of election according to their objectives and how these attitudes affect each other), it will be possible to determine the outcome. This is such an important requirement in order to achieve the objectives in the water sector. From this careful analysis it will be possible to implement institutional arrangements and managerial instruments for conducting the course of action of users in order to chose the selected practice and produce the desired outcomes in this sector.

In the case of water the complexity of the problem is larger due to its characteristics, its inter-relation with all sectors and users (water is essential for life and for this reason every human being becomes a user), and its multiple objectives.

The attributes of this resource enables water to influence all other sectors. On the other hand, it is highly sensitive to external factors and intensely exposed to uncertainties. Water managers must pay careful attention to these aspects.

The management arrangements need to consider this picture. One common problem is underestimated or idealise the conduct of the users. The result will be unused institutional arrangements and managerial instruments.

Suggestions

Consider the users since their objective function and trait to ensure the participation of user with the all perceptions about water.

Generally , according to the objective function of users, which determines their conduct, it is possible to distinguish large users, small users(who are able and unable to pay) , protection and environment.

- The first group is composed of larger water consumers, such as the industrial agriculture, the water supply companies and the industry. All these groups are part of the private sector. The objective function of these groups is to maximise their profits and they are the firsts who are willing to pay for this resource.
- The second group is constituted of small users, such as small agriculture, fishing, small towns, and people close to rivers. All these stakeholders use this resource for surviving. Since an economical and social point of view there are exit users whom are able to pay and others whom are unable to pay.
- Protection is part of the stakeholders from community; its main function is protect human beings against hydrological changes, such as floods and droughts.
- Environment is another stakeholder from society and is related to maintain the safe and habitable conditions of the environment. The controls of water quality and water quantity are the main objectives of this stakeholder, via minimum flow and water quality indicators.

Additional and useful classification is :

- Since a water use point of view there are three main groups, such as agricultural, industrial and domestic uses.
- Other sector that need to participate in water management is

- The urban planning participation
- Municipal authorities

The first problem is to ensure a balanced participation of the all users. The complexity of this task is even more in large urban centres where the deterioration of water, scarcity of this resource and its necessity for production activities in order to alleviate the generalised poverty condition is a great problem.

As a response of the current necessities in water sector and after considering the behaviour of users, the institutional design must take into consideration the following institutional framework.

The **legal framework** has to do with the creation, definition, access and transfer of water rights and is indispensable in order to standardise the access to its use . The legal aspect must clearly fix the rights and obligations of water users and define the possibility of the transfer of water rights. Additionally, the law establishes institutions for water management and confers legality and authority to these structures.

The **decision framework** is concerned with decision makers as regards policy, strategies, plans, programs, projects, authorities and rules.

The main activity of the evaluation and co-ordination framework is to estimate the effects from and specific strategy and judge its beneficial application. Promote co-ordination, in between the sectors and stakeholders in order to achieve policy and improve strategies for water sector.

The **administrative framework** has to do with the administration, management, supervision and control of the procedures establish for the law, regulations and norms. In this framework it is possible to distinguish: legal, financial, planning, technical, operational and control configurations.

Legal and administrative structures are designated to the control of the procedures for concessions, permits, regulations and prohibitions from water law. The administrative, works close to legal, financial, operational and technical structures, and manages the administrative information related to concessions, permits, contracts, owners of water rights, and other useful information.

Financial structure is a useful instruments that ensure the achievement of the financial policy. Its objective is to ensure funding for the water management system. Activities such as operation, control and planning besides of infrastructure, equipment and human resource improvements. The economical sustainability of the water policy depends on the effective and efficient performance of this structure. Common sources are funding from national and local sources, from water charge, international organisations and others.

An important structure is planning, which is related to producing information to add for the comprehension of the water system as a whole, related problems and the outcome of possible management strategies for the development, conservation and allocation of water. (Savanije 1998) . This information contribute to long time sustainability of the water management.

The principal issue for the operational and control framework being how implement the strategy selected. Its principal activities are: the physical running of the system for allocating this resource, and the control of water quality and water quantity, considering its environmental sustainability. The technical department is related to how measures and monitor considering regulations, restrictions and possibilities from water availability and water rights.

The **importance of the river basin** is great in water management, since it is possible to find almost all the frameworks within this territorial unit, such as planning, administrative, decision, operative and financial.

It is common that each framework comes into action at different levels, according to the institution involved. Co-ordination and co-operation at all levels in all frameworks will also exist.

4.8 Control, Operational and Informational Conditions

This chapter is related to run the water system and regulate the quantity and quality of this element. Additionally, it will be possible to control of the water rights.

There exists a necessity for information on water, economical and social aspects in order to implement the better policy and to measure the effects from its application.

Obtaining good and sufficient information on water takes a long time. Most developing countries have problems with the lack of reliable hydrological data.

These conditions are related to control the achievement of management instruments which works on; economic (such as charges, subsidies and taxes), operational rules (deals with the correct operation of the physical structures for allocating and preserving this resource), regulatory proceeding (legal and administrative procedures) and structural measures (water infrastructures, such as dikes, reservoirs and others.)

The main specific activities are to determine responsibilities, technical and operational procedures in order to control the water quantity and quality, previously determinate. It delimit responsibilities and identify clearly the department in charge. The operational procedures define time and space for an specific operational activity. The technical define the instruments and tools that will use for achieve the objectives of the control and operational tasks.

Problems

The quantity of the marketable good, use or ownership, is based on the balance of water in a basin working on hydrological information. Irregular water distribution over time and space obligates the use of a large amount of accurate hydrological information. The time for water access is around 30 years and water rights must guarantee water availability during this period. The trade of water over volume/ unit time requires knowledge about precipitation, evapotranspiration, infiltration, capillary raise, runoff, percolation, and river flows for calculating the recharge of the basin, and the quantity of water available. One of the most common problems in water management is the protection of the rights of all users in the river basin. Upstream users have the guarantee of their rights due to their position, the problem is how to ensure the water rights to downstream users. Information and technology will provide the solution. Programs for river basin simulation will describe the general conditions of the basin, considering long term hydrological information, the extraction for upstream users, the minimum flow (which is a requirement for the environment) , and with all these information determine the amount of water available for downstream users. Water rights based on this amount have more probabilities of ensuring the sustainability of the water management and the confidence of water rights.

Additionally , control and information conditions are related to other fields such as, protection against hydrological events and preservation of the environment.

Information related to inhabitants, economical and social conditions is useful for water management in order to define the water demand and the "movement" of the demand. The long term of the plans increase the value for these information. The current demand is not constant and it will change according to the population growth expectation. Rates of birth, death, immigration, emigration, creation of economical poles, poverty, habitat and others will strongly impact the water demand in space and time. These information need to be organised in the same pathway, as well.

The control of water is related to those water resource characteristics and technical conditions present in the river basin. In some places the natural conditions of the water and its cycle makes it difficult to control this resource, this being related to how easy is the access and how much it costs.

The presence of technology assists to obtaining hydrological (and even economical and social) information, determining the amount of water and protecting the water rights of all users. It is associated to technical equipment, technical human resources, and adequate technical information (precipitation, evaporation, runoff, etc).

Technology improve the probability for developing and succeeding the selected water management.

Suggestions

The hydrological network is based on the river basin and its main activities are the collection, storage, calculation and diffusion of information. According to the objective of the specific network, this system incorporates an organised group of equipment, data process centres, expert systems, and control procedures.

In the collection stage, the organised group of equipment is necessary. The objective of the specific network information determine the type of equipment to be used, and is related to measuring precipitation, evaporation, runoff, infiltration, percolation, capillary rise, water quality indicators, and river flow. This network should have permanent and mobile stations, according to the specific information that is required. The presence of equipment with high technology will ensure the data, and make easier to from the collection station to the process centre. The construction of hydrological network needs the organisation and standardisation of the water and hydrological data base at all levels, local, national and even international.

The storage activity is done in data treatment centres wherein the information obtained; in the collection stage; is organised, standardised and presented as practical and useful information. Unserviceable hydrological information is related to antiquated and improper data base organisation.

The next stage, calculation, is related to expert systems, where the organised and standardised information is used in order to obtain other information, for example, water availability and the possibilities of floods. The presence of high technology in hardware and software; such as, the use of last generation computers, mathematical models and physical models; will enlarge on the probabilities of accurate results. The objective of this activity is related to prevention and protection of the users and their water rights from undesired hydrological events.

The diffusion of all this information is essential activity for water for water management.

The running of the system is considering the practical information calculated in the previous phase. This has to do with the procedures for the transport of water in quantities previously defined. The control of discharges from households, industrial and agricultural activities is via measuring the water quality discharged. If previous stages were successfully faced it will be possible to run the system in the same way, as the visible result of the all work previously done. Additional activity is the legal and administrative control of the privileges from water rights. The protection of all stakeholder's rights depend on these activities.

Technical human resources are an essential part of this technical requirement, in fact, they are indispensable in order to guarantee the accuracy of the information and safely execution of the water policy. The technical capacity must be achieve from an integrated water resources management point of view. Technicians will need a clear comprehension of the water cycle, water quality indicators, water requirements of the environment, the legal framework, water users and uses, basic infrastructure, the social conditions, water demand, water supply, national and regional objectives in the water sector, and national objectives.

The development of water is in direct relationship to technology. Intermediate or low technology will be a constraint for water management.(by the absence of more accurate information) and increase the uncertainty of water rights.

Unfortunately this basic technology is not present in most developing countries.

Conclusion

The application of the Dublin Principles in water management in urban centres of Latin America requires a carefully study about the environmental considerations, urban reality, social relationships and economical problems.

The poverty and social deterioration already interfere to urban water management. The general poverty reaches to majority in theses centres. This population is unable to attend the most important necessities such as feeding, health, housing, basic services and feeding. As a consequence there exist an evident social deterioration that influence the most basic rights.

Under this conditions the water management must be carefully study: The participation of users is a important issue. The incorporation of marginal seems to be a hard activity. This group lives in illegality and informality.

It is necessary the participation of this sector in water management?

The clear interference of this group in water management is via the illegal use of land, normally close to water bodies, which causes the water deterioration.

In order to incorporate the appropriate managerial arrangements into water management is necessary a different view about the agents, the scenario and the conditions.

The informal sector is ignored and its incorporation to water management will face technical and cultural problems.

The scenario is different due to the critical urban reality. The constant population growth is the main reason of the stress of current water systems (water supply, sewage, drainage and water quality), some of which already show signs of high deterioration.

The social relationship shows a great marginality. There are few inhabitants that posses better conditions for living and the majority has almost nothing.

The current models of urban water management need to be improved in order to response to these conditions. These models have emerged in western countries, whit stronger governments, better respect to the law, different hydrological patterns, smaller river basin size, better organised cities, better access to basic services, enhance wealth distribution, less cultural diversity, more homogeneous societies, and low levels of poverty compared to L. A. countries. These tendencies have emerged in this scenario and responding to these natural, social, economic and cultural conditions.

References

Agarwal A. and Narain S., 1999. Making Water Management Everybody's Business: Water Harvesting and Rural Development in India. International Institute for Environmental and Development. London, UK.

Arendt H. Entre o Passado e o Futuro. Editora. Perspectiva. Brazil

Arroyo Juan, 1995. Guardianes de la tierra. Centro de investigaciones y publicaciones. Ediciones Puma. Lima, Perú.

Bhatia R., Cestti R. and Winpenny J., 1995. Water Conservation and Reallocation: Best Practice Cases in Improving. Economic Efficiency and Environmental Quality. A World

Bank-ODI Joint Study. *The World Bank, Washington DC, USA.*

Baptista J.D., 1996. Planificación Estrategica para Responder a la Globalizacion.

Bodley J. H., 1994. From Cultural Anthropology: Tribes, States and the Global System. Washington, USA

Briscoe J., 1996. Managing Water as *Economic good. The World Bank, Washington DC, USA.*

Cabral B.,1998. Tratados Internacionais de Recusos Hídricos. Senado Federal, Brasilia DF, Brazil.

Castro J. 1998. Agua e Ciudadania. La lucha por el Agua y los Derechos de la Ciudadania: El Caso del Valle de Mexico. Teoría y Pesquisa, Universidade Federal de San Carlos. San Carlos, SP. Brazil.

Chaui M., 1992. Etica. Adauto Novaeo organisation, Secretaría Municipal de Cultura, Companhia de letras. São Paulo, Brazil.

Coing. H., 2000. Decentralisation et gerance privee a Monagas: A quoi servent les contrats ? Europe-Amerique Latine, Seminaire international CNRS. Paris, France

Courtard O., 2000. La face cachee du service universel: Differenciation technique et tarifaire dans le secteur de la distribution deau potable en Europe. Institut des Hautes Etudes de I'Amerique Latine. Paris, France.

Davis K., 1990 Population and resources: fact and interpretation. In: DAVIS, K.; BERNSTAM, M. S. Resources, environment, and population: present knowledge, future options. Oxford University Press, Population Council. New York , USA.

De Soto H., 2000. El Misterio del Capital. Empresa Editora El Comercio.S.A. Lima, Perú.

De Souza M. and Pires J., 1992. A Cobranca sobre o uso dos recurso hídricos, Ambiente-Revista Cotest de Tecnologia, Volume 6, Numero 1, Page 25. Secretaria de estado do Meio Ambiente, São Paulo, Brazil

Dourojeanni A. and Jouraviev A.,1999. El código de aguas de Chile: entre la ideología y la realidad. CEPAL, United Nations. Santiago de Chile.

Folha de São Paulo, 02/07/1999. Especial report "Ano 2000 comida y energia". São Paulo Brazil.

García M., 1983. As Culturas Populares no Capitalismo. Brasiliense, São Paulo, Brazil.

Gunn Ph. Latin American Context and Contributions to Development Theory.

Gupta Joyeeta, 1998. Introduction to the Law . IHE. Delft, The Netherlands.

Juraviev A. 1998. Los precios, La Propiedad y Los Mercados del Agua. CEPAL . United Nations. Santiago de Chile.

Koudstaal R. and Savenije H.H.G., 1998. Management Arrangements. IHE. Delft, The Netherlands.

Kroeber A and Kluckhohn C.,1952. Culture: A Critical review of Concepts and Definitions. Cambridge, Massachussets, USA.

Lanna E. A., 2001. Sistemas de Gestao de Recursos Hídricos. Análise de alguns arranjos institutionaes. Instituto de Pesquisas hidráulicas. Universidade Federal do Rio Grande do Sul, Brazil

Laurie N., 2000. User identity in the Cochabamba Water conflict in Bolivia. Departament of Geography, Newcastle University. Newcastle UK.

Lee T. and Juravlev A., 1998. Los Precios, La Propiedad y Los Mercados en la Asignación del Agua. CEPAL . United Nations. Santiago de Chile.

Lovei Laszlo, 1992. An Approach to the Economic Analysis of Water Supply Projects. The World Bank. *Washington DC, USA.*

Marcuse P. Is Australia Different ? Globalisation and the New Urban Poverty. Ocasional Paper 3.

Marshall T. H. and Buttomore T., 1992. Citizenship and Social Class. London. UK.

Marvin S. and Laurie N., 1999. An Emerging Logic of Urban Water Management, Cochabamba, Bolivia. Urban Studies, Vol 36, No 2, 341-347. Centre for Urban Technology, Department of Town and Country Planing, University of Newcastle, Newcastle, UK.

Monteceli J. and Soares J.,1993. A Luta Pela Agua, São Paulo, Brazil.

Moran E. F., 1990. A ecologia humana das populações da Amazônia. Vozes, Petroposlis, Brazil

Perry C.J. Rock M., Seckler D., 1997. Water as an Economic Good: A Solution or a Problem? International Irrigation Management Institute. Colombo, Sri Lanka

Rios Monica and Quiroz J., 1995. The Market for Water Rights in Chile. The World Bank. *Washington DC, USA.*

Rogers Peter Bhatia R. and Huber A., 1998. Water as a Social and Economic Good:How to Put the Principles into Practice. Global Water Partnership. Stockholm, Sweden.

Rosegrant Mark W. and Binswanger Hans P, 1994. Markets in Tradable Water Rights: Potential for Efficiency Gains in Developing Country. Water Resource Allocation. International Food Policy Research Institute. *Washington DC, USA.*

Rosegrant Mark. W, Gazmuri Schleyer Renato and Yadav Satya N, 1995. Water Policy for Efficient Agricultural Diversification: Market-Based Approach. Water Resource Allocation. International Food Policy Research Institute. *Washington DC, USA*

Savenije H.H.G., 1998. Water Resources Management . IHE. Delft, The Netherlands.

Simpson L. and Ringskog K., 1997. Water Markets in the Americas. World Bank . Washington, DC, USA.

Solanes M., 1999. Institutional and Legal Issues Relevant to the Implementation of Water Markets. United Nations, Economic Commission for Latin America and The Caribbean.

Solanes M., 1997. Water Planning and Water Legislation From the Perspective of the Dublin Principles. Global Water Partnership.

Solanes M., 1997. Water Rights. Functions, Conditionalities. Harry S. Truman Research Institute, Hebrew University, Palestinian Consultancy Group. Istanbul, Turkey.

Solanes M. and Gonzales F., 1996. The Dublin Principles for Water Reflected in a Comparative Assessment of Institutional and Legal Arrangements for Integrated Water Resources Management. Global Water Partnership.

Solanes M., 1996. Water markets and the principles of Dublin. Dept. of Environment

Scienc, Policy, and Management University of California. California USA.
Van Wijk-Sijbesma Christine, 1987. What price Water?. Water and Sanitation Centre. The Hague, The Netherlands.
Vanier C., 1999. Patria, Empresa e Mercadoria. In: Arantes O., Vainer C. and Mericato E. Arantes O., Vainer C. and Maricato E., 2000 A Cidade do Pensamento Unico. Editora Vozes. Petrópolis R.J., Brazil
Villaca F., 1999. Uma contribuicao para a historia do planejamento urbano no Brasil. In: Deak C. and Shiffer S., 1999. O proceso de urbanizacao no Brasil. Edusp/Fupam. Sao Paulo, Brazil.

Part IV

New Research

19

Mexico City's Central Area Yesterday-Today-Tomorrow

A Vision of its Future Development based on Analysis of the Historic Transformations in the Heart of the Great City.

Alejandro Suarez Pareyón

Mexico City is a living example of the historic mixture of several cultures; the Mexican culture from the pre-Hispanic period which is internationally known as Aztec, the European culture from the start of Spanish colonial domination, the culture of an independent country whose liberty was forged by wars, revolutions and the industrial development of the 20th century, and finally, the culture of globalization at the beginning of the 21st century.

The material, human and cultural consequences of this complicated mixture of peoples can still be seen in Mexico City's Central Area, and the study of this particular space is the subject of the research proposal.

The period chosen for investigation starts at the middle of the 19th century and finishes at end of the 20th century. This period is considered sufficient to be able to make some informed comments on the future of the Central Area, and especially on the role that it should fulfil in relation to the development of the Mexico City metropolis in the 21st century.

In 1857 Mexico City's first railway line was inaugurated and with it a new form of urban development in the city was initiated. Mexico's first experience of globalization was during the decade 1900-1910 during the dictatorship of General Porfirio Diaz and during this time Mexico City was transformed by many public works and private investments. The immediate motive for these improvements in the city's infrastructure and buildings was the celebration of 100 years of Mexico's Independence from the Spanish. At the start of the Mexican Revolution in 1910 Mexico City had a population of 500,000 inhabitants. Twenty years later when the Revolution was over the city's population had grown to one million inhabitants and the process of industrialization was beginning. It was not until the 1950's that the phenomenon of metropolization got underway and with it the seemingly unstoppable demographic growth and the expansion of the urban area. In many cases the urban problems presented by these phenomenon could not be solved by local and national governments who did not have sufficient capacity to attend to the demand. At the end of the 20th century, when globalization had become a major influence, the population of Mexico City and its Metropolitan Area was more than 18 million inhabitants and its urban area was more than 1,300 square kilometres.

Today, the Central Area of the great metropolis occupies what was earlier the total urban area of Mexico City. The Central Area is of great importance in historical, economic, political and cultural terms and is known for the contrasts and contradictions between its different social groups. Sometimes these occupy urban and architectural spaces that have not significantly changed over the centuries, whilst other groups may occupy spaces that are associated with the most advanced type of economic, technological, cultural interchange, which is the product of globalization. However, it seems that the general dynamic of economic and spatial development in the Mexico City Metropolitan Area is being defined in different terms, and ones that could have an impact on the "centrality" of the Central Area. This could pose a threat to the identity of the historic city.

The challenge for the inhabitants of the Mexico City's Central Area, for the local government and for all those interested in conserving this special place that has enormous development potential, is to be able to articulate the development of the historic city with the city of tomorrow.

To sum up: the proposal seeks to look into the past and present of Mexico City's Central Area in order to examine what are the best possibilities for its future development.

The methodology consists in following the historic transformations of the environment in urban and sometimes architectural terms by analysing the evidence left by the railway system, industrial installations, the formation of neighbourhoods, the urban renovation projects, and specific actions associated with urban and housing regeneration. At a later stage the development policies and strategies pursued by local government during the last thirty years will be examined, and the research conclusions will look at possible scenarios for the future of the Central Area.

Some Preliminary Ideas For Discussion

1. Objective

The research proposes to trace the production of urban space, and sometimes the production of the built environment (architecture), in the Central Area from a historic perspective. The variables to be used are the remaining evidence of the railway system and industrial installations, the formation of neighbourhoods, the content and terms of reference of development plans, urban renovation projects, and specific urban renovation and housing projects. In a second phase, local government development policies and strategies during the last thirty years will be examined, and the conclusions will speculate about the future of the Central Area.

2. Preliminary Questions To Guide the Study

- How important is the historic city for the present urban structure of the Central Area?
- Which aspects of development have lasted over time and characterise different spaces in the city?
- What situations have had greater impact in the transformation of urban space than others?
- Which social groups have intervened in the transformation of the Central Area?
- What development policies and strategies have been applied to Mexico City?

- Is there a perspective for the Central Area and the Mexico City Metropolis?
- What is the role of the Central Area and what does Globalisation offer it?
- How can a new centrality be constructed or recuperated?
- What are the factors that policy should address?

3. The Study Area

How is the Central Area defined?

At the beginning of the third millennium Mexico City is a metropolitan area with more than 18 million inhabitants. The area extends over more than one political-administrative demarcation and includes the Federal District, 37 municipalities in the State of Mexico and one municipality in the State of Hidalgo. All of these demarcations have different governments and administrative systems and the level of development between them varies widely.

Given the size of metropolitan Mexico City the central space fulfils a particular function where the main economic, social, political and cultural activities are located. This situation is similar in other big metropolitan areas. Today the Central Area is still important in the era of Globalisation, the general dynamic of economic and spatial development in the Mexico City Metropolitan Zone seems to be leading to changes in the Central Area's historic role and could challenge its "exclusive centrality," which has remained relatively intact throughout the city's history, to develop a "poli-nucleated" urban structure.

4 The Period Under Study: 1850-2000

The study begins in the middle of the 19th century when the new neighbourhoods were established and the railway was constructed. The study ends at the end of the 20th century using paradigms of Globalisation, which are used to support reflections on the future of the Central Area and on the role that it could play in the development of the metropolis as a whole in the 21st century.

5. Methodology

Starting from the present situation with reference to urban space in the study area, the analysis proceeds to follow the interaction between seven components that have influenced its urban development

- The continued presence of elements from the past (pre-Hispanic and colonial)
- The development of neighbourhoods, housing estates or large residential areas and their particular architectural style
- The structural elements associated with the railway system
- The structural elements associated with industrial development
- Land-use changes
- Public investment in infrastructure, urban equipment, and development projects
- Public urban development policy

The research will pay particular attention to the analysis of urban space in the sense that it will be given priority in fieldwork, the analysis of historic plans and photographs, including aerial photographs, and the search for eyewitness accounts. The results of this work will be used to undertake a reconstruction plan of the area. A database will be built.

The documentary part of the research will be carried out in parallel to the field work and has two aims: one, seeking out information from the period in question, and two, revising the literature on the key themes explored in the project.

It is important to note that the experience acquired through previous, or ongoing, technical assistance and academic research will play an important role in the completion of the research.

Preliminary Structure

- **Introduction**
  An overall view of urban development in Mexico
- **The Development Model for Mexico City**
  A historical overview of the city's development from its foundation in 1325 to the start of the 21st century
- **Mexico City during the Second Half of The 19th Century**
  The first neighbourhoods, the railway and the new industries
- **Mexico City and the First Period of Globalization 1990-1910**
  The modernization of the city, public works and private investments (national and foreign capital)
- **The Mexican Revolution and its Impact on the Development of the City**
- **The Start of Industrial Development 1930-1950**
  Import substitution policy and industrial development; rural-urban migration; extensive urban development; and, increased population densities in the Central Area
- **The Metropolitan Process and the Emergence of New Central Areas 1950-1980**
  Explosive demographic growth and the growth of the urban area; the reduced importance of the Central Area, urban and housing deterioration; loss of housing and the expulsion of population; industrial decentralization. Urban renovation projects; the closing of the railways and the re-functioning of the area..
- **The Earthquake of 1985 and its Impact**
  Reconstruction after the disaster, poverty and marginality are evident
- **The Crisis of the Central Area**
  The new centres of the great metropolis; Old City vs. New City, the urban paradigms of globalization
- **Constructing A Project for the City**
  The first democratically elected government for Mexico City, a new urban development planning model; new plans for Mexico City's Historic Centre
- **Speculative Reflections On The Future of the Central Area**

References

Audefroy, Joel. Coordinador (1999). Vivir en los Centros Históricos, experiencias y luchas de los habitantes para permanecer en los centros históricos. México: Habitat International Coalition.

Barros, Cristina (1996). El Centro Histórico ayer, hoy y mañana. México: Instituto Nacional de Antropología e Historia.

Benévolo, Leonardo (1999). Historia de la Arquitectura Moderna. Barcelona, España: Editorial Gustavo Gili.

Carrega Lamadrid, Luz y Garay López, Begoña (1999). Un camino olvidado, Estaciones de ferrocarril en el estado de San Luis Potosí: Línea México-Laredo (Ferrocarril Nacional Mexicano). México: El Colegio de San Luis.

CONAPO (1998). Escenarios demográficos y urbanos de la Zona Metropolitana de la Ciudad de México, 1990-2010, Síntesis. México: Consejo Nacional de Población.

Coatsworth, John H. (1984). El impacto económico de los ferrocarriles en el Porfiriato, crecimiento contra desarrollo. México: Ediciones Era, Colección Problemas de México.

Connolly, Priscilla; Duhau, Emilio; Coulomb, René (1991). Cambiar de Casa pero no de barrio. México: Centro de la Vivienda y Estudios Urbanos A.C., CENVI, Universidad Autónoma Metropolitana Azcapotzalco.

Coulomb, Rene y Duahu, Emilio. Coordinadores (1988). La Ciudad y sus Actores. México: Universidad Autónoma Metropolitana Azcapotzalco.

Coulomb Bosc, René y Sanchez Mejorada, Cristina (1991). ¿Todos Propietarios?, vivienda de alquiler y sectores populares en la Ciudad de México. México: Centro de la vivienda y Estudios Urbanos A.C., CENVI.

Chanfón Olmos, Carlos. Coordinador (1998). Historia de la Arquitectura y el Urbanismo Mexicanos, volumen III El México Independiente, Tomo II Afirmación del Nacionalismo y la Modernidad. México: Universidad Nacional Autónoma de México UNAM y Fondo de Cultura Económica.

De Anda Alanís, Enrique X. (1990) La Arquitectura de la Revolución Mexicana, corrientes y estilos de la década de los veinte. México: Instituto de investigaciones Estéticas Universidad Nacional Autónoma de México.

Dirección de Obras Municipales de Santiago y Atelier parisien d'urbanisme (2000). Santiago Poniente, desarrollo urbano y patrimonio. Santiago, Chile: Dirección de Obras Municipales de Santiago.

Eibenshutz Hartman, Roberto y Rébora Togno, Alberto (2000). El Desarrollo Urbano en el Distrito Federal. México: Secretaría de Desarrollo Urbano y Vivienda.

Fideicomiso del Centro Histórico de la Ciudad de México (2000). Programa para el desarrollo integral del Centro Histórico de la Ciudad de México. México: Documento de Trabajo editado por el Fideicomiso del Centro Histórico de la Ciudad de México.

Fideicomiso de Estudios Estratégicos sobre la Ciudad de México (2000). La Ciudad de México Hoy, bases para un diagnóstico. México: Gobierno del Distrito Federal.

Garza, Gustavo (1996). Cincuenta Años de Investigación Urbana y Regional en México, 1940-1991. México: El Colegio de México.

Garza, Gustavo. Coordinador (2000). La Ciudad de México en el fin del segundo milenio. México: Gobierno del Distrito Federal y El Colegio de México.

Harms, Hans; Ludeña, Wiley; Pfeiffer, Peter. Editores (1996). Vivir en el "Centro". Viviendas e inquilinato en los barrios céntricos de América Latina. Hamburgo: Technische Universität Hamburg-Harburg.

Iracheta, Alfonso X. (1988). Hacia una Planeación Urbana Crítica. México: Universidad Autónoma Metropolitana y Ediciones Gernika.

Jimenez Muñoz, Jorge H. (1993). La Traza del Poder, Historia de la política y de los negocios urbanos en el Distrito Federal, de sus orígenes a la desaparición del Ayuntamiento (1824-1928). México: Codees Editores.

Kuntz Ficker, Sandra y Riguzzi, Paolo. Coordinadores (1996). Ferrocarriles y Vida Económica en México (1850-1950). México: El Colegio Mexiquense, Ferrocarriles Nacionales de México, Universidad Autónoma Metropolitana Xochimilco.

López Rangel, Rafael (1993). La Planificación y la Ciudad de México 1900-1940. México: Universidad Autónoma Metropolitana.
Mesías González, Rosendo y Suárez Pareyón, Alejandro (2001). Los Centros Vivos, alternativas de hábitat en los centros antiguos de las ciudades de América Latina. La Habana- Ciudad de México: Red XIV.B "Viviendo y Construyendo" Programa Iberoamericano de Ciencia y Tecnología para el Desarrollo CYTED.
Monnet, Jerome (1995). Usos e Imágenes del Centro Histórico de la Ciudad de México. México: Departamento del Distrito Federal y Centro de Estudios Mexicanos y Centroamericanos.
Ortiz Hernan, Sergio (1987-1988). Los Ferrocarriles de México, una visión social y económica, volumen I La luz de la locomotora, volumen II La rueda rumorosa. México: Ferrocarriles Nacionales de México.
Paz Arellano, Pedro. Coordinador (1988). La rehabilitación de la vivienda: una alternativa para la conservación de los centros históricos. México: Instituto Nacional de Antropología e Historia.
Perló Cohen, Manuel. Compilador (1990). La Modernización de las Ciudades en México: Universidad Nacional Autónoma de México UNAM.
Rivera Cambas, Manuel (1880-1883). México Pintoresco, Artístico y Monumental. México: Edición Facsimilar (1972) Editorial del Valle de México.
Romero, José (1910). Guía de la Ciudad de México. México: Librería Porrua.
Sanchez Ruiz, Gerardo G. (1999). La Ciudad de México en el Periodo de las Regencias 1929-1997. México: Universidad Autónoma Metropolitana Azcapotzalco y Gobierno del Distrito Federal.
Secretaría de Comunicaciones y Transportes y Ferrocarriles Nacionales de México (1996). Caminos de Hierro. México.
Secretaría de Desarrollo Urbano y Vivienda (1997). Programa General de Desarrollo Urbano del Distrito Federal. México: Departamento del Distrito Federal.
Secretaría de Desarrollo Urbano y Vivienda (2000). Programa Parcial de Desarrollo Urbano del Centro Histórico, Delegación Cuauhtemoc, Distrito Federal. México: Gobierno del Distrito Federal.
Sirvent Gutierrez, Gladis; Alfaro Salazar, Francisco Haroldo; Arciniega Avila, Hugo A. Coordinadores (1994). Colonia La Tabacalera, varias lecturas sobre un patrimonio.
Suárez Pareyón, Alejandro (2000). Escenarios Socioeconómicos y Espaciales de la Zona Metropolitana de la Ciudad de México, en El Mercado de Valores, mayo 2000.
Tello Peón, Berta (1998). Santa María la Ribera. México: Editorial Clio.
Ward, Peter M. (1991). México: una megaciudad, Producción y reproducción de un medio ambiente urbano. México: Consejo Nacional para la Cultura y las Artes, Alianza Editorial.
Yanes Rizo, Emma (1994). Los días del vapor. México: Consejo Nacional de la Cultura y las Artes, Instituto Nacional de Antropología e Historia y Ferrocarriles Nacionales de México, Museo Nacional de los Ferrocarriles.
Yanes Rizo, Emma (2000). Me matan si no trabajo y si trabajo me matan, historia de la comunidad tecnológica ferroviaria en México, 1850-1950. México: Instituto Nacional de Antropología e Historia, Serie Historia, Colección Científica.

20

Mobility in the Low-cost Housing Stock: New Housing Supply for the Poorest Sectors in Santiago, Chile

Ana Sugranyes

Introduction

Over the past 20 years, low cost housing financing policy has removed slums in Santiago. It has provided shelter to 20 % of the city's population through the construction of a large low-quality housing stock.

During 1996, in response to the demands of the private building sector, the government designed a "residential mobility programme" with the objective of granting innate value to low-cost dwellings and to facilitate its incorporation into the real estate market. This official mobility proposal, based on a market approach, has after five years not yet shown large-scale and effective results.

The focus of most housing research has largely been on access to dwellings and dwelling environment and, to a smaller degree, on the residential mobility of the low-income groups within the cities.

This research examines the following:

- The complex dynamics of residential mobility;
- Similar processes of low-cost housing mobility in other cities;
- The 300,000 low-cost housing stock in Santiago, in terms of its strengths, opportunities, limitations and threats in creating a new housing supply for the poorest sectors;
- An evaluation of the Chilean government's mobility plan from a theoretical and practical perspective.

The Issues

The financing policy for social housing was designed at the end of the 1970s, within the perspective of a market economy model, but following a long tradition of State intervention in low-cost housing. This policy combines user savings, state subsidies and private financial market loans; and assigns public resources through a widely supported and transparent system. Its application was consolidated in the 1980s. The Aylwin and Frei governments of the previous decade have maintained the same policy. During the past 20 years, Chile's top priority has been to reduce the high housing deficit and production rates reached the high average of 10 dwellings for 1000 inhabitants in the mid nineties (Consulta,2000).

During this period in Santiago, the mass production of low-cost dwellings —with nominal values of less that 10,000 Euro (400 UF), with State financing and the participation of huge construction companies—,

- has provided shelter to some 300,000 new property owners, or, to more than 20 % of the city's population;
- has contributed to a quantitative deficit reduction;
- has concentrated poor residential areas in very few of the 34 municipal territories (with autonomous municipal governments) that make up the city of Santiago;
- has increased spatial segregation and the social disintegration of the city.

The mass production model of low-cost housing, in the territory of Greater Santiago, is showing signs of failure. Land prices can no longer sustain the construction of houses with nominal values of less than 15,000 Euros (600 UF).

Lagos' government housing policy continues to produce houses of the same low quality, at the same rate as during the nineties (Minvu 2001). However, this emphasis has meant that, due to current land prices, housing the poor has to be undertaken further and further away from the consolidated areas of the city, outside the urban limit of Greater Santiago. This implies that the State is openly supporting the operations of the speculative real estate sector in various expansion zones of the city (Poduje 2001). Furthermore, that the State will now not be able to supply new public housing to the poorest sectors in the city.

The business construction sector -whose trade association, the *Cámara Chilena de la Construcción* (CChC) has essentially designed housing policy for the past 20 years-affirms that the low-cost housing stock in Santiago has been sufficient since the mid nineties. Seeking greater utilities, the CChC would like to leave the low-cost housing sector, and concentrate its activities on projects of greater investment and larger profits.

Therefore, the CChC advisers at the Housing and Urban Development Ministry, Minvu, developed the "housing mobility programme" (1996). This instrument proposes that the low cost dwelling owner (being the beneficiary of a State subsidy) can sell it in order to acquire another dwelling of a better standard. This instrument also proposes that the sold low-cost dwelling may be put on the secondary market and may be acquired by a recently subsidised family.

Minvu has made the necessary changes in the regulatory framework to allow for the sale of low-cost dwellings once the original loan has been repaid. This sale is financed through a new subsidy. An additional change is that Minvu now also subsidies used houses and not only new units.

The proposal of the CChC advisers to perfect the secondary market for low-cost housing has not yet shown effective and widespread results.

The Debate

Filtering theory serves to explain the housing stock supply dynamic from an economic point of view (Olsen, 1969). According to this theory, residential mobility develops when the following conditions exist:

- stability in the real estate market,
- constant demand,
- demand corresponding with stock volume,
- the number of unused dwellings cannot be more the 1 % of the stock,
- a highly diverse supply,
- levels of family income similar to housing expenditure levels, and
- low transaction costs.

Under these conditions, households can opt for better quality dwellings.

In the majority of Latin American cities, residential mobility is linked to the concept of social mobility, and especially that of labour mobility. "Of course, this problematic is of a highly complex nature… it is not easy to unravel all the intertwining threads of social status mobility, housing changes, tenure mobility, dwelling consolidations, and the many other processes interfering at the level of the domestic unit or that of the wider society" (Van Lindert, 1992).

At the beginning of the 21st century, Santiago shows:

- 15 years of sustained growth;
- a decrease in poverty levels; according to government sources: the poor reduced from 38.7% of the total population in 1987 to 14,8% in 1996; and the destitute reduced from 13.5% in 1987 to 2.7% in 1996 (Mideplan, Casen);
- a 300,000 unit low quality, low-cost housing stock, promoted and financed by the State with both explicit and hidden subsidies, produced by a very limited number of large construction companies;
- still an estimated demand of 100,000 new dwellings for the poor sectors.

Given this context, residential mobility should have worked. Nevertheless, the official government's housing mobility programme has had limited results.

The hypothesis of this research is that, in addition to economic factors, there are many other social and cultural variables that influence residential mobility, especially for the low-cost housing case. For the Santiago case, the variables, which greatly influence residential mobility, are:

- housing typology,
- construction technology,
- project size,
- public space improvement, and
- neighbourhood location within urban space.

Residential mobility may serve as a response to the risks associated with of a low quality housing oversupply. In addition to market pressure, cultural and social factors, mobility requires public private co-operation in order to tackle two main problems: deteriorated and obsolete construction and neighbourhoods isolated from urban sub-centres. Public private co-operation also may help in the improvement of public space and in the promotion of individual investment for residential consolidation. In the case of Santiago, the State should solve the technical aspects related to the processes of living together in condominiums, especially in those developments with more than 2,000 dwellings of prison-like design.

Given these hypotheses, the debate centres around three fundamental questions:

Why is mobility in the low-cost housing stock important in Santiago?

The "successful" system for low-cost housing financing -widely practised in Latin America- which combines contributions from the user, the State and the market, is experiencing difficulties in adapting to the current urban reality.

This situation became evident through two institutional crises in 1997. The first crisis was linked to administrative and political pressure on the executing bodies on the low-cost housing financing plans to achieve very high goals, and led to fraudulent actions. The second was associated to rainy conditions during 1997 that brought to light the limitations of the building technical specifications and, consequently, the quality of the low-cost housing (Consulta, 2000).

Both crises are linked to other deeper and structural issues:

- The demand subsidised housing model is a State incentive for private enterprise participation in the construction of low-cost housing. The financing system is, therefore, a guarantee that the Ministry of Housing and Urban Development provides to the entrepreneurial sector for very successful business activities in low-cost housing construction sector.
- The financing system has an impact on the social and spatial segregation of the city (Rodríguez, Winchester, 2000).
- The increase in land prices in Santiago limits the interest of companies in providing land for investments of less than 15,000 dollars per house (Consulta, 2000).
- The low-cost housing financing system is centred on the production of new units. It does not take into account the demands of renewal or recycling deteriorated and obsolete stock.
- The financing system's inertia inhibits innovation in housing management for the poor, and is ill suited to current city dynamics.
- The model is highly centralised in that the municipalities have practically no role in participation.

The direct consequence of these issues are such that that the poor can no longer access new housing in the consolidated area of the city. If the poor accept the rules of the game imposed by the government and the private sector, poor homeless families (principally those households which share a dwelling or site with another family, "los allegados" and in a lesser degree inhabitants of irregular settlements, "los de campamentos") only have access to low quality housing at great distances from their current residence.

The alternative that emerges from the research hypotheses, is that, under a residential mobility scheme, the poor would have access to used but renovated low-cost housing stock within the consolidated urban area.

What are the characteristics of the low-cost housing stock?

The 300,000 low-cost housing stock that accumulated over twenty years, in different urban areas of Santiago, is based on two typologies:

- single family housing, ranging from 35 to 45m², with one or two floors, on a lot of between 60 to 100m², detached in twin houses or attached in a continuous facade, with direct access to the street or a passage way;
- apartments in buildings of 3 or 4 floors, with units also ranging from 35 to 45m², in a

system of horizontal joint ownership, with a complex placing of the building in the middle of semi-public space or semi-private space of the condominium.

Each one of these types reveal different tendencies with regards to improvement or deterioration related to the following variables:

- *Typology*. The neighbourhood with single family dwellings has greater improvement, renovation and recycling possibilities than multiple floor housing. However, in almost all of the 3 or 4 floors buildings neighbourhood the inhabitants apply the Kiss principle building elements which protrude from the facades, like bubbles more or less anchored over sticks.
- *Individual or collective tenure*. The housing on sites with direct access to the street or passageway exhibit a certain respect for public space. The so called “condominiums”, that began to appear in Chile at the end of the 1960s, all have the same problems of how communal space around the buildings should be used. Because there is no tradition of communal living, the occupants of the apartments in the ground floor appropriate space to improve their housing, installing workshops and retail areas, or for parking and gardens. Given the numerous dwellings extensions and land occupations, the municipalities react by issuing fines.
- *Project size*. The average project size in Santiago is 330 units. This varies between 100 and 2000 units per project. In any project with a size greater than 200 units, the low cost housing developments present pathologies of communal living; the capacity of identification with public spaces decreases inversely to the size of the development.
- *Location of housing developments in the segregated city*. Although Santiago has good coverage of infrastructure and services, the differences in quality are great among the 34 municipal districts/territories. Low-cost housing is distributed among 29 districts/territories. The greatest concentrations are in five municipal territories in the south and west of the city (Puente Alto, La Pintana, San Bernardo, Maipú and Quilicura).
- *Time period in which the development was built*. There are differences in quality between the construction years of the neighbourhoods. The developments of greater quality are from 1980 to 1982 and 1998-2000. The moments of greatest political pressure to increase the annual number of housing and with a clear decrease in the quality are two: near the years 1985 and 1995.
- *Interventions and contributions of the municipality*. Traditionally the process of low-cost housing production is limited to the Ministry of Housing and Urban Development and private business construction companies. Where a local municipality has participated in some way, the elements of quality increase, especially in the configuration and maintenance of public space.

How does the residential mobility in the low-cost housing stock in Santiago function?

Opinions close to the business construction sector CChC maintain that the consolidation of the official program for residential mobility, designed by the State in 1996 to create a secondary market for low cost housing, is essentially a question of time and contribution by the State in:

- publicity campaigns for the potential buyer of a better dwelling,
- information campaigns oriented towards new low cost housing beneficiaries,
- additional subsidies for the buying of used housing, in the form of a location

premium,

- simplification of the transactions of the dwellings, that require, among others, a modernisation of the system of property registry.

Opinions that are more critical to the model maintain that the mobility process has to do with more complex dimensions than those relating to the market. These are:

- Cultural factors related to aspirations and the satisfaction with the dwelling. For popular urban sectors, with traditional rural origins, a house cannot be understood only as a product related to the market. It is a right and an acquired good, which remains with the family forever.
- The majority of low-cost housing beneficiaries, especially those from single family housing, do not demonstrate interest in selling their dwelling with the option of buying a better one.
- The condominium beneficiaries demonstrate more doubts about their permanent residence in the dwelling, mainly because of perceptions of fear and insecurity in the face of general criminality, and small-scale drug trafficking that is extensive in the popular neighbourhood (PNUD, 2000).
- In any case the intention of not selling the dwelling is linked to the labour situation, especially since 1999 with high rates of unemployment in the popular sector in Santiago.
- In other words, the general conditions of the physical deterioration, the social disintegration and the insecurity threats are determined by the neighbourhood - especially amongst the 3 or 4 floors apartments buildings- whose dwellings may be the principal supply source in the mobility scheme.

Future Directions: Methodology

To prove the hypothesis and to answer the three fundamental questions the present research proposes the following actions:

- Study of filtering theory through technical literature, in order to analyse the housing stock supply.
- A case study comparison on similar processes of residential mobility in the low-cost housing stock, in both Latin American and European cities.
- The study of the holistic impact of 300,000 low-cost housing produced in Santiago during the last 20 years, through direct observation, in order to analyse the location of the potential supply in the secondary real estate market.
- The analysis of general location tendencies of the 450 low-cost housing projects, through direct observation, comparing concentrations during the eighties and the nineties, in order to understand the tendencies on location of demand to low-cost housing in Santiago.
- The analysis of 10 different typical neighbourhoods in terms of their strengths, opportunities, limitations and threats to improvement, through direct observation and local interviews; this is done in order to understand the possibilities those neighbourhoods have in generating a low-cost housing supply to new subsidy beneficiaries.
- The study of the theory on which the official residential mobility programme is based, trough secondary sources and direct interviews with key informant persons, in

order to understand the correlation between the market perspective and the other social, cultural and physical factors which influence residential mobility.

- The evaluation of the official residential mobility programme, through direct interviews with key informant persons.

References

Benavides, Leopoldo y Eduardo Morales (1983). "Campamentos y poblaciones de las comunas del gran Santiago", Flacso, Santiago, Chile.

CEPAL (1996). "La producción de la vivienda en América Latina y el Caribe", Santiago.

"Consulta sobre la política habitacional en Chile" (2000). Oficina Regional de Desarrollo Urbano para Latinoamérica y el Caribe, USAID-RUDO/LAC.

Haramoto, Edwin (1992). "Espacio y comportamiento, estudio de casos de mejoramiento en el entorno inmediato a la vivienda social", Universidad Central, Facultad de Arquitectura y Bellas Artes, Santiago.

Laforest, Mireille (1999). "Lyon-Bron. Diez años de intervención en un barrio" en Proposiciones N°30, Urbanismo y democracia, experiencias en Lyon, Montreal, Santiago. SUR, Santiago

Mathéy, Kosta (1992). "Positions on Self-Help Housing" in Beyond Self-Help Housing, Profil Verlag, München, p. 387.

Ministerio de Vivienda y Urbanismo (2001). "Nueva política habitacional", Santiago, Chile

Odeplan, Programa de Adiestramiento en Preparación e Evaluación de Proyectos, "Costo nacional diferencial de localizar viviendas básicas", 1986

Olsen, Edgar (1969). "A Competitive Theory of the Housing Market", in American Economic Review, vol. 59, p 612-622.

Pérez-Iñigo, Alvaro (2000). "La movilidad habitacional", in "Consulta sobre la política habitacional en Chile", Oficina Regional de Desarrollo Urbano para Latinoamérica y el Caribe, USAID-RUDO/LAC.

PNUD, (1998) "El miedo al otro, seguridad ciudadana", en Desarrollo humano en Chile, Paradoja de la modernización"; capítulo 5, Santiago, Chile.

Poduje, Iván (2000) "La especulación inmobiliaria en la Región Metropolitana", Instituto de Postgrados, Facultad de Arquitectura, Urbanismo y Bellas Artes, Pontificia Universidad Católica de Chile.

Rodríguez, Alfredo y Lucy Winchester (2001). "Santiago de Chile. Metropolización, globalización, desigualdad", Eure, Revista Latinoamericana de estudios Urbano Regionales, Vol. XXVII, N° 80, p. 121-139

Simian, José Miguel (2000). "Eigentumorientierte Wohnungspolitik in Deutschland und Chile", Institut für Genossenschaftswesen der Universität Münster.

Sugranyes, Ana (2000) "Los desafíos de la política habitacional en Chile", III Seminario Internacional sobre Mejoramiento y Reordenamiento de Asentamientos Urbanos Precarios, MejorHab, Habyted, Cyted; Montevideo.

van Lindert, Paul (1992). "Social Mobility and Housing Advancement", in Beyond Self-Help Housing.

Vergara, Francisco y Palmer, Montserrat (1990). "El lote 9x18, en la encrucijada habitacional de hoy", Facultad de Arquitectura y Bellas Artes, Pontificia Universidad Católica de Chile.

21

The Virtual Network of the ITESM in Latin American Cities:

A Potential Vehicle for Collaborative Research in Sustainable Regional Design.

Ernesto Philibert-Petit

Introduction

In a world of cities, the international community is starting to address the issue of *urban sustainability*. The process began in Rio with Agenda 21 and continued at the 1996 UN City Summit in Istanbul. The Habitat Agenda, signed in Istanbul by 180 nations, states: 'Human settlements shall be planned, developed and improved in a manner that takes full account of sustainable development principles and all their components, as set out in Agenda 21. ... We need to respect the carrying capacity of ecosystems and the preservation of opportunities for future generations. ... *Science and technology have a crucial role in* ***shaping sustainable human settlements*** *and sustaining the ecosystems they depend upon*[101].

One of the most important resources for the global development of sustainable thinking on urban and regional issues is the network. The network scheme has foundations standing solidly on the emerging paradigm of holistic and collaborative approaches. This new paradigm is quickly displacing the mechanical and individualistic approach set in Western civilisation since the Renaissance. The rapid development of telecommunications and informatics has certainly fostered the growth of this emerging network approach to knowledge.

This paper is about a research proposal that relates sustainable design for regions and cities in Latin America with interdisciplinary virtual teams working and researching them simultaneously. The subject of study of the research proposal is dualistic: the sustainable regional design models proposed for the region or regions studied and the features of the collaboration within the virtual interdisciplinary teams.

This proposal to the Alfa-Ibis network has three main phases. The first is the development of a *virtual vehicle*, in which collaborative, interdisciplinary, integral, and simultaneous regional design research can be done, referred to the existing infrastructure of the Virtual University (VU) of the ITESM. The VU has facilities that can reach, in *real time*, up to 1200 sites in Latin America, by means of satellite broadcasting, videoconferencing and the internet.

The second phase will conduct the vehicle through a formal research project within a regional and urban sustainability subject of study, and with a specific object of study

101 Girardet, Herbert (2001). Cities and the Culture of Sustainability. Quarterly Journal of the Urban Design Group # 78.

still to be defined, on the vehicle devised in the first phase. The third phase would be the PhD thesis itself.

Regional Design. A Holistic Approach to Sustainability.

Recent discussion over urban form and its regional impact have raised serious questions in respect of the feasibility of the concept of the city as an isolated subject of study, when the emerging holistic thinking has been claiming the reality of the interconnections between the city and its environment. According to a number of authors, *ecology, traffic, pollution, even social life, are all regional, even though our political jurisdictions do not reflect this reality*[102], thus it can be awkward to identify the smallest appropriate unit for a given aspect of the environment[103].

We might consider that the systems of the global economy are in fact regional: only the larger, more diverse entity of the region has the multifaceted strength required to be part of the global market, which is why planners can now say with great conviction that if one part of a region suffers, the whole suffers and becomes less competitive. Therefore, *regional planning and a sense of the overall public interest must become a part of our lives*[104].

The first keyword in this project is *regional*, a holistic point of view for an approach to sustainability, rather than in terms of cities or even in terms of nations as a whole[105]. The region is a more suitable way of thinking about the interconnections discussed previously, given the fact that the country, or to be more specific - the city as a cultural phenomenon, has a deep relationship with its natural environment. The symbiotic relation between nature and culture has been denied in many cases and in many forms in our *civilization*[106] and daily city-actions. At this point, the notion of a *regional city* appears to be displacing the more commonly used term - *metropolitan region*. The latter suggests a pattern of growth with a city at its center, whereas a regional city suggests a pattern likened to a constellation with many centers. The concept of the *metropolitan region* conforms to the idea of the city as the origin and center, somehow implying a denial of interconnectivity. The term *regional city* accepts notions of sprawl that have been long resisted that it is in effect, eclipsing the old cities and the hierarchical, solar-system configuration. It implies a landscape in which the natural areas become interstitial, rather than encompassing[107].

Furthermore on this subject, Lewis has introduced the concept of *Regional Design*[108], as a collaborative node grouping different teams of various disciplines in terms of networks that seek to give form to the region. In spite of the fact that he still holds a "national" approach to the subject, our main interest in his proposal rests in the concept of collaboration between design disciplines in what he calls "design teams" in

---

102 Calthorpe. (2001). The Regional City.

103 Barton, Hugh (1996). Going Green by Design. Quarterly Journal of the Urban Design Group, #57.

104 Calthorpe, op.cit.

105 The city and its immediate interdependent region has overgrown, in many cases, the limits of nations and in many others is clearly linked to other cities, therefore we should approach urban sustainability in terms of regions rather than in terms of cities.

106 The word "civilisation", taken to its roots meaning city development.

107 Calthorpe, op.cit.

108 Lewis, Philip. (1996) *Tomorrow by Design.*

aiding the visualization of both the product and process to other nodes of the network. Here we find another keyword in our proposal: *integral design*[109].

Regional design is trans-disciplinary. The definition encompasses urban, landscape, architectural, industrial and graphic designers working in collaboration. This comprehensive approach to design and its correspondence to a holistic point of view are of fundamental interest to this research proposal.

Design as a Bridge over the Gap between Planning and Communication

Beyond the different scales, classifications or fields in which design is used to give form to a given cultural product (namely a book, a lamp, a room, a house, a building, cityscape, landscape, or even a whole city) design generally moves between an abstraction of that given object (the ideas, the concept) and concrete information concerning it. Design goes back and forth between planning and communication until the object is no longer an idea and exists in the physical world. Since design, planning and many other disciplines are changing rapidly from an isolated, mechanistic approach to practice, to a more integrated, systemic and holistic one, we may find in this another researchable question to answer:

Is design as a general discipline a feasible connection between the abstraction of planning and concrete information to get self-feedback, external feedback or execution? If it is, then we should deepen our knowledge about its application to a regional approach in order to propose feasible schemes for regional design as a subject of trans-disciplinary teamwork.

Empowerment of People in Sustainable Regional Design

Perhaps one of the most important tasks of having a feasible connection between abstract planning and concrete information is that of improved means in engaging people in the discussion of the form (in the widest sense of the word) of the region they inhabit and that region's design. Theory about sustainability emphasizes that development is about maintaining and enhancing the quality of human life - social, economic and environmental - while living within the carrying capacity of supporting ecosystems and the resource base. The two key principles that emerge from this definition are first, satisfying human needs, recognizing the obligation for intergenerational as well as intra-generational equity; and second, increasing the level of self-sufficiency at different scales: building, locality, town, region[110]. A third principle is the issue of people's participation at all levels of sustainable planning and design. Design occurs in a rich social context where the effectiveness and efficiency of social interaction and collective performance are key to successful outcomes. Increasingly, design is being explored and developed as a collective, collaborative, participatory, and even community process. The heightened recognition of design as a social process has stimulated interest in collaborative design[111]. Forester uses a variety of case studies to show how his ideas concerning deliberation have shaped planning practice. He perceives planning as the effort to build consensus towards commonly perceived goals. *Since the context of*

109 Integral design as integrative and trans-disciplinary in a wide length of design fields.
110 Barton, op.cit.
111 Linden J. Ball (Editor). (2000) Collaborative Design : Proceedings of Codesigning 2000.

planning is always fraught with differences, conflicts and inequalities, a planning process necessarily shapes opinion, creates values and transforms not just material conditions but human relationships[112]. At every level the designer or decision-maker should attempt to maximize the level of autonomy of the ecosystem while enhancing its life-giving qualities. That means, in essence, reducing dependence on the wider environment for resources, and reducing its pollution by waste products[113]. The emphasis on democracy and participation is central in research for effective planning and decision-making practices. But, in what measure is an integral design approach applied to regions helpful for the participation of people in the process?

Transdisciplinary implies Collaborative?

Not necessarily. The emerging paradigm regarding the value of collaboration has not displaced or even balanced that of competition. The idea of having trans-disciplinary design teams to aid in the visualization of the planning process might present operational problems not found in the lack of abilities or obtained knowledge of the team participants, but in their competitive attitudes, by definition, contrary to those of collaboration.

Our Western civilization has just started to question the individualistic and hierarchic organization, finding out the benefits of the collective network organization as a means of decision making and as a way of life.

This paradigm shift is and will be critical in many ways. This matter surely defines another issue in the research: team collaboration and, since in the near future it is expected to have distant team sessions (synchronic or asynchronic) within the project, an even more acute delimitation: inter and trans-disciplinary virtual team collaboration. Surely this issue currently means, as Kuhn has stated, the creation of new research problems, methods, and expected results. The current fragmented structure of knowledge and practice present tensions between different facets of environmental concern; each area often possessing its own set of experts and specialist agencies. The challenge is to make sense of these disparate elements, to produce fusions and inter-relations. This requires the collaboration of interests and the involvement of agencies and people at different levels to ensure that sustainability works[114].

A Dualistic Research Model

Interdisciplinary design teams and the city-regions in which they will perform their work are both subjects of study and representative of a dualistic model in this first phase of giving form to a vehicle for sustainable regional design research. Our present interest is on one hand, that of furthering the understanding of the performance and collaboration of integral design teams and on the other, that of going deeper into the concept of the regional city.

Defining the subjects of study (issues) are:

- A regional city concept
- Integral design

112 Forester, John (1999). The Deliberative Practitioner.
113 Barton, op.cit.
114 Barton, op.cit.

- Design as a connection between abstraction and information
- Participative design processes
- Virtual teams collaboration

In the first stage we expect to obtain the program of and to give form to a vehicle able to perform a specific regional design research in the second stage.

The ITESM, a Reference Framework

The academic space in which the project will be developed exists within the ITESM System, or Sistema Tecnológico de Monterrey in Mexico. It is pertinent at this point to make a brief reference to it.

The Monterrey Institute of Technology and Higher Education was founded in 1943 by a group of Mexican businessmen. It is a private institution without political or religious affiliations. It has 30 campuses in Mexico, a student enrolment of nearly 92,000 and a faculty of around 7,100. There is a graduate student enrolment of over 4,800 in presented programs and 5,700 in virtual programs. The Institute offers 34 undergraduate majors, 57 masters and 8 doctoral programs, in such fields as architecture, engineering, computer science, business administration, communications, food technology, law and medicine. The Institute's presence reaches throughout Mexico, and its educational services are currently being extended to other countries in Latin America. The System has a scholarship and loan program that benefits 30.25% of the students.

Monterrey Tech has an unusual strength in Informatics and Telecommunications (IT). The System is linked by a computer network and encourages faculty members and students to use the computer and telecommunication networks for academic purposes. Monterrey Tech has over 25,000 computers, of which 18,000 are for student use. More than 16,000 students own laptop computers. An increasing number of courses incorporate web pages, on-line homework and other internet based course materials. As a general condition, many courses are supported by specific technological IT platforms such as Lotus Notes' *Learning Space* and lately, Datatel's *Blackboard.* The Institute has a private communications network linking the campuses, with 14 connections and 4 satellite networks. The System includes the Virtual University that provides distance education via satellite for institutions in Mexico, and Central and South America[115].

The General Educational Model of the Virtual University of the ITESM.

One of the main strategies followed by the Monterrey Tech System has been the development of the *Virtual University*, within the System itself. This entity has been exploring, developing and operating with distance education formats for more than twelve years. The distance education - *virtual* - model has been developed in various areas and disciplines. Now the VU has over 42,000 students. The Virtual University network can currently reach, in real time, 1,430 different sites in Latin America, linking them via satellite, internet and intranet.

115 Taken from the Monterrey Institute of Technology web page: http://www.sistema.itesm.mx

The general model of the VU is based on three main groups of resources: the videoconferences resources, capable of broadcasting from many of the network nodes and even mixing audio and video signals from two, three or more different locations simultaneously; interactive web pages in which schedules, course materials and activities are posted and held through the course and interactive sessions with student teams and professors based on collaborative software; and what we might call the "feedback" resources such as an internal network of voice and data. This efficient system of resources is capable of bringing education on many levels to many people at the same time in many different places[116].

The Virtual University network has become a powerful tool for education, but nevertheless, not yet an equally powerful tool for research. This proposal is intended to help develop such potentials.

A Particular Research Model through Graduate Studies Regional Design.

One of our immediate interests in the project is that of building a vehicle in which collaborative, interdisciplinary, integral, and simultaneous regional design research can be done. We assume that the actual features of the Virtual University can also be used, with great advantages over other electronic (nowadays conventional) means, like the extent of the network, the infrastructure available and the feedback capabilities, but overall, the particular bonus of working simultaneously in a number of regions-cities in Latin America with a general standardised methodology and with the particular conditions of the regions-cities studied in the cases to be defined. This dynamic model would certainly include the possibility of direct links with academics, consultants and practices in places all over the world; with other universities and research centres or consolidated research networks such as Alfa-Ibis and, to what perhaps is its great advantage, with people - users - in all the nodes of the network. To have at least a component of community consultation, participation or self-help in the process is now conventional wisdom, and it would be unusual if we did not include it into our model.

The specific academic space for conducting the vehicle would be within a synergy of two graduate programs that form part of the Virtual University: the Master of Architecture (with speciality in Urban Design) and the Master of Sustainable Planning, with a number of possibilities for new links to be added to this synergy, still to be found.

Designing a VCRV (Virtual Collaborative Research Vehicle)

Unlike most traditional *cultural systems*, modern urban systems depend crucially on a vast system of external supply lines to rural areas and manufacturing centres, facilitated by global transport and communications infrastructure. This is not *culture*, or even *civilisation* in the traditional sense, but a *mobilisation* - of people, resources and financial capital[117]. That is a reason why we have adopted the metaphor *vehicle* to designate the whole set of conditions for developing research on regional design. Mobilisation or, movement is a sign of our times and demand dynamic models.

---

116 Average groups have a number of around 200 students in 20 or 30 different cities in Mexico. Graduate groups are smaller, but normally reach 25 to 35 cities in Mexico and Latin America. Statistics on this subject will be part of further investigations.

117 Girardet, op.cit.

The primary task to achieve in the first stage of the project is that of designing the vehicle for the second stage. We have already described some concepts around this object of design but certainly it is desirable to establish a formal design program, both quantitative and qualitative to be met functionally and formally to conduct formal research in it. One issue then is the development of the virtual environments systems to facilitate this and so we must consider areas such as computer graphics, interface technologies, user embodiment and networking. *However, alongside this, there is the matter of the design of the environment where the interaction takes place* [118].

Since one of the keywords in the project, and consequently of the VCRV, features is collaboration. It is important that the vehicle should provide a common space for virtual team interactivity. Plans and development briefs need to specify clearly the way the local network should link seamlessly into networks in surrounding areas, identifying key desire lines from suburbs to services, jobs and leisure activities[119]. Thus, a comprehensive program must include a useful network of information flowing in multiplicity and not linear patterns. The most recent developments have established multi-user three dimensional environments, or Collaborative Virtual Environments (CVEs,) which allow a number of people to interact with others in a simulated 3D space. However, most current CVEs are limited to relatively small numbers of users and usually do not support audio communication, resorting instead to separate text based conferencing [120].

A common language is central in the program to design the vehicle. Large-scale research projects like the *Urban Environment Differentiation* conducted by the Dutch National Planning Agency in recent years, have yielded useful tools such as the *Pattern Image Tool*[121]. The Pattern Image Tool proposes typological conventions for interpretation in spatial planning and furthermore, precise descriptions of urban characteristics and types of environments that can be useful as a common vocabulary when interdisciplinary, international and intercultural team members work together.

Another interesting and useful feature found in Urhahn and Bobiç´s work is the example comparison that gives, by relation, precise account of scales, dimensions, indexes, and images in a patterned framework. Common graphic symbolism and a number of pictograms, like that proposed in the document of reference, are certainly of great help in any given team interaction. Defining a particular typological tool, analogous to this for the use in the second stage, is very important and certainly will imply deeper study and documentation of the subject.

Constructing the VCRV

Collaborative tools from electronic sketchpads, to personal digital assistants and computer generated virtual worlds are of little use to us without substantial investment in online community building and design processes[122]. This enhances the need in carrying out a formal design process study (or the software) that will drive the vehicle (the hardware). After the first stage in the process, it is expected that during the next seminar presentation, the design for the vehicle will be finished thereafter constructing the model

118 Ingram, Rob. (2000) Building Virtual Worlds: A City Planning Perspective. Online Planning Journal

119 Barton, op.cit.

120 Ingram, op.cit.

121 v. Urhahn and Bobiç.

122 Paul, op.cit.

will be the following task. This "construction" will be directed to give if not physical, then real form to the project with the self-embedded features it will have by design and also academic, administrative and of infrastructure to make it feasible to conduct, with the specific regional design research project, in the second year. Thus, we are planning to have all the conditions set to work with empirical evidence in one year from now.

Defining the Research Avenues

Due to the nature of this project, at this point we should only consider short-length avenues to search in. During the following stages, these avenues will surely grow farther in temporal and depth ranges. According to the issues set and the discussion on the "program" for designing the vehicle, we could state at this point that the immediate research and study should be directed to define four main features for the prototype:

- The dynamic model or the conceptual form of the vehicle, which should not be static, should meet the needs stated in the general program considering the particular subjects or the probable map for the academic-research route that, the vehicle will follow.
- The virtual interactivity scheme, including the main features of the platform of the VU and the characteristics of the platform in which the vehicle will move.
- The design processes that are to be conducted inside the vehicle, including its relations with people, authorities, experts throughout the world and other processes.
- The typological tools and the common language, semantic and symbolic, that will be of common use in the project and of clear understanding for the externals to it.

Future Utility of Research

We propose three points of view in seeing out the future of this research. The *possible* future, the one of what we foresee liberally and intuitively, almost dreaming, that future that *can* be real.

The *probable* future, the one that considers not the possibilities but the probabilities and that is colder and speculative since it is the future that *should* happen. Lastly, the *preferable* future, that common place between the future that can and the future that should come true if possibilities and probabilities interact.

The Possible Future

The starting point for sustainable development is the satisfaction of the basic human needs of shelter, warmth, health, opportunities for work, access to facilities and a pleasant environment. Social and environmental goals are often mutually reinforcing, thus providing a broad constituency of support for policy[123]. The proposed research project can help to satisfy those basic human needs in our Latin American region, by

123 Barton, op.cit.

producing awareness, interest and participation of the people, the authorities and professionals in giving form to communities.

Currently, cities are not centres of *civilisation* but *mobilisation* of people and goods. We need to revive the vision of cities as places of conviviality and above all else of sedentary living. This means reviving more local lifestyles within cities themselves, focusing on the concept of the urban village within the city, where community living can be a reality. A calmer, more serene vision of cities is needed to help them fulfil their true potential as places not just of the body but of the spirit. The greatest energy of cities should be directed towards creating masterpieces of human creativity[124]. Integral design teams can help people to regain this vision by a thorough visualisation effort. Designers can retake the role they had, of giving form to solutions to help people, to give form to aesthetic and functional entities and most importantly, to give form to the civilisation's dreams.

The Probable Future

It is no longer valid to claim that while sustainable development is all very fine in theory, it is not technically feasible in practice. On the contrary, most of the principles and techniques of sustainable design are tried and tested, although admittedly on a dis-aggregated basis. What is new is the challenge and obligation to adopt them comprehensively[125]. Nevertheless, the shift in the value paradigm of Western civilisation should still take many years. We should accept that a global liberal democratic capitalism has been gaining, and will gain, more terrain for a number of years, and will have radically different meanings for different segments of the world system[126]. The immediate future should present a growing gap between the wealthy and poor communities. Research in sustainable region-city form should bring timely solutions in given cases, but it should also take some time to be fully fruitful. Participation of people, authorities and professionals in collaborative design efforts should start to grow steadily with the visualising help of regional designer teams.

The Preferable Future

Successful environmental planning is preferably seen as a matter of co-operation between public, private and environmental organisations[127]. Many of the world's major environmental problems will only be solved by urbanites conceptualising new ways of managing their cities. Integral design teams will be of key importance in giving form to that conceptualising and those new ways of managing and building cities. The city will no longer be conceived as isolated or as a centre but, intimately related to the region and to other cities, as a natural-cultural node in a network or as a cell in an organism.

Our knowledge system will start to inform us that the human species has changed the very same way as the 'the web of life' on earth itself functions: from the *geographically scattered interaction* of a myriad of living species, to which local cultures are intimately connected, into an assembly of *concentrated urban centres* into which the one species, humanity, funnels resources from all over the world and then this

---

124 Girardet, op.cit.
125 Barton, op.cit.
126 Wagar, W. The Next Three Futures, in Blumenfeld (ed.) (1999) Scanning the Future.
127 Barton, op.cit.

issue will concern everyone; *cities today take up only 2 per cent of the world's land surface, yet they use over 75 per cent of the world's resources*[128], and growing efforts to revert that trend will start to change -for better- that future.

What we truly need in a society of dispensable media and abandoned shopping malls is information and communication tools and processes that connect us, build diversity, strengthen community, and build partnerships. We need to share important information, and teach each other ways to address our problems and learn to envision the road ahead and prepare for change[129]. This project is expected to help doing so.

References

Ball, Linden J. (Editor). (2000) *Collaborative Design: Proceedings of Codesigning 2000*, CoDesign 2000, Coventry.

Blumenfeld, Yorick (Editor). (1999) *Scanning the Future,* Thames & Hudson, London.

Calthorpe, Peter, et.al. (2001). *The Regional City : Planning for the End of Sprawl,* Island Press, Washington.

Carmona, Marisa, Drewe, Paul, et. al. (2000-2001). *Globalisation, Urban Form and Governance.* Alfa-Ibis Conferences Proceedings Vols. 1, 2, 3. Delft University Press, Delft.

Castells, Manuel. (2000) *The Rise of the Network Society.* Blackwell, London,

Correa, Charles. (2000) *Housing and Urbanisation: Building Solutions for People and Cities.* Thames & Hudson, London.

Forester, John. (1999). *The Deliberative Practitioner: Encouraging Participatory Planning Processes.* MIT Press, Cambridge.

Grafland, Arie (Editor). (2001). *Cities in Transition.* 010 Publishers, Rotterdam.

Graham, Stephen and Marvin, Simon. (2001) *Splintering Urbanism. , Networked Infrastructures, Technological Mobilities, and the Urban Condition,* Routledge, London.

Golany, Gideon S. (1995). Ethics and Urban Design. John Wiley and Sons, New York.

Lewis, Philip. (1996) *Tomorrow by Design. A Regional Design Process for Sustainability.* John Wiley & Sons, New York.

Rykwert, Joseph. (2000) *Seduction of Place: The City in the twenty-first Century,* Schocken Books.

Urhahn, G.B. and Bobiç, M. (2000*). A Pattern Image. A Typological Tool for Quality in Urban Planning.* THOTH Publishers, Bussum, NL.

Articles

Barton, Hugh (1996). Going Green by Design, Quarterly Journal of the Urban Design Group, #57.

Girardet, Herbert (1999). Cities and the Culture of Sustainability, Quarterly Journal of the Urban Design Group # 78.

Ingram, Rob. (2000) Building Virtual Worlds: A City Planning Perspective Building a Virtual Community Design and Planning, Online Planning Journal

Paul, W.G. (1998), CDAC Online. Office, Online Planning Journal.

---

128 Girardet, op.cit.

129 Paul, op.cit.+

22

“Globalization In the Realm of Urbitecture”.

An Approach to an Alternate Theory of Architecture for Latin-America

Jorge Ozorno

I. Foreword

The proposed research is aimed towards a diagonal and multidisciplinary analysis of the process of the integration/assimilation of the “Global Language of Urbitecture[130]” into the “Local Reality language” of the city of Queretaro, Mexico, as a case study. (Queretaro[131] is a provincial city located 200 kilometers from Mexico City). As a result; the investigation will generate a frame of reference aimed to propose a conceptual approach to a Theory of Architecture for Latin-America[132]. In order to be consistent to the hypothesis that the globalization has accelerated the process of colonization and has impeded a Local form of Urbitecture, the research will include a comparative analysis of different cities in Latin-America.

The term **URBITECTURE** is placed here in the field of the “spatial”, the constructed spaces and the residual spaces. It is a term with all the implications and interrelations between the private and the public, the “other” and the “otherness”, the urban fillings and the urban voids, the “way of living” the city and the way all the spaces where human activities take place are designed or built. The difference between an Architect and an Urbanist is basically the scale; both deal with space. (Naturally there are many complex variables that make the difference in reality)

Although the word “Globalization” is a term that is commonly understood mainly in the realm of economy I will use it along the research in relation to the language of architecture and urbanism. Since most of the human activities take place basically in the cities, I will focus my investigation in the transformation of the constructed environment due to the process of Globalization and the generation/transformation of its urban objects such as constructions, buildings or architectural buildings, taking into account certain variables related to the process in which one foreign culture tends to impose its values

---

130 In the second half of the 20th century and defined by the “Economic Powers” i.e. “The group of 7”

131 Querétaro is a city of 1 million inhabitants and is part of the Macrometropolis of the Mexican Central Valley. Querétaro and another 5 cities (Puebla, Cuernavaca, Toluca, Pachuca and Leon) represents an urban concentration of 32 million inhabitants.

132 I will try to prove that using the case study of Querétaro is representative of the pattern of growing in which cities of Latin-America fall, and since in the near future the main growing will be in cities with the characteristics of the one in this case study.

over the local culture; such variables belong to the cultural sphere and are among many: interdependence, imitation, interpretation, adaptation, mutation, Clonation or, using a word with a more ample meaning, the term **colonization**.

It is my intention to investigate/analyze/catalogue the referred process of globalization, and confirm that our cities (Latin-American cities) have been through the process of "**Globa-Colonization**" for the last 5 centuries since the conquest by the Spaniards first, then by other countries in Europe, France and England mainly, and finally and most significantly by the American culture.

The process of Globa-Colonization although not new –as mentioned before-, is, at the beginning of the 21st century currently present in our cities vigorously and in every aspect of our daily life challenging not only the architects, builders, developers and many others involved in the self-construction but specially to the students of architecture to cope with the aspects of our identity specially under the powerful influence of the world trend of signing trade agreements or establishing strategic alliances, such as the European Community or the North America Trade Agreement between Canada, the United States and Mexico. (NAFTA). In consequence, many abrupt changes have taken place in our cities.

II. The aim of the Proposed Research.

I will be designing three tools that in the best case will improve the teaching of Architecture; 1. The Theory, 2. The Methodology for design teaching and 3. the Data Base center for city monitoring.

The main challenge will be to convert all the information and conclusions in a **wwwplatform,** that is to say that along the research process, the investigation not only will be open to scholars and students to question the presented facts but since the core of the job is to be as pluridisciplinary as possible the "Pier/Deck" will be open to the other disciplines.

1. Theory, Manifesto, Plan.

To develop certain elements for an Adequate "Theory of Architecture for Latin America". "Towards a Mexican Reconstructivism"

I will prove along the research that the production of writings related to our specific socio-cultural conditions have been very limited. In most cases the information is provided by images "Homovidens" eulogy to the object.....

I even say that as today it has become fashionable or necessary for many institutions (educational or public) to promote Lectures, Congresses or Seminars inviting the "Great living Design Stars" of the icons that define the new century.

- The graphic world mediatized
- Urgency to hold a Philosophical frame of reference
- In search of the Urban Genome of Latin-American Cities.

"Emergency", "Urgency", "Transitional", "Low technology", "Ephemeral", "Spontaneous", "Virtual", "Sponsored Architecture" and "Itinerant" are alternate concepts to "Global Theories of Architecture" to be part of the "Necessary Grammar" for the proposed transformation in Teaching architecture at least in my campus.

Conformation/Confrontation between different paradigms

"Glocal Architecture". How to face the Spatial demands of cities that experience an annual growth superior to 10%?.

The Theory (dictionary, plan, glossary, manifesto,...) will be presented as a theoretical tool which presumably will link in circular references the desirable architecture with the possible architecture.

The dynamic book is a platform of reference, its contents will be placed in the net as a deck.

The preponderance of the public space over the private space.

A Sacrifice in Aesthetics in counterpart for a more effective distribution of "space" among the population.

From the book I intend to generate a Methodology for design teaching and a frame for a continuous monitoring of the city. Setting the information in the **www** I intend to create a way in which professors, academics, and professionals will use it as a continuous form of actualization.

2. A Methodology for Design Teaching

Pretext-Text-Context

As a consequence of the reflection around the new paradigms I would like to develop a methodology for Architectural design teaching for the students of Architecture in my region. Methodology that will facilitate the approach to an adequate and appropriate way to present the problem of growing cities, the huge gap between different socio-economic groups, deterioration of the built environment and the incapability to produce all the required spaces for the different needs of society and to develop experimental projects which will include new proposals to solve the new spatial needs.

Such methodology will strongly confronts the socio-cultural aspects of a country that has been exposed in terms of its architectural language for the last 500 years to the influence of foreign cultures. On the other hand the genetics of the ground play an important role in the definition of the form , the lack of infrastructure to deal with the severe adverse conditions of nature (40 % of our territory is subject to cyclones, earthquakes, flodgings, etc.) versus the economic capabilities to built the constructed environment

In many schools of architecture (at least in Mexico) architecture is taught separated to the phenomena of the city I fell comfortable with the term Urbitecture because it links the architectural object to the environment in which it is placed or where it derives its function or utility. Since it will be complicated to find a word to establish other connections such as economy ...it willl be understood that the study of the city will imply the fields of economy, sociology, media, anthropology among many other disciplines.

The professor of design is such that has to bring up among many others at least 4 abilities in their students: Sensibility, Clarity (to read the problem and to organize) Imagination (in order to conceptualize different alternatives of solution) and Creativity to put together the thoughts and the solutions

A common design-practice among many students in the world consists not only to imitate the form of those successful buildings is defined by the exuberance of the form by the sophistication in many cases to forget the strength of the trinomy "form-function-meaning".

The achievement of the aesthetic excellence implies the escalation of the following levels to be able to differentiate from what is global and what is glocal:

- Description
- Construction
- Classification
- Interpretation
- Recreation

The need to be Multidisciplinary

3. University Data Base Center

Anatomy of the city.

This proposed tool will intent to create a structured "Index" of what is built, what is in process and 3. Certain Scenarios for the future

Since the city is the ground for all the architectural performance we need to understand

To develop the criteria for an Institutional Data base center (at the University) that is to say a pre-Catalogue to insert the new buildings and Urban achievements in order to constantly analyze the process of globalization. Quantify and Qualify what became Global, Clobal and Non- Global.

University- Society- Reality.

As you read this it might sound something that is normal in cities of the first world

- The Data-base Center
- The students as researchers
- The digitalization of the city

III. Research Methodology

1. Understanding the Meaning of Globalization

An Historical Analysis of Globalization in Architecture.

The journey of patterns, Clichés, shapes, or forms (Typologies) along the time path of different geographies and circumstances, trying to find a local expression in the best scenario or, in the worse to become part of accepted/admired history just because an urban object survived in time.

The idea is to design a diagram that will allow the reader to follow the evolution of certain symbols (*patterns, Clichés, shapes, or forms)* in architecture along history.

Just to mention two of the most important Trademarks in world architecture; The "Parthenon", its form and shape, or abstraction of it, has been used for the last 2500 years in the most indiscriminate and incredible contexts, from the original center of reverence to the Renaissance palaces all the way to the shopping mall and corporate centers in the 20th century as a symbol of power and elegance, and the MoMa exposition in New York city at the end of the 30's where the term "International Style" was coined by Ph. Johnson and a phenomena that was expanded from the United States to the rest of the world(Signifier/Signified/referent). Never before in the last century a style/trend/school/trend/ the idea of being global or international was spread in such a strong way as to find "International Style" type buildings in Jamaica, Bogota, Mexico City, Santiago de Chile, forgetting that the local conditions are in most cases opposite to each other.

An Historical Analysis of Colonization in Latin-America.

The continuous process of globalization along 500 years of colonization in Mexico produce an immense amount of buildings that honored in the best case those left behind

Imposition of the Spanish Model "The generic" style such as the Generic medicines sold without the famous brand. We know the author of "The Escorial" in Madrid, Spain I do not

Imposition of the French, US and European Models

(Certain Integration (2nd ½ XX C.)

Barragan's House (Integration of the "Global Spanish" to the Mexican Vernacular.

The process of being global is aggravated today by the fact that what used to take three months (The journey from Mexico City to Madrid in Spain) today can be done in a matter of hours or seconds if internet is included in the process of being global).

An Analysis of a Philosophical Frame of Reference.

I have attended many lectures by famous architects on architecture in Mexico, Latin-America, United States and Europe, good and bad ones, long and boring ones and a few, short and surprising, I particularly remember the Japanese Sugherio Ban's presentation lectured in incoherent English on how his "Board Structures" are being used in poor countries.

In many of these congresses, I always get the feeling of attending a rock concert where the lecturer is treated as a star as soon as the slides are projected on the screen. I have heard stories where the architect links his/her work to memories of his infancy such as the way Ghery used to play with live fish in the bathtub at the age of 6 meanwhile his grandmother was getting ready in the kitchen; there in the bathtub, he realized how intricate was the skin structure of the fish; flexibility and ungravity were concepts that he will use 50 years later.

Only because we like arithmetic excuses (the use on multiples of 10 years, centuries) at the end of one of them or the beginning of the next, the need to relate the making of architecture to philosophy is indispensable. At this stage I can only mention a few: 1, Emmanuel Levinas and the Prophetic voice of Posmodernity[133], 2,The Ethics of Deconstruction[134]" 3, Martin Heideger's "To build, Habitat and to think"

Contemporary analysis of Globalization. What is global today?.

"The World becoming One".

"Cities and City Objects in Continuous process of being similar".

133 By Anthony F. Beavers. The topic of the "Other"

134 Simon Critchley/Published 1992

It is my intention to match the diagrams of Globalization in architecture to the meaning of the concept of globalization in terms of its most used assertion, the socio-economy concept. I will try to establish the connection between the evolution of the Concept in the last 30 years. In the 70's we used to have three worlds as if the division were easily fabricated; the ***First World*** belonged to the **Western Industrialized Nations, the** ***Second World*** *to the* **Non-Aligned Socialist Bloc** and ***Third World*** *to the* **Poor Countries in** Latin-America, Asia and Africa.

Along the 80's and the 90's, mainly due to the accelerated process of communications and the convenience of the rich countries new definitions were spread through the world: ***Developed Nations*** referring to **The Industrialized World** and the ***Developing Nations*** in reference to **The rest of the World.**

At the end of the 20th century, at the end of the communist era and the spread use of the www (social decadence signs in the richest countries) it is easier to refer to the word defined in three categories ***World # 1.*** Advanced Nations & Social Classes in other Nations, living in prosperity wherever and however they want, ***World # 2.*** A vast range of people living reasonably well in all countries and ***World # 3.*** People Living in extreme conditions of poverty. (#2 & #3 are the main subject of study of this research).

It is my intention to state that the countries of Latin-America represent another type of Globalization. Poverty, irregular distribution of the income, high mortality, pollution both atmospheric and visual, less opportunities for employment, less accessibility to public spaces with aesthetic quality, poor public transportation systems and the "Slum" as a generic type of dwellings are some of the variables that define not only Latin-American cities, but cities in all continents, and in that way there is another kind of being "Global".

Comparative Study of Latin American Cities.

To be consistent with the hypothesis, and in order to redefine the future of the architecture one of the ways to alter or change it, is through the students of architecture or better said, through the teaching of architecture.

I will try to be partly global and will include an analysis of different cities in Latin-America trying to establish different analogies considering :

- -Cities from 1 to 2 million inhabitants
- -Cities with an "Historical Colonial Center"
- -Cities related to the Country's Capital in distance, power and economic dependence, such as:

Querétaro	to	Mexico City	Mexico
Valparaíso	to	Santiago	Chile
Guayaquil	to	Quito	Ecuador
Sucre	to	La Paz	Bolivia
Cordova	to	Buenos Aires	Argentina

Multidisciplinary Approach.

- Semiotics, The Media Factor.
  - "The American way of life"
  - WWW
  - International Congresses of Architecture:

- "Showrooms of the latest trends in the global language"
- Magazines/Books
- T.V. Programs (U.S. & Mexican) (Felicity ,Friends, Soap Operas)
- Cinema

- Anthropological Vision
    - Immigration
    - Fast demographic growth
    - Drug traffic
    - Religion
    - Violence

- Economy
    - The Imposed models by the World type 1 countries
    - Industrial Architecture
    - Real-estate Architecture
    - Government Architecture

- Politics
    - Democratization process
    - Government responsibility Vs. Your own responsibility

IV. Problem Setting

1. Some Hypothesis

Redefinition of the Global Language and its possible re-interpretations.

- **Globalization**, "Global Urbitecture"
- **Clobalization**, "Cloned Urbitecture"
- **Non-Globalization Globalization**. "Junk-Globalization",
- "Non-Global Urbitecture" ***Globalization***

General Signs: WWW World Wide Web, Multinational Enterprise, Green House effects, Tele-Work, Tele-Money, Tele-House, Mediatic Culture, Aids/Virus

Urban Signs : "Thematic Cities", "Smart Cities", New commercial districts, Infrastructure for communication, Infrastructure for Transportation, Residential areas for the new industrial parks.

Architectural Signs: Architects as "Citizens of the World" (Gehry in Spain, London, Tokyo, Mexico City)

The Shopping Mall as the Cathedral of the 20th. Century, The Corporate Tower, (Before and after the TWC.), Fast food containers, Airports, Amusement Parks

Clobalization

Clobalization = An apparent Cloning (Inserting the appearance of the "global seed" or "The gene's form" in our context). A Morphological cloning with physiologic mutation. What we sometimes call "Influences";Disguised Architecture

General Signs: Only a few have access to World Wide Web multinational enterprise: People as workers.

Urban Signs : New Industrial Parks generally lacking the proper infrastructure.

Americanized sectors of the cities, New Commercial districts: "American Sectors"

Franchises looking like the originals, but with incomplete Infrastructure for communication, infrastructure for transportation insufficient and not reliable and non durable, Proliferation of Slums, the relation $/Space is very poor.

Architectural Signs: The Shopping Mall. (Just do it, even if you have to import everything), The Corporate Tower (As high as possible).Airports. The bulk and appearance is what matters.

The basic rules for design these cloned structures are (among many):

- Vessel type shape
- Evanescent type of windows
- The indiscriminate use of grids
- Cantilever Access
- Crowing of the building
- Hollowed type of mass construction
- Pregnant shapes, vertically and horizontally

Non-Globalization Globalization

Another form of being "Global", Meaning the expression of "Poor Globalization"; globalization of poverty. In Latin America 50% of the city population living in Slums.

General Signs: No access to World Wide Web, Underemployment.

Urban Signs: "Urbis-Morbus-Virus" o a form of proliferation via the invasion of the land, inadequate systems of transportation, visual Pollution, uncontrolled Residual spaces, segregation of the city between the American Sectors and the other sectors, small Industrial Parks inserted in the most populated sectors in the
outskirts of the city

Architectural Signs: The image of really deconstructed houses and buildings.

2. The Urban Analysis Model

Platforms of Analysis

The proposed approach of this part of the research consists in analyzing the cities based on the model presented by Ignasi de Sola Morales at the International Congress of Architecture in Barcelona In 1996; which consists in the interaction of 5 platforms of analysis in which the architecture of our immediate future will recognize its own place, its own instruments and its own ability to intervene the wide web that is implied by the city.

The Form of Change: Mutations

A Casual Change in the genetic material , in this case the "Urbo-Genetic" material

The "Organs of the city" are subject to the Biological process; grow, adapt, transform and interact with the natural environment. The city is in a permanent readjust process in its form as in its function.

The process of city-conformation in Market Economies generally is :1). Planning, 2). developing of the infrastructure and 3). the process of construction.

The process of City Conformation in Developing, 3rd, world, and/or world type #3 countries generally is: 1). Invasion of the land, and construction, 2). Implementation of the minimum infrastructure and 3).Plan elaboration.

The form of Movement/Motion:Fluxes

The Juxtaposition of multiple urban Fluxes; webs that accumulate thousand of interconnections, specially those of "Global Interactions".

The aim would be to create "architectures" that will allow the transit and and facilitate the interchange between different urban nets or tissues.

The Form of Residence: Housing

This is the most important topic in terms of quantity and the one in which all the participants in society conformation should be involved. Some characteristics are:

- Collective atypical and marginal housing
- Housing for immigrants
- Single housing
- Housing for transitional situations
- Housing for homeless
- Special House. (Many times these house –freely designed- represent the experimental field that allows future innovations.
- Multi-components houses (industrial production)

The Form of Interchange: Containers

Industrial Societies depend on the forms of interchange. The meeting with merchandise requires a Scenario, a Stage. Shopping malls are the new Ritual Spaces of Modern Society. Airports that are in itself cities even with its own Police and churches

The Form of Absence: Residual Spaces

- The "otherness".
- Aggressive, anonymous and "Ugly"
- Fragmentation, illegibility, aggressiveness (Movies, painters, artists)
- The approximation to "empty spaces" improductive, obsolete, limitless
- Ex- industrial territories, train stations, ports, as a result of violence, nature disasters, freeways, etc.

3. Genealogy of the Global Family of architecture

To find out the origins of or architectural language. I currently base my personal classification of "Global Architecture under the concepts expressed by Jenks in his book: "Theories y Manifestos in contemporary architecture[135]"

Modern Architecture: 1919-1955

- Functionalism, Rationalism, Bauhaus et al.

Late Modern:1954…

- Technocratic and Pragmatic ideology
- Emphasizes the Technology. Autonomous of the form
- Refuses the "Silly Box" or the "Shoe Box" in favour of the "Articulate Box" (Structure, services, and Joints like in the high tech.
- *The Technophiles, Foster, Rodgers, Grimshaw*

Postmodern: 1955…

- The combination of modern thechnics and the philosophy of the Traditional Architecture to be able to communicate with the public and with the intellectual minorities (preferably architects). Adoption of an hybrid Language

Traditional Architecture: 1969

- Based on the models of the past, great attention to the context
- It is a reaction to the Urban dissolution and to the failure response to the habitat by the Modernism. *The Krier Brothers. Denise Scott Brown*

Postmodern-Ecologist: 1969….

- Double Agenda: Criticizes the modernism and the traditional and at the same time selects elements from both.

Neomodernism:1976

- Deconstruction of Modern forms & Ideas through a fragmented and dissonant code. Explosive and apparently inhuman.
- Works with opposites and deconstructs traditions to emphasizes the difference.
- It is a reaction to the Modern and Postmodern movements among many by Jackes Derrida.

V. Hypotheses/Intended Conclusions

The built environment is a social phenomenon produced by cultural determinants which need to be decodified in order to be redesigned.

- 1. There are many reasons to believe that a common language in Urbitecture is shared among Latin-American countries.
- 2. On the long run it might be possible to modify the "Reading of Latin-American" as not being part of the "Global Language of Urbitecture" and consequently generate a more adequate approach concerning Latin-American ways of

135 edited by Charles Jenks & Karl Kropf, 1997,)

design.

- 3. That we need to use the possibilities of the "Net" in order to develop a new relation between the Aesthetics and Ethics of Urbitecture.
- 4. That the schools of Architecture can play an important role in the redefinition of the city and all the urban objects in order fill in the gaps that 500 years of colonialism have produced.

Research Product

This research leads to three preliminary products:

- Theory, Manifesto, Plan.
- A Methodology for Design Teaching
- University Data Base Center Model for monitoring the city.

References

Burian, Edward R. (ed).1997. Modernidad y Arquitectura en México. GG. México
Grafland, Arie (Editor). (2001) *Cities in Transition. 010 Publishers, Rotterdam.*
Held, Gary et.al.(2000). *Global Transformations.Polity Press.*
Castells, Manuel. (2000). *The Rise of the Network Society. Blackwell, London.*
Koolhaas, Rem, et. Al. (2000). *Mutations. Harvard Project on the City .Actar.*
La Bienale de Venecia.(2000). *Less Aesthetics More Ethics. Marsilio.*
Poch, Moliner & Partners. (2001) *On the Limits. Actar.*
Robertson, Roland.(1995) *Globalization: Social Theory+Culture.* Sage Books.
Rykwert, Joseph. (2000). *Seduction of Place: The City in the twenty-first Century.*

23

Globalisation and Urban Morphological Transformation. Justification for a Second IBIS Research Program

Marisa Carmona

The first collective publication of the IBIS network that was called "Strategic Planning & Urban Projects: Responses to Globalisation from 15 Cities", illustrated the major spatial and social changes occurring in cities - from both advanced and emerging countries- over the past fifty years[136]. This collective publication was aimed at providing organised information about the effects of globalisation and the resultant changes in urban planning. It included theoretical as well as empirical knowledge. Based on this experience, the current initiative is to start a second research project on the transformation of urban morphology in similar cities as analysed in the previous publication and with a similar structure. This, we think, can help in the search for analytical categories on the organisation of space under globalisation.

The first collective publication is organised in two parts. The first part provides a historical framework on the main theories, structures and principles underpinning urban and architectural development in emerging countries and the second part is the presentation of the empirical analysis in chosen cities. In the conceptual framework, three developing periods over the past fifteen years have been identified.

Links between the Two Research Projects: Globalisation, Growing Financial Opportunities and the Social Inequalities materialised in Space.

It is remarkable to notice from our first publication "Strategic Planning & Urban Projects: Responses to Globalisation from 15 Cities" how governments in most emerging countries and especially in those with higher foreign debt are the most enthusiastic defenders of globalisation. They are constantly looking for tools and instruments to increase and enhance the benefits and opportunities for transfer of technology, logistics and capital from advanced countries to their main cities.

The general political discourse of most national governments and main city authorities is to intensify sub-national markets in order to increase resources available for social expenditure (education, health) and environmental policies. ECLA's 1998 report on Foreign Investments, and more recently the UNCTAD report 2000, show that in the 90's the FDI at world level grew from an annual average of US$245000 million between 1991 and 1996 to nearly US$400 000million in 1997, increasing the significance of

136 Bilbao, Bogota, Buenos Aires, Cordoba, The Hague, Montevideo, Mexico-City, Pretoria, Quito, Rotterdam, San Salvador, Santiago, Sao Paulo, Singapore and Tucuman.

transnational firms in the majority of developed and developing national economies. Although the inflows and outflows concentrated in developed countries (60% and 90% respectively) the participation of developing countries as receptors of FDI has grown to 38% in 1997. Latin America received 44% of these flows and Asia, despite retaining its dominance (53%), exhibited a slow down of FDI (ECLA, 1998). The international expansion of transnational firms was one of the central elements of the globalisation of Latin American economies over the decade. Since 1997 the principal dynamics has been the transference of public and private assets into foreign hands especially in the larger economies of Brazil, Mexico, Argentina, Colombia, Venezuela and Chile.

Currently FDI is focused on the acquisition by means of concessions of production and service activities previously delivered by the State. These include telecommunication, water and electricity, car industry, food drink and tobacco, commerce, electronic goods, mining, petroleum and chemical industries. Between 1994 and 1997, foreign firms increased their corporate presence in the largest 500 Latin American firms by increasing their share of total purchases from 29% to 33%. In Argentina and Brazil foreign firms have expanded their participation in the MERCOSUR market in order to compete with imports and to eliminate competition through the massive acquisition of local assets (e.g. in the food and drinks industries).

In most Latin American cities, private capital has become the main actor in the accumulation and growth processes driven by a new type of entrepreneur, that is more innovative than previously. Private capital has increased the horizontal diversification of investments and formed extended productive-financial networks geared towards export chains, services and manufacturing. A growing number of "economic groups" (Chile) and "multi focussed entrepreneurial groups" (Argentina) have emerged.

They have established relations with the international banking system, they control the movement of external loans and have become the main private beneficiaries of industrial development, the transfer of public assets and the capitalisation of foreign debt. De Mattos' research on globalisation indicates a progressive alliance between national groups and foreign investors (de Mattos 1998).

After decades of military regimes and the authoritarian imposition of economic and cultural neoliberalism, democracy is currently presented as the legitimate criterion that will permit the rapid expansion of political and civil freedom to overcome social exclusion. However some time has passed since some countries started privatising their natural resources and main regional and urban infrastructure to recover from the crisis of the Eighties.

The resulting financial liquidity was in some cases used to initiate the necessary industrial reconversion and modernisation of the communication and transport system and in general producing greater changes in the consumption domain. This is clearly visible in the urban transformation, the emergence of new financial urban centralities and in the infrastructure system. Urban agglomerations such as Mexico-City, Sao Paulo, and Santiago are apparently in a better financial state to proceed with the intensification of technological and capital transference than others, while their social and spatial structures are in relative terms significantly more polarised and social exclusion patterns are greater than before the whole process of adjustments. Thus together with a real modernisation of the productive and urban structure and an extensive diversification of society, absolute poverty has decreased but the socio-economic gap between rich and poor has increased.

It seems as if the more globalised countries are those that have most successfully enacted decentralisation, de-regulation and policies for the modernisation of state institutions. These are the countries searching for ways in which to incorporate logistics, strategic planning and civil society in the transformation of productive and social urban structure.

Considering the differences between advanced and emerging countries, it becomes clear that more globalised does not mean more equitable, more democratic and more participative. During the Sixties some global synthesis approaches to explain the phenomenon of increasing inequalities given the shortcoming of previous sectoral explanations started to develop. The concept of 'dependent capitalism' was introduced by the likes of Dos Santos, Cardoso and Castells etc. Later in the 70's and 80's the concept of "monopoly accumulation" was established (Aglietta 1977, Mistral 1978, Boyer 1990). Currently the "anti-globalisation movement" explains the problem of growing inequalities between nations, regions and social groups from the point of view of the increasing global polarisation enacted by communication technologies and capital mobility. The arguments are well defined in the UN report of the Sub-commission on the Promotion and Protection of Human Rights (J. Oloka-Ongango, Deepika Udagama 2000[137]). The concept of 'dependent capitalism' explained the growing inequalities from the position of the state in relation to internal market orientated industrialisation and the transnationalisation of economic, financial and production systems.

Later the concept of "monopoly accumulation" explained inequalities through a more holistic perspective, the accumulation regimes and modes of regulation. Currently the development of an 'elite society' typical of underdeveloped societies, and formation of 'economic groups' operating at cross border levels is seen as a product of the development of global communications, the hyper-mobility of capital that serve transnational corporations. In all these arguments that have been discussed, structural determinants underpin the relationship between the state, the market and civil society on the one side and the changing relation between the social and the spatial structure on the other side.

Because of increasing social polarisation, more intense discussions have developed around market forces and privatisation and their contribution to economic growth and social development. Opponents of this view argue that in most developing countries the link between increased productivity and growing consumption does not follow the same trend that allowed advanced capitalist societies to become post-industrial societies. In most developing countries the link between growth and development is not established, since markets are not capable of increasing productivity and consumption needs simultaneously. Rather an increasing impoverishment of large sectors of the population and growing contradiction in the urban system and the environment are produced.

Everybody accept the argument that 'globalisation' exists, that it is a fact and nothing can be done to revert it (Castells 1999, Krugman 2000[138]). From an economic perspective the link between globalisation and free market forces is explained as the result of the formation of the new geography of world politics that strengthen the formation of supranational and sub-national entities underpinning the role of national states. According to this point of view, the state with its centralised decision-making structures is incompatible with the objective to increase productivity (Boisier 99) and the region and its *capacity for social organisation* become a natural platform from which the

137 J. Oloka-Ongango, Deepika Udagama United Nations Sub Commission on the Promotion and Protection of Human Rights. The realization of Economic, Social and Cultural Rights.

138 "Globalización es la transferencia de tecnología y capital desde países ricos a pobres con el resultante crecimiento de las exportaciones del Tercer Mundo", Paul Krugman, economista del Massachusetts Institute of Technology (MIT) y que en estos días trabaja en la Universidad de Princeton

transition from economic growth and development can take place. Many argue that regardless of the amount of resources which the State may direct to a region and a city, if this region or city lacks a *regional society* with regional institutions, a political and entrepreneurial class, community-based social organisations and politically defined strategic project that enhances comparative advantages, the region and the city could be difficult to develop.

From a spatial perspective the revitalisation of the role of individual actors (individual, corporate, collective) within a socio-political framework, demand the acknowledgement that the conditions for materialisation of their ideals are intimately related with opportunities and options available within the space in which they live their daily lives.

The New IBIS Research on the Transformation of Urban Morphology

With the second network research we want to initiate a concern for the city structure from a regional dimension. It is about the transformation of urban morphology and constitutes a look inside the urban structure as the materialisation of social relations in time and space. Within the changing scenario steered by globalisation and development in telecommunications, in which the impact of external forces varies according to the position of each region, country and city in the global market, the idea is to analyse the transformation of urban morphology considering the complex relationship between the various urban processes that co-exist: renewal, consolidation, gentrification, downgrading, development and re-functioning.

The existence of different processes in the city is currently being analysed by several IBIS members (Suarez in Mexico City; Falu and Marengo in Cordoba, Sepulveda in Santiago). We will specifically focus on the middle and low-income residential prototypes that have developed as a reflection of the large changes occurring within cities. The idea is to understand the changes in urban form that result from the articulation of complex forces, flows, productive processes and functional interactions both in time and space, that transform the particular places, modifying the city and the relationships between production and consumption patterns as well. It seems as if the rapid transformation of activities and functions have prompted the obsolescence of formal concepts associated with relationships previously linked to the nation-state and internal-market-industrial-oriented society. Some dualities such as: form and function; public and private domain; work and residence relationships; formal as productive and informal as marginal; as well as direct associations of gentrification with exclusion, higher density with compact structures; and low floor rates with suburban developments, etc are functional interactions which must be revised within the scope of new social and functional manifestations. Some interactions can express conflict, others resistance to change and still others will be the real expression of new social relationships.

Amongst the factors that most clearly play a role in the new interaction between urban form, function and structure and that contribute to transformation in urban morphology, are those related to the technological changes brought about by and diffusing with globalisation; the demographic and social changes occurring in developing societies, and the overall institutional transformation resulting from the new relationship between the state and civil society.

1.Technological Changes

On the one hand technological changes have facilitated the mobility of global capital flows generating despatialised cross-border networks and contributing to the creation of new locations of massive concentration of resources (Sassen 2001[139]). Technological changes and the introduction of logistics have also contributed to changes in production processes and transformation at different spatial levels. The formation of regional economic blocks (European Union, NAFTA, MERCOSUR, APEC) and new networks and spatial corridors at regional and national level (Santos-Sao Paulo-Antofagasta; Santos-Sao Paulo-Montevideo-Buenos Aires-Valparaiso) are expression of these changes.

The old system of cities resulting from the planned location of activities that are functional for certain national development strategies, has been transformed into a centralised system of industrial de-concentration within larger metropolitan regions, which have significantly affected the urban form of the economically networked centres and of the spatially agglomerated cities. It has also contributed to the formation of new financial and economic centralities, new activity nodes and the consolidation of development corridors at the different spatial levels and scales. The studies of the Ibero American Network RII (de Mattos 2000) have shown how uneven the process of spatial restructuring has been in Latin America. Most small cities suffer from a lack of locational and managerial advantages and are experiencing great difficulty in transforming traditional development patterns. The cities that have gained the most are those within the area of influence of large metropolitan regions (e.g. Mexico City, Greater Buenos Aires, Sao Paulo). Despite major urban, social and environmental problems, they have been able -progressively- to restructure on the basis of a long term economic model.

Technological Changes and its Effect in Space and on Places

Technological development has contributed to new changes in space. The creation of new competitive advantages for flexible production systems and activities based on logistics has important impacts on the city. The changes in industrial production generate changes in the spatial structure at regional, metropolitan and local level. In and out flows, depending on the agglomeration size and other features, have moved modern and old fordist based production systems out of cities and new factories with intensive labour (maquilas) have moved in and out to particular export processing areas and regions. Some researchers speak of several processes taking place from a type of "industrial deconcentration" of intensive production units and capital in some large agglomerations, to manufacturing decay in many places and industrial reconversion and spatial production in others (Lotero 1998, Diniz & Crocco 1998, Brazil).

The re-organisation of the productive process has introduced new differences between regions and cities according to the size of the agglomeration, the internal markets, the resources and indigenous forces and the incentives for changes (Carmona, 2000). A change in the location pattern of residences, industries, services and retail from central areas to the suburbs or to the areas of influence within large spatial agglomerations has been identified in all 15 IBIS cities researched.

The processes of industrial modernisation, de-industrialisation, industrial reconversion, counter-urbanisation and movements of high-income groups to gated

---

139 S.Sassen, Lewis , Ralph (2001) The Global City and the New Information Technologies: Impacts on the Economy and Politics. Typed.

communities and the emergence of new industrial and commercial zones, are changing the morphology and compactness of cities and central urban areas rapidly. The effects on the regional scale include a change in the national system of cities. On the metropolitan scale massive changes in the use and function of land are experienced, including the disappearance of large traditional labour intensive industrial zones leaving behind residential development of unemployed and aged population. Other zones are suddenly affected by the arrival of new modern infrastructure, services, financial and commercial activities, high-income residential development, etc expressing more clearly the social fragmentation of the morphology and the complex diversification of interactions between the place of production and the place of consumption.

In Buenos Aires, large low-income residential areas developed nearby old industrial centres that are impoverished and downgraded by the loss of their income base. In some cases, complete cities suffer from de-industrialisation such as Valparaiso during the Eighties.

The creation of regional trade blocs particularly MERCOSUR have also contributed to the re-organisation of space and changes in the urban morphology. Many centrally located derelict industrial installations, port areas and old railway stations have been redeveloped and restructured.

2. Demographic and Social Changes

It is clear that current demographic changes affect the urban morphology. The southern countries in the Latin American cone and Venezuela have been the most urbanised countries of the continent for some time. Urbanisation levels are higher than 85%, many with more than 90% and the urban growth rate has reduced over the last decade (chart 1). In secondary cities in the South Cone, such as Cordoba and Tucuman (Argentina) and Valparaiso (Chile), demographic growth has declined. The growth of Cordoba has declined from 2,6 in 1970-1980 to 1,6% in 1980- 1991.

Within the context of high urbanisation rates such experienced for long periods of time in the southern countries of Latin America, where the urban experience of poor migrants stretches over more than two generations, the social and historical references are spatially well-developed. Social housing solutions based on mass housing ideologies, varying from medium high-density apartment flats to low-density detached core-house units expressed the social relations and production system of state-oriented policies of the 60s and early 70s, and have shaped the urban morphology of large areas of the southern countries.

The availability of vast stretches of land on the periphery and the need to separate poor dwellers from the central urban areas where the urban political struggle was taking place underpin the low-income urban development of the 60s. The spreading of communication and television contributed to the increase of urban demands during the next four decades. This situation is structurally different in the countries with lower rates of urbanisation during the sixties, in which the high rate of rural migration occurred later in the 80s and 90s as the case of San Salvador, Cochabamba, Mexico City, Pretoria and Quito. This has led to important differences in social housing developments.

National development strategies and the corresponding housing policies have structured the morphology of the city in the different periods. This is evident in the different urban rings of urban extensions. During the 70s and 80s, the self-built environments, supported by urban ideologies enhancing poor people's rights to build, had an important influence on the consolidation of the urban morphology. These ideas have deeply penetrated the resident organisations and powerless local authorities during the decade of general crisis. It also contributed to develop a system of land speculators and building developers that further influenced the morphology of cities in Latin America.

Structural adjustment measures and neoliberalism underpinned the residential developments of the 90s and contributed to change the urban structures through adding new morphologies, consolidating settlements and fostering obsolescence and depletion of others. The high urbanisation level of Southern countries added to the reduction of the urban growth also contributes to changes in household composition and housing typologies, which affect the urban morphology. In the case of Buenos Aires 18% of households consists of one family member.

The growth of unemployment resulting from cuts in state programs and institutions affects the middle-lower class and have consequences for housing overcrowding and occupation rate of dwellings, and affects the use of public space with increasing violence and personal insecurity in the poor neighbourhoods.

Table 1. Variation of Percentage of Population in the large metropolitan arearelated to the total population and the total urbanisation rate.

		Metropolitan					National	
		% total population			Growth rates		% Urbanisation level	
Country	**Metropolitan Area**	1970	1980	1990	1970/1980	1980/1990	2000	2005
Argentina	Buenos Aires	35.6	35.7	34.5	1.6	1.1	89.6	90.6
Bolivia	La Paz	13.0	13.8	17.4	2.6	3.6	64.6	68.2
Brazil	Sao Paulo	8.4	10.2	10.6	4.4	2.0	80.4	82.4
Chile	Santiago	32.3	34.8	35.4	2.7	1.8	85.7	86.9
Ecuador	Guayaquil	13.0	14.9	15.6	4.6	2.9	62.7	65.8
Salvador	San Salvador	13.9	---	11.5	2.38(1)	2.72(1)	55.2	57.8
Peru	Lima	24.4	25.9	27.9	3.7	2.6	72.3	73.5
Colombia	Bogota	14.4	14.8	15.8	3.0	2.4	73.7	75.7
Mexico	Mexico-city	18.5	20.8	18.5	4.2	0.8	76.4	78.4
Uruguay	Montevideo	48.2	49.5	41.6	0.7	0.6	91.2	91.8
Netherlands	Randstad (1)			14.02	0.82	0.33	89	90.5
Singapore	Singapore (1)	100	100	100	1.91	0.94	100	100
South Africa	Cape Town (1)			29.64	2.61	2.7	49.3	56.95
Spain	Madrid (1)			19.3	1.23	0.22	76.5	81.5

Source CEPAL 1998

(1)Source UNDP. org/hdro/urban.htm. Metropolitan total population is in cities of more than 750000 as % of total population 1995

% Urbanisation level 1995 and 2015 respectively and Growth rates 1970-1995 and 1995-2015

a. "Metropolitan Area

In the Andean countries the urbanisation rates are lower, although higher than those in Central America and South Africa, where urbanisation levels have just reached 50% and urban growth rates are maintained at almost 3%. In these countries there are even higher rates of overcrowding and large extensions of new squatter areas and inner city slums are to be found. Difficulties to supply urbanised land for sites and services increase high-density squatting on public land that are restricted for building (along railway line, in public spaces, in riversides etc). In the case of South Africa overcrowding in backyard shacks of township dwellers is increasing.

3. Agglomeration Economy and Institutional Changes

The opening of the economy to external markets brings about the revaluation of large spatial agglomerations and the accentuation of polarisation at national scale. The dual movement of centralisation and de-concentration processes, inwards and outwards, contributes to urban sprawl beyond the limits of metropolitan areas, as has been demonstrated in Buenos Aires, Mexico City, Santiago, Montevideo and Sao Paulo. Its consequences for urban structure is immense and complex, and it has fostered social fragmentation of space, changing locational opportunities, activities, land uses and centralities. The importance of transport and communication is accentuated, large intra and inter urban connectivities are generated together with the generation of networks, opening of corridors, nodes and intermodal transport. The new consumption patterns create new centralities, and these contribute to the vitalisation of some particular places and the downgrading of others. Too much accessibility or too much pedestrianisation can also produce opposite reactions to those expected, as in the case of the central area of Cordoba (Forne 2001). All these changes are contributing to changes in the urban morphology, and the way in which the city is used and experienced.

The new forms of management of the city have an important impact on the form of the city since it liberalises land and public services. Urban growth, land uses, transport systems and the accessibility and distribution of public services are left to market forces, thereby accentuating inequalities within a polycentric structure and limiting the possibilities of a network based city. The opening of stock markets to foreign investors and the privatisation of public sector firms have been crucial conditions for the development of a new spatial model of the city. From the IBIS research it can be concluded that after a long period of downgrading, many central areas of large cities are revitalising again, financial activities and ITC are once again choosing the central areas as best location (Santiago, Buenos Aires, Montevideo). The research of Valenzuela in Santiago during 1998 shows that the urban centres are attractive for many activities that fled some decades ago from pollution, traffic jams, vandalism and other negative externalities of agglomeration, and they are inserting themselves in a new modern environment with compatible land uses. The residential function in many large agglomerations is also returning to central areas, attracting middle and high-income groups. In some cases the image of an empty inner city, violent and insecure is being replaced by an image of modernity, multi-functionality and vitality. In some cases where urban re-regulation is taking place, through a flexible and more sophisticated urban managerial policy, the negative externalities of the unregulated system of multiple centres (containing free movement of individual and collective transport systems that increase energy expenditure, generate pollution, traffic jams and noise) have been reverted for the benefit of the whole city (e.g. the case of Santiago).

Institutional modernisation, combined with decentralisation of the state and the formation of smaller autonomous local governments, is contributing to new forms of management and citizen participation. In high-income areas "public opinion" plays a significant role in the formulation of programs while municipalities with concentrations of poverty are more sensitive to direct participative structures. The intensification of real estate activities is facilitated by governmental actions leading to the formation of partnerships with the private sector in order to negotiate tenure, land uses, urban functions concessions, etc.

Contrary to the great concentration of real estate activities in central and high-income areas, developments in the deprived areas of the cities are very limited and left to interventions of increasingly poor local authorities. Large areas containing middle-low and lower income residents, that are being affected by structural adjustments and that remains outside of the process of labour reconversion are added to the large and diversified marginal sector. It has produced descendent social mobility flows. The informal sector continues to be the source of employment for independent workers in a labour market, which has became more and more competitive. Modernisation and structural adjustments have increasing affected larger sectors of the population, and for many people the only possibility is to live under conditions of overcrowding with another family.

The changes of accessibility and mobility, which have taken place with globalisation and adjustments seem to have benefited the higher purchasing power of the population rather than to answer to social and urban objectives. The economic recuperation that took place on the middle of the 90s in many emerging cities, (Sao Paulo, Buenos Aires) which in many Latin American countries represented an economic growth of around 6%, temporarily concealed the unemployment rate that is currently becoming evident and frightening. The unequal changes of opportunities seem to be growing with the rapid changes in the economic structure, while changes in the urban structure seem not to follow the same pattern. When the amount of poor increases in relation to those few that become richer, it becomes a problem of the social system. The study of urban form and urban morphology in these conditions become complex; but represent the only way to understand the complex relationship between the changing social structure and the city, through its city fragments.

References

Aglietta, M. (1977) Regulation et Crisis du Capitalisme, Calman- Levy, Paris (1977)

Boyer R, Mistral J. (1978) Accumulation, Inflation, Crisis, PUF, Paris

Boisier, S (1999) Regions as the product of Social Construction. CEPAL Review N. 35. Santiago

Burgess, R; Carmona, M; Kolstee, T (1997). The Challenge of Sustainable Cities. Zed Books, London

Cardoso, F.H.,and Faletto.E., (1969) Dependencia y Desarrollo en America latina , Siglo XXI

Castells M (1974) La Cuestion Urbana. Siglo XXI, Barcelona

CEPAL-ECLACa. 1998. Panorama social de América Latina. Nacion.es Unidas. Santiago de Chile

CEPAL -ECLACb 1998. La Inversion Extranjera en America Latina y el Caribe., Dec, 1998

CEPAL- ECLACc 1998. Statistical Yearbook for Latin America and the Caribbean.

Cicolella,P.. 1998. "Transformaciones macroeconómicas en la Argentina y reestructuración territorial en la región metropolitana de Buenos Aires", en: C de Mattos, D. Hiernaux Nicolás y D. Restrepo Botero. (comp.) Globalización y Territorio. Impactos y perspectivas. Pontifica Universidad Católica. (Page 458-478)

De Mattos C.(1998) Reestructuración, Globalización, nuevo poder económico y territorio en el Chile de los Noventa. 1998. in Globalización y Territorio. De Mattos C;

Hiernaux Nicolas, D; Restrepo Botero, D. PUCE Instituto de Estudios Urbanos, Santiago (Pages 42-69)

Dos Santos,T.The Structure of Dependence, American Economic Review, Vol 60, N02, 1970. London

Davila, J. (1996) Bogota, Colombia: Restructuring with continued growth. In Cities and Structural Adjustment. Nigel Harris and Ida Fabricius. UCL Press, England. Pages

Daher,A. (1998) Privatización y Regionalizaciónen Chile. in Globalización y Territorio. De Mattos C; Hiernaux Nicolas, D; Restrepo Botero, D. PUCE Instituto de Estudios Urbanos, Santiago.

Deak, C. (2000) Sao Paulo, the development of an Elite Society. In Globalisation and Strategic Planning.Delft University Press, forthcoming

Diniz, C;Crocco,M (1998) Restructuración Economica e Impacto Regional el Nuevo Mapa de la Industria Brasilera, in Globalización y Territorio. De Mattos C; Hiernaux Nicolas, D; Restrepo Botero, D. PUCE Instituto de Estudios Urbanos, Santiago.(Pages 153-181)

Krugman, P.(1997) Requiem for the New economy

Lotero, J (1998). Crisis, Reconversion Industrial y Cambio Tecnico en el Sistema Urbano Colombiano, 1975-1991. in Globalizacion y Territorio. De Mattos C; Hiernaux Nicolas, D; Restrepo Botero, D. PUCE Instituto de Estudios Urbanos, Santiago. (Pages 209-235)

Pradilla.E. Las Politicas Neoliberales y la Cuestion Territorial, Revista Interamericana de Planificacion, 22, Abril-June, pp.77-107

Richardson, H (1980) Polarization Reversal in Developing Countries, in Papers of the Regional Science Association, vol 45.

Riffo,L; Silva,V (1998) Las Tendencias Locacionales de la Industria en el Marco de los Procesos de Reestructuracion y Globalizacion en Chile. in Globalizacion y Territorio. De Mattos C; Hiernaux

Sassen, S (1988) The Mobility of Labor and Capital, Cambridge University Press, Cambridge.

Sassen, S (1999) Globalisation and Telecomunications: Impacts on the Future of Urban Centrality. In Globalization, Urban Form and Governance. Conference Book IBIS Network. Ed. M. Carmona. Bouwkunde Publicatie Buro. Delft. (Pages 243-255)

Saskia Sassen, Lewis Ralph (2001) The global City and the New Informal Technology. Impacts on the Economy and Politics. Conference Paper to IBIS 5th Conference. Delft.

Silva, Toledo R; 1999Multi-utilities and Horizontal Monopolies in the Provision of Urban Infrastructure In Globalization, Urban Form and Governance. Conference Book IBIS Network. Ed. M. Carmona. Bouwkunde Publicatie Buro. Delft. (Pages 171-175)

Silva, Toledo R; 1997 The Environment and Infrastructure Supply in Brazil. In the Challenge of Sustainable Cities, Burgess, Carmona, Kolstee ed, Zed Books London.

Silva Toledo R. 1992. Urban Infrastructure, Privatisation and Public Regulation. The Limit of the Market. in Urban Restructuring in latin America. M.Carmona Publicatie Buro Bouwkunde Delft.

Glossary of Terms and Acronyms

AMBA	Metropolitan Area of Buenos Aires [Argentina]
APEC	Association of Petroleum Countries
APU	Urban Planning Assessment Office [Argentina]
BGE	Brazilian Institute of Geographic and Statistic [Brazil]
CAC	Charged Average Cost
CADU	Advisory Council for City Planning [Argentina]
CAI	Argentinean Engineering Centre [Argentina]
CAPU	Urban Planning Secretary and Council of City Planning [Argentina]
CASEN	Socio Economic Survey [Chile]
CBD	Central Business District
CBO	Community Based Organisation
CBS	Central Bureau of Statistics [The Netherlands]
CCHC	Chilean Chamber of Construction [Chile]
CMC	Charged Marginal Cost
CMD	Municipal District Board of Rosario [Argentina]
CMV	Housing Municipal Commission of Buenos Aires [Argentina]
CNRS	National Centre of Scientific Research of France
CONADE	National Development Commission [Argentina]
CONICET	National Commission on Scientific and Technological Research [Argentina]
CORMU	Urban Renewal Corporation [Chile]
COUT	Commission of Urban Territorial Ordering [Argentina]
CPF	Central Provident Fund [Singapore]
CPC	Community Participation Centre of Cordoba [Argentina]
CVE	Collaborative Virtual Environment
DNA	Does not appear
ECH	Economic and Confortable Housing [Singapore]
ECLAC/CEPAL	Economic Commission for Latin America and the Caribbean
EPH	Permanent Household Survey [Argentina]
FAO	Food and Agriculture Organisation of the United Nations
FDI	Foreign Direct Investments
FONAVI	National Housing Funds [Argentina]
FOS	Land Occupation Factor
FOT	Floor Space ratio
GCBA	City Government of Buenos Aires [Argentina]
GDP	Gross Domestic Product
GNP	Gross National Product
GSMT	Greater San Miguel de Tucumán [Argentina]
HPF	Housing Provident Fund [Singapore]
IBA	Internationale Bau Austellung [Germany]
IBDR	International Bank for Reconstruction and Development [See also World Bank]
IBGE	Brazilian Institute of Geography and Statistics [Brazil]
IDA	International Development Association
ICSID	International Centre for Settlement of Investment Disputes
ICT - ITC	Informational Communication Technologies
IDA	International Development Association
IFC	International Finance Corporation
ILO/OIT	International Labour Organisation
IAC	Initial Average Cost
IMC	Initial Marginal Cost
IMF	International Monetary Fund
INDEC	National Institute of Statistics and Census [Argentina]
ISP	Internet Service Provider

ITESM	Monterrey Institute of Technology at Higher Education [Mexico]
MABA	Metropolitan Area of Buenos Aires [Argentina]
MASP	Metropolitan Area of San Pablo [Brazil]
MCCA	Common Market of Central Andean Countries
MDQ	Metropolitan District of Quito [Ecuador]
MERCOSUR	Mercado Comun del Sur – Southern Common Market
MIDEPLAN	Ministry of Development and Planning [Chile]
MIGA	International Multilateral Investment Guarantee Agency
MINVU	Ministry of Housing and Urban Development [Chile]
MIT	Massachusetts Institute of Technology
MR	Marginal Revenue
NAFTA	North America Free Trade Agreement
NBI	Unfulfilled Basic Needs index [Argentina]
NGO	Non-Governmental Organisation
NICs	Newly Industrialised Countries
OMA	Office of Metropolitan Architecture [The Netherlands]
ONABE/ENABIEF	National Agency of State Assets [Argentina]
OPAMSS	San Salvador Metropolitan Area Planning Office [El Salvador]
OPS	Pan American Health Organisation
PGDT	General Territorial Development Plan of Quito [Ecuador]
PLANDEMET	Plan de Desarrollo Metropolitano de Cordoba [Argentina]
PMV	Predicted Mean Votes index
PYME	Small and Medium Enterprise [Argentina]
R&D	Research and Development
RANDSTAD	Urban Main Region in The Netherlands
RII	Inter-American Research Network on Globalisation and Territory
RP	National Government [Argentina]
RR	Residential Ring
SEPLADE	Sistema Nacional de Planeamiento y Desarrollo [Argentina]
SERVIU	Regional Service of Housing and Urbanism [Chile]
UNCHS	United Nations Commission for Human Settlements
UNCTAD	United Nations Commission for Trade and Development
UNDIESA	United Nations Department of International Economic and Social Affairs
UNDP/PNUD	United Nations Development Programme
UNESCO	Nations Educational, Scientific and Cultural Organisation
UNICEF	United Nations Children's Fund
UPS	Urban Public Space
USAID - RUDO/LAC	Regional office of Urban Development for Latin America and the Caribbean
VCRV	Virtual Collaborative Research Vehicle
VINEX	Forth Memorandum on Physical Planning [The Netherlands]
VROM	Ministry of Housing, Planning and Environment [The Netherlands]
VU	Virtual University
WHO	World Health Organisation
World Bank	International Bank for Reconstruction and Development
WTO	World Trade Organisation
WWII	Second World War

About the Authors

Marisa Carmona	Researcher and Senior Lecturer at the Faculty of Architecture of Delf. University of Technology, The Netherlands
Rosemann, Jurgen	Professor at the Faculty of Architecture of Delft University of Technology, The Netherlands
Schoonraad, Marinda	Researcher and Lecturer at the School of Planning of the University of Pretoria, South Africa
Toledo Silva, Ricardo	Full Professor at the Faculty of Architecture of the Universidade de Sao Paulo, Brazil
Drewe, Paul	Professor at the Faculty of Architecture of Delft University of Technology, The Netherlands
Ramos Schiffer, Sueli	Full Professor at the Faculty of Architecture of the Universidade de Sao Paulo, Brazil
Lungo, Mario	Professor at the Faculty of Architecture of the Universidad Centro Americana José Simeón Cañas and Executive Director of the Metropolitan Planning Office of San Salvador
Rocco, Roberto	PHD Researcher at the Faculty of Architecture of Delft University of Technology, The Netherlands
De Schiller, Silvia	Professor at the Faculty of Architecture of the Universidad de Buenos Aires, Argentina
Read, Stephen	Researcher and Lecturer at the Faculty of Architecture of Delft University of Technology, The Netherlands
Arrese, Alvaro	Professor of Architecture at the Faculty of Architecture of the Universidad de Buenos Aires, Argentina
Sepúlveda, Diego	PHD Researcher at the Faculty of Architecture of Delft University of Technology, The Netherlands
Villegas Ormachea, Américo	PHD Researcher at the Faculty of Architecture of Delft University of Technology, The Netherlands
Marengo, Cecilia	Researcher at the Faculty of Architecture of the Universidad Nacional de Córdoba, Argentina
Carrión M. Diego	Professor of Architecture at the Pontificia Universidad Católica de Quito and Head of the Metropolitan Planning Office of Quito, Ecuador
Bazan-Lopes, María J.	PHD Researcher at the Faculty of Architecture of Delft University of Technology, The Netherlands
Cuenya, Beatríz	Head of Research Centre for Urban Studies (Cipur) of the Universidad de Buenos Aires, Argentina
Falú, Ana	Professor of Architecture at the Faculty of Architecture of the Universidad Nacional de Córdoba, Argentina
Di Lullo, Raul	Professor of Urban Planning at the Faculty of Architecture and Urbanism of the Universidad Nacional de Tucumán, Argentina
Hu, Hou	Guest Researcher at the Faculty of Architecture of Delft University of Technology, The Netherlands .Former Lecturer University Singapoe
Chanez Mendía, José	PHD Researcher at the Faculty of Architecture of Delft University of Technology, The Netherlands
Suarez Pareyón, Alejandro	Professor at the Faculty of Architecture of the UNAM, Universidad Autónoma de México.
Suygranes, Ana	PHD Researcher at the Faculty of Architecture of Delft University of Technology, The Netherlands
Philibert-Petit, Ernesto	Head of the Faculty of Architecture of Instituto Politécnico de Monterrey, sede Querétaro, México
Ozorno, Jorge	Researcher and Docent at the Faculty of Architecture of the Instituto Politécnico de Monterrey, sede Querétaro, México